Yellowstone Place Names

YELLOWSTONE PLACE NAMES

"This is more than a Wonderland; it is the veritable fairyland of my childhood's dream."—Alice, a young maid, 1884.

by
Lee H. Whittlesey

A Montana Historical Society Guide
Montana Historical Society Press, Helena
1988

A Montana Historical Society Guide
The Montana Historical Society Press, Helena, 59620

Copyright © 1988 by the Montana Historical Society
All rights reserved
Printed in the United States of America

Cover photograph of the Upper Yellowstone River Valley by Tom Murphy, Livingston, Montana
Cartography by Ed Madej, Great Divide Graphics, Helena

Composed in Sabon by Arrow Graphics and Typography, Missoula.
Printed by Advanced Litho Printing, Great Falls.

Unless otherwise noted, all photographs are from the MHS Photograph Archives. Photographs by F. Jay Haynes or Jack Ellis Haynes or those credited to the Haynes Studio are part of the Haynes Foundation Collection of the MHS Photograph Archives.

Library of Congress Cataloging-in-Publication Data
Whittlesey, Lee H., 1950-
    Yellowstone place names / by Lee H. Whittlesey.
p. cm. — (A Montana Historical Society guide)
    Bibliography: p.
    ISBN 0-917298-15-2
    1. Names. Geographical—Yellowstone National Park. 2. Yellowstone National Park—History. I. Title. II. Series.
F722.W59 1988
917.87' 52' 0014—dc19   88-21610
                                                        CIP

To Mom and Dad, who introduced me to Wonderland, and who so generously and wisely made possible the experiences and opportunities that have enriched my life.

To my brother Curtis of Tower Fall, who has made me a better person.

And to the Park Rangers and Transportation Bus and Snowcoach Drivers, for they are the continuing history of Yellowstone.

Contents

Foreword
   by Timothy R. Manns   ix
Preface   xi
Introduction   xv

How to Use This Book   3
Map 1: Northwest Quadrant   4
Map 2: Northeast Quadrant   6
Map 3: Southwest Quadrant   8
Map 4: Southeast Quadrant   10

Yellowstone Place Names   13

Yellowstone Place Names Committee   28
The Washburn Expedition of 1870   56
The Folsom-Cook-Peterson Expedition   84
The Hayden Surveys   104
The Hague Surveys   120
Guides to Yellowstone Park   136

Bibliography   171

Foreword

We know distant and famous places first through their names. The name "Yellowstone" is one known around the world by millions who have come here and many more who have not. During the late 19th century, the explorers who made this country known encountered the place as one virtually without names. They did not know what Native Americans called the mountains, lakes, and geysers of the Park, nor do we. Those names and the people who used them have gone. Today, Yellowstone's history, from the 19th century to recent times, is written across the Park map in names given by trappers, prospectors, explorers, and officials.

The names of Yellowstone conjure up both past events and personalities. "Nez Perce Creek" recalls the tragic events that brought the Nez Perce Indians across the Park in 1877, following this creek along their flight from Idaho and the U.S. Army. The great wilderness panorama of the Hayden Valley recalls the role that geologist Ferdinand V. Hayden played in the exploration and establishment of the world's first national park. Many names of geysers describe some particular characteristic, from the obvious Steamboat Geyser to the more obscure Africa Geyser, the shape of whose vent resembles the continent. In 1870, the members of the Washburn-Langford-Doane expedition named Old Faithful Geyser for its regularity, which soon became legend. Recite the names of Yellowstone and you conjure up some of the wildest and most unusual scenes on earth and the longest span of history encompassed by any such institution.

In the 116 years since President Grant signed the Yellowstone Act, the place names of the first national park have become a litany recited by visitors headed to or returning from a trip to the place earlier writers nicknamed "Wonderland." Old Faithful, Lake, Canyon, Norris, and Mammoth Hot Springs are no longer merely places along the Grand Loop Road but stations in an experience with nearly the import of a pilgrimage. More than 85 million people have come to Yellowstone. Names such as "Old Faithful" have acquired mythical overtones in the degree of their fame and the depth of their symbolism. Here geology is no mere matter of cold rock and ancient events. Here the animals that populated the American West still abound. And here the national park idea first took shape.

This book, the first of its kind, will deepen the reader's appreciation and knowledge of Yellowstone's past. It will show you the history of which you are part simply by coming to these places. Many of Yellowstone's names and the places or things they label tie us to an era when the West was the scene of adventure and when wilderness did not have to be sought because it was everywhere. These names signify a place unique on the planet but also a time mostly past that is still fleetingly present in Yellowstone. In 1886, Secretary of the Interior L. Q. C. Lamar wrote that Yellowstone was to preserve "something of the original Wild West," and so it does.

The book's practical value will be readily evident. For a person traveling through the Park, this book will be a guide to places along the way, adding meaning that might otherwise be missed. The simple act of stopping to read and look will also help break the tiring pace of travel during the busiest months of summer. Stop, leave your car, and repopulate the scene with the people and events that placed Yellowstone's names on the landscape. Through Yellowstone's place names you can come to understand what Yellowstone National Park has meant to generations before us and can mean for many to come.

Timothy R. Manns
Yellowstone National Park Historian

Preface

In the history and landscape of the West, Yellowstone National Park has a special place—a place that has inspired half-believed stories about a region where water spouted "as high as a flag pole," where there were "burning plains, immense lakes, and boiling springs," "where hell bubbled up." Yellowstone became the world's first national park in 1872, and it remains one of the only really large areas in the lower 48 United States free of settlements, farms, fences, and other developments. Yellowstone is a place of wonder and incredible beauty.

When I first arrived to spend a whole summer in Yellowstone in 1969, it was the idea that this place had been changed so little in nearly 100 years that captured my imagination. During the first four years that I worked in Yellowstone, I became very curious about various aspects of this great park, especially the place names and the history behind them. As a bus tour guide for the Park concessionaire (now TW Services), I had to learn plant types, animal facts, geology, history, and a huge number of place names. Guide books were helpful for getting information on some of these subjects, but no one could answer my questions about place names. I soon found out that there was no comprehensive list of all of Yellowstone's place names. In 1972, I started writing down information about Yellowstone place names on file cards. As bibliography begat bibliography and as I added more and more information, I began to realize how much confusion existed in the maze of historical Yellowstone place names. I was amazed at the number of obsolete names included in older literature and the confusion that existed about the locations of many thermal features.

My project soon turned into a history of Yellowstone's features as well as its place names, for the two are intimately tied. The result was a manuscript that included more than 4,000 place names in Yellowstone National Park—the first comprehensive compilation of Yellowstone place names with detailed chronologies of activity for the major geysers. This book is a distillation of the larger study.

In writing this book, I have tried to make it as complete as possible and still be useful for tourists and general readers. Posterity will be the judge of how well I have accomplished the work, but I must acknowledge some of those individuals whose labors before me blazed the way: to Arnold Hague and Walter Harvey Weed, whose pervasive influences on Yellowstone's maps, place names, and history have been virtually uncredited; to the Washburn and Hayden expeditions who kept history alive by retaining the place names of earlier eras and without whom we might have a very different Yellowstone; to Hiram Chittenden whose early interest in the place names of Yellowstone resulted in the only work on the subject for many years; to George Marler whose *Inventory of Thermal Features* remains the standard work on the 20th century activity of Yellowstone's hot springs and geysers (I only wish he were alive to enjoy the newer source materials); to Aubrey Haines whose books and articles on Yellowstone's history remain the first ones to which we all go; and to Sen. George G. Vest of Missouri whose watchful eyes on the would-be despoilers of Yellowstone no doubt saved the Park several times. Although there are those of us who try, no one person can ever totally know the wilderness that is Yellowstone. May those of us who aspire to know it all remember the 1901 words of tour guide G. L. Henderson: "The wonders of Yellowstone Park are not half discovered and the guide who thinks he knows all about them is very much like the good Saint Augustine who thought it was possible for a finite mind to comprehend an infinite God."

As I reach the end of a project that occupied mind and soul for more than twelve years, I remember with gratitude the names and numbers of people and institutions without whom it could not have been done. In seeing this book to fruition, I have engendered many debts.

Gerry and Helen Pesman, my mentors, are the inspiration behind the project. Personal thanks are due to Aubrey Haines, the eminent Yellowstone historian who is truly an expert on the subject. Among other things, he taught me how to fully evaluate a source, and his vast knowledge kept me from making some key errors. "You know," he told me once, "every once in a while I run into something I've missed." So do we all, and it keeps us humble.

Rick Hutchinson, Yellowstone's thermal geologist, is a person with whom I have been, and will continue to be, constantly in contact. The hot springs and geysers of Yellowstone are his trusts, and he knows more about their current activity than anyone. Sam Martinez is a knowledgeable thermal researcher, and I trust what he says and writes.

Christina MacIntosh translated several obscure 1880s manuscripts from their original French. Because of her, that part of Yellowstone history is seeing the light of day for the first time since it was originally published.

Dr. Wick Miller of the University of Utah, Virginia Trenholm of Cheyenne, Wyoming, Wesley L. Kosin of Ft. Washakie, Wyoming, and Priscilla Hughes of Salt Lake City all provided important information on the Shoshone Indian language. William A. McKenzie of the Burlington Northern Railroad gave me information about Northern Pacific Railroad personnel of the 1880s that I could find nowhere else.

Yellowstone naturalists Fred Hirschmann, Tom Pittenger, and Scott Bryan have helped me time and again with field work. Bill Keller, Yellowstone Park photographer, allowed me to peruse his many historic photo volumes and traded pictures with me. Rocco Paperiello, Tomas Vachuda, and Grover Schrayer are three members of that fraternity of enthusiasts known as "geyser gazers," whose field observations have added a great deal to this project. Rocco has also been a valuable reader of this work.

John Varley of the U.S. Fish and Wildlife Service was never too busy to trade information with me on Yellowstone's lakes and streams. Lou Glover of the U.S. Forest Service in Washington, D.C., personally showed me the important historic maps of areas around Yellowstone. The descendants of key figures in the history of Yellowstone have helped me shed much new light on some obscure areas: Jesse and Polly Frost of Cody, Wyoming; Dorothy Hering Hanatschek of New York; Malin Craig, Jr., of Chevy Chase, Maryland; Herb Tutherly of Windsor, Connecticut; and Clarence Chadbourne of Chadbourne, Montana. In Reston, Virginia, Donald Orth was kind and generous with his time and expertise at the U.S. Board on Geographic Names.

General thanks go to Marie Wolf, Jeff Selleck, and Tom Carter of TW services, Inc. Laura Mann was a valuable contact at Yale University. Terri Ray, Charley White, Mike Plumlee, Michael Gibson, Gail and John Richardson, Charles and Saundra Dean, Larry Brown, and the notorious Sharp Brothers have all been friends when I needed them. My Yellowstone friends Bob Carnes, Ken Cummings, and Barry Smith lent impetus to the book by telling me for years I would never finish it. From H. A. Moore (Yellowstone's and surely the world's greatest horse packer) I learned the true spirit of the land.

Great thanks must go to the Transportation Department of TW Services for providing me with many years of job-related travel over the roads of Yellowstone, travel that is so important if one is to really learn the place.

At the University of Oklahoma, where the project began, Marvin Guilfoil and his assistant Bonnie Turner skillfully guided me through a maze of government documents. Claren Kidd provided expert assistance at OU's excellent geology library, and Glenn Jordan helped me in Oklahoma's renowned Phillips Collection of Western History.

At Montana State University, Kay Carey and Minnie Paugh were burdened with me for months in the interlibrary loan division and rare books room. William Walker assisted me at the National Collection of Fine Arts in Washington, D.C. Rex Myers, Amy Stark, and Lory Morrow showed me the materials I needed at the Montana Historical Society.

At the U.S. Geological Survey in Reston, Virginia, I drew on Mary Rabbitt's vast knowledge of the history of that survey. Her colleagues at Menlo Park, California, and Denver, Colorado, have helped me for years with maps and correspondence: Don White, Pat Muffler, Alfred Truesdell, Keith Bargar, J. M. Thompson, Raymond Hill, Irv Benes, and Robin Schumutzler.

In Yellowstone Park's wonderful research library, Illa Jane Bucknall, Val Black, and Bev Whitman were plagued by me constantly. Linda Young Green and Tim Manns have always been kind and helpful. Archivist Jim Peaco generously helped us locate photographs.

In Washington, D.C., Richard Crawford, Michael Goldman, and Ronald Grimm found crucial materials for me at the National Archives. Much of this material sees the light of Yellowstone's beautiful sunrises for the first time in this book thanks to them.

I found many pertinent materials at Baltimore's Enoch Pratt Library with its outstanding periodical collection and at Johns Hopkins University's Milton S. Eisenhower Library. Rite Renaud was helpful in my Baltimore endeavors. And the Library of Congress, as usual, proved to have some otherwise hard to find materials.

My editors William Lang and Marianne Keddington performed a superlative job of condensing 3,000 pages yet maintaining the rich essence of the stories. Chris Eby and Lorrie Hanson patiently typed reams of manuscript.

My in-laws, Dr. and Mrs. Albert Caywood of Ardmore, Oklahoma, helped make possible six months of residence in Washington, D.C. Mikelann Caywood, who loves Yellowstone as much as I do, believed in this project and in me when no one else did.

My parents Mr. and Mrs. Charles L. Whittlesey and my brother Curtis sacrificed my attention for too long while I researched, wrote, agonized, rewrote, dreamt, and lived this book.

And finally, I can do no better than to quote Yellowstone Ranger Wayne Replogle as to the way I feel at the end of this project:

> After hundreds of hours of reading—after hundreds of miles of hiking—after hundreds of evenings of recording and writing—I, myself, have come to the end of the trail. It is a little like finishing the last page of the most wonderful book you ever read: you close the cover slowly, almost tenderly, and with a feeling of infinite regret because there is no second volume. You plan to lose yourself immediately in something of like interest, you yearn for someone who has done the same reading so that you can talk it over together, and you recommend it to your friends so strongly that they shy away from you for weeks—or until they, too, have read the book. I find myself in a very similar predicament. The problem . . . has so monopolized thought and action for a number of years that whatever sense of accomplishment I might have is tempered with regret over the end of a completely absorbing study.

Completing this project is almost like losing a loved one. But I feel that I have come to know, understand, and love Yellowstone. I feel that we are the best of friends.

Lee H. Whittlesey
West Yellowstone
June 1988

Introduction

Place Names of Yellowstone is about the names on the face of Yellowstone National Park, who gave the names, when they first used them and why. It is a book about what Mark Wexler has described as the human psychological necessity "that cannot tolerate a place without a name." It is also a book that identifies which names are officially approved, which ones are accepted in local usage, and which ones are now considered obsolete. Embedded in the history of Yellowstone's place names is the earliest history of the region and the story of these names is also the part of the continuing history of Yellowstone.

Official names, in Yellowstone and elsewhere, also carry legal and administrative weight by demarcating political boundaries, identifying areas of administrative and cultural responsibility, and defining legal descriptions in property, water, and mineral rights. The choice of names, including form and spelling, is determined by the United States Board on Geographic Names (USBGN), which is located in Reston, Virginia. The USBGN does not give names but makes choices from existing names. Those names that are officially approved by the Board are included thereafter on government maps of the U.S. Geological Survey, the Forest Service, and the National Ocean Survey.

When a place name is approved by the Board, it is published in the Board's quarterly decisions list, with an entry such as:

Cook Peak: peak (over 9,500 feet high), in Yellowstone National Park, Wyo., near lat. 44°, 50′, 30″ N., long. 110°, 34′ 30″W. Not: Storm Peak. Sixth Report, approved May 7, 1924.

By using the *not* notation in the entry, the Board indicates that the name has been changed from a former Board decision, or that others had been considered and were vetoed.

New names that are proposed to the Board should be unique, euphonious, not unduly long or clumsily constructed, noncontroversial, and acceptable to local citizens. New names for places in national parks, forests, and wilderness areas must be coordinated with the agency that administers the area. The Board is quite strict about giving personal names to natural features. In general, the USBGN draws a distinction between honorable fame and mere notoriety, prefers that the size of the feature to be named should be in keeping with the stature of the individual being honored, and advises that the individual should have been directly associated with the feature or area. Names of living persons are rarely approved, and the Board usually requires that individuals be deceased for at least one year before approval of their names as place names for major features.

In determining official names, the Board refers to several cartographic sources: the quadrangle maps of the National Topographic Map Series published by the U.S. Geological Survey; administrative and recreation maps published by the Forest Service; nautical charts of coastal areas and inland waters published by the National Ocean Survey; and sectional aeronautical charts published by the National Ocean Survey. Names that appear on these maps *are considered official*, unless they conflict with a USBGN decision, unless there is a conflict with local usage, or unless there is a conflict among the maps. If there is a conflict, the Board weighs the variables and attempts to resolve it by tracing the competing names through historical documentation. Conflicts with local usage are usually resolved with the help of people in the area. Anyone may suggest a new name for a mountain or other feature, provided that the feature has no prior name and provided that there is no local name in current use.

The Domestic Geographic Names section of the Board deals with new names and clears up confusion about established names. It traces rivers backwards from their mouths to their sources, for example, and determines which is the main stem and which should be named branches. The Board also studies maps of mountain formations and places the same name on a mountain range for its entire length. The Board attempts to preserve suitable historic place names and names that have Native American and other non-English origins. The Board also tries to be true to the etymology of all names, although it usually retains names that have been corrupted by local usage. The Board tends to drop apostrophes in possessive names—*Gardner's Hole* becomes *Gardners Hole*. It also avoids hyphens in names and attempts to combine two words into one—*Hell Roaring Creek* becomes *Hellroaring Creek*.

The overriding principle that guides the Board's domestic names policy, however, is recognition of current local usage. Although the Board works closely with state and local governments, various geographic committees, and the general public, if there is confusing duplication of local names or if local names are derogatory to persons, races, or religions, the Board may disapprove those names and seek alternatives. In those circumstances, well-documented names and names with historical priority are usually given the strongest consideration. Duplicate names are sometimes unavoidable, because names become locally established before the duplication is noticed. But the Board usually refuses to officially sanction more than one name in an area. In Yellowstone National Park, there are four *Cascade Creek*s, three geysers named *Catfish*, three springs named *Fissure*, two *Glade Creek*s, and numerous other duplications. Not all of these names, however, are officially approved by the USBGN. In cases where local usage is very strong, the Board may slightly modify the name to avoid duplication.

Inappropriate or derogatory names may be changed. In Yellowstone, for example, "Squaw Lake" has been changed back to *Indian Pond*. Further, the Board will not place names on features against the wishes of local residents. In general, however, it is difficult to change existing names unless an extremely good case can be made and local people approve.

The sources of place names makes the determination of official names and the study of those names a matter for historical investigation. In Yellowstone National Park, place names have come from six basic sources: participants in the fur trade; gold prospectors during the 1860s; early explorers; government surveyors; local use by Park employees and visitors; and recognition of local use or origination by Park officials.

The oldest place names in Yellowstone came from the fur trade and prospecting eras. There are fewer of these names and it is nearly impossible to trace their origins to individuals. Names given by early explorers—the Folsom and Washburn parties—are easier to trace than their older counterparts. Names given by government surveyors often became accepted more quickly and had a better chance for retention, because they were the result of official government work and they were published on "official" maps.

The U.S. Geological Surveys, led by Ferdinand V. Hayden and Arnold Hague during the 1870s and 1880s, named many Yellowstone features. At first, the Hayden and Hague parties followed an example set earlier by the 1870 Washburn party by not naming any feature after members of their groups. Although this was a noble sentiment perhaps, it was one not destined to be totally observed. There are many places in Yellowstone that were named by their discoverers.

During the early days, the USGS named places all over the American West largely because they were often the first to survey these regions and names were needed for mapping and geological references. The men who staffed those government surveys were men of classical educations who often named features after characters, themes, and places mentioned in classical literature, such as Undine Falls and Castor Peak in Yellowstone.

Ferdinand V. Hayden, Arnold Hague, Henry Gannett, Albert C. Peale, and many others named much of Yellowstone as they contributed to the expansion of knowledge about the region. They named these places as they worked, and in many cases we do not know which of the survey members actually gave certain names; many may have even been suggested by packers and cooks around a campfire.

The origins of some of the names generated by the surveys are unclear. Features named by the 1878 Hayden survey, for example, were probably not given that year but were actually named at the time of the 1871-1872 surveys and were not mentioned in print until the publication of the 1878 report. Some names may have been given in Washington, D.C., between 1878 and 1883, when the final report was being prepared. The same is true of names given by Arnold Hague's survey crews during the 1880s and 1890s. Beginning with their initial map surveys in 1883, Arnold Hague and his men of the USGS added several hundred new place names to the Park and to the Absaroka Range, which was then largely outside the Park. In his report in 1887, Hague expressed his intentions:

> In consultation with Mr. Henry Gannett, geologist in charge of geography, it was agreed that the necessary new names to designate the unnamed mountains, valleys, and streams should be mainly selected from the beasts, birds, fishes, trees, flowers, and minerals found within the park or adjacent country (*Annual Report USGS*, 1887, p. 152).

Some names that arose from Hague's policy are not always meaningful. Just because a creek is called *Badger Creek*, for example, does not necessarily mean that a badger has been seen there.

The Hayden surveys had begun the task, but it was Hague and his men who did the real core of the work of surveying, naming, and mapping Yellowstone National Park. Although Hague was not as consistent as he set out to be and he sometimes allowed his own proclivities to enter into place-name decisions, his thoroughness and care make him one of the most important name-givers in Yellowstone history. As Hayden himself wrote, "We performed what we could, but you [Hague] will make the work thorough" (Hague Papers, Box 5, May 26, 1885).

Arnold Hague considered it "one of the hobbies of my life to see a proper nomenclature established in Yellowstone," and naturalist John Muir concurred in Hague's place names, saying that they were exhilarating and that they made his pulse dance.

During his survey work, Hague kept Park officials posted on how his naming procedures were progressing. In 1887, he sent Captain Moses Harris a letter with the names of features to be posted on signboards at Lower Geyser Basin, and in 1889, he sent Captain F. A. Boutelle a letter that included 201 names of features around the Park. For Hague, place names in Yellowstone was serious business. Showing concern that certain local names might come into permanent use, Hague wrote to Henry Gannett in 1886 that he wanted to add the names of certain hot springs and creeks to the new map:

> This is important as there are a number of places that unless they are on the map, the stage-driver names will become a fixture and in many cases they are exceedingly objectionable . . . (Hague Papers, Box 1, September 2, 1886).

The features the government surveys did not cover often carried names from local usage and still do. Someone in an area begins calling a feature by a name that might be suggested by its shape, color, or other characteristic, and the name sticks. Park stagecoach drivers, for example, originated and perpetuated many Yellowstone place names. Local origin names are sometimes the most difficult to track down as there is usually no record of who coined the name or when.

George L. Henderson, the builder of the Cottage Hotel at Mammoth and an early resident of the Park during the 1880s, named many places in Yellowstone. Beginning his career in Yellowstone as an assistant superintendent of the Park, Henderson later became a tour operator, and throughout the 1880s and 1890s he lectured widely and wrote articles about the Park for newspapers. He was a prolific name-giver. His newspaper-like guidebook, *Yellowstone Park Manual and Guide*, which was published in 1885 and 1888, and *Yellowstone Park: Past, Present, and Future*, a promotional pamphlet which he published in 1891, contained hundreds of his place names. These three publications, along with his letters and newspaper articles, constitute some of the rarest and most interesting of early Yellowstone literature.

When Henderson named places in Yellowstone, he paid no attention to historical priority and his names were usually high-sounding—wildly romantic, mythological, classical, political, or biblical. Most of his names reflected Henderson's classical education and are more imaginative, creative, and original than other names. Had he been more precise in giving exact locations for the features he named, however, it is quite likely that many more of his designations would have survived. Regardless of the number of his names that have survived, the study of Henderson's place names is a fascinating and relatively unknown part of Yellowstone's history.

In dealing with Yellowstone's place names, I have dealt only with names that have been recorded during the Park's history *unless* (and these exceptions are few) Park Service officials or other sources have convinced me that the name has been well-entrenched in local usage for many years. While not all of the active names included here are officially approved by the USBGN, all are generally accepted or have historical priority. Many of these names have not yet been submitted to the Board.

In some cases, especially with regard to more recent place names, it has been difficult to decide whether or not the local usage is adequate to justify the name's inclusion in this book. Some may criticize my omissions and inclusions saying "he left that one out and he shouldn't have" or "he put that one in and he shouldn't have." The distinctions I have made have often been difficult choices, and sometimes I have had to judge the amount of local usage of a recent place name based purely on conversations with Park personnel or on the appearances of the name in reports and other publications.

For older names, however, it is my contention that if no other name has supplanted or superseded an older historic name the original name should remain, regardless of the amount of usage it has received over the years. This philosophy is in keeping with other authorities. The U.S. Fish and Wildlife Service and the USGS dig up old names for lakes and creeks and reapply them when features show up unnamed on current maps. If a feature must have a name, it is only logical that it retain its historic name if it has one. As T. M. Pearce has written:

> Our place names tell the story of our historical and linguistic inheritance. By preserving their integrity, they tell the story with greater honesty, accuracy, and truth (Pearce, *New Mexico Place Names*, p. xiv).

While historical priority is paramount, local usage and suitability must also be considered. But suitability, being a matter of opinion, should be given less weight than priority or local usage.

Some historical Yellowstone names have been rescued from oblivion in this book. Many features received their names in earlier decades, when the tourist routes ran close to them. During the Park's 116-year history, roads and trails in the Park have changed many times and many features were seldom visited. Gradually they were dropped from newer maps and were virtually forgotten. Identifying those long-forgotten names and discovering which Yellowstone natural features have had names are two of the principal reasons for this book.

The place names in Yellowstone that are the most difficult to verify are those that have been applied to the Park's many thermal features. Because hot springs and geysers change so quickly, their names are sometimes fleeting in local usage. The latest hot spring, geyser, mud pot, or steam vent that the Park thermal geologist refers to as "Cradle Mud Spring," for example, may dry up tomorrow and leave a place name on a map or in the literature for a feature that no longer exists. Or the feature may change from a quiet hot spring to a spouting geyser, in which case its name may be locally changed from "spring" to "geyser." It all causes confusion. The use of the term *pool* in place names, for example, has been random and arbitrary, because both springs and geysers can be pools. In addition, all geysers are hot springs but not all hot springs are necessarily geysers.

When a name is lacking, Park personnel often refer to smaller, newer, or otherwise unnamed thermal features with a number. This avoids cluttering maps with printed names for hundreds of minor features that exhibit little activity, and it also prevents names from becoming invalid or confusing when a "Blue Spring" suddenly turns into a "White Mudpot." But it has definite disadvantages, as evidenced by this commonly heard conversation among naturalists, tour guides, and geyser gazers:

"I saw pool #9 erupt today."
"Oh, is that anywhere near spring #10?"
"No, it's over by unnamed geyser #17."
"Oh—I think I know where it is . . ."

People are more comfortable referring to features by name as opposed to number, and names are usually less apt to be forgotten or confused with other features than are numbers.

A well-established rule, which began with the 1870 Washburn party, has grown up in Yellowstone that no names of people are applied to thermal features. Ferdinand V. Hayden helped this tradition along when he wrote to Arnold Hague in 1885:

Dr. Peale informs me that you are opposed to placing personal names to geysers. I am very glad. What could be more absurd than a Sheridan or Arthur Geyser? There are still plenty of mountains to compliment people with if need be (Hague Papers, Box 5, May 26, 1885).

Unfortunately, four exceptions to this rule are well entrenched in Yellowstone literature. One of them is even officially approved by the USBGN. It is hoped that there will be no more exceptions made. Names of Yellowstone's thermal features are largely descriptive or otherwise characteristic of the feature's appearance, activity, or location.

There has also been confusion and disagreement about the use of terms such as "spring/springs," "pool/pools," and "geyser," as well as "fall/falls," "cascade/cascades," and "mountain/peak." To resolve these conflicts I have used the following priorities in choosing the names used in this book: 1) the USBGN designation, 2) designations on USBGN map references, 3) sheer number of references in literature, and 4) local usage. Because the choice of an active name in this book is a result of this priority order, it is not a simple matter to make minor changes in names. Even though a feature that is a geyser may be mistakenly approved by the Board as a named *spring* or a named *pool*, we are obligated to use the official designation. "Big Alcove Geyser," for example, is not correct, because the USBGN has officially approved the name *Big Alcove Spring*.

In the future, it is hoped that people who name places in the Park will observe some basic rules. Because of the seriousness and permanence of establishing place names and the possibility that the natural feature has already received a name at one time or another, namings should be kept to a minimum. New names should follow Park guidelines and should be compared with names in the unabridged version of this book to prevent further duplications. No name that appears in this book should be used again in any form. This is to prevent further confusion in an already chaotic literature. Thermal and microorganism researchers should beware of attaching their own names to springs and thus adding to the confusion.

In cases of new thermal features, names should not be given until the feature appears at least fairly stable in its activity. The terms "New" spring or pool or "Old" geyser or vent should *never* be used. These terms have already caused much confusion in the literature. No thermal feature is new for very long and old features can rejuvenate. This also applies to the use of the term "Little."

The thermal namer should also beware of overly simple descriptive names, such as "White Bubbler," because the term may have already been used and because the thermal feature may change. Because of the transitory nature of steam vents, names should not be given to them. Names should also not be given to springs in greatly varying water table (often acid) areas, because the potential for change is too great. Clichéd words should be avoided. Locations should be clearly shown, either on a good map or with precise descriptions. Finally, in the future, when a name is given, the individual giving the name, when they named it, and why should be recorded.

May you enjoy Yellowstone's place names as much as John Muir did. And as I have.

Yellowstone Place Names

So it may be said of names, as of constitutions, "they are not made, but grow."—G. L. Henderson, godfather to many Yellowstone names, 1888.

How to Use This Book

All entries of Yellowstone place names and their histories in this book are presented in alphabetical order. Names that have been officially approved by the U.S. Board on Geographic Names are marked with an asterisk; those that are official because they appear on officially recognized maps are marked with a dagger. Each entry is further identified with a map number that refers to one of the four quadrant maps on pages 4 through 9. The four maps, which show the main features in the Park and the major roads and streams, represent the northwest (Map 1), northeast (Map 2), southwest (Map 3), and southeast (Map 4) sections of the Park.

Each name in *Yellowstone Place Names* is listed on the appropriate map pages with map coordinate numbers and letters. Using these coordinates, you can find the location of each place by drawing an imaginary horizontal line from the letters on the left side of the map and a vertical line from the numbers at the bottom of the map. It will be helpful to supplement the maps in this book with one of the USGS topographic maps of Yellowstone (the standard 1961 Park topographic map, the 15-minute map quads, or the new 7½-minute maps) to more easily locate mountains, plateaus, and valleys.

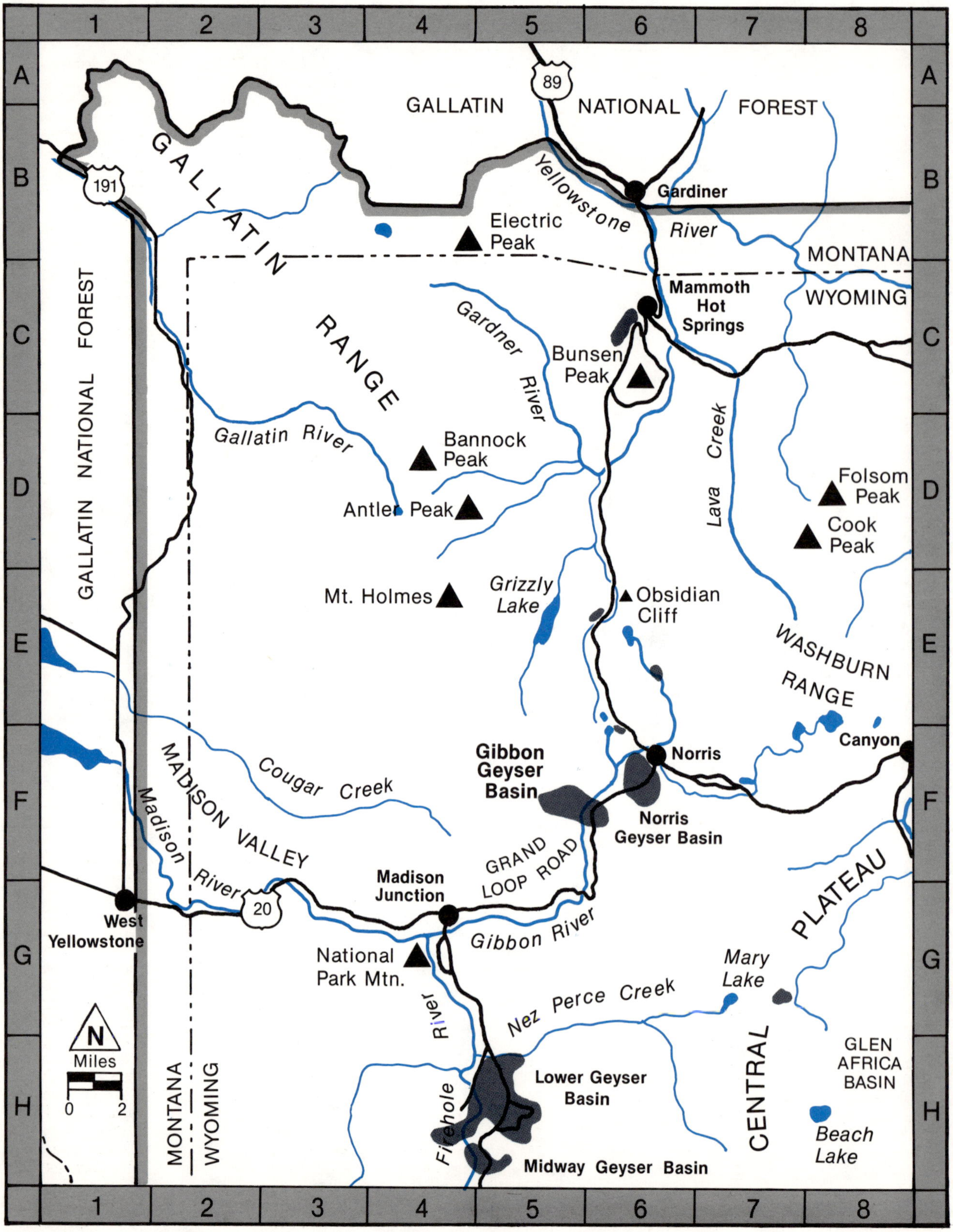

1
2
3
4
5
6
7
8
A
B
C
D
E
F
G
H
89
GALLATIN NATIONAL FOREST
GALLATIN RANGE
191
Gardiner
Yellowstone River
Electric Peak
MONTANA
WYOMING
Mammoth Hot Springs
Gardner River
Bunsen Peak
GALLATIN NATIONAL FOREST
Gallatin River
Bannock Peak
Lava Creek
Folsom Peak
Antler Peak
Cook Peak
Mt. Holmes
Grizzly Lake
Obsidian Cliff
WASHBURN RANGE
Canyon
Gibbon Geyser Basin
Norris
Cougar Creek
MADISON VALLEY
Madison River
Norris Geyser Basin
GRAND LOOP ROAD
Madison Junction
West Yellowstone
20
Gibbon River
CENTRAL PLATEAU
National Park Mtn.
Mary Lake
Nez Perce Creek
Firehole River
N
Miles
0
2
MONTANA
WYOMING
Lower Geyser Basin
GLEN AFRICA BASIN
Beach Lake
Midway Geyser Basin

MAP 1: Northwestern Yellowstone Park

Mammoth Hotel from Mound Terrace, 1895
F. J. Haynes

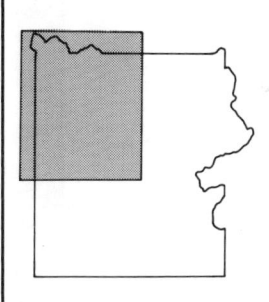

Ace of Hearts Lake, D7
Admiration Point, C6
Africa Lake, C6
Angel Terrace, C6
Anthony's Entrance, C6
Antler Peak, D4
Apollinaris Spring, D6
Arrow Canyon, E7
Arsenic Geyser, F6
Artists' Paintpots, F6
Arvid Lake, E4
Baby Spring and Terrace, C6
Back Basin, F6
Bacon Rind Creek, C2
Bannock Peak, D4
Bath Lake, C6
Bathtub Spring, F6
Beaver Lake, E6
Beryl Spring, F6
Bijah Spring, E6
Black Butte, B1
Black Canyon, C7,C8
Blacktail Deer Creek, C8
Blanding Hill, F7
Blood Geyser, F6
Boiling River, C6
Bottler's Lookout, C6
Brickyard Hill, E6
Bunsen Peak, C6
Campanula Creek, E2
Canary Spring, C6
Capitol Hill, C6
Cathedral Rock, C6
Chadbourne Hill, B6
Christmas Tree Park, E4,E5
Christmas Tree Park, G1
Clagett Butte, C6
Coffin Spring, F5
Congress Pool, F6
Constant Geyser, F6
Cook Peak, D8
Corporal Geyser, F6
Crevice Creek, B8
Crystal Spring, C6
Cupid Spring, C6
Dailey Creek, B1
Dante's Inferno, F5
Decker Island, F6
Devil's Kitchen, C6
Devil's Stairway, G7
Devil's Thumb, C6
Diana Spring, C6
Doctor Allen's Paintpots, F6
Duck Creek, F3,F4
Duck Creek, E1,E2
Eagle Nest Rock, B6
Earthquake Cliffs, G5
Ebony Geyser, F6
Echinus Geyser, F6
Echo Canyon, H2
Echo Peak, D4
Electric Peak, B4
Elk Park, F6
The Esplanade, C6
Fan Creek, C2,C3
Frog Rock, C8
Frying Pan Spring, E6
Gallatin Lake, D4
Gallatin Range
Gallatin River, C2
Gardner River, B6,C5,C6
Gardners Hole, C5,C6,D5
Gibbon Falls, G5
Gibbon Meadows, F5,F6
Gibbon River, F6,F7,F8
Gneiss Creek, E2,E3
Golden Gate Canyon, C6
Gray Lakes, F6
Grebe Lake, E8,F8
Green Dragon Spring, F6
The Grottoes, C6
Hals Lake, C5
Harding Geyser, F6
Harlequin Lake, G4
Hayden Valley, G8,G9
Hazle Lake, F6
Hibbard's Pass, E6
Highland Terrace, C6
The Hoodoos, C6
Hurricane Vent, F6
Hymen Terrace, C6
Ice Lake, F7
Indian Creek, D5
Iron Spring, G5
Jackstraw Basin, G2
Joffe Lake, C6
Jordan Falls, G5,G6
Joseph Peak, C4
Jupiter Springs, C6
Jupiter Terrace, C6
Kingman Pass, C6
Kite Hill, C6
Knowles Falls, B7
Ladies' Lake, C6
Lake of the Woods, E6
Landslide Creek, B6
Lava Creek, C6,C7,D7
Lemonade Creek, E6
Lemonade Lake, E6
Liberty Cap, C6
Lightning Hill, B2
Little Gibbon Falls, F7
Little Meadows, C6
Lone Tree Rock, F6
Lookout Cliffs, G3
Lookout Terrace, G5
Madison River, F2,G2,G3,G4
Main Springs, C6
Mammoth Hot Springs, C6
Marble Terrace, C6
McCartney Cave, C6
McMinn Bench, B6,C6
Medusa Spring, F6
Meldrum Mountain, B2
Minerva Spring, C6
Minerva Terrace, C6
Minute Geyser, F6
Mol Heron Creek, B4
Monarch Geyser, F6
Monument Geyser, F5
Monument Geyser Basin, F5
Monument Peak, C4
Mount Everts, C7
Mount Haynes, G3
Mount Holmes, E4
Mount Jackson, G3
Naiad Spring, C6
Narrow Gauge Springs, C6
Narrow Gauge Terrace, C6
National Park Mountain, G4
New Crater Geyser, F6
Norris Geyser Basin, F6
Norris Valley, E6
Nuphar Lake, F6
Nymph Lake, E6,F6
Oblique Geyser, F6
Obsidian Cliff, E6
Opal Terrace, C6
Orange Spring Mound, C6
Orpiment Spring, F6
Osprey Falls, C6
Oxbow Creek, C8
Painted Pool, C6
Paintpot Hill, F6
Palette Spring, C6
Palpitator Spring, F6
Paper Picker Spring, C6
Park Creek, F6
Pass Creek, D2
Pearl Geyser, F6
Pequito Geyser, F6
Phantom Lake, C8
Phelps Creek, B6
Phillips Caldron, F6
Pillar of Hercules, C6
Pinyon Terrace, C6
Poison Cave, C6
Poison Spring, C6
Porcelain Basin, F6
Porcelain Springs, F6
Porcelain Terrace, F6
Porkchop Geyser, F6
Puff 'n Stuff Geyser, F6
Pulpit Terrace, C6
Purple Mountain, F4,G4
Quadrant Mountain, D4,D5
Queen Elizabeth's Ruffle, C7
Rattlesnake Butte, B7
Realgar Springs, F6
Red Jacket Spring, G7
Reese Creek, B5
Rescue Creek, C7
Richards Creek, E2
River Styx, C6
Roaring Mountain, E6
Rosa Lake, E4
Rustic Falls, C6
Sand Spring, C7
Sandy Butte, E2
Semi-Centennial Geyser, E6
Sepulcher Mountain, C5
Sheepeater Cliffs, C6
Silver Gate, C6
Snow Pass, C6
Snowshoe Pass, C4
Soap Hill, C6
Soda Spring, C6
Solfatara Plateau, F8
South End Hills, E4
Squirrel Springs, C6
Squirrel Springs Ridge, C6
Steamboat Geyser, F6
Steamvalve Spring, F6
Stellaria Creek, C3
Stephens Creek, B5
Stone Mountain, E8,E9
Storm Pass, D8
Stygian Caves, C6
Sulphur Lake, G7
Sunday Geyser, F6
Swan Lake, C6
Tangled Creek, H5
Tantalus Creek, F6
Tantalus Geyser, F6
Terminal Monument Creek, C2
Terrace Mountain, C6
Thompson's Peak, C7
Three Brothers Mountains, G4
Three Rivers Peak, D4
Trilobite Point, E4,E5
Tuff Cliff, G4,G5
Turkey Pen Creek, B7
Turkey Pen Pass, B7
Turkey Pen Peak, B7
Twin Lakes, E6
Undine Falls, C7
Valentine Geyser, F6
Veteran Geyser, F6
Violet Creek, G8
Violet Springs, G8
Virginia Cascade, F7
Vixen Geyser, F6
Washburn Range, D8,E8,E9
Whiskey Spring, C6
White Elephant Back Springs Terrace, C6
Whiterock Springs, E6
Wraith Falls, C7
Yancey Creek, C9
Yellowstone River

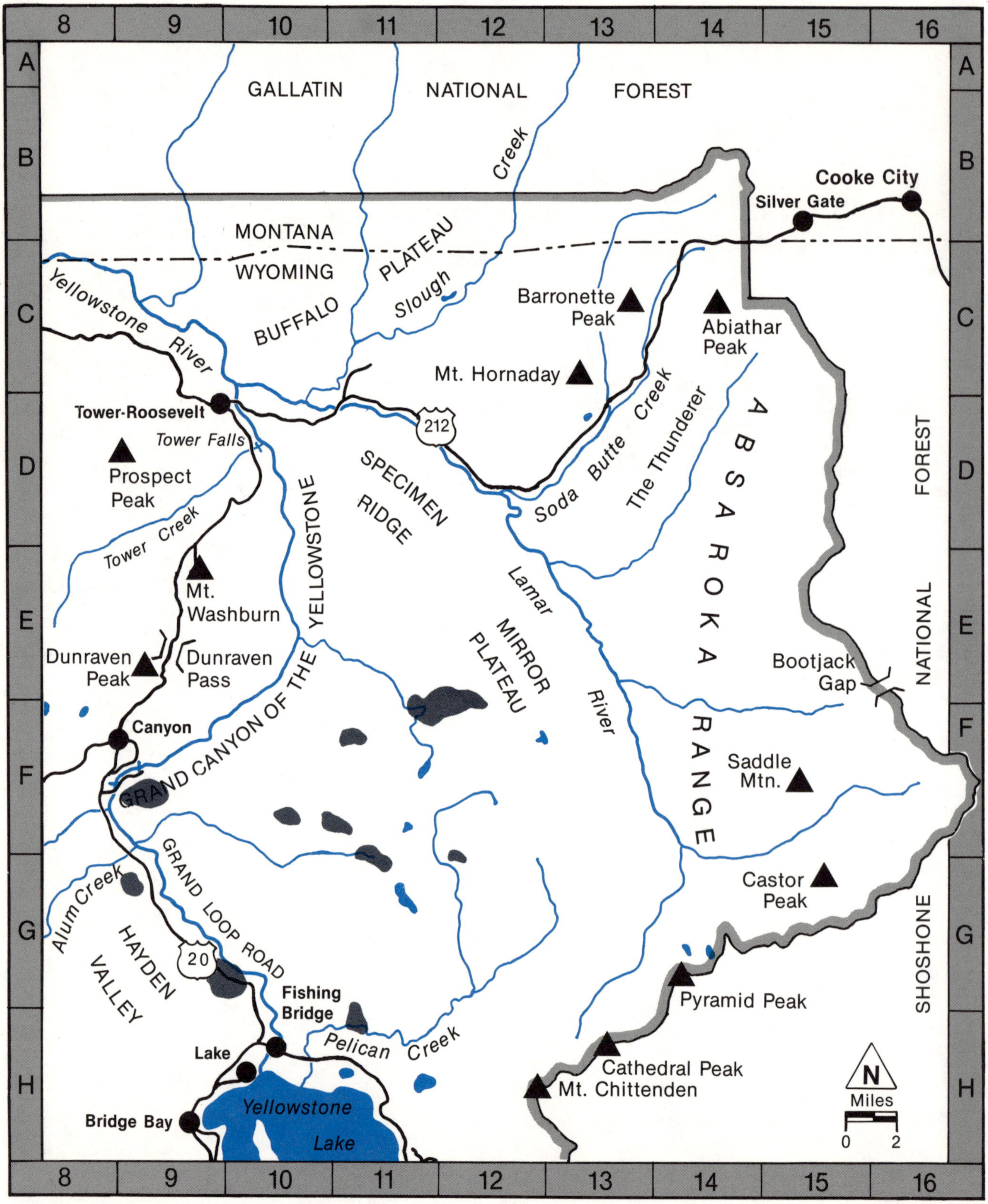

GALLATIN NATIONAL FOREST
Creek
MONTANA
WYOMING
BUFFALO PLATEAU
Slough
Cooke City
Silver Gate
Barronette Peak
Abiathar Peak
Yellowstone River
Mt. Hornaday
Tower-Roosevelt
Tower Falls
212
Prospect Peak
SPECIMEN RIDGE
Soda Butte Creek
The Thunderer
ABSAROKA RANGE
FOREST
Tower Creek
YELLOWSTONE
Lamar River
Mt. Washburn
MIRROR PLATEAU
Dunraven Peak
Dunraven Pass
Bootjack Gap
NATIONAL
GRAND CANYON OF THE YELLOWSTONE
Canyon
Saddle Mtn.
GRAND LOOP ROAD
Alum Creek
Castor Peak
HAYDEN VALLEY
20
SHOSHONE
Pyramid Peak
Fishing Bridge
Pelican Creek
Lake
Cathedral Peak
Mt. Chittenden
Bridge Bay
Yellowstone Lake
N
Miles
0 2

MAP 2: Northeastern Yellowstone Park

Fording the Lamar River, 1926.

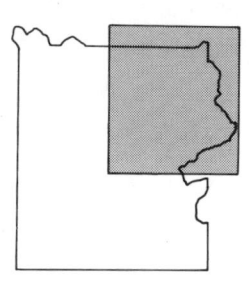

Abiathar Peak, C14
Absaroka Range
Alden Valley, D10
Alum Creek, G8
Artist Point, F9
Astringent Creek, G12
Bannock Ford, D10
Barronette Peak, C13
Bellow Spring, E11
Bell's Lake, D10
Bison Summit, E12
Black Dragon's Caldron, G9
Bliss Pass, C13
Bootjack Gap, F16
Buffalo Plateau, C11
Bumpus Butte, D10
Cache Creek, D14,E13
Calcite Springs, D10
Calfee Creek, E14,E15
Candlestick Mountain, G16
Canoe Lake, E15
Carnelian Creek, E9
Cascade Creek, F8
Castle Ruins, F9
Castor Peak, G15
Cathedral Peak, H13
Chalcedony Creek, D12
Cold Water Geyser, G9
Crescent Hill, C9
Crystal Falls, F8
The Cut, C9
Cutoff Creek, B13
Cutoff Mountain, B13
Death Gulch, E13
Devil's Den, D10
Dragons Mouth Spring, G9
Druid Peak, D12
Dunraven Pass, E9
Dunraven Peak, E9
Ebro Springs, G10
Fairies' Fall, D11
Fish Creek, D13
Flutter-Wheel Spring, G7
Folsom Peak, D8
Frederick Peak, C12
Frost Lake, G14
Garnet Hill, C9
Glade Creek, E10
Glen Africa Basin, G7
Grand Canyon of the Yellowstone, E10,F9
Grand View, F9
Grant Peak, G15
Green Grotto Spring, E11
Grotto Pool, F8
Hague Mountain, F15
Hayden Valley, G8,G9
Hedges Peak, E9
Hellroaring Creek, B9,C9
Hoodoo Basin, F16
Hornaday Creek, C12
Ice Box Canyon, C13
Indian Pond, H11
Inside Mountain, E9
Inspiration Point, F9
Jackson Grade, D12
Jay Creek, F8
Josephs Coat Springs, F11
Junction Butte, C10
Junction Valley, C10
Lamar River, C10,D11
Lamar Valley, D11,D12
LeHardys Rapids, G10
Little America Flats, D10
Little Specimen Creek, D11
Little Trumpeter Lake, D10
Lookout Point, F9
Lost Creek, D9
Lovely Pass, G13
Lower Falls, F9
Mae West Curve, D9
Mary Bay, H11
McBride Lake, C11
Miller Creek, E14,F15
Millers Valley, E14
Mirror Lake, F13
Mirror Plateau, E12,F13
Moose Pool, G9
Moran Point, F9
Mount Chittenden, H12
Mount Hornaday, C13
Mount Norris, D13
Mount Washburn, E9
Mountain Terrace, F14
Mud Geyser, G9
Mud Pots, G9
Mud Volcano, G9
The Needle, D14
The Needle, D10
Nez Perce Ford, G9
Nymph Spring, D10
Orange Rock Springs, F11
Painted Cliffs, F9
Parker Peak, F16
Pebble Creek, C13
Pelican Creek, H11
Pelican Creek Mud Volcano, F12
Pelican Valley, H11
Petrified Tree, D9
Phelps Peak, E10
Point Sublime, F9
Pollux Peak, F15
Ponuntpa Springs, F11
Porcupine Cone, G12
Prospect Pass, D8
Prospect Peak, D8,D9
Rainy Lake, D10
Red Rock, F9
Republic Pass, C15
Republic Peak, C15
Round Prairie, D13
Rowland Pass, E10
Ruddy Duck Pond, D10
Saddle Mountain, F15
Safety Valve Geyser, F9
Scorodite Spring, F11
Seven Mile Hole, E10
Shrimp Lake, D13
Silver Cord Cascade, F9
Sleeping Giant, G15
Slough Creek, C11,C12
Soda Butte, D13
Soda Butte Canyon, C14,D13
Specimen Ridge, D11
Sulphur Beds, D10
Sulphur Caldron, G9
Sulphur Mountain, G9
Sulphur Rock, D10
Sulphur Spring, G9
Sulphur Spring Creek, G9
Sunset Point, F9
Three Knob Peak, G16
The Thunderer, D14
Tower Fall, D10
Tower Pass, E9
Trumpeter Lake, D10
Twin Creek, E12,E13
Twin Falls, E10
Uncle Tom's Point, F9
Upper Falls, F9
Wahb Springs, E13
Whistler Geyser, F11
White Lake, G11
Wrangler Lake, F9
Wrong Creek, E12
Yancey's Hole, C9,C10
Yellowstone River

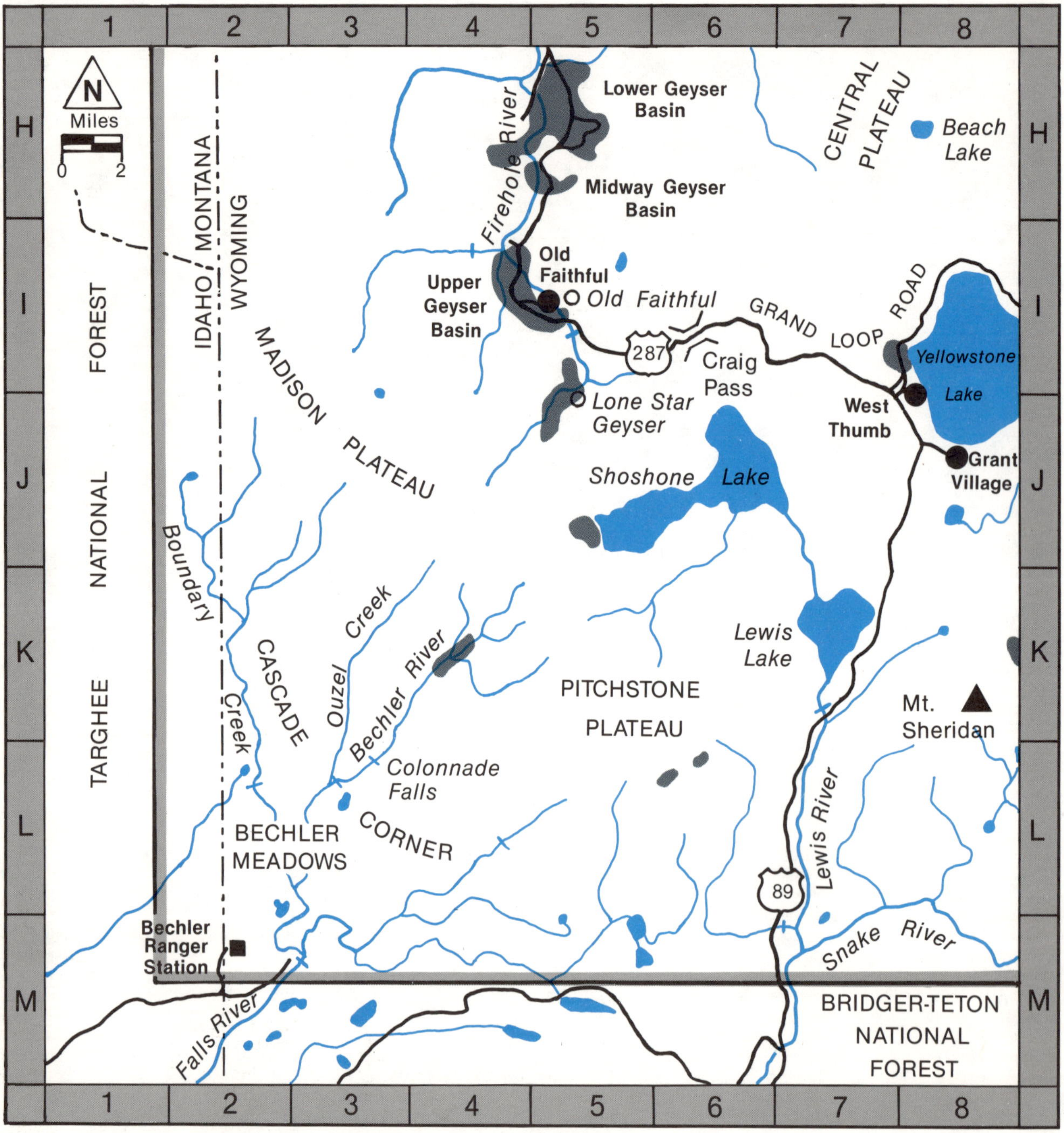

N
Miles
0
2
1 2 3 4 5 6 7 8
H I J K L M
TARGHEE NATIONAL FOREST
IDAHO MONTANA
WYOMING
Boundary
MADISON PLATEAU
Firehole River
Lower Geyser Basin
Midway Geyser Basin
Upper Geyser Basin
Old Faithful
Old Faithful
CENTRAL PLATEAU
Beach Lake
GRAND LOOP ROAD
287
Craig Pass
Lone Star Geyser
Yellowstone Lake
West Thumb
Grant Village
Shoshone Lake
Lewis Lake
Ouzel Creek
Bechler River
Cascade Creek
CASCADE CORNER
Colonnade Falls
PITCHSTONE PLATEAU
Mt. Sheridan
BECHLER MEADOWS
Bechler Ranger Station
89
Lewis River
Snake River
Falls River
BRIDGER-TETON NATIONAL FOREST

MAP 3: Southwestern Yellowstone Park

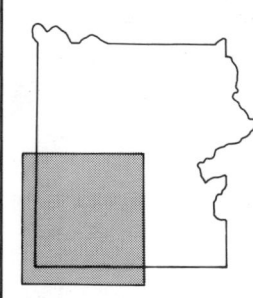

Abyss Pool, I8
Albright Falls, K4
Anemone Geyser, I5
Arnica Creek, H8,I8
Arrowhead Spring, I5
Artemisia Geyser, I4
Asta Spring, I4
Atomizer Geyser, I4
Bartlett Slough, L2
Batchelder Column, K4
Beach Spring, I5
Bead Geyser, H5
Bear Park, J4
Bears Playground, I5
Bechler River, K4,L3
Beehive Geyser, I5
Belgian Pool, I4
Bellefontaine Geyser, H5
Beula Lake, M5
Big Bear Lake, H2
Biscuit Basin, I4
Black Sand Basin, I4
Black Warrior Springs, H5
Bonita Pool, I4
Botryoidal Spring, H5
Boundary Creek, J2,K2,L2
Buffalo Meadows, H3
Butterfly Spring, I5
Calthos Spring, I4
Cascade Corner, K4,L3
Castle Geyser, I4
Catfish Geyser, H5
Cave Falls, M3
Celestine Pool, H5
Chinaman Spring, I5
Christmas Tree Rock, G4
Clepsydra Geyser, H5
Cliff Geyser, I4
Colonnade Falls, L3
Corkscrew Hill, I6
Coulter Creek, M8
Cowan Creek, G6
Craig Pass, I6
Crawfish Creek, L6,M6
Crested Pool, I4
Daisy Geyser, I4
DeLacy Creek, I6
Demon's Cave, I4
Devil's Gate, I5
Douglas Knob, K4
Dunanda Falls, L2
Ear Spring, I5
Economic Geyser Crater, I4

Egeria Spring, H5
Emerald Pool, I4
Excelsior Geyser Crater, H4
Factory Hill, K8
Factory Springs, G8
Fairy Falls, H4
Fairy Springs, H4
Falls River, M5
Fan Geyser, I4
Ferris Fork, K4
Firehole Falls, G4
Firehole Lake, H5
Firehole River, G4,H5
Firehole Spring, H5
Fountain Geyser, H5
Fountain Paint Pot, H5
Fungoid Spring, H5
Gentian Pool, H5
Giant Geyser, I4
Giantess Geyser, I5
Glen Africa Basin, G7
Grand Geyser, I4
Grand Prismatic Spring, H4
Grants Pass, J5
Gray Bulger Geyser, H5
Gray Spring, J5
Great Fountain Geyser, H5
Gregg Fork, K4
Grotto Fountain Geyser, I4
Grotto Geyser, I4
The Grumbler, I4
The Gumper, G9
Gwinna Falls, K4
Halfway Spring, F9
Handkerchief Pool, I4
Hering Lake, M5
Herron Creek, I6
Highland Hot Springs, G7
Hillside Springs, I4
Hot Lake, H5
Hourglass Falls, K4
Hygeia Spring, H5
Imperial Geyser, H4
Indigo Spring, H4
Inkwell Spring, I4
Iris Falls, L3
Iris Pool, H5
Iron Pot, H4
Iron Spring Creek, I4
Isa Lake, I6
Jelly Spring, H5
Jug Spring, H5
Kaleidoscope Geyser, H5
Kelp Pool, I4
Kepler Cascades, I5
Kidney Spring, H5
King Geyser, I8
Kitchen Spring, J5
Lactose Spring, I4
Lake View, I7
Lake Wyodaho, L3
Lambrequin Spring, H5
Laundry Spring, I4
Lavender Spring, I4
Leather Pool, H5
Lewis Canyon Falls, L7

Lewis Lake, K7
Lewis River, K7,L7
Liberty Pool, I5
Limekiln Springs, I4
Linen Spring, I4
Lion Geyser, I5
Littles Fork, K4
Lone Spring, H5
Lone Star Geyser, I5
Lost Lake, J7
Madison Lake, J4
Maidens Grave Spring, H5
Mantrap Cone, I8
Marble Cliff Spring, J5
Marshall's Park, G3,H3
Mary Lake, G7
Mastiff Geyser, I4
Microcosm Basin, H5
Midway Bluff, H5
Midway Geyser Basin, H4,H5
Model Geyser, I5
Morning Falls, L4
Morning Geyser, H5
Morning Glory Pool, I4
Mottled Pool, I5
Mud Volcanoes, H5
Mushroom Pool, H5
Mustard Springs, I4
Myriad Creek, I5
Mystic Falls, I4
Narcissus Geyser, H5
Narrow Gate, I2
New Handkerchief Pool, I4
Nez Perce Creek, G6,G7
Niobe Creek, I4
Norris Pass, I6
Ojo Caliente Spring, H4
Old Bath Lake, H5
Old Faithful Geyser, I5
Opalescent Pool, I4

Ouzel Falls, L3
Peanut Pool, I5
Pentagonal Spring, I4
Phantom Fumarole, L6
Phillips Fork, K4
Phillips Fork Fall, K4
Pinto Spring, I4
Pitchstone Plateau, K5,L5
Pocket Lake, J6
Porcupine Hills, H5
Primrose Springs, H5
Proposition Creek, M4
Prospect Point, H5
Pseudo Geyser, G7
Punch Bowl Spring, I4
Queens Laundry, H4
Rabbit Geyser, H5
Ragged Falls, K4
Ranger Pool, H5
Red Spouter Geyser, H5
Red Terrace Spring, H4
Restless Geyser, I4
Restless Geyser, I4
Riverside Geyser, I4
Robinson Creek, L1
Rock Creek, M1
Rocket Geyser, I4
The Ruin, I5
Sand Geyser, H5
Sapphire Pool, I4
Savage Hill, J7
Sawmill Geyser, I4
The Seashell, I4
Sea Weed Spring, I4
Seismograph Pool, J8
Sentinel Creek, G4
Serendipity Springs, H5
Shoshone Lake, J5, J6
Shoshone Point, I6
Silent Pool, H5

Silex Spring, H5
Silver Globe Spring, I4
Silver Scarf Falls, L2
Sinking Water Canyon, L2
Skeleton Pool, H4
Sluiceway Falls, K4
Smoke Jumper Hot Springs, I3
Solitary Geyser, I5
Spa Geyser, I4
Spirea Creek, L6
Splendid Geyser, I4
Sponge Geyser, I5
Spring Creek, I5
Steady Geyser, H5
Sullivan Creek, J4,J5
Sunset Lake, I4
Surprise Pool, H5
Tardy Geyser, I4
Tempe Cascade, K4
Tendoy Falls, K4
Terra Cotta Spring, I4
Three River Junction, K4
Three Sisters Springs, I4
Till Geyser, H5
Tortoise Shell Spring, I4
Treasure Island, L3
Trischman Knob, J4
Turquoise Pool, H4
Twilight Geyser, H4
Twister Falls, K4
Union Falls, L4
Wahhi Falls, K4
Whiskey Flats, H5
Whistle Geyser, I4
Winegar Lake, M3
Wylie Hill, I4
Yellowbell Brook, I4
Zomar Spring, H5
Zygomatic Arch, I4

Shoshone Lake, October 1899

F.J. Haynes

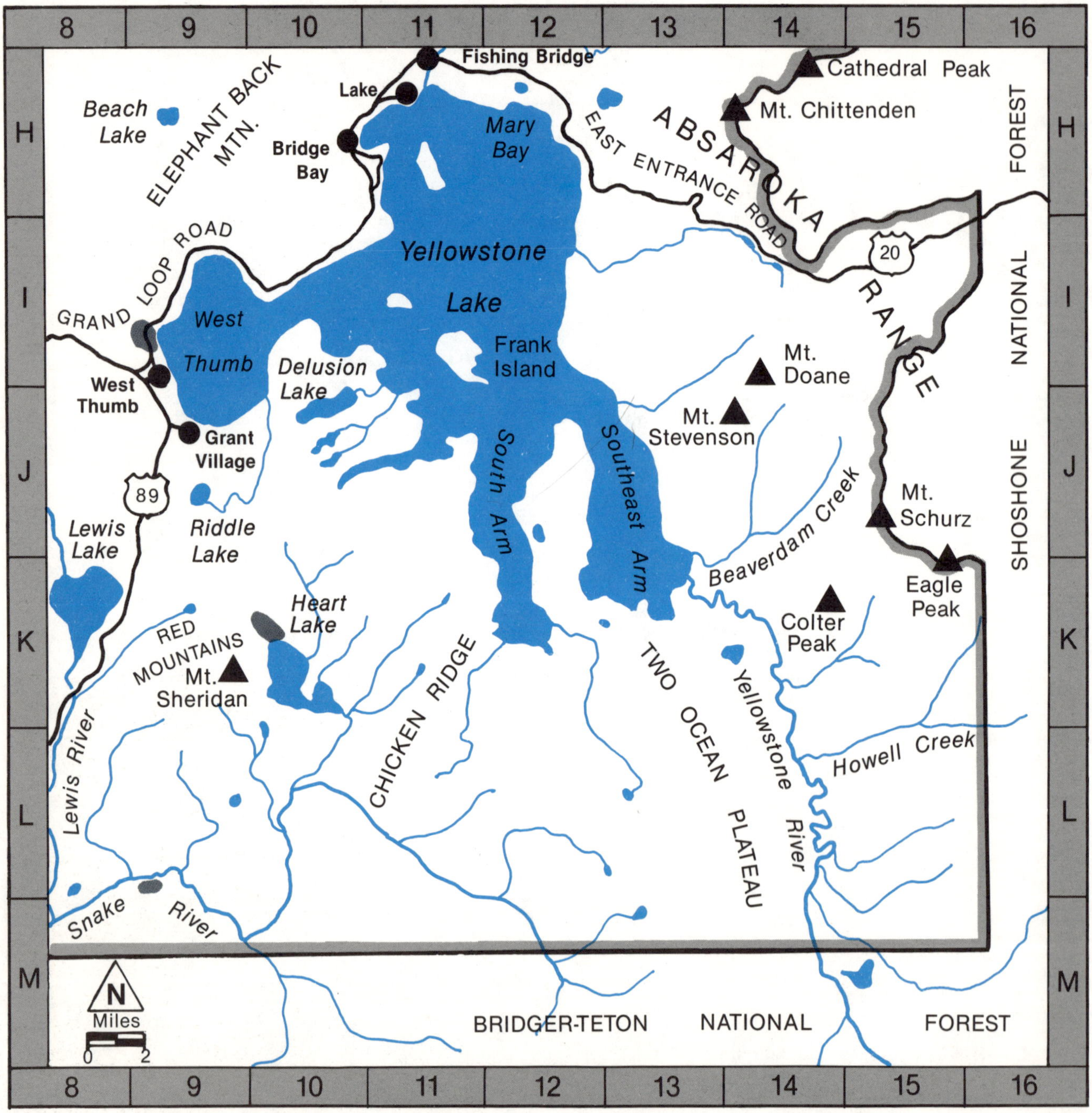

8
9
10
11
12
13
14
15
16
H
I
J
K
L
M
Fishing Bridge
Lake
Bridge Bay
Beach Lake
ELEPHANT BACK MTN.
Mary Bay
EAST ENTRANCE ROAD
ABSAROKA RANGE
Cathedral Peak
Mt. Chittenden
FOREST
NATIONAL
SHOSHONE
20
GRAND LOOP ROAD
Yellowstone Lake
West Thumb
West Thumb
Frank Island
Delusion Lake
Grant Village
Mt. Doane
Mt. Stevenson
South Arm
Southeast Arm
89
Lewis Lake
Riddle Lake
Beaverdam Creek
Mt. Schurz
Eagle Peak
Heart Lake
RED MOUNTAINS
Mt. Sheridan
CHICKEN RIDGE
TWO OCEAN PLATEAU
Yellowstone River
Colter Peak
Howell Creek
Lewis River
Snake River
N
Miles
0
2
BRIDGER-TETON NATIONAL FOREST

MAP 4: Southeastern Yellowstone Park

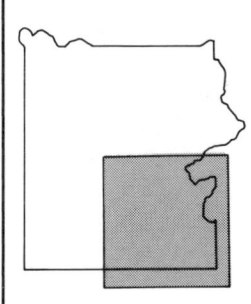

Absaroka Range
Arthur Peak, I14
Atkins Peak, J14
Barlow Peak, L10
Beaverdam, I13,J13
Beaverdam Creek, J13
Big Game Ridge, L9,M9
Breeze Point, I9
Bridge Bay, H9,H10
Brimstone Basin, J12
Camellia Mud Pots, H11
Carrington Island, I8
Channel Mountain, K10
Chicken Ridge, K10,L10
Cody Peak, H14
Colter Peak, K13
Concretion Cove, H11
Crecelius Cascade, I13
Delusion Lake, J9
Diamond Beach, H10
Dot Island, I10
Dryad Lake, H8
Eagle Peak, K14
Eleanor Lake, I13
Elephant Back Mountain, H9
Ephedra Spring, J8
Explorer's Creek, I11
Fishing Cone, J8
Frank Island, I10
Glade Lake, J13
Grizzly Creek, G10
Heart Lake, K9
Heart River, L9
Hidden Lake, J9
Howell Creek, K14
Hoyt Peak, I13
Indian Pond, H11
Jones Pass, H12
Knotted Woods Hill, H8,I8
Langford Cairn, J12
Lily Paint Pots, K12
Mammoth Crystal Spring, I13
Mariposa Lake, M12
Mary Bay, H11
Molly Islands, K11
Mount Chittenden, H12
Mount Doane, J13
Mount Hancock, M9,M10
Mount Humphreys, J14
Mount Langford, J13
Mount Schurz, J14
Mount Sheridan, K8
Mount Stevenson, J13
Mountain Creek, L14
Natural Bridge, H9
No Name Creek, K11
Outlet Canyon, K10
Outlet Creek, K10
Park Point, I11
Passage Creek, L11
Paycheck Pass, K8
Peale Island, K11
Pelican Roost, H11
Plenty Coups Peak, J14
Plover Point, J10
Potts Hot Spring Basin, I8
Prometheus Spring, K8
The Promontory, J11
Red Canyon, L9,M9
Red Mountains, K7,K8
Reservation Peak, I14
Riddle Lake, J8
Sage Creek, G12,H12
Sandy Creek, J8
Sickle Creek, L10
Signal Hills, I12
Signal Point, I11
Snake River, L10,M7,M11
Solution Creek, J8
Steamboat Point, H11
Steamboat Springs, H11
Stevenson Island, H10
Storm Point, H10,H11
Surprise Creek, K9,K10
Terrace Point, J12
Teton Point, I12
Thorofare Creek, M13
Topping Point, H10
Trappers Creek, K13
The Trident, L14
Trout Bay, H10
Two Ocean Plateau, L12
Wells Creek, H9
West Thumb, I8,I9
Witch Creek, K8
Yellowstone Lake
Yellowstone River

Monad formed by Trout Creek in the Hayden Valley

Elliott W. Hunter, Haynes Studio

Tourists along the Lamar River, 1917

ABIATHAR PEAK*   Map #2

This 10,928-foot peak (pronounced uh BI uh ther) of the Absaroka Range is located west of Barronette Peak above Soda Butte Creek, about 4.5 miles from the Northeast Entrance. In 1885, members of the Arnold Hague parties of the USGS named this peak after paleontologist Charles Abiathar White (1826-1910). White helped the USGS in its western explorations during the 1860s and 1870s and wrote numerous scientific reports on western America. Although he never visited Yellowstone Park, White collected and classified fossils from areas surrounding the Park.

ABSAROKA RANGE*   Map #2

Forming the eastern boundary of Yellowstone National Park, the Absaroka Range stretches some 80 miles long and is dominated by 11,000- and 12,000-foot peaks. During the 1870s, explorers called the range "Yellowstone Range," "Yellowstone Mountains," or "Upper Yellowstone Mountains." One of F. V. Hayden's men, W. H. Holmes, used the name "Great Yellowstone Range" in 1878. In 1881, Wyoming Territorial Governor John Hoyt referred to the range as the "Stinkingwater Mountains" (from the early name of the Shoshone River); and in 1888, T. B. Comstock called the range the "Snake Mountains," a reference to some bands of the Shoshone Indian tribe.

In 1885, USGS geologist Arnold Hague placed the name Absaroka Range on his new maps, evidently on specific instructions from his boss, John Wesley Powell. In the Hidatsa language, "Absaroka" was the name that Crows used to refer to themselves. It has been interpreted to mean "children of the large beaked bird," "forked-tail bird," "bird people," or "sparrowhawk people."

ABYSS POOL*   Map #3

In 1935, Chief Park Naturalist C. M. Bauer named Abyss Pool, a hot spring of the West Thumb Geyser Basin, for its impressive deepness. Bauer may have taken the name from Lieutenant G. C. Doane's 1870 description of a spring in this area: "the distance to which objects are visible down in [its] deep abysses is truly wonderful" (Bonney and Bonney, *Battle Drums*, p. 330). Abyss Pool may also be the spring that visitors referred to during the 1880s as "Tapering Spring" because of its sloping walls.

Nineteenth century observers were impressed with the pool's beauty. In 1871, F. V. Hayden reported that this spring's "ultramarine hue of the transparent depth in the bright sunlight was the most dazzlingly beautiful sight I have ever beheld" (*Preliminary Report*, p. 101). And W. W. Wylie (see Wylie Hill) observed in 1882 that the spring's walls, "coral-like in formation and singular in shape, tinted by the water's color, are surely good representations of fairy palaces" (*Yellowstone*, p. 47).

ACE OF HEARTS LAKE   Map #1

In 1884, USGS geologist J. P. Iddings took note of the shape of this lake, located 2 miles east of Horseshoe Hill, and named it Ace of Hearts Lake.

ADMIRATION POINT   Map #1

Since early days in the Park, Admiration Point has been a celebrated spot for observing the Main Terrace of Mammoth Hot Springs. A nearby point with about the same view was named "Arthur's Seat" in 1883 for the time that President Chester A. Arthur sat here to view the terraces. But Park tour guide G. L. Henderson gave the point its present name in 1883. Henderson had guided G. M. Von Rath of Bonn, Germany, around the area that summer. When Von Rath first looked from this viewpoint and saw the cerulean hot spring lakes below, "he lifted his hat from his venerable brow and letting his grey locks flutter in the wind, exclaimed: 'Vonderful! Vonderful! Most Vonderful' " (*Helena Weekly Herald*, June 7, 1888).

AFRICA LAKE   Map #1

This small lake is located on the east side of the Grand Loop Road about 2 miles south of Mammoth. Park tour bus drivers probably entered "Africa Lake" into local usage during the 1960s because of the lake's shape. The lake had been called "Beatty Lake" since 1931, when Park truck driver Roy Beatty had driven a new pickup truck into it. The small lake was also known as "Hays Lake" for Howard Hays, former president of Yellowstone Park Camps Company, and "Kidney Lake" because of its shape.

ALBRIGHT FALLS*   Map #3

Formerly called "Batchelder Column Cascade," this sloping, 260-foot cascade of an unnamed branch of the Bechler River is located near Batchelder Column. The falls was renamed Albright Falls by Yellowstone Park Superintendent Robert Barbee in 1986 in honor of Horace Marden Albright (1891-1986), one of the chief architects of the National Park Service and Yellowstone's superintendent from 1919 to 1929. Albright helped save this section of the Park when he lobbied against flooding the Bechler River with an irrigation dam.

As Yellowstone superintendent, Albright oversaw the change from army to civilian administration of the Park in 1916 and the ousting of undesirable concessionaires. Through his dealings with John D. Rockefeller, Jr., he was responsible for the creation of Grand Teton National Park. In 1933, he persuaded President Franklin Delano Roosevelt to add more than 50 military parks, historic sites, and national monuments to the National Park system.

On naming the waterfall for Albright, Superintendent Barbee wrote in 1986: "A few weeks before his death on March 28 of this year I discussed with Mr. Albright the idea of naming this . . . waterfall in southwestern Yellowstone in his honor. While naturally somewhat reticent, he was positive about the idea."

ALDEN VALLEY   Map #2

This small valley is located on the east side of the Yellowstone River in the Tower Fall area bench above the prominent columnar basalt layers. In about 1935, geologist Arthur D. Howard named the valley for W. C. Alden, a geologist who had postulated in the 1920s that the Yellowstone River once flowed through this valley. Alden theorized that glacial ice later diverted the Yellowstone from a course through the valley—between the Grand Canyon and the western slope of Specimen Ridge—to its present course.

ALUM CREEK*   Map #2

"Alum Creek" first appeared as a name on 1865 and 1869 maps, referring to a creek (possibly present-day Broad Creek or Sour Creek) that flowed into the Yellowstone River from the east. Prospectors or hunters probably named the creek "Alum" because of the sour waters caused by thermal springs dumping into the streams.

Members of the 1870 Washburn expedition named the present-day Alum Creek. In 1873, N. P. Langford, a member of the expedition, wrote: ". . . at two miles above the [Upper] falls we crossed a small stream which we named 'Alum' creek, as it is strongly impregnated with alum" (*Discovery of Yellowstone*, p. 98). The creek's waters do taste a little like alum, and many stories tell about its odiferous properties. Yellowstone tourist Andrew Weikert, for example, reported in 1877 that

> the headwaters of this stream are so strong with alum that one swallow is sufficient to draw ones [sic] face in such a shape that it is almost impossible to get it straightened again for at least an hour or so ("Journal of the Tour," p. 160).

Some writers have wrongly attributed a Park tall tale about Alum Creek to fur-trapper Jim Bridger. In one version of the story, a fur trapper rode his horse across the creek only to find that his horse's hooves had shrunk to the size of a pony's. In another version, sprinkling water from Alum Creek on Park roads caused the distances to shrink. These stories cannot be traced back to the fur-trade era and are probably of more recent origin.

ANEMONE GEYSER*   Map #3

Geologist Walter Weed named this geyser in the Geyser Hill Group of Upper Geyser Basin in about 1886. He probably named it for the sea anemone, a small animal with spiny projections that look a lot like geyser nodules. But some have suggested that Weed named the geyser for the anemone flower, even though "the resemblance is not that noticeable today." In recent years, the central (largest) vent of Anemone Geyser has erupted every 3 to 8 minutes with a duration of 20 to 30 seconds and a height of 3 to 12 feet. The southern vent frequently fills and erupts after the central vent drains.

ANGEL TERRACE†   Map #1

This long-dormant terrace of Mammoth Hot Springs was named in about 1895, possibly by photographer F. Jay Haynes. Haynes probably chose the name "because of the purity of the deposit and the resulting snowy whiteness of the terraces when inactive and the algae are not covering it" (*Haynes Guide*, p. 20). Several parts of Angel Terrace have been active over the years, exhibiting intermittent activity from 1883 to at least 1938.

Sections of the terrace have been known by different names. In 1883, guide G. L. Henderson toured New York Senator Roscoe Conkling over the Mammoth Hot Springs, and they named the terrace "Bethesda Plateau" for the Jerusalem pool in the Bible that supposedly had healing properties. Bathers used the Mammoth hot pools because of "the health restoring waters." Hearing that bathing appeared to have helped some ailing visitors, Conkling stated: "Behold the angel hath descended and touched the water, and whoever next bathes therein shall be made white [like an angel]!" And so the valley of Bethesda was named. Henderson added, "In this baptism we all concurred. So it may be said of names, as of constitutions, 'they are not made, but grow'" (*Helena Weekly Herald*, May 17, 1888). The terrace would ultimately be named Angel, but not for another dozen years.

Also in 1883, Henderson referred to another part of the terrace as "Chameleon Terrace" because it seemed to change color several times a day. He also named an upper southwestern side of Angel Terrace for German geologist G. M. Von Rath, who visited the springs in 1883. As early as 1885, Henderson named "Haynes Terrace," a few yards below "Rath Spring and Terrace," for photographer F. Jay Haynes. Also in that year, Henderson named other springs of the Angel complex. He considered "The Minnehaha Terrace" to be "the most beautiful of all the living springs on this plateau," but those springs had ceased flowing by 1888.

In 1884, Henderson guided agnostic orator Robert Ingersoll around Mammoth and named the lowest eastern edge of Angel Terrace "Ingersoll Spring and Terrace." By the next year, Henderson had applied his last name for the Angel area, calling it "White Sulphur Spring Plateau." This name probably had its roots in an early name, "White Mountain" (used to refer to *all* of Mammoth Hot Springs), and was no doubt a reference to the sulphur smell of the springs.

ANTHONY'S ENTRANCE   Map #1
See Cupid Spring

ANTLER PEAK*   Map #1
This peak of the Gallatin Range lies west of Indian Creek campground on the Grand Loop Road about 4 miles south of Mammoth. Antler Peak, which rises to an elevation of 10,023 feet, was named in 1885 by members of the Hague USGS parties for the elk and deer antlers that are commonly found shed in the Park. In 1878, the peak had been named "Bell's Peak," probably by geologist W. H. Holmes. Locals used that name into the mid-1890s, when, according to geologist Arnold Hague, "the name of Bell was dropped as it was [named for] a man who really had no interest in the Park. There was no good reason why his name should be put on the map" (Hague papers, Box 3, Book 3B, p. 443).

APOLLINARIS SPRING*   Map #1
Since at least the 1880s, thirsty Yellowstone tourists have stopped at this cold mineral water spring, located 1.5 to 2 miles north of Obsidian Cliff on the Grand Loop Road. As early as 1885, Constance Gordon-Cummings noticed that the Park contained "springs of natural Apollinaris water, sparkling fountains charged with carbonic acid" (*Overland Monthly*, January 1885, p. 13). This observation contradicted the prevalent and false idea that water in the Park should not be drunk because of the geysers and hot springs.

Carter Harrison, an 1890 traveler to Yellowstone, appears to have been responsible for giving the spring its formal name (in literature if not local usage). He wrote:

> Guide books tell us not to drink the water. I think their writers were in collusion with the hotel management to force guests to buy [bottles of] lager [beer] and apollinaris at 50 cents a bottle. By the way, there is on the first days [sic] drive [from North Entrance] an apollinaris spring. It seems to me the simon pure thing. We drank freely of it at the spring and afterwards from bottles carried for several hours. One of the bottles was tightly corked, and, when opened, popped as if well charged. . . . A gentleman in the party who has drank [sic] only Apollinaris since he came into the Park, tasted from my bottle and declared it quite equal to the pure stuff. . . . The hotel people are inclined to disparage the waters of the springs generally, and discourage their use, thereby . . . largely increasing the consumption of lager and bottled waters. . . . The enormous number of empty bottles along the road sides and at the hotels testify to the thirst and timidity of the traveling public (*A Summer's Outing*, pp. 68-70).

The "pure stuff" that Harrison referred to was Apollinaris Water, a well-known commercially bottled product (still available today) taken from a spring at Rhenish, West Germany.

ARNICA CREEK*   Map #3
In 1885, geologist Arnold Hague named this creek, which flows south into the north side of West Thumb bay. Hague had a particular interest in the yellow arnica flower that grows in the Park and once recommended that his fellow survey members rub it on their skin to ease sore muscles. Northern Pacific Railroad surveyors had named the stream "Beaver Creek" in 1882, and guidebook writers referred to it as "Hot Spring Creek" in 1883.

ARROW CANYON†   Map #1
Arrow Canyon is located northeast of Norris on the west side of the Washburn Range. Members of the Hague parties of the USGS named this canyon sometime between 1896 and 1904 to reflect its long, straight, arrow-like shape.

ARROWHEAD SPRING   Map #3
Park Geologist George Marler named this hot spring in the Geyser Hill Group of Upper Geyser Basin sometime before 1959. He selected the name because "during an attempt to remove Park-visitor rubble from this spring an obsidian arrowhead was retrieved."

ARSENIC GEYSER   Map #1
In 1887, geologist Arnold Hague named Arsenic Geyser, located in the Porcelain Basin of Norris Geyser Basin. Hague reported in about 1915 that the geyser had a "large amount of arsenic held in solution by the hot waters before reaching the surface" (Hague papers, Box 13, p. 20). He described the geyser as being 4 feet high with eruptions at short intervals for a 20-minute duration. The waters of Arsenic Geyser contain no more arsenic than other waters of the area, but Hague may have thought that the green scorodite particles in the area were arsenic.

ARTEMISIA GEYSER*   Map #3
Artemisia Geyser is part of the Cascade Group in Upper Geyser Basin. In 1883, geologist Walter Weed named this

Tourists at Apollinaris Spring, 1925

Horace M. Albright (left) with C. W. Cook and Dixie Anzer at the Park's semi-centennial celebration, 1922

geyser "Artemisia Spring" because of "the sage color of its deposits" (USGS, Box 56, vol. 3, pp. 106-107). *Artemisia* is the Latin name for the type of sagebrush that grows in Yellowstone, and the name has nothing to do with the color of water in the geyser or its eruption pattern. Geologist Arnold Hague described Artemisia Geyser in his paper on "The Geyser Basins":

> It lies back from the river, not far from the edge of the forest, a large, irregular-shaped pool 55 by 60 feet.... The pool is turquoise-blue in color, highly transparent.... The water rises and falls quietly and periodically, being only ruffled by escaping gas bubbles.... In an eruption an enormous volume of water is ejected, which slowly builds up, by evaporation, an area of beaded sinter of varied structure.... The deposits lining the pool are pure white except along the border, or where they are under water much of the time, in which case they present a peculiar olive-green tint characteristic of this particular spring (Hague papers, Box 11, pp. 76-77).

It was this coloring that inspired Weed to name the geyser Artemisia.

Geologists did not identify Artemisia as a geyser until 1886, when Hague recorded that it had been "playing very frequently" since his return to the Park that year.

ARTHUR PEAK* Map #4

This peak, located in the Absaroka Range 4.5 miles southwest of the Park's East Entrance, rises to an elevation of 10,438 feet. Yellowstone Park Superintendent Roger Toll named the peak in 1932 for President Chester A. Arthur, who in 1883 was the first president to visit Yellowstone.

ARTIST POINT* Map #2

Located on the south rim of the Grand Canyon of the Yellowstone River, Artist Point is the most famous of the Grand Canyon viewpoints. Park photographer F. Jay Haynes probably named the spot in about 1883, and the earliest known written use of the name is in his 1890 guidebook. Haynes may have thought, as others have, that Thomas Moran sat at this vantage point when he created the sketches for his famous 1872 painting of the canyon. But Moran actually made his sketches from the north side of the canyon at a place now called Moran Point. It is also possible that Haynes named Artist Point for himself.

ARTISTS' PAINTPOTS* Map #1

In about 1884, geologist Walter Weed named Artists' Paintpots, a thermal area in the Gibbon Geyser Basin north of Gibbon Canyon. The bright, varied, colorful mud in the area reminded Weed of an artist's palette. Artists' Paintpots is well-known for its bright red, emerald, yellow, blue, and cream-colored mud springs, which reach the surface through brilliantly colored clays. Yellowstone Park Superintendent P. W. Norris explored Artists' Paintpots in 1878 and later referred to it as "Paint Pool Basin." It was also known as "Gibbon Paint Pot Basin" and "Devil's Paintpots." The term "paint pot" comes from early visitors describing mud hot springs as resembling vats of bubbling paint.

ARVID LAKE Map #1

This small lake, located just west of Mount Holmes between Echo Peak and the White Peaks, drains into the head of Indian Creek. Carl Hals and members of a Northern Pacific Railroad survey team named Arvid Lake in 1882, but there is no record of the reason for the name. In recent years, some have referred to Arvid Lake as "Echo Lake" because of its proximity to Echo Peak, but the name Arvid Lake has historical priority.

ASTA SPRING Map #3

Asta Spring is the main, gushing spring of the Hillside Springs in Upper Geyser Basin. In about 1884, geologists with the Hague parties of the USGS (probably Walter Weed) named the spring for a shortened form of *astacin*, a red carotenoid ketone pigment found especially in crustaceans, such as lobsters, but also in plants. Algae growing along the runoff channels of Asta Spring are bright red in color.

ASTRINGENT CREEK* Map #2

Astringent Creek is a northern tributary of Pelican Creek, northeast of Mary Bay on Yellowstone Lake. In 1878, members of the third Hayden survey named this stream "Lake Creek" because they thought it originated from what is now called White Lake. Geologist Arnold Hague gave the stream its present name in 1886 because of the contracting laxative-like acid quality of the water. In 1886, Hague recorded in his field notebooks:

> Started out with [Thomas J.] Ryder [packer] from Camp just before 9 o'Clock and traveled northward up the creek on which we camped, which as yet has no name but which should have some designation. Some name suggestive of its alum and iron waters or its numerous springs (USGS, Box 55, vol. 2, p. 78).

ATKINS PEAK* Map #4

An 11,043-foot-high peak of the Absaroka Range, Atkins Peak is located directly east of the Southeast Arm of Yellowstone Lake and just south of Plenty Coups Peak. In 1885, geologist Arnold Hague named the peak for John DeWitt Clinton Atkins (1825-1908), the newly appointed U.S. Indian Commissioner. Originally from Tennessee, Atkins had been active in Tennessee politics until the Civil War, when he fought for the South as a lieutenant colonel of the Fifth Tennessee Regiment. After the war, Atkins won election to five terms as a congressman from Tennessee. Hague gave Atkins's name to the peak in recognition of the congressman's role in establishing the U.S. Geological Survey.

ATOMIZER GEYSER   Map #3

Located in the Cascade Group of Upper Geyser Basin, Atomizer Geyser was named in 1885-1888 by tour operator G. L. Henderson. Henderson saw a similarity between the geyser's appearance and an atomizer, which breaks liquids into small particles and a very fine spray. Atomizer Geyser is in all probability the spring that the Hayden survey named "Restless Geyser" in 1878.

BABY SPRING and TERRACE   Map #1

Baby Spring is located just west of and across the road from Cupid Spring at Mammoth terraces. Park naturalists named Baby Spring in about 1932 because of its small size. Apparently active in 1932 and then almost dry in 1933, the spring rejuvenated in 1934 and was also active in 1936 and 1938. There are no records of any further activity until 1962-1965, and the spring has been dormant since 1966. Only the terrace remains.

BACK BASIN   Map #1

Back Basin is one of the three major subdivisions of Norris Geyser Basin. During the 1880s, members of the Hague surveys called this area "Tantalus Basin." But much of the surveyors' work was never published, and that name slipped into obscurity. Park Geologist George Marler applied the name Back Basin in 1964, perhaps adopting it from local usage.

BACON RIND CREEK*   Map #1

Bacon Rind Creek flows east to the Gallatin River from the Park's west boundary, about 20 miles north of West Yellowstone on U.S. Highway 191. There is no record of who named the creek, but U.S. Army scouts called it Bacon Rind Creek as early as 1898, probably referring to their breakfast around the campfire. Geologist Arnold Hague thought that contractors who surveyed the Park's west boundary may have named the creek. In a June 1904 letter, Hague disparaged the name, calling it "a common, vulgar name" that "should have no place in the nomenclature of the Park" (Hague papers, Box 5). Despite Hague's criticism, Bacon Rind Creek appeared on official maps in 1907 and has survived.

BANNOCK FORD   Map #2

Bannock Ford is on the Yellowstone River near the Sulphur Beds at the bottom of the trail down to Tower Fall. This famous ford, which is at the point of a small island, is one of the few on the river north of Yellowstone Lake. The Great Bannock Trail crossed the Yellowstone at this "crossing of immemorial antiquity," and Indians crossed the river and scaled the steep ravines on the east side as they followed the trail across the Park. This is also probably the place where John Colter, the first white to explore Yellowstone, crossed the Yellowstone River on his 1807-1808 trip.

BANNOCK PEAK*   Map #1

This peak of the Gallatin Range can be seen directly west of Indian Creek campground on the Grand Loop Road, about 4 miles south of Mammoth. Park Superintendent P. W. Norris named this peak "Norris Mountain" during the early 1880s. It received its present name in 1885 from members of the Hague parties of the USGS for the Bannock Indian tribe and the Great Bannock Trail, which passed a few miles to the south.

The Bannocks, who were closely related to the Shoshones, lived southwest of Yellowstone in Idaho. Their name has been translated to refer to their upswept hairstyles or to mean "people from below," "southern people," or "people from across the water." In 1878, dissatisfied with conditions on their Fort Hall reservation in Idaho, a small band of Bannocks left the territory and entered the Park. At Mammoth, the Indians stole 20 horses and left the Park by heading northeast up the Lamar River. This raid may have influenced the Hague survey's naming of the peak.

BARLOW PEAK*   Map #4

Located 9 miles southeast of the South Arm of Yellowstone Lake, Barlow Peak rises to 9,622 feet. Geologist Arnold Hague named this mountain in 1895 for Captain John Whitney Barlow (1838-1914), an army engineer officer who led a party of explorers on the first official exploration to the headwaters of the Snake River in 1871. Barlow's name had been given to the Snake River above Harebell Creek in 1872, but Hague transferred Barlow's name to this peak in the same area.

Barlow worked in tandem with F. V. Hayden's expedition in 1871, sharing the same military escort and following the same route through the Park. Barlow also occasionally separated from Hayden, discovering and breaking new ground on his own. He named Mount Sheridan, Mount Hancock, and Mount Humphreys; he discovered Heart Lake, Fairy Falls, and a number of geysers; and he explored unknown territory around the headwaters of the Snake and Lamar rivers.

Barlow helped Hayden lobby Congress for the establishment of Yellowstone National Park by publishing a portion of his report in the Chicago *Evening Journal* on January 13, 1872. Unfortunately, Barlow's specimens and photographs were lost in the Great Chicago Fire, but his official report and map remain key pieces of Yellowstone literature.

BARRONETTE PEAK*   Map #2

This 10,404-foot-high peak is located in the Absaroka Range just west of the road between Tower and Cooke City, about 7 miles west of the Northeast Entrance. Named for Collins Jack (John H. "Yellowstone Jack") Baronett (1829-1901), this peak has the dubious honor of being the only place name in Yellowstone that is officially approved in a misspelled form. When members of Hayden's third survey named the peak for Baronett in 1878, they misspelled his name.

Baronett was born in Glencoe, Scotland, in about 1830. Before coming to Yellowstone in 1864 to prospect for gold, Baronett had traveled in the South Pacific and in western America. He guided and prospected in Montana and the Southwest and scouted for George Custer in 1868. Baronett was also the man who found Truman Everts, the lost member of the 1870 Washburn expedition, and received a reward. In 1871, he built the first bridge across the Yellowstone River at the confluence of the Yellowstone and Lamar rivers, where he collected tolls.

Baronett also served as one of Yellowstone's first guides. He guided Gen. Philip H. Sheridan on several trips through Yellowstone and was the only member of the civilian police force to be retained when the army took over the Park in 1886. He was even considered for the superintendency of the Park in 1884. Baronett lived in Livingston until his death in 1901.

BARTLETT SLOUGH†   Map #3

Bartlett Slough is an intermittent stream that flows east to Boundary Creek just north of the Bechler River Ranger Station on the west side of Bechler Meadows. The name of the stream honors the Bartlett brothers (first names unknown), who kept several hundred head of cattle in this area during the 1860s. During the late 1890s, U.S. Army scouts used the Bartletts' old cabin for patrol purposes. It is not known when this place name was given or by whom, but the name was in general use by the 1940s.

BATCHELDER COLUMN*   Map #3

This 50-foot-high column of volcanic rock stands alone on a hillside about 2 miles and a little west of Three River Junction, on the trail from Bechler River to Old Faithful. Explorer W. C. Gregg discovered this "sentinel" rock in 1920 and named it in 1921 for Amos Grant Batchelder (1868-1921). Batchelder, who died in a plane crash in 1921, was well-known for his work in America's national parks.

As chairman of the American Automobile Association, Batchelder did "invaluable" work to help open Yellowstone Park to automobile tourists. In 1915, he studied the feasibility of allowing automobiles into the Park and reported in favor of the idea. On July 31, 1915, a Ford Model-T Runabout driven by two people from Minnesota was the first motor vehicle to legally pass through Yellowstone's North Entrance.

BATH LAKE   Map #1

G. L. Henderson named Bath Lake, a small hot spring at Mammoth Hot Springs, in 1882 or 1883. Bathing was allowed in the Park in the early days, and bathers probably began using this spring in 1883. (Bathing has not been allowed in Yellowstone's hot springs for many years because of the potential for damage to the springs and danger to the bathers.) Geologist Walter Weed, who studied the spring that summer, described the lake's shores as strewn with discarded garments. George Thomas, a waiter at the new National Hotel at Mammoth in 1883, recalled in his "Recollections":

> It was a wonderful swimming hole and had a long plank floating in the water and a swimmer could lie full length at one end of the plank and still be deep enough in the water to paddle around and be happy. One afternoon I and three other young fellows from the Hotel Waiters force, went to this lake for a swim. We had no bathing suits on, and the lake was surrounded by a growth of shrubbery that hid the water from sight, so we figured that we would not be disturbed by any passers-by. We had been in the water about an hour when we were surprised by a shower of stones that were being thrown by four young women who wanted their turn in the lake. As we were reasonable gentlemen, we left the water, grabbed our clothes and took to the brush, leaving the victorious women to enjoy their bath . . . (pp. 5-6).

Although at one time women were allowed to take their turn in Bath Lake, by 1885 they had been barred. Henderson reported in the June 27, 1885, *Livingston Enterprise*:

> It is to be regretted that both sexes cannot share this delightful bath. Ladies cannot even see it, for in pleasant weather [a] large number of nude male bathers occupy it exclusively. The government ought to regulate this matter by either constructing or permitting the construction of dressing rooms in which both sexes could have bathing suits and together "bask in the glare and stem the tepid water."

Bath Lake, Mammoth Hot Springs, 1884

Gen. John W. Barlow, 1861

Jack Baronett's toll bridge across the Yellowstone River, c. 1879

There was so much trouble with nudity at Bath Lake that army Capt. Moses Harris finally closed it to daytime bathing. Henderson had suggested that one solution might be to "enclose" a nearby spring for ladies (see Ladies Lake), but that never occurred. By 1912, both sexes could bathe at Bath Lake "provided they are properly dressed," and by 1919, the government had built a small bath house. The bath house was removed in 1928, after the Mammoth swimming pool was built in 1925. Bath Lake went dry in 1926, and in 1927 it became "Old Bath Lake." The lake remained dry until 1959, when the Yellowstone earthquake restored its water and gave it back its name. Bath Lake dried up again in 1984 and has been dry since.

BATHTUB SPRING*   Map #1

Bathtub Spring is a hot spring located just west of the Norris Museum in the Back Basin of Norris Geyser Basin. This ear-shaped spring was a favorite of travelers who took the stage road through the Park from 1880 to 1915. In the early days of the Park, the main stage road made a turn just as it reached the spring on the west side of the road. The track of the old dirt road can still be seen near the spring.

Many early visitors described the spring as reaching heights of up to 20 feet. It was variously called "Devil's Bathtub," "Devil's Ink Well," "Devil's Inkstand," "Slum Kettle," "Devil's Inkpot," "Schlammkessel" (German for "mud kettle"), "Mud Geyser," "Demon's Washtub," and "Blue Volcano."

In more recent years, Bathtub Spring—which is still shaped like a bathtub—has been a muddy yellow spring that responds to changes in the surface water table and sometimes bubbles actively. The spring had minor eruptions during the early 1950s, but it has not been an active geyser for a very long time.

BEACH SPRING   Map #3

Geologist Walter Weed named this geyser, which is located in the Geyser Hill Group of the Upper Geyser Basin, in 1886 or 1887. The spring became well-known to tourists during the 1890s because of the wide border of sinter (the residue of evaporations from springs) in its central bowl. This formation resembles a beautiful sandy beach in color and form.

BEAD GEYSER*   Map #3

Bead Geyser is located in the Pink Cone Group of the Lower Geyser Basin. In 1873, T. B. Comstock probably gave this name to present-day Labial Geyser or to one of the vents near Labial. He named it for the "aggregation of minute, shiny, globular grains" that he found in the geyser (in Jones, *Report*, p. 248). The name was later transferred to present-day Bead Geyser.

BEAR PARK   Map #3

This large meadow is located at the head of the Firehole River, just northwest of Madison Lake and west of the river. In 1882, Carl Hals and other members of a Northern Pacific Railroad survey team named the meadow and put Bear Park on their map. Bear Park was included on Park maps for many years afterward. For reasons unknown, the name does not appear on current maps of the Park.

BEARS PLAYGROUND   Map #3

This small pond, which is dry at times, is located just west of the bridge that crosses the Firehole River on the Grand Loop Road downstream from Kepler Cascades (1.5 miles from Old Faithful). By 1912, locals were calling this area "Bears Feeding Grounds" because a bear-feeding show for tourists was often staged near the pond. By 1914, however, maps identified the pond as Bears Playground. Bear-feeding shows were common during the early days of the Park, but the practice has long been discontinued as being incompatible with protecting and preserving the Park's natural ecosystem.

BEAVER LAKE*   Map #1

Park Superintendent P. W. Norris discovered and named this lake at the foot of Obsidian Cliff in 1878. Norris took the name from a story supposedly told by fur-trapper Jim Bridger:

> So [it is] with his [Bridger's] famous legend of a lake with millions of beaver nearly impossible to kill because of their superior "cuteness, with haunts and houses in inaccessible grottoes in the base of a glistening mountain of glass" [which Norris thought was nearby Obsidian Cliff] . . . (*Report Upon the Yellowstone*, pp. 989, 980).

Norris does not identify which Bridger story he meant, but he may have heard it from Bridger in 1844 when the trapper told Norris other stories about the canyons of the upper Snake River. The Beaver Lake story may also be a variant of Bridger's tale of a mountain of glass that included a description of a nearby lake filled with beaver.

Visitors have noticed beaver dams at this lake since early days. In his *Practical Guide* (1890), A. P. Guptill wrote that "more than a dozen beaver dams are constructed across the lake" (p. 34), and Maturin Ballou reported in 1892 that a "colony [of beaver] have built a series of thirty dams, thus forming a sheet of water . . . half a mile in width, and two miles long . . ." (*New El Dorado*,

p. 30). More recent references (see *Haynes Guide*, p. 60) mention a 1,000-foot-long beaver dam that runs the entire length of the lake's northern shore.

BEAVERDAM   Map #4

Beaverdam is the long and prominent ridge that connects Top Notch Peak to Mount Langford directly south of Sylvan Pass. P. W. Norris named the ridge in 1881 and put it on his map of the Park. It is not clear why Norris selected this name. Perhaps he mistakenly thought that the ridge was the head of Beaverdam Creek, which empties into the Southeast Arm of Yellowstone Lake.

BEAVERDAM CREEK*   Map #4

Beaverdam Creek is located east of the Southeast Arm of Yellowstone Lake. Members of the Hayden survey named the creek in 1871. In his diary of the expedition, survey member A. C. Peale recorded the great numbers of beaver dams in the area.

BECHLER RIVER*   Map #3

The Bechler River is the major river in the southwest corner of the Park. Frank Bradley, a member of the second Hayden survey in 1872, named the river for Gustavus R. Bechler, the chief topographer on the expedition. In 1878, Henry Gannett wrote that Bechler was the "discoverer" of the river, but fur-trapper Osborne Russell had explored the area 40 years earlier.

Not much is known about Gustavus Bechler. He drew many of the maps of the 1872 Hayden survey, including the first one of Shoshone Geyser Basin and two very important and little-known maps of Upper, Midway, and Lower geyser basins. Sidford Hamp, a young man who accompanied the survey party that year, wrote to his mother on August 16, 1872: ". . . I am with Mr. Bechler the map maker and he is rather slow so we don't get into camp so soon as the others" (YNP Research Library). Bechler also accompanied the survey on its attempted ascent of Grand Teton in 1872 and sustained a bad fall in the process. He also explored and mapped Cliff Lake (west of Yellowstone Park). Bechler stayed with Hayden until 1878, accompanying him on later surveys of Colorado and other parts of the West, but his cantankerous ways and his jealousy of other division leaders made him a difficult companion.

BEEHIVE GEYSER*   Map #3

This important geyser is part of the Geyser Hill Group in the Upper Geyser Basin. On September 19, 1870, members of the Washburn party made the first recorded sighting of the geyser:

> Opposite our camp, on the east side of the Firehole River, is a symmetrical cone resembling an old fashioned straw beehive with the top cut off. . . . We named this geyser the "Bee Hive" (Langford, *Discovery of Yellowstone*, p. 173).

The expedition listed the geyser's duration at 10 to 18 minutes and carefully triangulated the height of Beehive's eruption. Their measurement of 219 feet is still accepted. The height of the water column is spectacular—usually 100 to 219 feet—and observers over the years have often likened the eruption to a firehose nozzle.

Beehive has always been a favorite of Park visitors. Upon hearing "The Beehive is playing!" early tourists reportedly ran screaming in delight from the lobby of the Old Faithful Hotel to see the spectacular eruption. In the September 10, 1887, *Livingston Enterprise*, G. L. Henderson described one eruption of Beehive that occurred during a church service being held nearby:

> In September, 1882, the Rev. Geo. Comfort was giving out a hymn to be sung by assembled worshippers at the Upper Geyser Basin when a young lady, just to see the effect on the audience, cried out "Bee Hive!" The worshippers broke loose and scampered for the footbridge, George Comfort following, hatless, with glasses on head, hymn book in hand, as eager as his audience to see the famous Bee hive [*sic*] hurl its torrid waves 200 feet into the air. The young lady had no idea that the Bee Hive would erupt, and was more astonished than anyone else when she saw the chambers of the deep let loose its liquid swarm of hissing hot drops and atomized vapor with such prompt response to her timely, or untimely, exclamation. George Comfort good-naturedly comforted his audience by the assurance that a great geyser was also an ordained agent of the Almighty to proclaim his power and glory to man, and that it was no discredit to him or his flock to suspend their services for a quarter of an hour to hear and see one of the natural agents of God's infinite power and wisdom. The young lady is yet in doubt whether the same exclamation that dispersed the assembly did not also arouse the Bee Hive into premature activity.

As geologist Arnold Hague noted in 1911, the Beehive is a spectacular sight:

> In full action the Beehive has no superior for beauty of its jet and sharpness of outline. The height of a measured column gave 222 feet, and probably frequently attains 200 feet. A feature of the Beehive is the relatively small amount of water thrown out during its eruptions, as compared with the volume of steam (Hague papers, Box 11, "The Geyser Basins," pp. 27-29).

Beehive Geyser has a history of being irregular. After long periods of dormancy, the geyser will sometimes erupt 3 or 4 times per day. Beehive was very active from 1870 to 1900, with some 221 known eruptions occurring during this period. From 1900 to 1920, Beehive was dormant some of the time; it was somewhat active from 1920 to 1930, and it lay dormant until 1946. The geyser rejuvenated in 1946-1947 and has been in an active cycle ever since.

BELGIAN POOL   Map #3

Belgian Pool is a hot spring located in the Sawmill Group of the Upper Geyser Basin. Because of its appearance, this spring became known as the "Oyster" or "Oyster Spring" in about 1900. The name was in common usage from 1900 to 1915, but then it fell into obscurity. In 1929, an accident gave the pool its present name. Georges Landoy of Antwerp, Belgium, who was visiting the Park with a group of European journalists, fell into this Upper Basin hot pool and later died (the local paper erroneously reported that Landoy died from the water of Castle Geyser splashing onto him). Sometime after the incident, this spring was named Belgian Pool, but who gave the name and when are not known.

BELLEFONTAINE GEYSER*   Map #3

Located in the Fountain Group of the Lower Geyser Basin, Bellefontaine Geyser is about 260 feet southwest of Jelly Spring. Walter Weed's use of the name Bellefontaine in 1888 makes him the likely namer of this geyser. He described the spring's eruption as "a profuse bubbling and the formation of a foaming water hillock." *Bellefontaine* means "beautiful fountain" in French, and certainly geologists Weed and Arnold Hague thought it was. In about 1911, Hague described Bellefontaine as "a circular spring of clear blue water of great beauty . . . bubbling more or less all the time, accompanied by a copious runoff of highly heated waters" (Hague papers, Box 11, "Firehole Geyser Basin," pp. 51-52). Weed recorded the temperature of the "eruption" at 177.5°F., too cool for a steam eruption; he suggested that gas was a factor.

BELLOW SPRING   Map #2

This hot spring is located on an overhang on the north bank of Wrong Creek, just west of Green Grotto Spring in the Rainbow Springs group on Mirror Plateau. Geologist Walter Weed named Bellow Spring in 1888 for its resemblance to a fireplace bellows. Weed described the spring as projecting 4 feet out over the stream below. In 1980, Bellow Spring expelled water into Wrong Creek through the tip of its rock "bellows."

BELL'S LAKE   Map #2

This small lake is located 4 miles northeast of Mount Washburn and about a mile east of Antelope Creek. In 1879, P. W. Norris may have named this lake because it is shaped like a bell. The possessive form of the name, however, makes it more likely that Norris named the lake for a person, possibly A. Bell, who was acting Secretary of the Interior during the late 1870s.

BERYL SPRING*   Map #1

A hot spring in the Gibbon Canyon, Beryl Spring is located about 5.5 miles south of Norris Junction on the Grand Loop Road. In about 1884, a member of the Hague parties of the USGS (probably Walter Weed) seems to have added the name to one of his 1883 notebooks. The spring was named for its resemblance to the color of a blue-green gemstone. Like the gem, the name is pronounced "burl," not "barrel."

With a temperature above the boiling point, Beryl Spring is one of the hottest springs in Yellowstone. In 1885, the main road was moved to the west side of the river, and tourists were able to drive right by the spring, just as they can today.

BEULA LAKE*   Map #3

Members of the second Hayden survey in 1872 named this small lake, which is located near the Park's southern boundary. Topographer Rudolph Hering may have named the lake in his report, spelling it "Beulah" instead of "Beula," as it appeared on Hayden's map. The name given to the lake may be from Beulah, the mystical land of sunshine and delight in Bunyan's *Pilgrim's Progress*. In that book, pilgrims rested in Beulah until they were called to cross the river to the Celestial City. At Beula Lake, the pilgrims resting were probably the Hayden survey members who camped at the lake before crossing the Falls River to continue their work. If this speculation is correct, the "h" should be returned to the name.

BIG BEAR LAKE†   Map #3

Big Bear Lake is located near the Park's western boundary, about 10 miles west of the Lower Geyser Basin. USGS topographer Raymond E. Hill named the lake in 1958 because of these circumstances:

> A packer, a rodman, and myself had packed back in to a ranger cabin quite some distance south of West Yellowstone, where there was reputed to be a flowing spring. When we reached the cabin, all that remained [of the spring] was mud and bird feathers. Since it was quite late, we dug down and managed to get a small amount of water of questionable purity for drinking. . . . Consulting our photographs, we identified what appeared to be a small pond in heavy timber, and the rodman and I set off at first light on foot through dense

Auto stage parties at Beaver Dam just east of the Lava Creek crossing

G. C. Axelrod, Haynes Studio

jack pine to verify this. We did indeed find water and though rather stagnant, [it] was a welcome sight. . . . We set up a working base at this pond, and the first night there the animals were badly frightened and got out into the pond with hobbles on, stirring up the mud so badly the water was near unusable the next morning. Tracks in the mud disclosed the presence of a bear of remarkable size. That same morning while riding out to continue surveys we arrived at the rather shallow lake, and the fresh tracks of what was presumed to be the same bear were found there. Hence the name proposed . . . Big Bear Lake (Hill to author, April 28, 1980).

BIG GAME RIDGE†   Map #4

This precipitous ridge, which forms a wall that blocks much of the Park's southern boundary, has been called "the heart of big game hunting" because it extends into the Teton National Forest where hunting is permitted. Members of the 1872 Hayden survey named it "Elk Ridge," but geologist Arnold Hague changed the name in 1895 to Big Game Ridge because "in former years it furnished abundant sport for the hunter in search of bear, elk, deer, and mountain lion" (*Geology of the Yellowstone National Park*, p. 167). Theodore Roosevelt, the most famous hunter to shoot on Big Game Ridge, wrote about his experiences on the ridge for *Century Illustrated* in 1892.

BIJAH SPRING*   Map #1

Bijah Spring is a large hot spring located about a mile north of Nymph Lake and 3 miles north of Norris Junction on the west side of the Grand Loop Road. Bijah Spring is one of Yellowstone's place-name mysteries. Geologist Walter Weed reported in 1888: "Bijah Spg seems a rather inapp[ropriate] cognomen for the large spring near the Twin Lakes, but [it] will probably be retained as [a] sign board has been up a couple of years" (USGS, Box 48, vol. 21, p. 71). When making corrections to one of his 1884 notebooks, Weed added the possessive form of the name, making it "Bijah's Spring," suggesting that the spring might have been named after someone or something.

Bijah is a tree that grows in India, but there is no evidence that this has anything to do with the origin of the spring's name. It is possible that the original signboard for the spring was badly lettered, and that the name was supposed to be "Bijou," which is a jewel or exquisite trinket. It has also been suggested that Bijah was a corruption of "Big Joe," who might have been a Park worker or even one of the roadside beggar bears in the area.

BISCUIT BASIN*   Map #3

A. C. Peale named this part of Upper Geyser Basin "Soda Geyser Group" in 1878 after its main geyser (present-day Jewell Geyser). Hague survey members also referred to the basin as "Sapphire Basin" because of its major hot spring, the Sapphire Pool. Known for a time as "Silver Globe Basin" (after the Silver Globe Spring), Biscuit Basin received its current name during the late 1880s because of the knobby, biscuit-like geyserite formations around Sapphire Pool and Cauliflower Geyser. In 1887, Walter Weed recorded that the deposit around Sapphire Pool was "forming 'biscuit basins', on the west side of the spring" (USGS, Box 53, vol. 28, p. 105). These biscuits became quite well-known through the work of Park photographer F. Jay Haynes. Unfortunately, many of the biscuits were destroyed by the Yellowstone earthquake in 1959, which caused hot spring runoff channels to wash them down into the Firehole River.

BISON SUMMIT   Map #2

This is a summit of Specimen Ridge, which is located 3 to 4 miles southeast of Amethyst Mountain. Park Superintendent P. W. Norris named the summit in 1879, and it appeared on his maps in 1880 and 1881. Bison Summit is near one of Norris's early trails and is probably the hill marked "9468" on topographic maps.

BLACK BUTTE†   Map #1

Black Butte is located in the extreme northwestern corner of the Park, between Black Butte and Specimen creeks. It was named in local usage as early as 1910 for its dark-colored lavas.

BLACK CANYON (of the Yellowstone)†   Map #1

Early fur trappers and prospectors referred to this canyon—located north of the Blacktail Deer Plateau—as the "Third Canyon" of the Yellowstone. Rock Canyon, at Livingston, Montana, was the "First Canyon," Yankee Jim Canyon was the "Second Canyon," and the Grand Canyon of the Yellowstone was the "Fourth Canyon."

The Folsom expedition in 1869 and the Washburn expedition in 1870 had to bypass this canyon because its passage was so difficult. The canyon walls are literally black in some places, and Lt. G. C. Doane wrote in 1870 that Black Canyon was "grand, gloomy, and terrible; a solitude peopled with fantastic ideas, an empire of shadows and of turmoil" (in Bonney and Bonney, *Battle Drums*, p. 245). From his dark descriptions, it is apparent that Black Canyon made an impression on Doane, and he probably gave it its name in 1876 during his winter trip through the Park.

BLACK DRAGON'S CALDRON Map #2

This giant, black, seething mudpot in the Mud Volcano area came into existence sometime in February 1948. As it grew, the mudpot shifted to the south until it is now 200 feet from its original location. Shortly after the mudpot developed, Chief Park Naturalist David Condon named Black Dragon's Caldron for its color and its lashing, tongue-like agitation. The explosion that created this "demon of the back woods" blew trees out by their roots, and the weight of disgorged mud killed other nearby trees. Today, Black Dragon's Caldron is an awe-inspiring spectacle of the violent forces of the earth's processes.

BLACK SAND BASIN* Map #3

Black Sand Basin is a separately designated part of the Upper Geyser Basin, located just west of Old Faithful. In 1878, A. C. Peale named this area the "Emerald Group" of springs, taking the name from Emerald Pool. During the 1890s, locals called it Black Sand Basin because of one spring, present-day Black Sand Pool. In 1927, the place-names committee officially transferred the name from the spring to the entire area. The name refers to the tiny obsidian fragments that make up the sand in Black Sand Pool and in the entire area.

BLACK WARRIOR SPRINGS* Map #3

This hot spring feeds Black Warrior Lake and is part of the Black Warrior (Firehole Lake) Group in the Lower Geyser Basin, located just east of the lake and north of Flake Spring. In about 1887, Park tour operator G. L. Henderson applied the name "Black Warrior Geyser" to nearby Steady Geyser (or perhaps to the second "jet" of Steady Geyser). Some have speculated that the name refers to either the color of deposits or to the water near the spring. As early as 1885, Henderson had named this part of the valley "Ebony Basin" because of the dark color of the deposits or the water of Tangled Creek. That may explain the "black," but discovering the reason for "warrior" is more difficult. At the time, there was a Black Warrior mine near Cooke City, Montana, and Henderson had friends (if not a financial interest) at Cooke City. It is possible that he borrowed the name from that mine.

In 1927, the place-names committee accepted Steady Geyser as the name for the perpetual spouter, and moved the name Black Warrior to these nearby springs in order to save the historic name.

BLACKTAIL DEER CREEK* Map #1

A tributary of the Yellowstone River, Blacktail Deer Creek is located 2.5 miles east of the Lava Creek Campground on the Grand Loop Road. Prospectors named this stream before 1870, and it first appeared on Barlow's 1871 map. The reason for the name is unknown, but it probably referred to the blacktail deer (a subspecies of mule deer) that inhabit the Park. Prospectors were very familiar with another Blacktail Deer Creek near Virginia City, Montana, and it is also possible that it was the inspiration for the name.

BLANDING HILL Map #1

This hill on the Norris Canyon Road is located just east of the Gibbon River crossing (below Little Gibbon Falls). Road-builder Ed Lamartine named Blanding Hill in about 1885 for his road foreman, James C. Blanding, who worked on Park roads for many years. In 1885-1886, Blanding, Lamartine, and Oscar Swanson built the first road from Canyon to Norris. The road passed over the original Blanding Hill on the line of the telephone poles just west of and below the point where the present-day road turns northwest. Road construction during the early 1950s moved the road farther north, and the name Blanding Hill moved with it.

According to Pete Nelson, an early telephone man in the Park, Jim Blanding was the first man to drive a wagon across the new road in 1885-1886. Blanding later worked at Great Falls, Montana, ran a livery business, and was a miner at Sand Coulee, Montana. As late as 1908, Blanding was back in the Park, heading up a road crew camp near Beryl Spring. "Blanding Station," north of Gardiner, Montana, is also named for him.

BLISS PASS† Map #2

Bliss Pass is located in the Absaroka Range at the head of Elk Tongue Creek, a tributary of Slough Creek in the northeastern corner of the Park. Park Superintendent Horace Albright probably named this pass sometime after 1922 for the Bliss brothers, wealthy eastern friends of Albright's. In order to give the Park the "right" kind of neighbors, Albright persuaded the brothers to buy the Silver Tip Ranch (just north of and bordering the Park) after owner Frenchy Duret died from a grizzly bear mauling in 1922.

BLOOD GEYSER Map #1

Located at the north base of Paintpot Hill, Blood Geyser is a thermal spring of the Artists' Paintpots group. It appears that guidebook writer W. W. Wylie named the geyser or adopted a local name for it in about 1882. In his 1883 guidebook, Herman Haupt included the observation that Blood Geyser "throws a column of water through a stratum of red mud, which stains the water of the creek flowing from it and gives rise to the name..." (*Yellowstone*, p. 62).

BOILING RIVER*   Map #1

Believed by many to be part of the underground outflow of Mammoth Hot Springs, this famous hot stream has probably never been hot enough to deserve its official name. The stream emerges from beneath a travertine ledge and rushes for only 145 yards before emptying into the Gardner River. At 6 to 9 feet wide and about 2 feet deep, Boiling River is the largest discharging hot spring in the Park. Park tour operator G. L. Henderson named the hot stream between 1883 and 1885. Henderson had a vivid imagination, and his guidebooks played the stream up as the spot where a person could catch a trout and cook it on the hook.

Boiling River had been described several years earlier. Ascending the Gardner River on their way to Mammoth Hot Springs, the members of the 1871 Hayden party discovered this stream and other nearby hot springs:

> ... from underneath this crust a stream poured a volume of water into the river, six feet wide and two feet deep, with a temperature of 130°. A little farther up the stream were a number of hot springs of about the same temperature, with nearly circular basins six to ten feet in diameter and two to four feet deep. Around them had already gathered a number of invalids, who were living in tents, and their praises were enthusiastic in favor of the sanitary effects of the springs. Some of them were used for drinking and others for bathing purposes (*Scribner's Monthly*, February 1872, p. 389).

This rude encampment of invalids was called "Chestnutville" for its founder, a "Colonel Chestnut" of Bozeman. Matthew McGuirk later claimed and "improved" the springs, and by March 1872 he had built a house, a fence, a ditch, and a barn at the site. McGuirk operated his springs, which he called "McGuirk's Medicinal Springs," for the treatment of rheumatism until 1874, when Park Superintendent N. P. Langford made him leave the Park.

In 1914, years after Henderson had named the stream Boiling River, geologist Arnold Hague lamented the use of the name. Hague preferred the name "Hot River," but the USBGN approved the name Boiling River in 1930.

BONITA POOL   Map #3

Bonita Pool is a hot spring in the Daisy Group of the Upper Geyser Basin. It appears that geologist Walter Weed gave the name to the spring in about 1886. *Bonita* is the Spanish word for beautiful, and the spring must have been much prettier then than it is now.

BOOTJACK GAP†   Map #2

Bootjack Gap is a pass of the Absaroka Range, located near the head of Miller Creek on the Park's eastern boundary. The name was apparently given to the pass sometime between 1931 and 1934. The shape of the gap must have reminded someone of a bootjack, a notched tool used to remove boots.

BOTRYOIDAL SPRING   Map #3

Botryoidal is a hot spring that erupts to heights of 6 to 8 feet in the White Creek Group of Lower Geyser Basin. Park Geologist George Marler named the spring sometime before 1973. *Botryoidal*, which means beaded or nodular, is from the Greek word meaning "bunch of grapes."

BOTTLER'S LOOKOUT   Map #1

From this point on the south side of Bunsen Peak visitors can see Osprey Falls and Sheepeater Canyon. P. W. Norris named this point in about 1883 for Frederick, Phillip, and Henry Bottler, brothers who lived on a ranch with their mother just north of the Park on the Yellowstone River. Norris described the point in his *Calumet of the Coteau* in 1884:

> Near this point a trail blazed through the small pines and aspens leads within half a mile to Butler's [Bottler's] Lookout, on the edge of a cliff rising fully 1000 feet from the winding thread of silver [Gardner River], about half a mile below the [Osprey] falls. This cliff, though at so great a distance and elevation from the falls, is the best point from which to obtain a good view of the nearly 200-foot leap, and also of the terrible cañon and looming cliffs of basalt, portions of which are uniquely or fan-shaped (p. 247).

The Bottlers lived near Emigrant Peak in Paradise Valley and in 1868 were the first settlers between Bozeman, Montana, and the Park area. Norris traveled with Frederick Bottler to the top of Electric Peak in 1870, where they glimpsed what would become Yellowstone Park to the south; but Bottler was injured while crossing a stream and the pair was forced to turn back. Norris maintained a close friendship with the Bottlers, whose ranch became an important stopover for visitors traveling to the Park before the railroad was built in 1883.

Bottler's Lookout was later called "Observation Point" and "Lookout Point," but the name used here is the original one. It is appropriate that the Bottler brothers, those "moral, temperate, and industrious mountaineers," should be honored with a place name in Yellowstone.

Yellowstone Place Names Committee

In the summer of 1927, geologist A. L. Day, working on thermal research in Yellowstone, grew concerned that there was a lack of consistency in Park place names. He and Park photographer Jack Haynes conferred with Superintendent Horace Albright about the problem, and the three of them with Ranger Marguerite Lindsley formed the first Yellowstone place-names committee. The team's purpose was to clarify the names situation in the Park. The 1928 editions of *Haynes Guide* and the *Ranger Naturalists' Manual* reflected this committee's work. The team submitted over 500 new place names to the USBGN, which approved most of them in 1930.

During the 1930s, in connection with Chief Naturalist Clyde Bauer's research on Yellowstone place names, the National Park Service put together a Yellowstone place-names file. The compilation was never very extensive, was far from complete, and was not kept current after 1946; but it served as an aid to the Yellowstone place-names committee. Spearheaded by Bauer, the committee sent more place names for approval to the USBGN in about 1937 and in 1943. In 1953-1954 and in 1962, when Chief Naturalist David Condon headed the Yellowstone place-names committee, the group submitted a number of both old and new place names to the USBGN.

The Yellowstone place-names committee—now composed of the Park superintendent, chief naturalist, assistant chief naturalist, historian, geologist, chief ranger, and knowledgeable advisors—continues to function in the Park whenever the need arises. The committee met most recently in 1980 and submitted a number of recommendations to the USBGN, including dropping "Squaw Lake" and "Buffalo Ford" in favor of the historic names Indian Pond and Nez Perce Ford.

The complicated rules involving the choice of place names and their forms, spellings, applications, and submissions are detailed in the 3,300-page unabridged edition of this book, available from the Montana Historical Society.

Indian Pond, with Yellowstone Lake in the distance, 1935

J.E. Haynes

BOUNDARY CREEK*   Map #3

Boundary Creek flows south from the Madison Plateau to the Bechler River in the southwestern corner of the Park. Surveyor A. V. Richards, who conducted surveys of the western boundary of Wyoming Territory, called this stream "Cascade Creek" in 1874. In 1904, members of the Hague surveys placed the name of Boundary Creek on their maps. The name is a reference to the stream's proximity to the Wyoming-Idaho state line.

BREEZE POINT*   Map #4

This point on Yellowstone Lake is located north of Delusion Lake and near West Thumb bay. In about 1885, members of the Hague USGS parties named Breeze Point for the prominent winds that sweep across this promontory from the southwest. Three years earlier, Carl Hals and members of a Northern Pacific Railroad survey team had named it "Clough Point" for "Colonel" Joel B. Clough (1823-1887). Clough was the engineer in charge of the Montana branches of the NPRR and the man who built the Yellowstone branch railroad to Cinnabar, Montana, in 1883. A guidebook writer in 1883 called the point "Delusion Point" because of its proximity to Delusion Lake.

BRICKYARD HILL   Map #1

This low hill is located about 1.5 miles north of Roaring Mountain on the west side of Grand Loop Road and just north of Clearwater Springs. Army scout Felix Burgess mentioned the "Brick yard" in his diary as early as 1898. The name crept into local usage at about that time, because brickmakers obtained clay here to make bricks for Fort Yellowstone chimneys.

BRIDGE BAY*   Map #4

Bridge Bay, a natural bay on Yellowstone Lake southwest of the Lake Hotel, was deepened in the early 1960s to be used as a marina. Park Superintendent P. W. Norris named it Bridge Bay in 1880 because of a natural bridge of stone near the bay and a stream nearby that had been named Bridge Creek.

BRIMSTONE BASIN*   Map #4

Brimstone Basin is a nearly extinct thermal area located east of the Southeast Arm of Yellowstone Lake and just south of Columbine Creek. Lt. G. C. Doane of the Washburn party inadvertently named the area in 1870:

> On the slope of this [Absaroka] range covering an area of three square miles is a formation known as a Brimstone Basin. The whole lower range of the slope for that space is covered with masses of either blue clay or yellow calcareous deposit perforated by millions of minute orifices through which sulphur vapor escapes, subliming in masses around the vent (Bonney and Bonney, *Battle Drums*, p. 306).

Doane's capitalization of Brimstone Basin was apparently inadvertent, as several early exploring parties used the term to describe similar areas. The word "brimstone," which is sulphur, was often used to represent Hell. "Hot Spring Brimstone" appeared on the earliest map of the Yellowstone area (William Clark, 1806-1811), and it is appropriate that the name survives somewhere in the Park.

BUFFALO MEADOWS*   Map #3

Buffalo Meadows is located on the Madison Plateau about 5 miles north of Little Firehole Meadows. Chief Park Naturalist David Condon named this large meadow in 1958. The name is an appropriate one. During the late 1880s and 1890s, the U.S. Army scouted this area in an attempt to locate the few buffalo that still lived in Yellowstone.

BUFFALO PLATEAU*   MAP #2

Located north of the Northeast Entrance Road, Buffalo Plateau is one of 7 named plateaus that make up the Yellowstone Plateau. In 1870, a group of prospectors—including A. Bart Henderson, James Gourley, Adam Miller, and Ed Hibbard—named the area. Henderson recorded the naming in his diary:

> We turned to the left, crossed a low divide or gap, and came to a beautiful flat which we gave the name of Buffalo Flat, as we found thousands of buffalo quietly grazing. This flat is something like 10 miles by 6, with numerous lakes scattered over it, and the finest range in the world" (YNP Research Library, p. 50).

BUMPUS BUTTE*   MAP #2

This small, square-shaped butte, located between Rainy Lake and Calcite Springs was named by Park Ranger E. LeRoy Arnold in 1945. As early as 1938, Park photographer Jack Haynes had suggested that something be named for Hermon Carey Bumpus (1862-1943), but he was turned down because Bumpus was still living. Bumpus, a director of the American Museum of Natural History, first came to Yellowstone in 1924 when he was chairman of the executive committee on museums in national parks for the American Association of Museums. Bumpus made a thorough study of Yellowstone's museum needs and later became a member of the president's commission on educational work in national parks. He supervised the building and equipping of museums at Madison Junction, Norris, Old Faithful (now gone), and Fishing Bridge, as well as many roadside exhibits. Bumpus wrote two pamphlets on Yellowstone (*Trailside Notes*) and named at least four places in the Park. As Jack Haynes said, "the work [Bumpus] did in Yellowstone will forever stand as a monument to his career" (Bumpus, *Herman Carey Bumpus*, p. 109).

BUNSEN PEAK*   MAP #1

Located directly south of Mammoth Hot Springs, Bunsen Peak is an Eocene igneous intrusion of dacite related to Absaroka volcanics. Many geologists believe that it is the neck or stock of an ancient volcano.

Although F. V. Hayden and Capt. J. W. Barlow ascended this 8,564-foot-high mountain in 1871, they did not name it. In 1872, members of the second Hayden survey named the peak for Robert Wilhelm Eberhard von Bunsen (1811-1899), an eminent German physicist. Bunsen studied geysers in Iceland and developed a long-accepted theory about them. He was also a chemist, an inventor (the spectroscope and the Bunsen electric cell), and the discoverer of the elements caesium and rubidium. The Bunsen burner was named for him, but he probably was not its inventor.

In 1872, E. S. Topping ascended the peak, which he called "Observation Mountain." In his first references to the peak, Hayden called it "Mount Everts," probably because he misinterpreted an early map.

BUTTERFLY SPRING   Map #3

Butterfly Spring, a hot spring in the Geyser Hill group of Upper Geyser Basin, is located east of Infant Geyser and south of Mottled Pool. The name derives from the shape of the spring's two craters, which together resemble a butterfly. During the early days of the Park, this spring was important and much admired. In 1878, A. C. Peale labeled it spring number 2 of the "Giantess Group" and described it as a "fissure 4 feet long, yellow sputterer." In 1881, Walter Weed described the spring as "Butterfly 2. Two noisy splashers," the earliest known use of the name, which he may have taken from local usage. In 1895, J. Sanford Saltus wrote in his *A Week in the Yellowstone*:

> The Butterfly is a hole in sandy rock, not many inches wide, full of dark brown water which has deposited sediment and coloring matter for several feet around, forming a marvelously life-like semblance to a gigantic butterfly. It is almost impossible not to believe it the work of some clever artist. Head, body, and outspread wings are perfectly outlined, filled in, in the most vivid manner, with red, yellow, brown, orange, and black, reproducing almost line for line the markings of a well-known species of butterfly (p. 45).

CACHE CREEK*   Map #2

A tributary of the Lamar River, Cache Creek flows southwest from the Absaroka Range. A party of about 40 prospectors—including George A. Huston, Adam "Horn" Miller, H. W. Wayant, Bill Hamilton, and a Mr. Harrison—named the creek in the spring of 1864, making it one of Yellowstone's earliest place names. The prospectors ascended the Yellowstone and Lamar rivers to the south side of present-day Cache Creek, where Indians stole their horses, leaving the men with only two donkeys. The party "cached" some of their belongings here and split up. A small contingent of men, including Wayant, went east to prospect while the others headed downstream.

CALCITE SPRINGS*   Map #2

Calcite Springs is a group of hot springs located between the Yellowstone River and Bumpus Butte. Although USGS geologists Arnold Hague, Walter Weed, and G. M. Wright probably named the springs in 1885, others had described them much earlier. The name refers to thin layers of calcite found in nearby deposits. On the 1814 map that showed John Colter's 1807-1808 route, this area or the Sulphur Beds farther south were called "Hot Spring Brimstone."

The Cook-Folsom-Peterson party saw these springs in 1869 and described the smell of sulphur, the delicate frost-like sulphur crystals, and the rising steam. They added:

> While we were standing by, several gallons of a black liquid ran down and hardened upon the rocks; we broke some of this off and brought it away, and it proved to be sulphur, pure enough to burn readily when ignited (*Western Monthly*, July 1870, p. 63).

This description probably accounts for the area appearing on 1870 maps as "Burning Spring." Eight years later, A. C. Peale referred to Calcite Springs as "Junction Valley Springs," because of their proximity to Junction Valley.

During the 1930s, researchers found the Park's highest percentage of hydrogen sulphide gas at Calcite Springs, along with deposits of calcite, gypsum, and sulphur.

CALFEE CREEK*   Map #2

A tributary to the Lamar River, Calfee Creek flows west from the Absaroka Range, joining the Lamar about 8 miles south of Soda Butte Creek. In 1871, members of the Hayden survey named this stream "Lodgepole Creek" for the lodgepole pine trees that are found in so much of Yellowstone Park. In 1880, while on an exploratory trip,

Park Superintendent P. W. Norris renamed the creek for his friend Henry Bird Calfee, who accompanied the party: "Some seven miles above Cache Creek we passed the mouth of another stream in a deep, narrow timbered valley, which we named Calfee Creek, after the famous photographer of the park" (*Annual Report*, p. 7).

A photographer in Bozeman, Montana, Calfee first visited the Yellowstone area in 1871 and over the years took some very early panoramic stereopticon photographs of the Park. Calfee toured geyser areas with a companion, Macon Josey, and at one point carried Josey to safety after he had suffered burns in a hot spring—probably Yellowstone's earliest recorded hot spring injury. In 1877, Calfee helped Mrs. George Cowan, her injured husband, and their party get to Bozeman in a wagon following their escape from the Nez Perce Indians.

In 1879, Calfee photographed Yellowstone and played a minor role in naming Lone Star Geyser. Shortly afterward, in 1881-1882, he and W. W. Wylie conducted a short-lived and unsuccessful Yellowstone lecture tour. Wylie used engravings from Calfee's photographs in his 1882 guidebook, *Yellowstone National Park or the Great American Wonderland*.

CALTHOS SPRING   Map #3

Calthos Spring—a hot spring located in the Cascade Group of Upper Geyser Basin—is one of Yellowstone's place-name mysteries. *Calthos* is not the Greek word for hot, as some had thought, nor is it a Spanish, French, Latin, or Shoshone word. The word's application to a hot spring in addition to its *cal* beginning (as in *calida* and *caliente*) suggest that calthos relates somehow to heat, but its origin and meaning remain unknown.

CAMELLIA MUD POTS   Map #4

Camellia Mud Pots are located on a bare, white slope about 200 feet above Steamboat Point (near Mary Bay on Yellowstone Lake) and 200 yards east of the point. Facing Sedge Creek, the mud pots are on the south slope of the spur that forms Steamboat Point. Hague survey geologist Walter H. Weed named Camellia Mud Pots in 1886 or 1887. Weed described the mud pots as 5 feet in diameter, and he saw the form of a rose-shaped flower—the camellia—in the splashing mud. It was, he wrote, "blobbing and forming camellia-like forms" (USGS, Box 53, vol. 23, pp. 91-92). It was spring #1 of the several springs that Weed found at this location.

CAMPANULA CREEK*   Map #1

Campanula Creek flows west from the Crags into Gneiss Creek. Because of some confusion with nearby Grayling Creek, on some maps Campanula Creek became known as "Prospect Creek." The present name was given sometime between 1895 and 1904 by members of the Hague parties of the USGS. They named the creek following the practice of naming natural features for local flora, in this case a blue flower called harebell (*Campanula sp.*). *Campanula*, a diminutive of the Italian *campana*, means "little bell."

CANARY SPRING   Map #1

Canary Spring is a hot spring of Mammoth Hot Springs, located on the southeastern edge of the Main Terrace. Members of the Hague parties of the USGS—possibly Walter Weed himself—appear to have named Canary Spring sometime before 1904, when the name appeared on their map. None of the known writings of the survey members mentions the name, but it probably referred to the filamentous, sulphur-depositing, yellow-colored bacteria that Weed had seen at the spring.

CANDLESTICK MOUNTAIN   Map #2

Candlestick Mountain, a peak of the Absaroka Range, is located just southeast of Castor and Pollux peaks and north-northeast of Notch Mountain. Geologist T. A. Jaggar, Jr., a member of the Hague survey, named the peak in 1897. Jaggar wrote:

> On the NW are Castor and Pollux [peaks], on SW is Notch Mt., a remarkable table capped with basalt, next to it 3-Knob Peak and next to it E[ast]. the "candle extinguisher"—so-called from its form (notebook, vol. 1, p. 33).

In the same notebook, Jaggar referred to the peak as Candlestick Mountain.

CANOE LAKE†   Map #2

This small lake is located east of the headwaters of Calfee Creek and near the Park's eastern boundary. By 1927, Canoe Lake had appeared on maps of the U.S. Forest Service. The reason for the name is undocumented, but it could refer to the long, narrow shape of the lake. It is possible that the Nez Perce used a pass near here in 1877. A stone cup made by Indians was found nearby, and one part of the Great Bannock Trail crossed the mountains here.

CAPITOL HILL†   Map #1

Capitol Hill, a low glacial hill just east of Mammoth Hot Springs, was named "Lookout Hill" in 1878 by members of the third Hayden survey. Because of its view of the Mammoth area, it was later known as "Observation Hill" or "Observatory Hill." The name Capitol Hill came into local usage sometime after 1879, when Park Superinten-

Castor Peak and Pollux Peak in the Absaroka Range, 1924

J.E. Haynes

dent P. W. Norris built Yellowstone's first administration building on the hill. The building resembled a fort made of wood, which included a slitted metal-plated cupola for defense purposes. Norris and other civilian superintendents used the building as both office and home. Because the building on the hill was the center of authority for the Park, the hill became known as Capitol Hill. Walter Weed recognized the use of that name in 1887. After the army constructed the first Camp Sheridan buildings in 1886-1887, the old capitol building was used for private quarters. It was finally torn down in 1909.

CARNELIAN CREEK*   Map #2

Carnelian Creek flows north to Tower Creek from Hedges Peak in the Washburn Range. Members of the third Hayden survey named the creek in 1878 after a form of chalcedony (a type of quartz) that is reddish or reddish-white in color.

CARRINGTON ISLAND*   Map #4

Carrington Island is located a couple of miles northeast of Bluff Point on Yellowstone Lake. Members of the Hayden survey named the island in 1871 for E. Campbell Carrington, a zoologist with the survey. Carrington had accompanied Hayden on his 1869 surveys of Colorado and New Mexico. During the summer of 1871, Carrington made extensive observations on Mud Geyser, and he prepared a report for Hayden on the worm that infests cutthroat trout in Yellowstone Lake.

During that summer, Carrington spent a week exploring Yellowstone Lake with Henry Elliott in *The Anna*, the first recorded boat on the lake. The two men sketched the shoreline of Yellowstone Lake and named many of its islands, points, and bays. One or both of them probably named Carrington Island.

CASCADE CORNER†   Map #3

There are numerous cascades and waterfalls in Cascade Corner, the southwest, or Bechler River, area of Yellowstone. Explorer W. C. Gregg and Park Superintendent Horace Albright named the area in 1921. Maps of the Hayden surveys during the 1870s and the Hague survey in 1904 had shown the southwest corner of the Park as a swampy area. But in 1920, when congressmen introduced a bill to dam Bechler Meadows to create a reservoir for Idaho irrigation interests, Gregg explored the area and found beautiful waterfalls and cascades. He reported on his discoveries in the November 20, 1920, *Saturday Evening Post* and the November 23, 1921, *Outlook*, which helped foil the reservoir plan.

CASCADE CREEK*   Map #2

Cascade Creek flows south from Cascade Lake to the Yellowstone River near the Lower Falls. Cornelius Hedges of the Washburn expedition named the creek in 1870 for its "cascade," which expedition members named Crystal Falls. In 1883, Park Superintendent P. W. Norris wrote "Afar from the Cities and Hamlets of Men," his tribute to this stream, which he treasured for its respite from the cares of the world:

> Unselfish I've struggled to benefit men,
> Regretless I leave them, my refuge the glen,
> Where mist-nourished flowers and carpets of green
> Commingling in bowers like Eden are seen
> (*Calumet of the Coteau*, pp. 117-118).

Norris called this place "the glen of the Cascade," a

> rainbow-spanned refuge from the guilded haunts of fashion and pleasure, and the crafty wiles of the politician, the speculator, or the money-lender, in these days when proffered friendship is too oft a lure, and real friendship a cherished vision of the past,—in these enlightened but degenerate days, when far too often robbery and betrayal of public trusts are viewed and punished in inverse ratio to the magnitude of the crime. . . . Hence my changeless attachment to these unpolluted scenes of the grandest handiwork of nature's God as a refuge . . . (*Calumet of the Coteau*, p. 204).

CASTLE GEYSER*   Map #3

Castle Geyser is a major geyser located in the Castle Group in the Upper Geyser Basin. Lt. Gustavus C. Doane and N. P. Langford, members of the Washburn expedition, named this geyser in 1870 because of its strong resemblance to "an old feudal tower partially in ruins" (Bonney and Bonney, *Battle Drums*, p. 349).

In 1871, Capt. J. W. Barlow found Castle's resemblance "to a ruined castle or tower" to be "wonderfully striking. . . ." Its interesting eruptions and its large prominent cone, which has been heavily vandalized since the early days of the Park, have long attracted Yellowstone visitors.

CASTLE RUINS   Map #2

This myriad of yellow altered-rhyolite rock formations on the north wall of the Grand Canyon of the Yellowstone is located just northeast of Inspiration Point. In about 1897, Olin Wheeler either named this area or took the name from local usage because the formations resembled castles. Wheeler wrote that the yellow colors "run riot" here, and another writer observed that the Castle Ruins were "a thousand castellated pinnacles shaped by the elements in their thousands of years standing there" (Campbell, *Complete Guide*, p. 122).

CASTOR PEAK* Map #2

Located in the Absaroka Range, this 10,854-foot-high peak is southwest of Pollux Peak on the Little Lamar River. In about 1893, members of the Hague parties of the USGS named the peak apparently because it was a twin of nearby Pollux Peak. In Greek mythology, Castor and Pollux were half brothers who were finally placed among the stars as "the Twins" (Gemini). They protected travelers and were the gods of hospitality.

CATFISH GEYSER Map #3

Catfish Geyser, part of the Midway Geyser Basin, is located on the right bank of the Firehole River just below the Fountain Freight Road bridge, about 100 feet northwest of Pebble Spring and across the river from Silent Pool. Named in 1871 by members of the Hayden survey, Catfish Geyser is a low, 1 to 1.5-foot-high cone at the river's edge with a vent in its top about one foot in diameter. The Hayden survey report included only a drawing of the geyser with no additional information or reason for the name. A crack in the river's bed just to the north has been separately named River Spouter.

CATHEDRAL PEAK* Map #2

This 10,760-foot-high peak of the Absaroka Range is located northeast of Mount Chittenden. Members of the Hague parties of the USGS named this commanding summit in 1885 because it inspired reverance and reminded them of a cathedral.

CATHEDRAL ROCK* Map #1

This large dacite rock is located on the northern slopes of Bunsen Peak. During road construction through the Golden Gate Canyon in 1883 or 1884, Cathedral Rock was so named because of its majestic appearance. It is likely that Dan Kingman (who built the road), G. L. Henderson (a Park assistant superintendent who wrote about building the road), geologist Arnold Hague, or members of the the road crew named it. Hague wrote in 1884: "Cathedral Point [sic] is a spur of the mountain jutting out to the north . . . [it] receives its name from its rather spire-like forms" (Hague papers, "Notes on Mammoth Hot Springs," Box 12, p. 14).

CAVE FALLS* Map #3

A waterfall on Falls River in the extreme southwest corner of the Park, Cave Falls is 20 feet high and 250 feet wide. Explorer W. C. Gregg and topographer C. H. Birdseye named the falls in 1920 or 1921 because of a 50- by 50-foot cave they found just below the falls on the north bank of the river.

CELESTINE POOL Map #3

Celestine Pool is a hot spring of the Fountain Group in Lower Geyser Basin. Members of the Hague parties of the USGS apparently named the pool sometime before 1904. The reason for the name is undocumented, but the men may have named it for the blue form of the mineral celestite or celestine (strontium sulphate), or they might have taken the name from the Latin word *celestinus*, which means heavenly.

CHADBOURNE HILL Map #1

Chadbourne Hill is on the old stagecoach road between Gardiner and Cinnabar near Devil's Slide on the west side of the Yellowstone River. This hill is the first one east of the old Cinnabar townsite, where the road curves abruptly south then east. During the 1880s, this name was in local usage, referring to Allen W. Chadbourne (1842?-1943), who owned the ranch property from 1882 until 1901. The lakes on the upper hills nearby (probably present-day Rainbow Lakes) were known as "Chadbourne Lakes."

Chadbourne drove cattle on the Chisholm Trail, operated bull and mule trains on the Kansas and Wyoming frontier, and hunted buffalo before moving with his wife Dolly to Belgrade, Montana. He came to Cinnabar in 1882 and carried tourists in his own wagons from Cinnabar into the Park from 1884 until 1901. Chadbourne claimed to have hauled the first load of lumber to Mammoth for the construction of the first Mammoth Hot Springs Hotel. The Chadbourne ranch house has been moved to Gardiner, where it still stands on the far eastern end of Park Street on the north side of the street. In 1901, the Chadbournes moved north to a ranch in the Clyde Park area, where Chadbourne died in 1943 at the age of 101.

The first of many steep hills encountered by stagecoaches on the Park tour, Chadbourne Hill often became so slippery in wet weather that it was almost impassable. At those times, Mammoth was isolated and no visitors or supplies could get through.

CHALCEDONY CREEK* Map #2

This small stream flows northeast from Amethyst Mountain to the Lamar River. Geologist Arnold Hague named the creek in 1885 for chalcedony (kal SED o nee), a waxy, smooth form of quartz found in the Park. Chalcedony often lines cavities, fills cracks, or forms crusts in rocks and may be white, gray, blue, brown, or black. This quartz is sometimes formed when water carrying silica gel dries slowly.

CHANNEL MOUNTAIN* Map #4

Channel Mountain is an 8,745-foot-high peak of Chicken Ridge, located just southwest of the South Arm of Yellowstone Lake. Members of the Hague parties of the USGS named this peak sometime between 1889 and 1895. In 1889, the geologists discovered an ancient outlet channel (see Outlet Creek) of Yellowstone Lake, when the lake emptied into the Snake River. The channel is located immediately south of the mountain.

CHICKEN RIDGE* Map #4

This ridge is located south and west of the tip of the South Arm of Yellowstone Lake. Members of the Hague parties of the USGS named the ridge sometime between 1889 and 1895. No one knows for certain why the geologists called it Chicken Ridge, but they were probably referring to the sage chickens and grouse found in the area.

CHINAMAN SPRING* Map #3

This hot spring (occasionally a geyser) in the Old Faithful Group in the Upper Geyser Basin is located 120 feet west and slightly north of Blue Star Spring. Early guidebooks list Chinaman Spring as a geyser, and an 1896 guidebook claimed that Chinaman could erupt 40 feet high for 2 minutes at regular intervals.

The spring was named in 1885, probably by Park tour operator G. L. Henderson, who often told tourists that "a tent was stretched over an effervescent spring situated between Old Faithful and the Firehole River, in which the laundry work for the hotel was done by a Chinaman" (*Livingston Enterprise*, September 10, 1887). In an 1885 letter to geologist Arnold Hague, Supreme Court Chief Justice Morrison R. Waite claimed that he saw an eruption of Chinaman Spring at the Chinese laundry. Mrs. James Hamilton, a tourist, remembered "the little pool that was said to be the Chinese laundry" from her 1888 trip to the Park ("Through Yellowstone," pp. 6-7). Isidor Rothschild, a bicycle tourist, reported that the laundryman was still there in 1894:

> I had the guide go with me for a three hour walk. We passed the laundry where Joe the Chinaman always has hot water. It is borax mineral and he puts the clothes into a box. The water keeps turning them until it requires very little rubbing to make them clean ("Bicycling Through Yellowstone," p. 4).

There is some evidence that two Japanese, M. A. Sunada and H. Kurose, ran a laundry at Chinaman Spring sometime before 1915. Susan Sunada, Sunada's daughter-in-law, told Park Geologist George Marler that the two men set up business at the spring and were paid in money and often in trout. . . . At the end of the summer, these two "Chinamen" really Japanese, disappeared. They never returned. "We buried our barrel of soap. We had every intention of returning the following spring," Kurose often remarked, but "That soap is still there" (*Pacific Citizen*, December 1972).

Unfortunately, it is not known what year this occurred nor where the barrel of soap was buried.

CHRISTMAS TREE PARK Map #1

Christmas Tree Park is a valley of woods and meadows at the south base of Mount Holmes near the headwaters of Winter Creek. The valley was named in 1883-1885 by members of the Hague parties of the USGS, because of the spruce trees in the Park that resembled Christmas trees. Joseph Iddings, who may have named the area, called it a "most beautiful natural park" (USGS, Box 53, vol. 10, p. 13). Arnold Hague noted that it was "a characteristic feature of many localities in the Park—openings and glades on the plateau dotted over with spruces. It is moreover, a very beautiful spot . . . (Hague papers, Hague to L. F. Schmeckebier, January 6, 1913, Box 5).

CHRISTMAS TREE PARK Map #1

This Christmas Tree Park is a wooded area located near West Yellowstone, Montana, which Park stagecoach drivers named at the turn of the century. The area extends from the Park's west boundary to near the Montana-Wyoming state line and along both sides of the entrance road.

CHRISTMAS TREE ROCK Map #3

This large boulder sits in the center of the Firehole River about one-quarter mile above Firehole Cascades on the Grand Loop Road. The rock was probably named during the 1960s by Park tour bus drivers for the single lodgepole pine that grows out of it. When tour guides pass the rock, they often tell tourists about "Christmas in Yellowstone," which Park employees celebrate each August 25. The tradition began in about 1940, when tourists at Old Faithful were stranded in one of Yellowstone's summer snowstorms. Looking for something to do, they decided to celebrate Christmas. "Christmas in Yellowstone" is now an annual event, which Park employees often celebrate by decorating the tree on Christmas Tree Rock.

CLAGETT BUTTE* Map #1

This small butte near Mammoth Hot Springs is located between Terrace Mountain and Clematis Creek. In 1926, Park

Colonnade Falls on the Bechler River, 1921

J.E. Haynes

photographer Jack Haynes and Superintendent Horace Albright named the butte in honor of Montana Territorial Delegate William Horace Clagett. In late 1871, Clagett introduced the bill in the U.S. House of Representatives that designated Yellowstone as the world's first national park. Clagett, formerly of Nevada, was one of the leading lawyers in Montana Territory during the early 1870s.

Park tour operator G. L. Henderson first named this butte "Temple Mountain" in about 1885, perhaps referring to his Cottage Hotel (his "temple"), which he built at the foot of the hill that year. Locals called the butte "Temple Mountain," and the name became entrenched in the literature; it is the name the butte should really bear. Members of the Hague parties called the butte "Sentinel Butte" in about 1887 and "Signal Butte" in 1897.

CLEPSYDRA GEYSER*   Map #3

Clepsydra is a geyser in the Fountain Group of the Lower Geyser Basin. The geyser was named in 1873 by its discoverer, Theodore Comstock, who wrote in 1875:

> The third member of the group is one of the most regular in the basins, and on this account the name Clepsydra is proposed for it. Like the ancient water-clock of that name, it marks the passage of time by the discharge of water. It would be unwise to number this among the constant geysers without knowing more concerning its movements than has yet been gathered, but it was in action during the whole of the two hours and a half that we were in its vicinity. A large mass of water is forced up in a rolling wave, ending in a vigorous but not greatly elevated spurt, at intervals of three minutes (in Jones, *Report*, p. 245).

The 1959 earthquake stimulated Clepsydra Geyser into nearly constant eruption to heights of 20 to 40 feet.

A *klepsydra*, from the Greek *kleptein* (to steal) and *hydor* (water), was a metal vessel with a perforated base and a narrow neck for drawing water. The vessel was also used as a water clock in the courts of ancient Athens.

CLIFF GEYSER*   Map #3

Cliff Geyser is located in the Black Sand Basin of the Upper Geyser Basin. A. C. Peale and Walter Weed saw Cliff Geyser in action in 1883. Arnold Hague named it "Cliff Geyser as it lies so close under the abrupt wall which skirts the west bank of Iron [Spring] Creek" (Powell, *Fifth Annual Report*, p. 16).

CODY PEAK*   Map #4

This 10,267-foot-high peak of the Absaroka Range is located just north of the East Entrance to the Park. The peak was named in 1931 by the Cody Club of Cody, Wyoming, for William F. "Buffalo Bill" Cody (1846-1917). Cody was a rider for the Pony Express, a showman who presented his famous Wild West shows throughout the world, and a hunter who helped to nearly exterminate the American bison. He founded the town of Cody in about 1896 and lived there for much of his later life.

COFFIN SPRING   Map #1

Coffin Spring is a hot spring in the Sylvan Springs group in Gibbon Geyser Basin. It is located over a ridge northeast of Evening Primrose Spring and on the east side of the entire complex. The largest black mudpot in the area, Coffin Spring was named in about 1927 by Ranger Charles Phillips because it slopes toward the west and resembles an open coffin.

COLD WATER GEYSER   Map #2

Located on the left bank of the Yellowstone River below Nez Perce Ford, Cold Water Geyser is on the Grand Loop Road about 5 miles north of Fishing Bridge. This spring drew considerable attention during the 1930s as a "cold geyser" that spouted soda water. Newspaper stories reported that people added flavoring and made sodas at the spring, which appeared to erupt to heights of 18 inches because of carbon dioxide gas. Park naturalists named Cold Water Geyser in 1954 when they made a study of its activity. The geyser's eruptions seemed to last about 10 minutes with some degree of regularity through 1982. In 1983, however, eruptions were irregular, and by summer Cold Water Geyser was dormant.

COLONNADE FALLS*   Map #3

This double waterfall is located on the Bechler River near the Iris Falls campground on the Bechler River Trail. The upper falls is 35 feet high; the lower falls is 67 feet high. Members of the Hague parties of the USGS named Colonnade Falls in 1885. The reason for the name of the falls is undocumented, but it probably referred either to the nearby columnar basalt layers or to the fact that there were two waterfalls. A colonnade is a series or row of columns placed at regular intervals.

COLTER PEAK*   Map #4

This 10,683-foot-high peak of the Absaroka Range is located directly east of the tip of the Southeast Arm of Yellowstone Lake. Members of the Washburn expedition ascended this peak in 1870, and Walter Trumbull wrote:

> Near the south-east end of the [Yellowstone] Lake is the highest peak in the vicinity. It is steep and barren, and from

the lake-shore appears to taper to a point. On the south side is a precipice, nearly a thousand feet high. Two of the party ascended it (*Overland Monthly*, June 1871, p. 490).

From the top of the peak N. P. Langford and G. C. Doane saw the surrounding country, and Langford made the first known sketches of Yellowstone Lake. As a result of the ascent, Gen. H. D. Washburn named the peak "Mount Langford" and named its lower northern summit "Mount Doane." The 1871 Hayden survey moved those names to peaks farther north. For reasons not known, Park Superintendent P. W. Norris named this prominent peak "Mount Forum" in 1881.

In 1885, geologist Arnold Hague named the peak in honor of John Colter (1775?-1813), "the first white man of whom we have any record who penetrated this rough and rugged country" (in Powell, *Eighth Annual Report*, p. 152). Colter has been credited with being the white discoverer of the Yellowstone area in 1807 and its earliest explorer of record. Colter was a member of the Lewis and Clark expedition and an early fur trapper in Montana and Wyoming.

CONCRETION COVE   Map #4

This small cove or bay is located on the west side of Mary Bay on Yellowstone Lake. Along the beach of this cove, north of Storm Point, early visitors found strangely shaped rocks, which resembled cups, boxes, spoons, and other common objects. Prospector A. Bart Henderson saw these rocks in 1867, and in 1870 members of the Washburn party named the place "Curiosity Point" or "Curiosity Shop." In 1877, another group referred to the area as "Specimen Beach." Park Superintendent P. W. Norris gave the small bay its present name in 1880:

> The prolongation of Mary's Bay near the Indian Pond, between the mouth of Pelican Creek and Steamboat Point, upon the Yellowstone Lake, was by myself named Concretion Cove, from the countless numbers and various forms of concretions which there fairly shingle the wave-lashed beach (*Calumet of the Coteau*, p. 186).

Souvenir hunters removed these oddly shaped rocks long ago. We are all a little poorer because of those who have removed natural resources from the Park. Today, souvenir hunting is prohibited in all national parks.

CONGRESS POOL*   Map #1

Congress Pool is a hot spring in the Porcelain Basin in Norris Geyser Basin. The breakout of Congress Pool in 1891 (from an earlier feature called "Teakettle" or "Steam Vent") occurred in the same year that Arnold Hague and 50 other geologists from all over the world gathered for the Fifth International Geological Congress in Yellowstone. The pool was named for this Congress, not for the 53rd U.S. Congress, as has been suggested.

CONSTANT GEYSER*   Map #1

This geyser in the Porcelain Basin of Norris Geyser Basin was once in nearly constant action. Named in about 1881 by P. W. Norris, in the early days Constant Geyser was known as "Minute Man" or "Minute Geyser." The geyser put on an amazing performance from at least 1881 until about 1920, erupting regularly and at short intervals. The eruptions were from 4 to 50 feet high (usually 20 to 40 feet) and occurred about every minute, lasting about 10 seconds. During all those years, the geyser was dormant for only two short periods. It was so popular that even its runoff channel was given a name—"Fairy River." After 1920, Constant Geyser became erratic and unpredictable.

After years of studying the geyser, geologist Arnold Hague wrote that the geyser was "strangely persistent in a region of constant change" (USGS, Box 55, vol. 1, p. 85) and that its "name was cleverly chosen, for it has all the impressiveness of steady action and is as constant and regular in movement as Old Faithful" (Hague papers, Box 13, p. 21).

COOK PEAK*   Map #1

This 9,742-foot-high peak of the Washburn Range is located about 7 miles northwest of Mount Washburn. In 1880, Park Superintendent P. W. Norris named this mountain "Thompson Peak," although later maps sometimes put this name on nearby Folsom Peak. Norris had named the peak for Frank Thompson of the Northern Pacific Railroad. In 1885, members of the Hague parties of the USGS renamed the peak "Storm Peak."

In 1922, Park Superintendent Horace Albright renamed the mountain Cook Peak for Charles W. Cook (1839-1927). Cook had been a principal of the 1869 Cook-Folsom-Peterson party of Yellowstone explorers, and he had co-authored (with David Folsom) the first magazine article describing the region (in *Western Monthly*, July 1870, pp. 60-67). Cook had come to Montana Territory from Maine in 1864 with his boyhood friend, David Folsom. He settled in the Smith River Valley near present-day White Sulphur Springs, Montana. In 1922, Cook returned to Yellowstone to celebrate the Park's 50th anniversary.

CORKSCREW HILL*   Map #3

Corkscrew Hill is located just west of Herron Creek and north of Craig Pass on the Grand Loop Road. Built in 1891, the first road between Old Faithful and West

Thumb dropped east down Corkscrew Hill after leaving Craig Pass. There were many more successive turns than the present-day road has, and sometime between 1891 and 1903 stagecoach drivers named it Corkscrew Hill. As H. M. Chittenden described it in his 1903 guidebook: "Besides its picturesque scenery, its chief interest to the tourist lies in the exhilarating [sic] speed at which coaches are bowled down the hill after the slow and tedious pull up the other side" (*Yellowstone*, p. 302). Local wits maintained that Corkscrew Hill was "so crooked that you pass one place three times before you get by it, and then meet yourself on the road coming back" (Peabody, *Yellowstone*, p. 10).

Stagecoach drivers delighted in terrifying dudes by rushing them down the narrow and torturous Corkscrew Hill. This hill and "Devil's Elbow" (see Virginia Cascade) were considered the two most dangerous hills in the Park, and both were the scenes of a number of early stage wrecks. The name Corkscrew Hill was officially approved in 1937, just one year before the present road realignment was finished, straightening some of the turns on the hill.

CORPORAL GEYSER* Map #1

Geologist Arnold Hague named this geyser, which is located in the Back Basin of Norris Geyser Basin, in about 1889. The reason for the name is undocumented, but it probably related to nearby Veteran Geyser, which Hague apparently thought was older or larger than Corporal Geyser.

COULTER CREEK* Map #3

Coulter Creek flows northwest to the Snake River from the Teton National Forest outside the Park's southern boundary. Members of the second Hayden survey named the creek in 1872 for their botanist, John Merle Coulter (1851-1928). Coulter later founded and edited *Botanical Gazette* and served as president of Indiana University. Survey members named the creek because of an incident that occurred at the stream. Dorothea G. Doubt, one of Coulter's students, described it in a September 7, 1933, letter to the Park's "Secretary of the Museum":

> Dr. Coulter was fishing one day on the bank of a stream when he felt a slap on the shoulder and turned expecting to see one of his companions, but there was a large, black bear. Coulter plunged in and swam across the stream, then looking around saw that the bear had not followed, but was back there grinning at him. The party called this stream Coulter Creek, a name it still bears (YNP Archives).

In 1889, three Yellowstone guides found a large pine tree with a deep blaze on it, including the initials "J.C." The tree was on the left bank of Coulter Creek some 50 feet from the water and about 1.75 miles above the creek's mouth. The guides thought that the blaze was over 80 years old and the work of John Colter, but later historians believe that it was the work of John Merle Coulter.

COWAN CREEK† Map #3

Cowan Creek flows southwest to Nez Perce Creek from Mary Mountain and crosses the Mary Mountain Trail about 6 miles east of the Grand Loop Road. In about 1881, Park Superintendent P. W. Norris appears to have given this stream two names: "Willow Creek," apparently for the low shrubs of the willow family that grow in the Park, and "Yellowstone Creek." Chief Park Naturalist David Condon named the stream Cowan Creek in 1956 in honor of George F. Cowan.

It was near the mouth of this creek that Nez Perce Indians attacked Cowan during their retreat through Yellowstone in 1877. Cowan was with a group of tourists, the Radersburg party, when Nez Perce Indians captured them and took them up Nez Perce Creek. Cowan was shot twice and left for dead at the west foot of Mary Mountain; the rest of the party was taken away. Cowan survived the attack and crawled about 9 miles in 60 hours to reach the Lower Geyser Basin, where soldiers who were pursuing the Indians found him, gave him rations, and left him a fire with instructions to wait until ambulance wagons arrived. Cowan seemed doomed to misfortune, for while he slept the fire spread and burned him. Later, while in a wagon on the way to Fort Ellis, the wagon overturned. Still later in Bozeman, a doctor sat on Cowan's convalescent bed and the bed collapsed. All in all, it was a tough few days.

CRAIG PASS* Map #3

Craig Pass is at 8,262 feet at the Continental Divide, about 8 miles west of Old Faithful on the Grand Loop Road. In 1891, U.S. road engineer Captain Hiram Chittenden discovered Craig Pass while he was surveying for the first road between Old Faithful and West Thumb. It was probably Chittenden who named the pass for Ida M. Craig (Wilcox), "the first tourist to cross the pass" on Chittenden's new road, on about September 10, 1891. At the time that her name was given to the pass, Ida Wilcox (1847-1930) had been married 24 years. So why did Chittenden use her maiden name? Perhaps it was to honor her singularly for being the first tourist to cross the pass. It is also possible that through his connection with the military, Chittenden knew her father (Gen. James Craig) or her brother (Malin Craig, Sr.) and was really honoring the Craig family.

The George F. Cowan party near Bottler's Ranch, 1877

Chinaman Spring in the Upper Geyser Basin

CRAWFISH CREEK*   Map #3

Crawfish Creek flows southeast to the Lewis River from Pitchstone Plateau. The South Entrance Road crosses the creek about 2 miles north of the South Entrance. In 1882, Northern Pacific Railroad surveyors first named this stream "Loud Creek" for Charles H. Loud, an engineer in the party. Loud later became a rancher and practiced law near Miles City, Montana.

In 1885, members of the Hague parties renamed the stream Crawfish Creek in accordance with the USGS practice of naming natural features for local fauna. Warmed by upstream thermals, this stream was a hospitable habitat for crayfish. Researchers in 1974 discovered that Crawfish Creek contains the largest and most abundant crayfish population in the Park.

CRECELIUS CASCADE   Map #4

Crecelius Cascade is a waterfall of an unnamed tributary to Eleanor Lake on the lake's east end. The waterfall is visible from the East Entrance Road about one mile west of Sylvan Pass. Hiram Chittenden apparently named Crecelius Cascade in about 1901 for his employee, S. F. Crecelius, who was directly responsible for constructing this section of road in 1901. Before that time, there was only a trail crossing Sylvan Pass. Crecelius Cascade was later known as "Eleanor Cascade" from nearby Eleanor Lake. Still later it was called "Snow Fall." But the name Crecelius Cascade was the earliest and has priority.

CRESCENT HILL*   Map #2

This low hill is located east of The Cut and west of Floating Island Lake, about 4 miles west of Tower Junction on the Grand Loop Road. In 1885, geologist Arnold Hague named Crescent Hill because it had a crescent shape on his early maps. The hill is the most imposing of the volcanic piles bordering the Yellowstone River. This hill was used as a signal station in 1885 by members of the Hague parties, and for that reason geologist G. M. Wright called it "Signal Hill."

CRESTED POOL*   Map #3

Crested Pool is a hot spring in the Castle Group of Upper Geyser Basin. The spring has had a number of other names, and its deep blue color has been a subject of conversation and fascination since the earliest days in the Park. In 1871, F. V. Hayden wrote that its water was of "an almost unnatural clearness" and called it "a marvel of delicate tracery of pure white silica." At that time the temperature of Crested Pool was 172°F. In 1872, when the temperature had risen to 180°F., Hayden referred to it as "Fire Basin." Hayden's assistant, A. C. Peale, stated that the pool looked as though it were lined with white marble.

Guidebook writer Harry J. Norton visited the Park in 1872 and gave the spring the romantic name "Circe's Boudoir," after the mythological sorceress who transformed the companions of Ulysses into swine. Norton described the magical pool in *Wonderland Illustrated*:

> Upon the same mound, a few steps from the Castle, is one of those calm, lovely prismatic springs, the most beautiful in the whole geyser region. For delicacy of coloring and beauty of ornamentation it surpasses any we visited. It is more quiet than the others, yet its surface is gently rippled by constant vibrations. The handsomely-scalloped rim rises seven or eight inches above the water, describes a complete circle of about sixty feet, and inside is festooned and embroidered in many a fantastic design. The water is unnaturally transparent, and one can look an unknown depth into its fairy regions, discovering caves, bowers, castles, and grottoes, painted in every color of brightest rainbow, and magically carved. . . . It seemed as if our eyes would never cease feasting upon its unearthly beauty; there was an intense longing to know what mysterious treasures lie hidden deep down in its tranquil bosom; and as we regretfully, unsatisfiedly retired to rest, we wondered who would care if we explored its deepest recesses—to return to earth never again (pp. 17-18).

During the 1880s, guidebook writers referred to Crested Pool as the "Devil's Well," "Diana's Spring" (from Diana, the goddess of mountains, streams, and hunting), "Blue Crested Spring," "Pool Beautiful," and "Diana's Well." Other names were "Castle Pool" and "Diana's Bath." Members of the Hague surveys during the 1880s used the name "Crested Spring" and some of the other names as well. The name Crested Pool was accepted by a 1927 place-names committee, referring to the 1872 map by Gustavus Bechler, which showed the feature as "Crested Hot Spring."

The temperature of the 42-foot-deep pool has fluctuated over the years. Before the 1959 earthquake, for example, Crested Pool was 200°F.; after the quake, it dropped to 155°F. and took about four years to recover. The spring's temperature at the bottom is known to have reached at least 236.7°F.

Crested Pool has claimed at least one life. A young boy died in the hot spring in 1970, and a resulting court case threatened to close national parks across the nation. Because of this case, a protective railing was put up around Crested Pool.

CREVICE CREEK*   Map #1

Crevice Creek flows south into the Yellowstone River from the Gallatin National Forest, about 7 miles upstream from Gardiner. Prospectors in 1867 named the stream canyon "Crevice Gulch." In 1888, E. S. Topping reported in his *Chronicles of the Yellowstone*:

42   *Crystal Falls*

Early in the summer of 1867, Lou Anderson . . . with [A. H.] Hubble, [George W.] Reese, Caldwell, and another man, went up the [Yellowstone] river on the east side. They found gold in the crevice at the mouth of the first stream above Bear [Creek], and named it in consequence, Crevice Gulch (pp. 62-63).

According to an 1893 newspaper article, "another man" was probably William Simms, an ex-city marshal from Helena, Montana, who was a placer miner in Emigrant Gulch during the 1860s. The nearby gold-mining ghost town and the mountain received their names "Crevasse" from a misspelling on the 1871 maps of Capt. J. W. Barlow.

CRYSTAL FALLS*   Map #2

Crystal Falls is a 129-foot-high waterfall of Cascade Creek located just below the Lower Falls of the Yellowstone. Crystal Falls was probably named in 1870 by Cornelius Hedges of the Washburn party, who made his way down the creek and discovered the falls. Crystal Falls was one of Superintendent Norris's favorite spots in the Park. He wrote poetic tributes to it (see Grotto Pool), such as this one from 1875:

> Never more do I wish to leave it,
> My lovely last retreat,
> Evermore be this my music,
> And here my winding sheet ("Meanderings").

Over and over in Norris's writings and poems it is apparent that he loved Crystal Falls and Grotto Pool so much that he wanted to be buried there. His 1884 poem, "Rustic Bridge and Crystal Falls," described his attachment:

> Skipping rill from snowy fountains
> Dashing through embow'red walls,
> Fairy dell 'mid frowning mountains,
> Grotto pool and Crystal falls.
>
> Here we part perchance forever,
> In our pilgrimage below;
> Yet in scenes like these together,
> Above may we each other know
> (*Calumet of the Coteau*, pp. 132-134).

CRYSTAL SPRING   Map #1

This hot spring is located in the One Hundred Spring Plain of Norris Geyser Basin. It appears that geologist Walter Weed named Crystal Spring in 1884 for the abundance of crystal-like quartz sand grains nearby. In 1891, geologist Arnold Hague observed Crystal Spring and wrote that it was "one of the best places for observing the collection of quartz grains and crystals derived from the [underground] rhyolite" (USGS, Box 55, vol. 2, p. 94). The spring has been difficult to find, so Weed's entire description is reproduced here:

No 183 On a low mound situated in an alcove in a low spur of the hill, & close to the slope, is a curiously interesting spring. (a) hole, 6 in[ches] by 15 inches, filled with water bubbling quietly—no overflow at present. Sinter slope below [is] white. (b) quiet simmering sulphurous pool 2 ft. in diameter with soft muddy lining; no deposit—slight overflow at times to "c". (c) Crystal Spring. Hole a foot in diameter with perpendicular sides of corrugated soft white geyserite—1 ft. deep—lining on bottom of black perlite sand. Water nearly transparent; simmers quietly—temperature 187.5°[F.]. (d) 6 inches in diameter, & exactly similar to (c). 161.5°[F.]. The deposit around c & d is white—the overflow runs out of the small & shallow basin surrounding them, & down the slope coloring a few ft. red, & the rest of the slope brown (USGS, Box 52, vol. 15, p. 90).

CUPID SPRING*   Map #1

Cupid Spring is a hot spring on the Main Terrace of Mammoth Hot Springs. The name refers to the springs that formed what was called "Cleopatra's Bowl" during the 1880s. In 1883, geologist Walter Weed used the names "Cupid's Cave" and "Cleopatra's Bowl" to refer to a cave at the north end of the hollow and the spring on top of it. Weed described "Cleopatra's Bowl" as a flat-topped mound about 10 feet in diameter with a spring about 1 foot in diameter in the center. The top of the bowl was level with Fissure Ridge just to the east, and the overflow from the bowl flowed into a gaping crack nearby. Below "Cleopatra's Bowl" was "Cupid's Cave" (sometimes called "Cupid's Cove"), a cleft in the hot spring deposit whose "marvelous coloring . . . induced . . . many to enter its vapory precincts" (*Livingston Enterprise*, June 27, 1885). Drippings from "Cleopatra's Bowl" in 1882-1883 caused colorful algae to grow in "Cupid's Cave."

Park tour guide G. L. Henderson gave the names Cleopatra and Cupid in 1882 or 1883 for the beautiful queen of ancient Egypt and the blind Roman god of love. Henderson led tours into the small cove at the south end of Fissure Ridge at a place he called Anthony's Entrance (for Mark Anthony). As Henderson imaginatively described the spot for the May 31, 1888, *Helena Weekly Herald*:

Anthony's Entrance admits you at the east and to this mysterious labyrinth where the blind god hides in his rose-tinted cave, and the voluptuous queen has her toilet and dressing room and a washbowl that all the wealth of ancient Rome, with all the artists of Greece, could not produce or even imitate. At this entrance there is the round chimney of an extinct geyser with a rim closely resembling a horse shoe, and there is a legend that lovers must sit upon it for good luck, before venturing into the presence of the blind god who haunts the cave. We all sat down on Gluck Auf.

Henderson had given the name "Gluck Auf," which means "Good Luck," to a travertine rock (which now cannot be located) at Anthony's Entrance because its rim was shaped like a horseshoe. It was here that Henderson wished his tour parties good luck. In 1884, an earthquake closed off water to both "Cleopatra's Bowl" and "Cupid's Cave." Tourists could safely enter "Cupid's Cave" without its carbon dioxide gases, but part of the fun was gone.

The features remained essentially dry until about 1888 when another bowl sprang up close to the old one. By 1910, guidebooks reported that hot spring deposits had almost completely filled the cave, giving the impression that some spring in the area rejuvenated enough to cause the deposition. Between 1931 and 1935 there was activity at "Cupid's Cave," and references to "Cupid's Cave Spring" at that time finally resulted in the official approval of the name Cupid Spring in 1937.

THE CUT†   Map #2

The Cut is a small canyon that separates Blacktail Deer Plateau from Crescent Hill; the canyon is located on the west side of Crescent Hill. Blacktail Deer Plateau Drive off Grand Loop Road about 7 miles east of Mammoth runs through The Cut. The Great Bannock Trail passed through this canyon, and that trail led the Washburn expedition through the canyon in 1870. An emaciated Truman Everts, nearly dead from 37 days of being lost in the wilderness, was found near The Cut on the west slopes of Crescent Hill.

Superintendent P. W. Norris apparently called the canyon "Devil's Cut" or "Dry Canyon." Norris later decided that he did not like "Devil's Cut," so he used "Dry Canyon." The other name still held on in popular usage, sometimes becoming "Devil's Gut." Engineer Hiram Chittenden referred to the canyon as "Crescent Hill Canyon," but "Devil's Cut" still survived. Geologist Arnold Hague modified the name to its present form in his drive to rid the Park of all place names that contained "Hell" or "Devil." Norris probably got the name The Cut from N. P. Langford's account of the 1870 party's trip through the canyon. Langford wrote:

> Following the [Bannock] trail up the ascent leading from Antelope [Rescue] creek, we entered a deep cut, the sides of which rise at an angle of 45 degrees, and are covered with a luxuriant growth of grass. Through this cut we ascended by a grade entirely practicable for a wagon road to the summit of the divide separating the waters of Antelope [Rescue] creek from those of [Lost] creek, and from the summit descended through a beautiful gorge to a small tributary of the Yellowstone . . . (*Discovery of Yellowstone*, p. 75).

The "beautiful" gorge appears to have been The Cut, rather than the earlier "deep cut," but the name nevertheless remains.

CUTOFF CREEK† and MOUNTAIN†   Map #2

Cutoff Creek flows west to Slough Creek from Cutoff Mountain on the Park's northern edge, about 7 miles northwest of the Northeast Entrance to the Park. It is not known whether the mountain was named from the creek or vice versa, but the name Cutoff appears to refer to the Park boundary or to the mountain's very abrupt cliff on its western end.

DAILEY CREEK†   Map #1

Dailey Creek, which appears on the map as "Daly Creek," flows southwest to the Gallatin River from the far northwestern Park boundary. This stream was named at least as early as 1908 for Andrew J. Dailey, one of the earliest settlers of Paradise Valley, Montana. The valley is just east of and over the ridge from the headwaters of Dailey Creek. Dailey's parents, Ebenezer and Katharine Dailey, brought their family to Paradise Valley in 1866, where they wintered at the mining town of Yellowstone City at the mouth of Emigrant Gulch. They moved to Oregon in 1868 and returned to the Paradise Valley four years later. In 1883, the Northern Pacific Railroad named a siding on the new Yellowstone branch in honor of Andrew's brother, Samuel. Buildings still stand at this ghost town on the west side of U.S. Highway 89 near Meditation Point. By 1887, a lake in Paradise Valley was named Dailey Lake for Andrew. For a time, Dome Mountain at Yankee Jim Canyon was known as "Dailey Mountain." As late as the 1930s, there was still a Dailey Ranch in Paradise Valley.

DAISY GEYSER*   Map #3

Daisy Geyser, located in the Daisy Group of the Upper Geyser Basin, received its name in 1884 or 1885. A note in the Arnold Hague papers reports that Daisy was named on a "Superintendent guide-post," a sign that had been put up during the superintendency of David Wear. Because Wear assumed the superintendency on July 1, 1885, and because traveler Burt Buffum was using the name in August of that year, the name was probably given to the geyser that summer or the summer before. J. W. Weimer, an assistant superintendent stationed at Upper Geyser Basin during the summers of 1884 and 1885, possibly named Daisy Geyser and put up the sign.

Daisy Geyser may have been named for a popular expression of the day: "Hey, it's a daisy!" It could also have been named for Weimer's assistant, J. D. Gorman, who was called "Daisy Gorman." It is also possible that Arnold Hague named the geyser for his favorite mule, "Daisy." The geyser could also have been named for the flower. Geologist Walter Weed's 1884 notes showed the name

Tourists entering the Devil's Kitchen, c. 1915

F.J. Haynes

Daisy applied to spring #6 (present-day Brilliant Pool), and his map drawing showed "Daisy" as three concentric circles, somewhat resembling a flower.

DANTE'S INFERNO (SPRING) — Map #1

Dante's Inferno is a hot spring in the Sylvan Springs of Gibbon Geyser Basin. Park Naturalist Al Mebane named the spring in 1959. Since the earliest days in Yellowstone, various writers have used "Dante's Inferno" to describe various hot springs in the Park, so it is appropriate that one spring officially carries the name. The spring is a very large, gas-driven, heavily roiling pool. It is continually in the process of laying down extensive sinter terraces, suggesting the several levels of Dante's Hell.

DEATH GULCH* — Map #2

Death Gulch is a 75-foot-deep V-shaped trench located on the south side of Cache Creek about 4 miles above the stream's mouth. The gulch begins on the south bank of Cache Creek and twists upward for some 300 yards, ending abruptly on a small glacier-deposited bench. A second, smaller gulch then continues upward. In 1888, geologist Walter Weed discovered and named Death Gulch because animals were killed by its escaping gases. Weed found six bears, elk, squirrels, pikas, and many other small animals and insects dead from inhaling heavy carbonic acid gas and hydrogen sulphide gas in the gulch. He surmised from the scene that the elk carcass had attracted the first bear, which then served as bait for the others. Weed theorized that each year snowmelt and spring freshets washed carcasses into Cache Creek. In Weed's report on his discoveries in *Science* (February 15, 1889), he compared Death Gulch to "Death Valley," a similar place on the island of Java.

In 1897, Hague survey geologist T. A. Jaggar, Jr., and F. P. King visited Death Gulch. In the February 1899 issue of *Appleton's Popular Science Monthly*, Jaggar described the gulch as a "frightfully weird and dismal place, utterly without life, and occupied by only a tiny streamlet and an appalling odor" of gases and 8 decomposing bear carcasses. The inhalation of heavy gases put a peculiar pressure on the men's lungs and gave them slight headaches for several hours afterward. Jaggar noted that Death Gulch was a perfect place for fossilization of large mammal bones to occur.

DECKER ISLAND — Map #1

Decker Island is a small grove of trees on the braided stream channel of the South Fork of Tantalus Creek. The stream is located in the Back Basin of the Norris Geyser Basin near the thermal feature that was known as "Decker Geyser" from 1967 to 1981. This place name commemorates Hazel Decker of Two Harbors, Minnesota, who waited here for weeks at a time during the 1960s for major eruptions of nearby Steamboat Geyser. When she was in her late 60s and early 70s, Mrs. Decker waited for over 130 days to see the geyser erupt. Once she spent 52 consecutive days in the area, sleeping in her car in the parking lot.

On July 24, 1967, when a new geyser erupted where Mrs. Decker had kept her vigil, a seasonal naturalist dubbed it "Decker Geyser." This broke a long-standing tradition against naming features for people, but the name "Decker Geyser" continued to be used in the annual reports about the Norris area and in a popular guidebook until the early 1980s.

The spring erupted to heights of 35 feet for two weeks in 1969, and there were small eruptions in 1980. Otherwise, the geyser was a quietly bubbling murky green or muddy pool. "Decker Geyser" was renamed Tantalus Geyser in 1984.

DeLACY CREEK* — Map #3

DeLacy Creek flows south from DeLacy Lakes to Shoshone Lake. Park Superintendent P. W. Norris named the creek in 1881 for Walter Washington DeLacy (1819-1892), the leader of a prospecting expedition that passed through the Yellowstone region in 1863. DeLacy, a surveyor and engineer, compiled the first accurate map of the Yellowstone Park area in 1865.

In 1863, DeLacy led a group of prospectors from Jackson Hole across Pitchstone Plateau and discovered Shoshone Lake, which he named "DeLacy's Lake." He was the first to note the "strange" drainage of that lake south to the Snake River rather than west to the Madison River. But he did not publish his discoveries until 1876, which kept him from receiving credit for being the man who discovered Yellowstone and from leaving his name on present-day Shoshone Lake.

DeLacy also recognized the importance of Yellowstone's thermal features. In a published letter in 1869, he wrote: "At the head of the South Snake, and also on the south fork of the Madison [present-day Shoshone Lake and Firehole River], there are hundreds of hot springs, many of which are 'geysers' " (Raymond, "Mineral Resources," p. 142). In 1871, Hayden changed the name of "DeLacy's Lake" to "Madison Lake." In 1872, Frank Bradley criticized DeLacy for the "numerous errors" on DeLacy's map and named the lake Shoshone.

Park Superintendent P. W. Norris felt sorry for DeLacy and named the present stream for him in 1881, stating:

> The . . . narrative, the high character of its writer [DeLacy], his mainly correct descriptions of the region visited, and the

traces which I have found of this party [campsite remains, etc.], proves alike its entire truthfulness, and the injustice of changing the name of De Lacy's Lake [to Shoshone Lake]; and fearing it is now too late to restore the proper name to it, I have, as a small token of deserved justice, named the stream and Park crossed by our trail above the Shoshone Lake after their discoverer" (*Fifth Annual Report*, p. 44).

DELUSION LAKE*   Map #4

Delusion Lake, the fifth largest lake in the Park, is located 4 miles east of Grant Village and 2 miles north of the Flat Mountain Arm of Yellowstone Lake. Incorrectly mapped in 1871 by the Hayden survey as an arm of Yellowstone Lake (probably because the surveyors saw only part of it from atop a peak), the lake was named by members of the 1878 survey who discovered this "delusion." Recent studies have shown that the outlet of Delusion Lake is intermittent and disappears underground about a quarter mile from the lake. There are no fish in Delusion Lake, which has a maximum depth of 30 feet.

DEMON'S CAVE   Map #3

Demon's Cave is a hot spring located a short distance southeast of Black Sand Pool in Black Sand Basin of Upper Geyser Basin. This was probably the spring shown as "Cave Geyser" on one of Gustavus Bechler's 1872 maps. Capt. J. W. Barlow described the cave in 1871 as having "its cavity extending beneath the surface of the ground in the form of a cavern" (in Baldwin, *Enchanted Enclosure*, p. 33). Guidebook writer W. W. Wylie named Demon's Cave (or took it from local usage) in about 1881. Herman Haupt, a guidebook writer during the 1880s, described Demon's Cave as "a deep pit in the geyserite, which has been washed out, leaving a crust suspended over a boiling caldron, from which steam is constantly arising, filling the cave with a cloud of mist, which at times obscures the surface of the water below" (*Yellowstone*, p. 109).

DEVIL'S DEN   Map #2

Devil's Den is the name given to the canyon of Tower Creek above Tower Fall. In 1807, the Washburn party gave this name to the canyon of Cascade Creek above Crystal Falls, but that name was soon changed to Cascade Canyon. In 1871, F. V. Hayden transferred the name Devil's Den to the dark, tangled draw above Tower Fall, probably naming it after the terrible thicket at the Battle of Gettysburg known as the "Devil's Den."

DEVIL'S GATE   Map #3

Devil's Gate is the canyon of the Firehole River just below Kepler Cascades. In 1872, topographer Gustavus Bechler indicated this canyon on his map as "Narrow Gate." But in 1883, geologist Joseph Iddings of the Hague surveys referred to the canyon as Devil's Gate, probably because of its dark, narrow, torturous, and spooky appearance.

DEVIL'S KITCHEN   Map #1

The cave known as Devil's Kitchen was formed from an extinct hot spring located east of Bath Lake in the Mammoth Hot Springs area. Now rarely visited, this cave was a popular attraction during the early days of the Park. Apparently, Charles Millard, a tourist from Fort Ellis (near present-day Bozeman, Montana) discovered and named the cave. In 1884, Park tour operator G. L. Henderson built a ladder into the Devil's Kitchen, so he could lead visitors into the cave. By 1925, two women had opened an ice cream and soft drink stand there. They built a small log shelter for their business, which was used during the 1930s as the actual entrance to Devil's Kitchen. The Park Service closed the area in 1939 when it became aware of the dangers of carbon dioxide gases in the cave.

DEVIL'S STAIRWAY   Map #1

Devil's Stairway is a hill on the Mary Mountain Trail, which begins at the east side of the large meadows at the head of Nez Perce Creek and climbs to Mary Lake. The name Devil's Stairway had been applied to this steep stretch of wagon road by 1889. At one time, the road was the only route to Yellowstone Lake from Upper Geyser Basin, but it fell into disuse when the West Thumb-Old Faithful road was opened in 1891. West-to-east travelers often had to get out of their wagons and walk up the hill to save wear and tear on tired horses. In 1890, a coach driver asked Park visitor Guy R. Pelton, a former congressman from New York state, to walk up the hill. Pelton died of a heart attack at the side of the road, which prompted the government to cancel the transportation contracts of that Park concessionaire.

DEVIL'S THUMB   Map #1

Devil's Thumb, located near Palette Spring at Mammoth Hot Springs, is an extinct travertine cone built up from hot water that once flowed from it. In 1871, F. V. Hayden named this cone the "Beehive"; in 1878, A. C. Peale called it "Liberty #2" after nearby Liberty Cap, which it resembled. Later observers sometimes called the cone "Giant's Thumb," but apparently Park Superintendent P. W. Norris named it Devil's Thumb in 1879.

DIAMOND BEACH   Map #4

This long, sandy beach on Yellowstone Lake is located between the Yellowstone River outlet and Mary Bay. Although Capt. W. A. Jones named it "Crystal Beach" in 1873 "for the benefit of future poets and sentimentalists," locals already called it Diamond Beach because of the sparkling and flashing of tiny particles of sand. According to visitor Harry J. Norton in 1872, the sand was "composed almost entirely of obsidian and those minute and beautiful crystals known as California diamonds" (*Wonderland Illustrated*, p. 70).

DIANA SPRING* Map #1

Diana Spring is another acceptable and official name for Cleopatra Spring of Cleopatra Terrace at Mammoth Hot Springs. G. L. Henderson or another local person named the spring in about 1885 for Diana, the Roman goddess of animals and hunting and of mountains, woods, and streams.

DOCTOR ALLEN'S PAINTPOTS Map #1

This group of mudpots is located in the Back Basin of Norris Geyser Basin, just southeast of Emerald Spring. In 1927, a Park superintendent's place-names committee named the area for Eugene T. Allen, who apparently sustained minor burns in this area while working on thermal research. Allen was one of the authors of the treatise, *Hot Springs of the Yellowstone National Park* (1935). This place name is one of three or four in Yellowstone that breaks the rule against naming thermal features for people.

DOT ISLAND* Map #4

Dot Island, located east of West Thumb, is one of the 7 named islands of Yellowstone Lake. Members of the Hayden survey named the island in 1871 because it was a mere dot on the map. From 1896 to 1907, boat operator E. C. Waters kept buffalo and elk in pens to show tourists who stopped there on the boat trip from West Thumb to Lake Hotel. Because the animals were mistreated, Park officials forced Waters to release the animals in 1907.

DOUGLAS KNOB† Map #3

Douglas Knob is a low hill on the south end of the large meadow located at the head of the Little Fork of the Bechler River. Assistant Chief Ranger William S. Chapman named the hill in 1962 for Joseph O. Douglas (1872-1939), "a prominent member of the oldtime Yellowstone Ranger Force . . . and a colorful figure in Yellowstone's transition from army to civilian operations" (USBGN folder file). Douglas was Assistant Chief Ranger in Yellowstone in 1921 and was the Park's chief buffalo keeper. He had a great reputation as a mountain man, and one of his adventures made it into the November 12, 1927, *Saturday Evening Post*. One day on winter patrol when in his 50s, Douglas started across the frozen Yellowstone Lake at West Thumb and fell through thin ice:

> He scrambled out of the icy water into a thirty-below-zero atmosphere. Two miles behind was Thumb station and fifteen miles ahead, Lake.
> Douglas stripped, wrung out of his clothes what water had not already congealed, resumed his ice-stiffened garments and hiked the fifteen miles. The next day he did twenty more. "Why didn't you go back, you old fool?" they asked him at Lake. Douglas grinned sheepishly and spoke from long knowledge of the glee with which the service lays upon knowledge of a member's discomfort.
> "They'd have kidded me to death," he explained.

DRAGONS MOUTH SPRING* Map #2

This spring in the Mud Volcano area has had at least 17 different names. Warren Gillette of the 1870 Washburn party named it "Cave Spring" from its appearance. Lt. G. C. Doane's description of it as a perfect grotto was responsible for naming it "The Grotto," "Grotto Spring," "Grotto Sulphur Spring," "Gothic Grotto," and "Devil's Grotto." Since the earliest days, visitors have commented on the violent seething, surging, and rumbling of Dragons Mouth Spring, caused by explosive bursts of steam. Because of this seemingly "preternatural activity," it has also been called "Devil's Kitchen," "Devil's Workshop," and "Devil's Den." Its surging action earned it the names "Blowing Cavern," Holmes's "Arch Spring," and the "Belcher" or "Belching Spring." An unknown visitor seems to have given the name Dragons Mouth in about 1912. In 1913, Louise Elliott recorded in *Six Weeks on Horseback Through Yellowstone Park*: "The guide books call this fascinating cave the Green Gable Spring, but some tourist, thinking to improve upon the name, tacked a card on a nearby tree, rechristening it the Dragon's Mouth and I like that name better, because it suggests Fairyland" (p. 113).

DRUID PEAK* Map #2

Druid Peak is a low, 9,583-foot-high peak north of the mouth of Soda Butte Creek. This mountain is probably the "Soda Hill" named by the Hayden surveyors in 1878, because of its proximity to the extinct hot spring known as Soda Butte. P. W. Norris named the peak "Mount Longfellow" or "Longfellow's Peak" in about 1880, perhaps as a tribute to his friend Jack Baronett who Gen. W. E. Strong had characterized as "built like Longfellow's ship, 'for strength and speed' " (*A Trip to the Yellowstone*, pp. 47-48). Members of the Hague survey party in 1885 named it Druid Peak for unknown reasons.

Tourists at Excelsior Geyser, 1888

Boiling trout at Fishing Cone, 1892

Six-horse stagecoach in the Gardner Canyon near Eagle Nest Rock

DRYAD LAKE*   Map #4

This small lake is located west of Elephant Back Mountain, about 5 miles east of Beach Lake. Members of the Hague survey named it Dryad Lake in 1885 for unknown reasons. They may have been referring to the dryad flower that grows in the Park or for dryads, female forest fairies in Greek mythology, who were responsible for the welfare of trees.

DUCK CREEK*   Map #1

Duck Creek flows west to Maple Creek from opposite the headwaters of Straight Creek. Either Northern Pacific Railroad surveyors named this stream in 1882 or they took it from an incident in 1871. Members of an 1871 tourist party—which included R. W. Raymond, A. J. Thrasher, C. C. Clawson, and Gilman Sawtell—named a creek in this area Duck Creek because Raymond fell into it and was "ducked." In 1871, Raymond wrote: "The way to christen a creek is to immerse something in it; and the article immersed, in this case, was a member of the party . . . so we christened it Duck Creek and went our dripping way" (*New Northwest*, June 15, 1871).

DUNANDA FALLS*   Map #3

Dunanda Falls is a 150-foot-high waterfall on Boundary Creek in the southwest corner of the Park. Explorer W. C. Gregg (see Gregg Fork) discovered the falls in 1920 and named it Dunanda the following year. *Dunanda* is a Shoshone word meaning "straight down."

DUNRAVEN PASS*   Map #2

The 8,859-foot-high pass of the Washburn Range is located on the Grand Loop Road about 6 miles north of Canyon. In 1878, W. H. Holmes called the pass "Washburn Gap," but the next year Park Superintendent P. W. Norris named it for Windham Thomas Wyndham-Quin, the Fourth Earl of Dunraven (1841-1926). The Earl visited Yellowstone Park during his sightseeing and hunting trip to western America in 1874. He described his Yellowstone travels in *The Great Divide* (1876), which played a large role in introducing Yellowstone to Britain and Europe and in attracting foreign tourists to the Park. In his autobiography, *Past Times and Pastimes* (1922), Dunraven recalled eating antelope steaks on the south slopes of Mount Washburn near this pass.

Dunraven visited the American West in 1869 on his honeymoon, in 1871 when he was guided by Buffalo Bill Cody, in 1874, and in 1877 when he built the English Hotel at Rocky Mountain National Park, Colorado. Dunraven was educated at Oxford and in Paris, where he "acquired all sorts of agreeable bad habits and an appreciation of fine wines and pretty girls." "It is most annoying," he later wrote, "that everything that is pleasant is all wrong."

DUNRAVEN PEAK*   Map #2

This 9,900-foot-high peak of the Washburn Range is located just west of Dunraven Pass. Henry Gannett of the third Hayden survey named it for the Earl of Dunraven in 1878 (see Dunraven Pass), "whose travels and writings have done so much toward making this region known to our cousins across the water" (in Hayden, *Twelfth Annual Report*, p. 478).

EAGLE NEST ROCK*   Map #1

The name of this pinnacle of McMinn Bench, located about a mile south of the North Entrance, is a misnomer. The birds that have nested on this rock "from time immemorial" are not eagles; they are ospreys, or fish hawks. Several sources report that ospreys have nested here since at least the discovery of the Park.

Eagle Nest Rock apparently received its name from Park tour operator G. L. Henderson in about 1884. It is possible that Henderson took the name from the local usage of stagecoach drivers. Stagecoach drivers pointed out the rock and nests to tourists in the early days, and many drivers wrongly thought that the birds were eagles.

EAGLE PEAK*   Map #4

At 11,358 feet high, this peak of the Absaroka Range is the highest mountain in Yellowstone Park. Eagle Peak was named in 1885 by members of the Hague parties of the USGS. In 1897, geologist T. A. Jaggar, Jr., described the peak as being "shaped like a spread eagle," which was apparently the reason for the name.

In the early days, observers believed that Electric Peak was Yellowstone's highest peak. The battle for the honor came to the attention of the national press during the 1930s, and Eagle Peak was determined to be the highest.

EAR SPRING*   Map #3

Shaped like a human ear, Ear Spring is a hot spring of the Geyser Hill Group in Upper Geyser Basin. In 1890, geologist Walter Weed dubbed the spring "Oyster Spring," "whose form it somewhat resembles." In 1897, Weed used the name Ear Spring. He had not been in the Park for about 5 years, so perhaps he had found the name in local usage that summer.

By 1912, Ear Spring was referred to as the "Devil's Ear," and stories were told about messages being transmitted from the spring to the infernal regions below. Joe Mitchell

Chapple told this humorous story in *A Top O' the World* in 1922, wrongly attributing it to fur-trapper Jim Bridger:

> Suddenly coming upon the Upper Basin, we are told a good Jim Bridger yarn about the "Ear," a hot spring of only about three feet in diameter, but which has, near the lobe section of its ear-shaped circumference, a tiny geyser, whose pool is about the size of a silver dollar, and whose spouting power is only a few inches. Jim said that when the old-time trappers failed to make good in their expectations for the day, they would come here and tell their tales of woe into this giant's ear. At last the old man grew so tired of listening to their troubles that he placed a tiny button [the little geyser] on one side, so that he could fasten the flap of his ear over and turn a "deaf ear" to their complaints (p. 48).

EARTHQUAKE CLIFFS   Map #1

These rhyolite cliffs on the south side of the Gibbon River extend east and west from about 2 miles west of Canyon Creek to about 3 miles east of the Cascades of the Firehole. In about 1880, Park Superintendent P. W. Norris named the cliffs because of the frequent rockslides there, some probably caused by earthquakes. Norris built a road in 1878 that passed along the foot of these cliffs. Robert Strahorn passed over the road in 1880, and as he remembered in *The Enchanted Land*: ". . . we passed through a picturesque defile at the base of Earthquake Cliff, where earthquakes have been shaking up things generally within the past century" (p. 16).

EBONY GEYSER   Map #1

Ebony Geyser is in the Porcelain Basin of Norris Geyser Basin. In about 1915, geologist Arnold Hague wrote that "Black Ebony Spring" had been named for its "ochreous deposits." It appears that Hague or another survey member had named another spring "Black Ebony" (present-day Crown Jewels Spring) in or before 1904, but in 1927 the name was moved to this thermal feature.

EBRO SPRINGS*   Map #2

Ebro Springs is a group of thermal springs located on the south slopes of Sulphur Hills. Members of the Hague parties named these springs in about 1885. The name is probably a shortened form of *eborinous*, which means ivory or white and refers to the color of the thermal area.

ECHINUS GEYSER*   Map #1

Echinus Geyser (ee KI nus) is located in the Back Basin of Norris Geyser Basin. Mineralogist Albert C. Peale of the Hayden survey named this geyser in 1878 "because the pebbles around the basin" had "some resemblance to the spine-covered sea urchin" (Hayden, *Twelfth Annual Report*, p. 129). *Echinos* is Greek for spine, and *echinus* is a Latin genus of spiny sea urchins. During the 1970s and 1980s, Echinus Geyser has been a star performer. It is the largest predictable geyser in the Norris area, and between 1976 and 1980 its intervals lasted from 23 to 91 minutes.

ECHO CANYON†   Map #1

This mostly dry canyon is located near the Park's western boundary about 10 miles south of West Yellowstone and just southeast of South Riverside Cabin. How this canyon got its name or who named it is not known, but it appeared on an 1877 map, showing it just south of the point in the Park where Idaho, Montana, and Wyoming touch. The *Haynes Guides* from 1939 to 1966 ascribe the name to a "well-known Jim Bridger story, that upon retiring at night he would holler, 'Wake up, Jim,' and by morning the echo would return just in time to arouse him for the new day" (pp. 70-71).

ECHO PEAK*   Map #1

This 9,685-foot-high peak of the Gallatin Range is located northwest of Mount Holmes. In 1884, geologist Joseph P. Iddings named this peak while he was conducting geological investigations and mapping the Gallatin Range. Why he named it Echo Peak is unknown, but the prevalence of echoes in various parts of the Park has been noticed since the earliest days.

ECONOMIC GEYSER CRATER*   Map #3

Economic Geyser Crater is a long-extinct geyser in the Grand Group of Upper Geyser Basin. A star performer in Yellowstone between 1888 and 1913, this geyser has had very few eruptions since the 1920s. When active, it spouted from 25 to 30 feet high every 4 to 6 minutes. As Arnold Hague explained, the geyser was known as "Economy," "Economical," and finally Economic Geyser because "the water is ejected as a single column, all of it falling back into the pool, and thence down the open tube, leaving the basin dry, only to be again rapidly replenished" (Hague papers, Box 11, "The Geyser Basins," p. 44). In the August 17, 1901, *Livingston Enterprise*, tour guide G. L. Henderson answered the question this way: "first, it [Economic Geyser] never wastes its own time; second, it never wastes your time; third, it never wastes a drop of water."

In about 1889, Park photographer F. Jay Haynes took a photo of Economic Geyser. This name first appeared in Haynes's guidebook, and the photographer may have given the feature its name. Economic Geyser appears to have become dormant in about 1923, although it erupted three times in 1957 and a number of times in 1959 after the great earthquake in the Park.

EGERIA SPRING   Map #3

This hot spring is part of the Rabbit Creek Group of Midway Geyser Basin. Park Geologist George Marler named this spring sometime before 1973 to perpetuate the historic name of Midway Geyser Basin—"Egeria Springs." In Greek mythology, Egeria was a nymph spirit of springs. She married King Numa, and after his death retired to the woods in the valley of Aricia. Diana changed Egeria into a fountain, and she evermore foretold the fates of newborn babies.

ELEANOR LAKE*   Map #4

Eleanor Lake is near the top of Sylvan Pass, about 6 miles from the Park's East Entrance. Road engineer Hiram Chittenden named this small lake sometime during the building of the East Entrance Road (1901-1902). He named it for his daughter, Eleanor, who was five months old during Chittenden's first tour of duty in the Park (1891-1893). Eleanor Chittenden married James Bell Cress in 1916 and helped prepare a number of revised editions of her father's famous book, *The Yellowstone National Park*.

ELECTRIC PEAK*   Map #1

Electric Peak is a 10,992-foot-high mountain in the Gallatin Range, just west of Gardiner, Montana. It was once thought to be Yellowstone's highest peak, but it is actually the sixth highest. The peak's name comes from an incident that A. C. Peale of the 1872 Hayden survey described in his diary for Friday, July 26, 1872:

> We reached the summit of the peak about 4 o'clock. There was a storm cloud all about us. [Henry] Gannett was a little ahead and we saw him hurrying back to us with his hair standing on end. As he neared us we could hear a crackling noise as though there were a lot of frictional electrical machines all about him. We soon began to feel it ourselves. Gannett said [that when] he got to the summit the electricity was so strong that he was obliged to put down the gradienter and hurry down. [A. E.] Brown tried to go up and get it but got a shock on the top of his head and came back in a hurry also. We then descended about 100 feet, having the noise all about us as though there were a lot of electrical machines about us (p. 6).

A proposal in 1908 to rename this peak "Edison Peak" for Thomas A. Edison failed when Gannett opposed the change. "I attached the name of 'Electric Peak' to the mountain referred to in the year 1872," Gannett wrote, "because at that time and on this summit I first acted as a lightning rod—a rather unique experience" (USBGN folder file).

ELEPHANT BACK MOUNTAIN*   Map #4

Elephant Back Mountain is a low ridge located about 3 miles northwest of Bridge Bay of Yellowstone Lake. F. V. Hayden gave the name Elephant Back to this rather innocuous ridge in 1871 because "of the almost vertical sides of this mountain, and the rounded form of the summit" (Hayden, *Fifth Annual Report*, p. 99). Hayden had taken the name from the map of the explorations of Capt. W. F. Raynolds in 1859-1860, which had applied it to present-day Mount Washburn. The name probably came directly from Jim Bridger, one of Raynolds's guides on the expedition. Hayden, who was a member of the expedition, wrote to Arnold Hague on May 2, 1885: "I have to say that both [Robert] Meldrum and [Jim] Bridger spoke of the mountain which they called Elephants Back from its resemblance to the back of that animal—the name was given by the old trappers and has never been known by any other name" (Hague papers, Box 5, May 2, 1885).

ELK PARK*   Map #1

Elk Park is a large meadow located about a mile southwest of Norris Geyser Basin. Tourists who used this meadow for camping probably named it for the elk that frequented the area. As early as 1880, travelers used the name Elk Park. Some parties appear to have confused this camping area with a spot at nearby Gibbon Meadows, and this confusion seems to have been the reason for the maintenance of separate names.

EMERALD POOL*   Map #3

Emerald Pool is located in the Black Sand Basin of Upper Geyser Basin. One of Yellowstone's most famous hot springs, Emerald Pool got its name in 1872 during the second Hayden survey. It may have been named by Gustavus Bechler, whose 1872 map showed it as "Great Emerald Spring." In 1878, A. C. Peale described the pool as being of "beautiful emerald tint with yellow-green basin and ornamented edge . . ." (Hayden, *Twelfth Annual Report*, p. 245). The pool's deep green color is caused by the blue of its water combining with yellow algae growing in its bowl. Peale recorded the pool's temperature in 1878 at 148°F.; today it is about 155°F.

J. Sanford Saltus visited Emerald Pool in 1894 and summed up its magical properties:

> Emerald Pool . . . is the most beautiful thing in the way of wonderland water I have ever seen, and I have seen many wonderful and beautiful lakes, lagoons, ponds, and pools in Europe, Asia, Africa, South America, Canada, Mexico, the Mediterranean and West India Islands. . . . Fill a thin goblet with Creme de Menthe, on the top drop a few "beads" of absinthe, and you will have a faint, only a faint idea of the glis-

Muddy road between Norris and Madison Junction

Hiram Chittenden with daughter Eleanor at far left

Looking at the Gallatin Range from Indian Creek

tening green glory of Emerald Pool, which can be compared to nothing unless one can imagine liquefied Chinese fire or the unknown, unnamable tones seen under the influence of an anesthetic or during delirium. Round the edge is a rim of sediment, exactly the color and apparent texture of rough-grained gold. Truly this is a jewel—an emerald set in gold! Were there nothing else to be seen in the Park, Emerald Pool would be worth the journey (*A Week in the Yellowstone*, pp. 49-51).

EPHEDRA SPRING   Map #4

This hot spring in the West Thumb Geyser Basin received its name during the 1960s. The spring got its name from *Ephedra Brusei*, a species of brine fly that inhabits thermal areas and feeds off hot water algae. In 1959, naturalists named the spring "Little Blue Funnel Spring" because of its proximity and resemblance to nearby Blue Funnel Spring.

THE ESPLANADE   Map #1

The Esplanade is a travertine terrace located just southwest of and above Minerva Terrace. A turnout on the road on top of The Esplanade allows a good view of Mammoth. This terrace seems to have been named in about 1889 by geologist Walter Weed. An esplanade is a level, open space between a citadel and a town, which left attackers exposed to fire from the fortress. The name appears to have been given for the terrace's view and for its appeal to strolling visitors on the "citadel" above the "town" of Mammoth.

EXCELSIOR GEYSER CRATER   Map #3

Excelsior Geyser Crater is a large (276 by 132 feet) hot spring in the Midway Geyser Basin. In 1881, Park Superintendent P. W. Norris named this geyser after seeing its impressive eruption. Norris found the eruptions "so immeasurably excelling any other [geyser], ancient or modern, known to history, that I find but one name fitting, and herein christen it the 'Excelsior' until scientists, if able, shall invent a more appropriate one" (*Fifth Annual Report*, p. 62). Excelsior is the Latin word for *higher*.

One of Yellowstone's largest and most celebrated geysers, Excelsior became famous during the 1880s for its giant eruptions, which sometimes measured 300 feet in height and 300 feet in width. Two observers in 1881 reported to Norris that Excelsior's

> subterranean rumblings and earth tremblings were often so fearful as to prevent sleep—so great the cloud ascending from the Excelsior Geyser, and so dense and widespread the descending spray, as to obscure the sun at mid-day, and the united mists and fogs as to saturate garments like the spray from a cataract . . . (*Fifth Annual Report*, pp. 54-55).

During its heyday from 1882 to 1888, Excelsior erupted every 20 to 120 minutes with heights varying from 50 to 350 feet.

In the July 28, 1888, *Livingston Enterprise*, tour guide G. L. Henderson reported:

> The close of each eruption was accompanied by violent earthquake shocks that tore down the geyserite walls and added much both to the danger and sublimity of the spectacle. These masses of broken wall were at each eruption hurled into the air several hundred feet above the topmost waves, clashing together in their descent . . . with a deafening noise that was most terrific. . . . As the waters rose into a vast dome the hissing noise increased until the rocks broke through, and then all was clatter and confusion for a few seconds, and while the water sank back with a gurgling noise from three to seven shocks were so strong as to render it necessary for lookers-on to support each other to avoid falling.

For a long time, there was general agreement that Excelsior last erupted in 1888, but newspaper articles and letters from observers document eruptions in 1890. There is also some evidence of activity in 1891 and 1901.

When it was active, Excelsior must have been awesome. Only Steamboat Geyser at Norris was as high, and probably no other geyser ever discharged so much water and in so wide a column. In 1985, the geyser astonished naturalists by suddenly becoming active again, with small 6- to 7-foot eruptions.

EXPLORER'S CREEK   Map #4

Explorer's Creek flows northwest to Clear Creek. Its confluence with Clear Creek occurs less than a mile east of Yellowstone Lake. Park Superintendent P. W. Norris named this stream in 1880 or 1881 to honor his boat, the *Explorer*. He, Jack Davis, and W. H. Parker (see Parker Peak) used the boat to explore Yellowstone Lake in 1880, "encountering many mishaps and dangers." The name may also have been given in tribute to themselves as explorers.

FACTORY HILL*   Map #3

Factory Hill is a 9,607-foot-high peak in the Red Mountains. By 1876, the peak was called "Red Mountain," a name that had been originally given to present-day Mount Sheridan by members of the 1871 Hayden survey. Eventually, the name "Red" was applied to the entire small mountain range.

Members of the Hague parties named Factory Hill in about 1885 because of N. P. Langford's description of steam vents near the mountain. In the June 1871 issue of *Scribner's*, Langford wrote: "Through the hazy atmosphere we beheld, on the shore of the inlet opposite our camp, the steam ascending in jets from more than fifty craters, giving it much the appearance of a New England factory village" (p. 120).

FACTORY SPRINGS Map #3

Factory Springs is a group of hot springs in the Hayden Valley located along both sides of Alum Creek, about 3.5 miles above the creek's mouth. Guidebook writer Harry J. Norton named these springs in 1872 because he thought they resembled a factory. Various observers noticed this phenomenon in Yellowstone thermal areas: ". . . the escaping steam from numerous cracks and blow-holes and the boiling water in pools and crevices produce a combined effect which suggests the humming spindles and whirling wheels of a great . . . factory" (Linton, "Mount Sheridan," p. 12).

FAIRIES' FALL Map #2

This 30-foot-high waterfall is located about a mile above the mouth of Amethyst Creek. In about 1882, guidebook writer Herman Haupt, Jr., gave this beautiful name to the waterfall, probably taking the name from local usage. During the 1880s, a tourist trail passed just to the north of the falls along the south bank of the Lamar River. In about 1903, an attempt was made to rename the falls "Amethyst Falls," but it failed.

FAIRY FALLS* Map #3

Fairy Falls is a 197-foot-high waterfall on Fairy Creek and is the fourth highest named waterfall in Yellowstone. Capt. J. W. Barlow and F. V. Hayden discovered the falls when standing on the top of one of the nearby Twin Buttes in 1871. Barlow named it "from the graceful beauty with which the little stream dropped down a clear descent . . ." (Hayden, *Fifth Annual Report*, p. 112).

FAIRY SPRINGS* Map #3

Fairy Springs is a group of hot springs located on the west side of Lower Geyser Basin. G. W. Burton, an early-day tourist, wrote in 1909: "As you look into an emerald pool, or a sapphire pool, you would scarcely be surprised if a fairy clad in gauze and gems, crowned with stars and floating on dazzling wings were to emerge" (*Burton's Book*, p. 18). But members of the Hague parties named Fairy Springs in about 1885 from the creek that drains the springs.

FALLS RIVER* Map #3

Falls River flows west to the Henry's Fork of the Snake River from above Beula Lake and alongside the Cave Falls road in the southwest corner of the Park. This major river, which rises from large springs at the foot of Pitchstone Plateau, officially received its name in 1872 from members of the Hayden survey. Fur trappers had already named the river much earlier. As trapper Osborne Russell reported in his 1838 journal:

> . . . we fell onto the middle branch of Henrys fork which is called by hunters "The falling fork" from the numerous Cascades it forms whilst meandering thro. the forest previous to its junction with the main river (*Journal of a Trapper*, p. 92).

FAN CREEK* Map #1

Fan Creek flows southwest to the Gallatin River about 15 miles north of West Yellowstone, Montana. In 1885, geologist Joseph P. Iddings named this stream from the shape of the large valley at its headwaters. A fellow geologist, George M. Wright, wrote:

> The headwaters of Fan Creek lie in a large valley of peculiar shape . . . which is divided by radial ridges into several minor radiating valleys all of which unite producing somewhat the form of *a fan*—the dividing ridges being the "ribs." Mr. Iddings has suggested for this combination valley the very appropriate name of "The Fan" (USGS, Box 50, no. 2, p. 12).

FAN GEYSER* Map #3

Fan Geyser, located in the Morning Glory Group of the Upper Geyser Basin, got its name from members of the 1870 Washburn party because its eruption was shaped like a feather fan. N. P. Langford recorded that the geyser had two radiating sheets of water that crossed each other and shot up 60 feet. The geyser's eruption can reach as high as 125 feet, and it nearly always erupts along with nearby Mortar Geyser. The eruptions are unpredictable and rare, but visitors who have seen Fan and Mortar geysers erupt have found the spectacle strange and wonderful. In 1878, W. H. Holmes saw an eruption of Fan and found himself "quite weak from excitement":

> On the opposite side of the river, which here is comparatively quiet and some 40 feet wide, stand two low geyser cones or piles set into the gray domes bank and projecting slightly into the river. The upper one suddenly ceased as I reached the bank and the lower one began to sputter; very quickly a splendid fan-shaped jet was thrown into the air . . . its thousand darted jets trembling from right to left. To the left, and beyond this, within 6 feet a second stream of steam water of unexampled beauty was projected into the air to the distance of 100 to 200 feet and what was most surprising was that it stood at an angle of 40°, another little jet nearer me shooting but at a similar angle towards me. It is quite impossible to describe the wonderful spectacular display that followed or to give any adequate idea of the beauty of the two principal jets or of the resistless force with which they were projected upward (diary, pp. 22-23).

Both Fan and Mortar geysers went dormant in about 1912 and apparently did not erupt at all until 1938. From 1938 to 1968, only 16 eruptions are documented. In 1969, the geysers rejuvenated in grand style, erupting at least 79 times in two years. Since that time, Fan and Mortar have been sporadically active. To see them erupt is to see one of the most spectacular sights in Yellowstone.

FERRIS FORK (of the Bechler River)*   Map #3

Ferris Fork flows southwest from Pitchstone Plateau to become one of the three streams that form the Bechler River. In 1921, explorer W. C. Gregg wrote: "J. E. Haynes and I tried hard to find names of men identified with that [Bechler] region not already honored [with a name]" (*Outlook*, November 23, 1921, pp. 274-275). Their search turned up Warren Angus Ferris, a fur trapper and clerk of the American Fur Company who visited the Upper Geyser Basin in 1834 with two Indians. Because his motive was curiosity rather than business, Ferris deserves to be called Yellowstone's first known tourist. Ferris also was the first person to provide an accurate description of the Yellowstone country and the first to apply the word "geyser" to Yellowstone thermal features. His account is also the earliest known record of a visit to Upper Geyser Basin, where he saw a geyser erupting—probably Splendid Geyser. It is doubtful that he ever saw the stream that now bears his name.

FIREHOLE FALLS*   Map #3

This 40-foot-high waterfall is located on the Firehole River south of Madison Junction. A. C. Peale and F. H. Bradley of the Hayden survey both recorded seeing this falls in 1872, but neither of them named it. The name seems to have been applied during the early 1890s. A later attempt to call it "Fish Falls" failed.

FIREHOLE LAKE*   Map #3

Firehole Lake is a hot spring in the Firehole Lake Group (or Black Warrior Group) of the Lower Geyser Basin. As early as 1896, this large hot spring was known as Firehole Lake. The lake was named for nearby Firehole Pool (*not* for the Firehole River), which is the principal source of hot water for Firehole Lake. Locals called the lake Firehole because rising gases caused a "flickering" effect on the water that resembled blue flames, making it one of the Park's most famous "burning springs."

Guidebook author Reau Campbell described the spring in 1909 as "a lake of fire holes emitting blue blazes in globules of sulphuric looking fire, the most astonishing phenomena in the world" (*Complete Guide*, p. 57). Similar "flames" effects can be seen elsewhere in the Park at Firehole Spring, Flash Spring, Turban Geyser, and several other springs.

FIREHOLE RIVER*   Map #3

The Firehole River flows north from Madison Lake to the Madison River. The name Firehole dates from the early 1830s and is probably the Park's fifth oldest place name. During the 1820s and 1830s, fur trappers often referred to mountain valleys as "holes," such as Jackson Hole and Pierre's Hole. Trappers used "Burnt Hole" or "Fire Hole" to refer to a burned-over valley near present-day Hebgen Lake, and other trappers later transferred the name "Firehole" to the area now known as the Firehole, thinking that it referred to hot springs and geysers along the river. It is an understandable confusion. Fur-trader and explorer Benjamin Bonneville, for example, confirmed what his men thought were geyser areas during the 1830s. He wrote in 1876: "You ask me if I know of the thermal springs and geysers. Not personally, but my men knew about them, and called their location the 'Fire Hole' " (letter, MHS *Contributions*, I:109).

The name seems to have been first applied to the river in about 1850, when Jim Bridger, Kit Carson, Lou Anderson, James Kruse, O. P. Wiggins, Soos, and about 20 other men on a prospecting trip "saw the geysers of the lower basin and named the river that drains them the Fire Hole" (Topping, *Chronicles of the Yellowstone*, p. 16). In 1851, Fr. Pierre DeSmet included the name "Fire Hole Riv." on the map he drew using information from Jim Bridger, so Bridger may be responsible for naming the river. One of Bridger's stories, as reported by Capt. W. F. Raynolds, for whom Bridger guided, concerned the stream that "flowed so fast down the side of the hill that the friction of the water against the rocks, heated the rocks" (*Report*, p. 77). This story is not as farfetched as you might think, because hot springs in a riverbed can literally heat the rocks on the bottom. In 1870, when the Washburn expedition entered Yellowstone, N. P. Langford attempted to wade barefoot across the Firehole River, near Castle Geyser. He wrote:

> When I reached the middle of the stream I paused a moment and turned around to speak to Mr. [Cornelius] Hedges, who was about entering the stream, when I discovered from the sensation of warmth under my feet that I was standing upon an incrustation formed over a hot spring that had its vent in the bed of the stream. I exclaimed to Hedges: "Here is the river which Bridger said was *hot at the bottom*" (*Discovery of Yellowstone*, p. 175).

FIREHOLE SPRING*   Map #3

The name of Firehole Spring, a hot spring in the White Creek Group of Lower Geyser Basin, has nothing to do

The Washburn Expedition of 1870

In 1870, having heard rumors and stories from prospectors about strange wonders at the head of the Yellowstone River, a party known as the Washburn expedition set out from Helena, Montana, to see for themselves. This group was to receive credit for discovering the area now known as Yellowstone National Park. Accompanied by 40 horses and a dog, the 19 men in the party included some of Montana Territory's brightest stars, among them the state surveyor general, the assessor and collector of internal revenue, a bank president, a lawyer, and a dashing career army officer.

The men spent more than 40 days traveling to and through Yellowstone and gave names to more than 20 Park features. They named Tower Fall and climbed and named Mount Washburn for their leader. They viewed the Grand Canyon of the Yellowstone with both of its waterfalls and named two other waterfalls in that area. Traveling past the Crater Hills and Mud Volcano areas, the party proceeded east around Yellowstone Lake to the Heart Lake area, where party member Truman Everts was accidentally separated from the expedition (he was found 37 days later after a harrowing ordeal). Advancing west past West Thumb Geyser Basin, these adventurers crossed the difficult, timbered terrain between West Thumb and Old Faithful. They saw Old Faithful Geyser erupting just as they broke out of the trees on September 18, 1870. They stayed several days in the Old Faithful area, viewing and naming many of the major geysers before traveling down the Firehole and Madison rivers toward home.

Because of the Washburn party's explorations and the subsequent magazine and newspaper reports and speeches given by party members, the U.S. government sent the first of three Hayden surveys to Yellowstone the following summer. The movement to establish Yellowstone as the world's first national park had begun.

Paint pots in the West Thumb Geyser Basin, 1889

F.J. Haynes

with the Firehole River. W. H. Holmes (see Mount Holmes) of the second Hayden survey discovered this beautiful hot spring in 1872. Holmes thought that it deserved "in quiet way to be one of the great attractions of this attractive region" (in Hayden, *Sixth Annual Report*, pp. 144-145). Members of the 1878 Hayden survey (probably A. C. Peale) named the spring "Beauty Spring," but sometime between 1890 and 1894 someone noted the "flickering flame" effect of rising gases (see Firehole Lake) and named it Firehole Spring.

Park tour operator G. L. Henderson called this spring "Seraph" after a member of the highest of the nine orders of angels. He described it in 1888 as

> one of the most beautiful of the gas-aqueous variety [of springs]. Its action is incessant but variable. Every few seconds there arise great globes that seem to revolve like chariot wheels as they rise toward the surface. Then they come faster and faster until they seem to glide into each other and rise into one magnificent dome of liquid splendor, upon which the sunlight is reflected with a glory of coloring that equals the rainbow's prismatic hues (*Manual and Guide*, p. 3).

Today's visitors can look down into Firehole Spring and see the same phenomena that Henderson described a hundred years ago.

FISH CREEK Map #2

Fish Creek flows through Trout Lake to Soda Butte Creek about 3 miles east of Soda Butte on the Northeast Entrance Road. The name commemorates an early name of Trout Lake, which was "Fish Lake." As early as 1883, a Park assistant superintendent named the lake for its great fishing or for Assistant Superintendent Edmund Fish, or perhaps for both. By 1910, army scouts were calling the stream that drained the lake Fish Creek.

FISHING CONE* Map #4

Fishing Cone is a hot spring located in the West Thumb Geyser Basin. The Folsom party probably saw it in 1869, but the first recorded description of Fishing Cone comes from the 1870 Washburn party. Party member Walter Trumbull wrote about Cornelius Hedges's experience fishing:

> A gentleman was fishing from one of the narrow isthmuses or shelves of rock, which divided one of these hot springs from the [Yellowstone] lake, when, in swinging a trout ashore, it accidentally got off the hook and fell into the spring. For a moment it darted about with wonderful rapidity, as if seeking an outlet. Then it came to the top, dead, and literally boiled (*Overland Monthly*, June 1871, p. 492).

From that time on, and perhaps even earlier, visitor after visitor performed this feat, catching fish from the cold lake and cooking them on the hook. Hayden survey members did it in 1871, and the next year they named the spring "Fish Pot" or "Hot Spring Cone." Later names were "Fisherman's Kettle," "Fish Cone," "Fishpot Spring," "Crater Island," and "Chowder Pot." The name Fishing Cone came about gradually through the generic use of the term in guidebooks.

The cooking-on-the-hook feat at Fishing Cone soon became famous. For years, Park Superintendent P. W. Norris (1877-1882) demonstrated it to incredulous tourists, and in 1894 members of Congress hooted at their colleagues who described the process. A national magazine reported in 1903 that no visit to the Park was complete without this experience, and tourists often dressed in a cook's hat and apron to have their pictures taken at Fishing Cone. The fishing and cooking practice, regarded today as unhealthy, is now prohibited.

Fishing at the cone can be dangerous. A known geyser, Fishing Cone erupted frequently to the height of 40 feet in 1919 and to lesser heights in 1939. One fisherman was badly burned in Fishing Cone in 1921.

FLUTTER-WHEEL SPRING Map #2

This hot spring in Glen Africa Basin of the Hayden Valley is located on the east bank of Alum Creek just below Red Jacket Spring and partially under a sinter bridge that spans the stream. Flutter-Wheel Spring lies mostly hidden beneath the overhang of a large mound, but its violent rolling edge is visible.

Traveling on what was then the main road from Canyon to Lower Geyser Basin, the Rev. Edwin J. Stanley gave the spring its name in 1873 because of the noise it makes. As Stanley later described it in 1878:

> My attention was arrested by an unusual, fluttering kind of sound, which was caused by the forcible discharge of a small volume of hot water from a fissure right in the bed of the creek, and which comes through and above the surface of the main channel, giving off a vibrating noise, much like that of a flutter-wheel. So different from the rest, it appears quite comic and curious, and will attract the attention of the passer-by (*Rambles in Wonderland*, p. 90).

This interesting noise, which in 1871 Capt. J. W. Barlow likened to "the spindle of a spinning machine" (*Report of a Recognizance*, p. 19), is still audible.

FOLSOM PEAK* Map #2

This 9,326-foot-high peak is located in the Washburn Range northwest of Mount Washburn. In 1895, geologist Arnold Hague named the peak for David E. Folsom (1839-1918), a member of the 1869 Folsom-Cook-Peterson party and the first man to write a complete report of a tour of the Park. In 1870, Folsom published "Valley of the Upper Yellowstone" in *Western Monthly* under the by-line of his friend, C. W. Cook. He also gave information to Walter DeLacy, which resulted in a better map of the territory that guided the Washburn expedition in 1870.

Folsom came to Montana Territory in 1862 to search for gold. Becoming discouraged, he tried ranching and surveying before joining Cook and William Peterson in what would be the first step in the definitive exploration of what is now Yellowstone National Park. Folsom was also the second person to suggest that Yellowstone should be preserved for public use. He later became prominent in the affairs of the state of Montana.

In 1882, Folsom Peak was probably one of the summits that was given the name "Thompsons Peak," for Frank Thompson of the Northern Pacific Railroad.

FOUNTAIN GEYSER* Map #3

Fountain Geyser is part of the Fountain Group of Lower Geyser Basin. Lt. G. C. Doane of the Washburn expedition described the area as having "clear fountains" in 1870, but members of the 1871 Hayden survey gave the geyser its name. In the early days, Fountain Geyser erupted often and became one of Yellowstone's most famous features. The Fountain Hotel was built near the geyser in 1891, and the mud springs just to the south of Fountain Geyser were named Fountain Paint Pot.

Fountain Geyser's eruptions have varied, spouting a water column of from 10 to 70 feet and lasting from 10 to 60 minutes. It has had long periods of dormancy and can have very powerful eruptions. On July 13, 1983, the author and six others saw Fountain explode to 120 feet high. It felt as if we were watching Grand Geyser.

Fountain Geyser was most active between the 1870s and 1910. It was erratic between 1911 and 1929, dormant (with two possible exceptions) until 1947, and active irregularly from 1947 to 1958. Since the 1959 earthquake, Fountain Geyser has behaved irregularly, becoming active during some years and dormant during others. Because it is subterraneously connected to nearby Morning Geyser, when one geyser is active the other is often dormant.

FOUNTAIN PAINT POT* Map #3

Fountain Paint Pot is a group of mud springs in the Fountain Group of Lower Geyser Basin. Fountain is Yellowstone's most famous mudpot. Early observers, beginning apparently with William Ludlow in 1875, thought that the springs looked like a vat of bubbling paint—hence, the term "paint pot." Hydrogen sulphide gas and heat bubbling through water and mud are responsible for the phenomenon, but a century ago these mud springs must have been more colorful than they are today. Early descriptions listed many colors, including greens and yellows, and visitor George Thomas wrote in 1883 that "every imaginable color of paint is to be seen here" ("Recollections," p. 9). Tourist John H. Atwood remembered in 1918 that Fountain Paint Pot impressed visitors:

> Imagine a circular basin some fifty feet in diameter, some fifty feet across, surrounded by a ridge of clay four or five feet high, and perhaps a little more, looking for all the world like the outer rim of a huge circus ring. This rim confines a mass of this paint, liquid and boiling. So perfect is the resemblance to the lead paint of commerce that when a quizzical soldier told me that all the buildings in the Park were painted with paint taken from this pot, I bethought me of glass mountains, and apollinaris springs, and never dreamed of doubting the statement until I happened to think that none of the buildings were painted white, and then looked for and saw the twinkle in my informant's eye (*Yellowstone Park*, pp. 15-16).

Members of the Hayden survey named the springs "Mud Puff" in 1871, describing it as an area 40 by 60 feet and white to pink in color. The spring was later known as "Chalk Vat," "Paint Vat," "Devil's Paintbox," and the most used of early names, "Mammoth Paintpot." Usage of "Fountain Geyser and Paintpots" in guidebooks led to the name Fountain Paint Pot, which was accepted by a 1927 Park superintendent's place-names committee.

FRANK ISLAND* Map #4

Frank Island is the largest island in Yellowstone Lake. During his trip around the lake aboard the *Anna* with zoologist Campbell Carrington, Henry Wood Elliot of the Hayden survey named the island in 1871 for his brother Frank. We know virtually nothing about Frank Elliot, but his brother Henry was an artist whose drawings documented Hayden's early surveys. There was an attempt in 1875 to rename Frank Island "Belknap Island" for then Secretary of War William W. Belknap, but it failed.

FREDERICK PEAK† Map #2

Frederick Peak, at 9,422 feet high, is located west of Mount Hornaday and north of Druid Peak. In 1966, former Yellowstone National Park Superintendent Horace Albright named this peak for his friend Karl T. Frederick (1881-1963), "noted sportsman and conservationist who played a prominent role in the movement to establish Grand Teton and Mount McKinley [now Denali] National Parks." Frederick, an activist conservation lawyer, "made summer photographic and wildlife study pilgrimages to Lamar Valley, near the yet unnamed peak for many years [during the 1920s] . . . [and was a] staunch supporter of the conservation objectives of Yellowstone."

When Frederick died in 1963, Albright suggested to the Camp Fire Club of America (a group of which Frederick had once been president) that a mountain be named after him. The club then asked Albright to locate a suitable peak.

FROG ROCK   Map #1

Frog Rock is a large glacial erratic (boulder) located just south of the Grand Loop Road between Mammoth and Tower about 2 miles east of Blacktail Pond. The rock resembles a squatting frog, complete with eyes and a tongue. The name has been in use since at least the 1930s.

FROST LAKE*   Map #2

This small lake in the Absaroka Range is located 2 miles northeast of Pyramid Peak. The lake was named in 1893-1895 for Ned Ward Frost (1881-1957), an early Yellowstone packer and guide and a big game hunter. Frost came to the Cody, Wyoming, area in 1885 with his family and first visited Yellowstone when he was four years old. By the time he was thirteen he was heading his own outfitting parties into the Park. He discovered Frost Cave (near Cody) in 1903, and in 1910 he built a ranch on the North Fork of the Shoshone River on the site of the present-day Skytel Ranch. Frost also helped build the Corkscrew Bridge on Yellowstone's original East Entrance Road.

FRYING PAN SPRING*   Map #1

Frying Pan Spring is near the road about 2 miles north of the Norris Ranger Station and just east of Nymph Lake. The name seems to have come into local usage during the late 1880s when small hissing springs of this type were called "frying pans," because they sounded like hot grease sputtering on a griddle. The spring was called "Frying Pan" by 1890, and H. M. Chittenden described it in 1895 as "stewing away in a manner which reminds one of a kitchen spider in operation" (*Yellowstone*, p. 219). The spring was also called "Devil's Frying Pan" or "Devil's Frying Spring."

Early stagecoach drivers in the Park told their passengers "that the woods around [Frying Pan Spring] are full of boiled eggs, because when the birds drink of the water, the next eggs they lay are hard." Frying Pan Spring has a *pH* of about one, acidic enough to eat through a pair of jeans.

FUNGOID SPRING   Map #3

Fungoid Spring is a geyser in the Thud Group of Lower Geyser Basin. In 1871, this spring was named the Thud or "Thumping" Geyser "from the dull, suppressed sound which is given off as the water rises and recedes" (Hayden, *Fifth Annual Report*, p. 106). But in 1872, Hayden survey members renamed it Fungoid Spring (*fungoid* means like a fungus) from the spring's "margin of siliceous material that resembles a row of fungoid growths on short pedestals." A spring east of Fungoid is called Thud Spring.

Although A. C. Peale of the 1878 Hayden survey concluded that Fungoid was not a true geyser (no column of water was thrown out), the spring did function as a geyser in 1929, in 1948, and in 1972. Geologist Walter Weed recorded in 1883 that "the thumping appears to be produced by large bubbles of steam (in the same manner as the thumping of a liquid in a beaker, when heated). These bubbles are frequently 2 ft. or more in diameter" (USGS, Box 56, vol. 1, p. 90). Georgina M. Synge, an 1889 visitor, mentioned Thud Geyser and Thud Spring:

> On the other side [from Fountain Geyser] are the "Thud Springs," from which accumulations of steam burst forth every few minutes, with a mysterious muffled "thud" which seems to palpitate from some great living heart beneath (*Ride Through Wonderland*, p. 41).

Thinking the U.S. Geological Survey names unimaginative, Park tour operator G. L. Henderson called Fungoid Spring "Evangeline Geyser" in reference to the spring's shape and its heart-like thudding, which reminded him of Longfellow's famous poem, "Evangeline."

GALLATIN LAKE*   Map #1

This small, shallow lake—only 47 feet deep—lies at the head of the Gallatin River, just north of Three Rivers Peak. Members of the Hague survey named the lake in 1885 because it is the source of the Gallatin River.

GALLATIN RANGE*   Map #1

This major range of mountains extends north about 60 miles through Yellowstone from Mount Holmes. Capt. W. P. Raynolds's map in 1860 showed a "Mt. Gallatin" in the position of present-day Mount Holmes and is probably the original name of the Gallatin Range—the Gallatin River rises in these mountains. The Hayden surveys during the 1870s used various names for the range, including Gallatin Range, "West Gallatin Range," "Upper Madison Range," and "East Gallatin Range." The name "Pyramid Mountains" was also applied quite early, probably because of the pyramidal shape of present-day Antler Peak.

GALLATIN RIVER*   Map #1

The Gallatin River flows north from the Gallatin Lake through the northwest section of Yellowstone to form the

Road construction crew at Golden Gate, 1884

Auto stages on the Gibbon Junction bridge, east of Madison Junction, c. 1916

Missouri River at Three Forks, Montana. One of the three branches of the Missouri, the Gallatin was called "Cut-tuh-o'-gwa" by Shoshone Indians, meaning "swift water." Lewis and Clark named the river when they reached the headwaters of the Missouri River in 1805. Lewis described the naming of the three forks:

> ... we called the S.W. fork, that which we meant to ascend, Jefferson's River in honor of that illustrious personage Thomas Jefferson. The Middle fork we called Madison's River in honor of James Madison, and the S.E. Fork we called Gallitin's [sic] River in honor of Albert Gallitin [sic] (in Thwaites, *Original Journals*, 2:280-281).

Albert Gallatin (1761-1849) was Thomas Jefferson's brilliant Secretary of the Treasury, the negotiator of the Treaty of Ghent (1812), and the founder of the American Ethnological Society in 1842.

GARDNER RIVER*   Map #1

The Gardner River flows south and then north from the Gallatin Range to the Yellowstone River at Gardiner, Montana. The river carries one of the Park's oldest place names, which Johnson Gardner himself may have applied to the river during the early 1830s. Fur-trapper Osborne Russell referred to the river as "Gardners fork" in his diaries in 1835, and this name found its way onto an 1839 map by Capt. Washington Hood. A topographical engineer, Hood used information from two trappers who traveled through Yellowstone with Capt. Bonneville in 1833.

Johnson Gardner was one of the rougher characters to participate in the fur trade. He probably came up the Missouri River in 1822 or 1823 as part of the famous Ashley-Henry enterprise, which came into conflict with British fur trappers during the late 1820s and trapped in the northern Rockies during the 1830s. Stories of Gardner's fights with Indians are part of the lore of the mountain-man era.

There has long been confusion about the spelling of the Gardner River and of Gardiner, Montana. Jim Bridger called the stream "Gardener Creek" in 1851, which may have been a phonetical rendering of Gardiner. The name Gardiner or Gardner for the river was in common usage from about 1831 until the 1860s, when it was called "Warm-Stream Creek" or "Warm Spring Creek." Maps in 1869 returned the name of Gardner to the stream, and members of the 1870 Washburn party were apparently responsible for reinstating the "i," probably because N. P. Langford had talked to Jim Bridger in 1866 and had heard him pronounce the word. In this way, the name Gardiner was established for the river, and it appeared that way on Park maps and in literature until 1959. In that year, the USGS petitioned the USBGN to change the name to Gardner to accord with the 1830s usage of Osborne Russell and Washington Hood.

The origin of the spelling of Gardiner, Montana, is another story. The name simply comes from the river, but there are many erroneous but interesting stories that continue to be told about how the town got its name. Some have proposed that the name came from early pioneers "Tom Gardiner" or "Roy E. Gardiner" or from mountain man John Gardiner; others have even suggested that it came from mail delivered to James C. McCartney (see McCartney Cave), as "Jim on the Gardiner."

GARDNERS HOLE*   Map #1

Gardners Hole is a large valley at the head of the Gardner River located southwest of Mammoth. Fur-trapper Johnson Gardner (see Gardner River) may have named this valley for himself during the 1830s. Fur trappers called mountain valleys "holes" and named them for the trapper who liked to hunt there. During the 1830s, mountain men Osborne Russell and Joe Meek called this valley Gardner's Hole.

GARNET HILL*   Map #2

Members of the third Hayden survey in 1878 discovered and named Garnet Hill just north of Pleasant Valley and Tower Junction. W. H. Holmes, who wrote a geological report on the area and may have named the hill, described it as an outcropping of Precambrian granitic gneiss, which is believed to be some of the oldest rock in the world (perhaps 4.5 billion years old). Small, imperfect garnets are found in the schists associated with this gneiss formation, but as Holmes noted in 1878 "all [garnets] are very much flawed and so filled with impurities that they can never have any particular value" (in Hayden, *Twelfth Annual Report*, p. 43).

GENTIAN POOL*   Map #3

Beginning with the opening of nearby Fountain Hotel in 1891, Gentian Pool in the Sprinkler Group of the Lower Geyser Basin received a lot of attention. This nearly 90- by 25-foot pool is probably the spring that Park tour operator G. L. Henderson named "Thanatopsis" as early as 1885. Henderson took the name from William Cullen Bryant's poem, "Thanatopsis," which proposed a life without fear of death. *Thanatopsis* is Greek for "view of death." Gentian Pool has thin ledges that extend over the spring, which reaches temperatures of more than 160°F.

Sometime in or before 1889, the spring became known as Gentian Pool from a blue wildflower (*Gentiana thermalis*) that grows nearby. Geologist Arnold Hague used the name in 1889, and he may have given the spring its new name. Today, the blue gentian is the official flower of Yellowstone National Park.

GIANT GEYSER*   Map #3

Giant Geyser is the namesake geyser of the Giant Group in the Upper Geyser Basin. Except for Excelsior and Steamboat geysers, Giant Geyser is probably Yellowstone's most powerful geyser. Named in 1870 by the Washburn expedition, Giant Geyser's eruptions can reach from 100 to 250 feet, can consist of up to a million gallons of water, and can last from 1 to 1.5 hours. Geyser watchers believe that the Giant erupts only during one of its "hot periods," which are spaced at about hourly intervals and last about 5 minutes.

Giant Geyser greatly impressed the Washburn party in 1870, as Walter Trumbull wrote: "We thought it deserved to be called 'The Giant,' as it threw out more water than any other geyser which we saw in operation" (*Overland Monthly*, June 1871, p. 493). N. P. Langford, another expedition member, wrote in his diary that the Giant erupted 140 feet high continuously for 3 hours. And Lt. G. C. Doane observed that the "great geyser played several times while we were in the valley, on one occasion throwing constantly for over three hours a stream of water 7 feet in diameter from 90 to 200 feet perpendicularly" (Bonney and Bonney, *Battle Drums*, p. 350).

The Giant was active from 1870 to 1900, was somewhat active from 1920 to 1949, and was most active between 1949 and 1955. Since 1955, it has erupted 4 times: in 1978, 1982, 1984, and 1987. Giant Geyser has two types of activity—one usual and one rare. In the usual type, it erupts to more than 200 feet. In the rare type of activity, the "Mastiff function," it erupts in concert with large spouts of nearby Mastiff and Catfish geysers. This activity is known to have occurred only in 1951.

GIANTESS GEYSER*   Map #3

Giantess is the major geyser in the Geyser Hill Group of Upper Geyser Basin. Members of the Washburn expedition named Giantess Geyser on September 18, 1870, when they saw it erupt to a height of 250 feet. They thought it was the largest geyser they had seen. N. P. Langford wrote:

> All that we had previously witnessed seemed tame in comparison with the perfect grandeur and beauty of this fine display. Two of these wonderful eruptions occurred during the twenty-two hours we remained in the valley. This geyser we named the "Giantess" (*Scribner's Monthly*, June 1871, p. 125).

The party "unhesitatingly agreed that this was the greatest wonder of our trip" (*Discovery of Yellowstone*, p. 174).

When Giantess erupts, it often ranges in height from 100 to 250 feet. The eruption can be long, sometimes lasting from 12 to 43 hours, but the first hour is usually the best. During eruptions, water phases and stream phases will usually occur in generally unpredictable combinations. During steam phases, steam is ejected under great pressure, resulting in a deafening roar. Observers have given different descriptions of the geyser over the years because its eruptions can last many hours and they do different things. Four types of eruptions are known today for Giantess Geyser: steam phase eruptions, water phase eruptions, mixed steam and water phase eruptions, and aborted eruptions. During these eruptions, the water column can change shape and height and subterranean concussions can be "steady regular thumping" or, as one 1873 writer described, "heavy concussions like the firing of cannon underground."

Giantess Geyser was active in almost every year during the 1870s and every season during the 1880s. In general, it was considerably more active before 1930, and it has become very active again in the 1980s. The rejuvenation occurred on February 19, 1980. There were 13 known eruptions in 1980, 23 in 1981, 35 in 1982 (including aborted eruptions), and 41 in 1983 (including aborted eruptions). The 1983 eruptions represent what is believed to be the most ever recorded in one year for Giantess Geyser.

GIBBON FALLS*   Map #1

Gibbon Falls is an 84-foot-high waterfall located on the Gibbon River about 5 miles east of Madison Junction on the Grand Loop Road. According to A. C. Peale of the Hayden survey, photographer W. H. Jackson and botanist John M. Coulter discovered the falls in 1872. The name, which was taken from the river, was in general use by 1877. For many years, visitors had to make a side trip to the top of a cliff to look down at the falls because the main tourist road passed on the east side of the falls. Gibbon Falls is believed to drop over part of the wall of the Yellowstone Caldera, which is thought to be 600,000 years old.

GIBBON MEADOWS*   Map #1

These meadows are located on the Gibbon River about 3.5 miles west of Norris and a mile southwest of Gibbon River Rapids. The name came into local usage as early as 1881, probably because visitors used the meadow as a camping area. Park Superintendent P. W. Norris either established the name or took it from local usage.

GIBBON RIVER*   Map #1

One of the Park's major streams, the Gibbon River flows southwest from Grebe Lake in the Washburn Range to the

Madison River. Although it was later called "Hoppin River" and "East Fork of the Madison," members of the second Hayden survey named the river in 1872 for Gen. John Gibbon (1827-1896). Frank Bradley of the survey wrote:

> We had supposed ourselves the only travelers in this region, when suddenly we encountered a party of officers and soldiers from Fort Ellis [near present-day Bozeman, Montana] and other northern posts, under the leadership of General Gibbon, who had been visiting the wonders of the Yellowstone and geyser regions. After a brief exchange of courtesies and information, both parties were again on the march, and we soon emerged from the cañon and camped at the forks of the river [present-day Madison Junction]. While the main stream came from the southward [Firehole River], yet the real continuation of the valley we had been following was occupied by the stream coming from the eastward with perhaps 40 feet of water. As this stream had been partially explored by General Gibbon, who gave us some useful information concerning it, we have called it Gibbon's Fork of the Madison (in Hayden, *Sixth Annual Report*, p. 230).

Gibbon knew Hayden, having accompanied him in 1868 on explorations of the Snowy Range near Laramie, Wyoming. And Gibbon had told Hayden about the existence of present-day Terrace Spring near Madison Junction.

Gibbon was better known for his military exploits outside Yellowstone, including a Union generalship during the Civil War and his fighting in the Seminole War on the southern frontier. He served on the frontier in Montana during the 1870s and had the sad duty of identifying and burying the dead at the Custer battlefield in 1876. In 1877, Gibbon attacked Nez Perces at the Battle of the Big Hole and helped chase the fleeing Indians through Yellowstone National Park.

GLADE CREEK   Map #2

Glade Creek flows southeast from Mount Washburn to the Yellowstone River; it is the first stream northeast of Sulphur Creek. The creek was named in about 1881 by Park Superintendent P. W. Norris, probably for the large open meadow on its south branch. (There is also a Glade Creek that flows through Grassy Lake on the south side of Yellowstone Park.)

GLADE LAKE   Map #4

This small lake is located on the northern slopes of Mount Schurz and near the headwaters of Beaverdam Creek. Park Superintendent P. W. Norris named the lake in about 1881 when he explored this region of the Park. A later attempt was made to name this lake "Schurz Lake," but Glade Lake has historical priority.

GLEN AFRICA BASIN   Map #2

Glen Africa Basin is a hot spring area at the forks of upper Alum Creek on the western edge of the Hayden Valley. Park tour operator G. L. Henderson named this area in about 1887, when he guided tourists over the stagecoach route across the Central Plateau, over Mary Mountain, and down Nez Perce Creek. Henderson's 1888 guidebook included this description:

> Glen Africa Geyser Basin is about half way from the Grand Canyon to the Lower Basin. A walk of two hundred yards from the usual camping ground [at the crossing of Alum Creek] takes you through one of the most remarkable glens in the whole Park. The volcanic energy that could have cut through the mountains leaving great scoriated and half melted rock, must have been very great. Under the cliffs on the west side of the Glen there are still to be seen circular basins where geyser action had decomposed the rock, leaving admirable dens for the shelter of the carnivora. . . . An hour can be profitably spent in Glen Africa while the horses are resting (*Manual and Guide*, p. 2).

Henderson seems to have named the area for the many wildlife that his visitors were almost certain to see in the glens through the Hayden Valley, which was his fancied Africa.

GNEISS CREEK*   Map #1

Gneiss Creek (pronounced *nice*) flows west to Duck Creek from the south end of The Crags located in the Gallatin Range in the northwestern sector of the Park. In 1885, members of the Hague parties of the USGS named the creek for the outcroppings of gneiss that geologist W. E. Sanders discovered on the headwaters of this stream. Gneiss is a metamorphic rock that is granite-like in appearance but banded. The geologists had earlier named the creek "Aspen Creek," but they changed their minds in favor of Gneiss. This creek is probably the stream that Northern Pacific Railroad surveyors named "Mount Herring Creek" in 1882 for the "mountain herring," an early name for mountain whitefish.

GOLDEN GATE CANYON†   Map #1

Golden Gate Canyon is located just below Rustic Falls and about 2.5 miles south of Mammoth. Lt. Dan Kingman, Oscar Swanson, or Ed Lamartine (the road bosses in charge of the project) probably named the canyon when they were building the first stagecoach road through Glen Creek in 1883-1884. The canyon could also have been named by Park tour operator G. L. Henderson, who reported on the construction project in 1884:

U.S. Army Corps of Engineers' truck and trailer, August 1916

Military baseball game at the Mammoth campground, July 4, 1917

To avoid the terrible hill on the only passable route from Mammoth Hot Springs to the upper districts of the Park, the government has begun a road along the west fork of the Gardiner River [Glen Creek].... When complete this new route—the Golden Gate—will present an easy road and one that will be accessible fully two weeks earlier than that over the mountain [present-day Snow Pass] up which the road now leads (*Livingston Enterprise*, August 6, 1884).

The name Golden Gate referred to the golden color of the canyon's rock walls (caused by lichen) and to the road as a "gateway" into the upper Park. Originally built of wood in 1885, the Golden Gate bridge was replaced in 1901 with a concrete structure. It was widened in 1934 and totally rebuilt in 1977. The pillar of rock that stands on the north end of the bridge, known as the Pillar of Hercules, was originally part of the canyon wall.

GRAND CANYON OF THE YELLOWSTONE RIVER*   Map #2

Trappers and prospectors originally called this famous gorge on the Yellowstone River the "Fourth Canyon," because it was the fourth canyon up the Yellowstone from present-day Livingston, Montana. But in 1870, members of the Washburn expedition named it the Grand Canyon of the Yellowstone. Later called the "Great (Painted) Canyon" and the "Great Gorge," the canyon may have been named after the Grand Canyon of Arizona, which had already been named. The Grand Canyon of the Yellowstone is 800 to 1,200 feet deep and up to 4,000 feet wide.

The canyon has captivated and entranced visitors for over a century. Charles Cook of the Folsom-Cook-Peterson party of 1869, the first credited discoverer of the canyon, described the scene at the canyon's rim: "I sat there in amazement, while my companions came up, and after that, it seemed to me that it was five minutes before anyone spoke" (in Haines, *Valley of the Upper Yellowstone*, p. 31). Others, including H. Banard Leckler in 1881, had similar experiences. "George [our guide]," Leckler wrote, "has been with parties who have been so taken with the great sight that nearly a half hour would go by without a word being spoken, or their being aware of the passing time" (*American Field*, March 22, 1884).

The canyon's spectacular colors have inspired artists such as Thomas Moran, Albert Bierstadt, and Lucien Powell. The canyon's beauty has also stimulated writers who often react to the dramatic changes that cloud cover and sunlight can have on the colors of the dramatic rock walls. In 1870, N. P. Langford described the canyon as "sombre stillness a mile below. There all was darkness, gloom, and shadow; here all was vivacity, gayety and delight" (*Scribner's Monthly*, May 1871, p. 13). As Harry J. Norton expressed it in 1872: "The subject is beyond the conception of the most vivid imagination—language is inadequate to express the unapproachable picture presented—the eye only can photograph the gorgeous scene" (*Wonderland Illustrated*, pp. 38-39).

GRAND GEYSER*   Map #3

Grand Geyser, the namesake geyser of the Grand Group in the Upper Geyser Basin, has been in recent years the world's tallest predictable geyser. In 1870, the Washburn party missed seeing the geyser, but one year later members of the Hayden survey saw it erupting. As Hayden later wrote: "We called this the Grand Geyser, for its power seemed greater than any other of which we obtained any knowledge in the valley" (*Fifth Annual Report*, p. 116). The Hayden party saw two eruptions within 32 hours, one of which shot a column of water 6 feet in diameter to a height of 200 feet.

Grand Geyser's explosive eruptions, which can reach 100 to 200 feet in huge fountain-type bursts, have always impressed Park visitors. Guidebook writer W. W. Wylie described Grand Geyser in 1881:

> This is without doubt the most satisfactory Geyser in the whole Park, and all seeing it in action will pronounce it most aptly named.... The Geyser acts irregularly about twice in twenty-six hours. There is no warning of any certain character before an eruption; but as the Geyser seldom acts for less time than twenty minutes, tourists can get to it in time to witness its best action. The under-ground pulsations can be heard and felt to a great distance. This Geyser's action is entirely different from all the others. The first action is very violent, a series of charges and surges, shooting jets to great heights and at different angles. This action lasts eight or ten minutes; then it all settles down quietly at the Geyser orifice. The water covers over, no steam escapes, and for a little more than a minute it is calm and quiet, when suddenly it is heaved as by a mighty impulse, and the column rises perfectly straight up to a height of 200 feet, and is held there for several moments; then is followed by jet after jet for some minutes, ... [and] is repeated usually until seven or ten pulsations, or periods of action after repose, are completed ... (*Yellowstone National Park*, pp. 37-38).

Before 1969, Grand's long, tall bursts numbered anywhere from 6 to 45 (usually 8 to 12) per year; but between 1970 and 1984 there were only from 1 to 5 distinct bursts. The duration of the total eruption is often from 9 to 16 minutes, and the interval is from 6 to 15 hours.

GRAND PRISMATIC SPRING*   Map #3

This large, 250- by 350-foot hot spring in the Excelsior Group in the Midway Geyser Basin has the distinction of being the earliest described Yellowstone thermal feature. In 1839, fur-trapper Osborne Russell reported it in his journal, describing the spring's intense colors and noting that the colors were reflected in the spring's stream.

Members of the Hayden survey used the name Prismatic in 1871 to apply to a number of springs in the Lower Geyser Basin—perhaps today's Quagmire Group. Hayden wrote: "We called the most delicately colored springs Prismatic Springs" (*Fifth Annual Report*, p. 104). But on Gustavus Bechler's 1872 map, Grand Prismatic Spring is called "Great Spring." For the next 20 years, the spring had no fewer than 10 other names applied to it, including "Great Hot Spring," "Mammoth Hot Spring," "Hot Spring Lake," "Boiling Coral Well," "Prisim Lake," "Prismatic Lake," "Emerald Lake," and "Paradise Lake."

In 1878, after A. C. Peale had returned to the Park to confirm the brilliant colors in Thomas Moran's 1871 sketch of the spring, Peale wrote: "I have named it Prismatic on account of the brilliant coloring displayed in it" (in Hayden, *Twelfth Annual Report*, pp. 180-181). Since that time, visitors have agreed with Peale that the colors of Grand Prismatic Spring are indescribably brilliant. Park tour operator G. L. Henderson reminisced in 1899:

> This terrace, to be seen in all its transcendent, golden glory, must be seen between the hours of noon and 2 p.m. Before noon, standing with your back to the lake [spring], and looking eastward, the reflected light from the golden floor at your feet is so dazzling that the eye cannot endure it (*Livingston Post*, January 11, 1900).

Grand Prismatic Spring is the largest spring in the Park, and it is believed to be the third largest spring in area in the world—only two others in New Zealand are larger.

GRAND VIEW*   Map #2

It is not known who named this viewpoint on the north rim of the Grand Canyon of the Yellowstone River, but the name seems to have been perpetuated by F. Jay Haynes's photographs and captions. Haynes may have named the lookout, and it was in general usage as early as 1893.

GRANT PEAK†   Map #2

This 11,015-foot-high peak in the Absaroka Range, just west of Notch Mountain, was named in 1931 when east boundary surveyor W. R. Bandy selected it to honor President U. S. Grant. Park Superintendent Roger Toll had suggested naming a mountain for Grant, but the peak he selected was already called Plenty Coups Peak. Bandy then selected this nipple-shaped peak as a memorial to the president "who signed the bill creating Yellowstone National Park."

GRANTS PASS†   Map #3

This 8,000-foot-high pass on the Continental Divide is on the trail between Lone Star Geyser and Shoshone Lake. In 1882, Carl Hals, S. P. Panton, and other members of a Northern Pacific Railroad surveying team named the pass for M. G. Grant, the locating engineer of their survey. The NPRR survey, conducted between July 1 and September 28, 1882, charted a railroad route through Yellowstone Park. But Congress rejected railroad building in the Park, and the line was never built. Under Grant's leadership, the surveyors later plotted the route from Livingston, Montana, to the north boundary of Yellowstone for the railroad branch line that was built to the Park in the summer of 1883.

GRAY BULGER GEYSER   Map #3

This geyser in the Firehole Lake (Black Warrior) Group of the Lower Geyser Basin is located east of the Young Hopeful Geyser complex and has often been confused with Young Hopeful Geyser. It is possible that the names were reversed at some point.

Members of the 1878 Hayden survey, possibly A. C. Peale, named the geyser Gray Bulger because it bulged through a hole in gray geyserite.

GRAY LAKES*   Map #1

These two large hot springs, along with several smaller ones in the Back Basin of Norris Geyser Basin, received their names because of their color. Geologist Walter Weed named them in 1888, even though Park tour operator G. L. Henderson had already called one of them "Leap Frog Lake" for reasons unknown.

GRAY SPRING*   Map #3

This hot spring in the Orion Group of Shoshone Geyser Basin is also called Marble Cliff Spring. The spring actually has two officially approved names. The second Hayden survey in 1872 named Gray Spring for its color and included it on Bechler's 1872 map. Six years later, members of the Hayden survey renamed it Marble Cliff Spring.

GREAT FOUNTAIN GEYSER*   Map #3

One of the Park's premier geysers, Great Fountain Geyser is located in the Great Fountain Group in Lower Geyser Basin. It erupts in 75- to 200-foot fountain-type displays. In recent years, its eruptions have lasted from 35 to 60 minutes every 5 to 17 hours. During the Park's early years, the geyser attracted comparatively little attention because of its isolated location. Even so, an 1877 tourist party found hundreds of names written in pencil on the geyser's formation, some dating back to 1866 and 1867.

W. H. Holmes (see Mount Holmes) of the Hayden survey named Great Fountain Geyser in 1872 because he thought it was the only geyser in the Lower Basin that compared to those in the Upper Basin. Holmes watched it spout 60 to 80 feet high "for nearly an hour." He wrote in his diary that the eruption was spectacular, with

> exquisite jets and columns of water, enormous in quantity... sent upward. Jets from the central part of the basin reached the height of 140 or 150 feet, the cluster of jets breaking from the main columns in dartlike points and trembling into the surrounding pools in showers of crystal drops ("Extracts from the Diary," pp. 28-29).

Walter DeLacy's 1863 prospecting party had passed right by Great Fountain Geyser but apparently did not see it erupt. In 1869, however, David Folsom, Charles Cook, and William Peterson saw the geyser erupt "at least 80 feet" high without naming it. Cook wrote: "We could not contain our enthusiasm; with one accord we all took off our hats and yelled with all our might" (in Haines, *Valley of the Upper Yellowstone*, p. 42). In 1871, F. V. Hayden named it "Architectural Fountain."

Great Fountain Geyser has a number of "burst cycles," each one lasting between 5 and 7 minutes and of varying height during a total period of activity that lasts about an hour. Great Fountain is known to have occasional "super-bursts," usually the first one or two bursts, which soar to 225 feet.

GREBE LAKE*   Map #1

This small lake is located on the Solfatara Plateau about 2 miles east of Wolf Lake. It was probably named in 1883 by J. P. Iddings, a geologist with the Hague surveys, for the western grebe.

GREEN DRAGON SPRING*   Map #1

Naturalist Charles Phillips named this hot spring in the Back Basin of Norris Geyser Basin in 1926. Phillips called the spring Green Dragon because of its color and its flashing belches of steam and sulphur.

GREEN GROTTO SPRING   Map #2

Green Grotto is a hot spring in the Rainbow Springs on Mirror Plateau located on the right bank of Wrong Creek a hundred yards or so above Bellow Spring. In 1935, scientists reported that the spring was the most notable feature of the area, "lined and bordered with sinter, ... about 12 feet across, its deeper portion 3½ feet in diameter, expanding outward into a shallow pool" (Allen and Day, *Hot Springs*, pp. 356-357). In 1962, thermal area researcher Harry Majors named the pool Green Grotto because of its color and appearance.

GREGG FORK*   Map #3

Gregg Fork is the middle of three streams that form the Bechler River at Three River Junction near the head of Bechler Canyon. Horace Albright and Jack Haynes named this river in 1930 for William C. Gregg (1862-1946) of Hackensack, New Jersey, who had explored and studied the Bechler area in 1920 and 1921. He took some of the first photographs of the area's features, and his magazine articles in *Saturday Evening Post* and *Outlook* helped defeat the proposal for a dam that would have inundated Bechler Meadows. Called "Cascade Gregg" for his work in protecting the Cascade Corner area of Yellowstone, Gregg visited this area in 1923, 1926, and 1928.

GRIZZLY CREEK   Map #4

This creek, named in about 1881 by Park Superintendent P. W. Norris, flows north and west from a pond west of Sulphur Hills to the Yellowstone River. Norris named Grizzly Creek for the bears that often feed on spawning cutthroat trout here during the spring.

GROTTO FOUNTAIN GEYSER   Map #3

This geyser in the Grotto Group of Upper Geyser Basin got its name in 1949 when Yellowstone Park staff took the name that Park Geologist George Marler had given it. Grotto Fountain has also been known as "Surprise Geyser," "Grotto Drain Geyser," and "Strange Geyser," but its proximity to Grotto Geyser suggested its current name. As early as 1886, geologist Walter Weed identified Grotto Fountain as a geyser when he investigated a hole in the formation just below Grotto Geyser that was said to spout 30 feet high.

GROTTO GEYSER*   Map #3

Grotto Geyser is the namesake geyser of the Grotto Group in the Upper Geyser Basin. It was named in 1870 by members of the Washburn party "from its singular crater of vitrified sinter, full of large sinuous apertures" (N. P. Langford, *Scribner's Monthly*, June 1871, p. 124). Grotto Geyser erupts 8 to 40 feet high in 2- to 12-hour intervals. In 1870, the Washburn party reported that Grotto Geyser erupted with a column of water 2 feet in diameter to a height of 50 feet for half an hour.

The apertures in the geyser crater intrigued early visitors, who often reported crawling through them. Capt. J. W. Barlow observed in 1871 that the crater of Grotto Geyser was "hollowed into fantastic arches, with pillars and walls of almost indescribable variety" ("Reconnaissance of the Yellowstone," p. 26). The crater of Grotto

Superintendent E. B. Rogers at Grizzly Lake, July 9, 1940

Tourists at Handkerchief Pool, 1917

Geyser also attracted vandals. As William Ludlow wrote in 1875, "after seeing the injury done to its crater by visitors, the large majority of whom are residents of the [Montana] Territory, we could not help wishing the discharge of boiling water were absolutely continuous" (*Report of a Reconnaissance*, p. 132).

The sinter projection in the center of Grotto Geyser, geologist George Marler believed, is a tree stump that has been covered with deposits.

GROTTO POOL   Map #2

This idyllic pool on Cascade Creek is located just above Crystal Falls in a cavelike grotto. Park Superintendent P. W. Norris named the pool in 1875 and often said that it was his favorite place in Yellowstone. In his 1881 report, he wrote:

> This pool is caused by the sheet of water in the upper fall [above Crystal Falls] being at right angles with the stream, thus facing and undermining the eastern wall, and beneath it forming a broad, deep pool of placid water, nearly hidden under the narrow shelf of rocks between the two leaps of the cataract, and from its peculiarities named by me, in 1875, Grotto Pool (p. 21).

In 1881, Norris built a bridge just above Grotto Pool and set up ladders for the convenience of tourists exploring the area. H. Banard Leckler, a visitor that year, described Grotto Pool as "a strange, wild, romantic spot, and we could not resist lingering several minutes to enjoy it . . . (*American Field*, March 22, 1884, p. 286).

THE GROTTOES   Map #1

In 1880, Park Superintendent P. W. Norris may have called one of these small shallow caves the "Devil's Grotto." The Grottoes are located along the north side of White Elephant Back Terrace at Mammoth Hot Springs. The Grottoes place name has been in general use since at least 1926.

THE GRUMBLER or GRUMBLER SPRING   Map #3

In about 1899, Park tour operator G. L. Henderson named this hot spring in the Black Sand Basin of Upper Geyser Basin. The spring is located a few feet from the mouth of Spouter Geyser, and it is subterraneously connected to it. The Grumbler erupts simultaneously with Spouter Geyser to heights of 1 to 2 feet. The sound made by the spring prompted Henderson to name the geyser as he did.

THE GUMPER   Map #3

Located about 100 yards west of Sour Lake and Moose Pool in the Mud Volcano area, this new hot spring developed in 1974. Park naturalists named the spring because of the thumping, "gumping" action of its churning mud. Some 70 feet in diameter, the Gumper claimed a bison in 1984.

GWINNA FALLS*   Map #3

In 1921, explorer W. C. Gregg (see Gregg Fork) named this 20-foot-high waterfall on the Ferris Fork of the Bechler River, a half mile above Tendoy Falls. *Gwinna* is the Shoshone Indian word for eagle.

HAGUE MOUNTAIN*   Map #2

Hague Mountain lies between Little Saddle Mountain and Saddle Mountain, south of the upper Lamar River. Arnold Hague (1840-1917), a prominent geologist who named more places in Yellowstone than any other individual, is the namesake of this 10,565-foot-high peak in the Absaroka Range. Park Superintendent Roger Toll named the mountain in 1930 to honor Hague's studies of the Park and his support of conservation.

Born in Boston in 1840, Hague graduated from Yale University and later studied under Robert Bunsen (see Bunsen Peak). He worked for the U.S. Geological Surveys from 1867 to 1878 and took over as the chief of the Yellowstone Park surveys in 1883. The study of Yellowstone absorbed him for the rest of his life. Hague spoke out stridently in defense of Yellowstone's sanctity and integrity. As one of his assistants, Joseph Iddings, wrote:

> He was an ardent advocate of the preservation of the striking features of the region in their natural state, for placing hotels and other buildings where they would not mar the attractiveness of the localities to which they were tributary. . . . The writer recalls with emotion the interest Arnold Hague took in conducting his young assistant, with eyes shut, to the brink of the Yellowstone Falls, so that he might have the pleasure of a sudden view of the many-colored canyon beyond.

HALFWAY SPRING   Map #3

Halfway Spring, in the Seven Mile Hole Hot Springs, is about halfway down the trail to Seven Mile Hole on the Yellowstone River. The name of the spring, which has a large striking cone, was in local usage by 1929.

HALS LAKE   Map #1

Hals Lake is a small intermittent lake at the east base of Quadrant Mountain that drains into the Gardner River by way of an unnamed stream. In 1882, Northern Pacific Railroad surveyors named the lake for Carl Hals, an NPRR surveyor and topographer. Hals worked with

A. Rydstrom, S. P. Panton, M. G. Grant (see Grants Pass), and others to survey a proposed railroad line through Yellowstone Park, which Congress refused to approve.

HANDKERCHIEF POOL*   Map #3

One of the most famous thermal features in Yellowstone, this small spring in the Black Sand Basin of Upper Geyser Basin is no longer accessible by walkway. The pool got its name from visitors or Park employees at around the turn of the century. Park visitor Mrs. James Hamilton described it in 1888:

> It was a small pool that would suck the water down and in a few minutes it would come gushing out again. If you put a handkerchief in the handkerchief would be sucked down and would come up in a few minutes nice and clean ("Through Yellowstone," p. 7).

Over the years, hundreds of Yellowstone visitors watched their handkerchiefs go down into the pool and then come up again. The pool became so famous that scientists came to the Park to study it. By 1906, tour guides were telling visitors that this was where the devil took in washing, and by 1913 some were calling it the "Devil's Laundry."

Sometime in late 1926 or early 1927, Handkerchief Pool became dormant. Nevertheless, visitors continued to throw handkerchiefs and other objects into the pool. On June 21, 1929, Ranger Carlos Davis removed 1.5 bushels of foreign objects from Handkerchief Pool, including "one broken bottle, portion of a spark plug, over one hundred hair pins, nails, stove bolts and nuts, a small horse shoe, badges, about one dozen handkerchiefs and bits of material not belonging to the surrounding formation" and U.S. coins totaling $1.98. This cleaning somewhat restored the circulation of the pool, but it still remained dormant even with additional work in 1933. In 1950, Park Geologist George Marler pried a log out of its vent, and water jetted once more into the bowl of Handkerchief Pool.

HARDING GEYSER (CRATER)   Map #1

This geyser, which lies just east of the museum at Norris Geyser Basin, was probably named in 1923 by Park Superintendent Horace Albright or Ranger W. J. Cribbs. Albright wrote in 1923:

> A new geyser appeared the last winter, above the road from Black Growler. This geyser for a time erupted twice daily to an altitude of about seventy-five feet. Informal and unofficial suggestions have been made that this geyser be called the Harding Geyser, in honor of the President's visit (*Monthly Report of the Superintendent,* June 1923, p. 4).

Dorothy Day remembered watching President Harding's entourage go by when she was a little girl living in the Park. Just a month after his visit to Yellowstone, the president died. In deference to Harding, all Yellowstone Park traffic and services came to a complete stop for 5 minutes on August 11, 1923.

Harding Geyser has had a number of eruptions since 1975—the period of its greatest thermal activity—many of them to heights of about 50 feet for around 5 minutes. This place name is one of only four exceptions to the Park rule prohibiting the naming of thermal features for people.

HARLEQUIN LAKE†   Map #1

This small lake, located near Madison Junction, was known as "Secret Lake" during the 1940s, because a pair of trumpeter swans spent summers on the lake. In 1958, the official name became Harlequin Lake, named for the harlequin duck.

HAYDEN VALLEY*   Maps #1 and 2

It is appropriate that this magnificent treeless valley along the Yellowstone River, which is habitat for so many animal species in the Park, was named for Ferdinand V. Hayden. There is confusion, however, about when the valley was named and who named it. Railroad surveyor S. P. Panton wrote that the Earl of Dunraven (see Dunraven Pass) named the valley when he toured Yellowstone in 1874, but William H. Holmes (see Mount Holmes) of the 1878 Hayden survey claimed that he named the valley for his boss.

F. V. Hayden (1829-1887) conducted three government surveys of Yellowstone and surrounding areas in 1871, 1872, and 1878. The results of his 1871 survey—the first official exploration of the Yellowstone Park area—established the factual basis for establishing Yellowstone as the world's first national park in 1872. As much as any other individual, Hayden was responsible for the creation of Yellowstone.

Originally a medical doctor, Hayden became a geologist and explored the West for the USGS from 1867 to 1886. At least 44 genera and species of various organisms, "from a living moth to a fossil dinosaur," are named for him, and more than 50 volumes of reports with their related maps were issued under his supervision.

Yellowstone's geysers and hot springs fascinated Hayden, reportedly moving him to tears. "It is said of Prof. Hayden," Harry J. Norton wrote, ". . . that he cannot compose himself in the presence of a geyser in eruption; but, losing recollection of the material world for the time, rubs his hands, shouts, and dances around the object of his admiration in a paroxysm of gleeful excitement" (*Wonderland Illustrated,* p. 30). When Hayden died in 1887 of locomotor ataxia at the age of 58, he left an important legacy for Yellowstone in his work and accomplishments.

HAZLE LAKE   Map #1

In about 1888, Park tour guide G. L. Henderson named this small shallow lake, which is located north of Norris Geyser Basin and just south of Frying Pan Spring. He named the lake for its color, misspelling hazel—an error that has been retained in the name. Henderson included Hazle Lake on his 1888 tour along what he called "Seven Lake Avenue," which also took visitors past Lemonade Lake, North and South Twin Lakes, Nymph Lake, and Geyser Lake.

HEART LAKE*   Map #4

Lying in the Snake River watershed, west of Lewis Lake and south of Yellowstone Lake, Heart Lake was named before 1871 for Hart Hunney, an early hunter. The name does not refer to the heart shape of the lake. During the 1890s, historian Hiram Chittenden learned from Richard "Beaver Dick" Leigh, one of Hunney's cronies, about the naming of the lake. Evidently, Capt. John W. Barlow (see Barlow Peak), who explored Yellowstone in 1871, made the incorrect connection between the lake's name and its shape. Chittenden wrote to Barlow, who could recall nothing about the naming, but Leigh "was so positive and gave so much detail" that Chittenden concluded that he was right. Chittenden petitioned Arnold Hague of the USGS to change the spelling back to "Hart Lake," but Hague refused, convinced that the shape of the lake determined the name.

As for Hart Hunney, Leigh said that Hunney operated in the vicinity of Heart Lake between 1840 and 1850 and died in a fight with Crow Indians in 1852. Chittenden thought it was possible that Hunney was one of Capt. Benjamin Bonneville's men.

HEART RIVER*   Map #4

Heart River, the outlet of Heart Lake, got its name in 1872 from members of the second Hayden survey. A side note to the Hayden survey and naming the river is Lt. G. C. Doane's 1876 winter reconnaissance of Heart River and Snake River. Doane and his men nearly froze and starved to death during this futile and useless exploration. During their attempt to descend the Heart River, they threw water on the cracks in their boat. The water immediately froze and sealed the cracks.

HEDGES PEAK*   Map #2

In 1895, Arnold Hague named this 9,700-foot-high peak in the Washburn Range for Cornelius Hedges, a member of the 1870 Washburn expedition. Located southwest of Dunraven Peak, Hedges Peak was first named "Surprise Peak" by geologist J. P. Iddings in 1883. He also suggested "Three Bucks Peak," but the reasons for either name are unknown.

Cornelius Hedges (1831-1907) deserves at least partial credit for the creation of Yellowstone National Park. Hedges wrote in 1870: "I think a more confirmed set of skeptics never went out into the wilderness than those who composed our party, and never was a party more completely surprised and captivated with the wonders of nature" (*Helena Daily Herald*, November 9, 1870). Hedges retained an interest in Yellowstone for the rest of his life, calling the Park "a sacred trust for our national government." He died in 1907 after a long and distinguished career as a lawyer and cultural leader in Montana.

HELLROARING CREEK*   Map #2

Hellroaring Creek is a tributary to the Yellowstone River northwest of Tower Junction. In 1867, A. H. Hubble, Lou Anderson, George W. Reese (see Reese Creek), and a Mr. Caldwell discovered the stream on a prospecting trip. E. S. Topping recorded in his *Chronicles of the Yellowstone* in 1888 that "Hubbel [sic] went ahead . . . for a hunt, and upon his return he was asked what kind of stream the next creek was. 'It's a hell roarer,' was his reply, and Hell Roaring is its name to this day" (p. 63).

HERING LAKE*   Map #3

Members of the third Hayden survey in 1878 named this small lake located about 5 miles west of the South Entrance to the Park. Rudolph Hering (1847-1923) had been one of Hayden's topographers and the chief meteorologist on the 1872 survey of Yellowstone. In 1872, Hering had identified possible railroad routes to the Park, because, as he put it, "the Park will soon become an object of general interest, and . . . the resort of thousands of visitors" (in Hayden, *Sixth Annual Report*, p. 92). A hydraulic and sanitary engineer, Hering was an engineer for Philadelphia, Chicago, Los Angeles, and other cities. He also served as president of the American Public Health Association. Hering himself referred to this lake near the Park's southern boundary as "Lower Beulah Lake," because of its proximity to Beula Lake.

HERRON CREEK*   Map #3

Located near DeLacy Park on the Grand Loop Road, Herron Lake was named in 1885 or 1886 by members of the Hague parties of the USGS for William H. Herron, a topographer who assisted John H. Renshawe on those surveys.

HIBBARD'S PASS   Map #1

The trail up Solfatara Creek from the Norris Ranger Station takes hikers over Hibbard's Pass. This pass, just one

Arnold Hague next to a giant cedar in F. J. Haynes's yard, Mammoth, 1896

Superintendent H. M. Albright in the Hoodoo Basin with Hoodoo Peak at right, September 1924

mile west of the Lake of the Woods, was on P. W. Norris's original Park road in 1878. Norris named the pass in 1880 for his friend and exploring companion Timothy Ed Hibbard, a mountaineer who had been in the Yellowstone area since the 1860s. Hibbard accompanied A. Bart Henderson and Adam "Horn" Miller (see Miller Creek) in 1867 on a prospecting trip and helped name Hellroaring, Bear, and Slough creeks. In 1870, Hibbard also joined with others in discovering gold at Cooke City, Montana, and he rode with Norris into the Upper Geyser Basin in 1878 accompanied by "the first wagon ever there." Born near Chittendon, Vermont, Hibbard was one of Yellowstone Park's earliest tour guides during the early 1870s. He lived his last years near Big Piney, Wyoming, where he was a rancher and stockman.

HIDDEN LAKE   Map #4
Yellowstone Ranger Frank R. Oberhansley named this lake in 1938 for its hidden location. The more northerly of two lakes in the area, Hidden Lake is located about a mile south of Delusion Lake or about 1.5 miles north of the Flat Mountain Arm of Yellowstone Lake.

HIGHLAND HOT SPRINGS*   Map #3
In about 1885, members of the Hague parties of the USGS named Highland Hot Springs, which are near the Mary Mountain Trail about one mile east of Mary Lake. Hague's 1886 map showed Highland Hot Springs as unmistakably referring to two areas, one north of the Mary Mountain-Trout Creek stage road and one south of the stage road. This southern area should be included under the name Highland Hot Springs because it is much larger and more extensive than the springs to the north. But maps in 1887 and 1888 showed the name "Highland Hot Springs" only on the more northerly area, and maps in 1896 and 1904 followed this usage. Thus, although the major thermal area was to the south, the name was mistakenly consigned to a rather unimportant area. The Highland Hot Springs area contains two individually named features—Sulphur Lake and Miniature Geyser.

HIGHLAND TERRACE†   Map #1
This travertine terrace of the Mammoth Hot Springs, located just west of and above Prospect Terrace, has carried many names, including "Sulphur Pit Plateau" (1883) and "Blaine Terrace" (1884). G. L. Henderson named it "Sulphur" for pits of sulphur located in the meadow north of White Elephant Back Terrace, and either he or photographer F. Jay Haynes named it "Blaine" for presidential candidate James G. Blaine. When Blaine lost to Grover Cleveland in 1884, the terrace quickly became known as "Cleveland Terrace." In about 1889, members of the Hague parties of the USGS named it Highland Terrace.

HILLSIDE SPRINGS*   Map #3
Hillside Springs break out of the high rhyolite plateau on the west side of Upper Geyser Basin, north of Black Sand Basin and south of Biscuit Basin. The brilliant red color of this group of hot springs misled A. C. Peale of the Hayden survey to call it the "Iron Spring Group" in 1878. Algae that grows in the hot water actually accounts for the color. In 1883 or 1884, members of the Hague parties of the USGS (possibly Walter H. Weed) renamed the springs Hillside Springs because of their location on the steep hill.

HOODOO BASIN*   Map #2
In 1870, a party of miners discovered this remote area of strangely eroded rock formations in the Absaroka Range at the head of the Lamar River. The miners—Adam "Horn" Miller (see Miller Creek), Jack Crandall, and a man named Adams—named the area "Hoodoo" or "Goblin Land." Indians in the Park killed Crandall and Adams and kept Park Superintendent P. W. Norris from exploring the area until 1880.

Impressed by the strangely shaped rocks, Norris wrote a poem in 1883 in tribute "To monster stone-gods" titled "The Goblin-Land." His "monster stone gods" were tall, eroded lava pinnacles, sculptured into shapes resembling an old woman with a shawl, chickens, cathedrals, towers, palaces, camels, goats, and "nearly every form, animate or inanimate, real or chimerical, ever actually seen or conjured by the imagination" (*Annual Report . . . 1880*, p. 8).

Henry J. Winser, a guidebook author in 1883, described the Hoodoo Basin as a place where

> the frosts and storms of ages have worn numberless deep, narrow, crooked channels amid the slender tottering pillars, shafts, mounds and pyramids which form this singular maze. . . . One mound is described as looking like a large altar pyre, 125 feet in height, resting on a pyramidal base, the sacrificial victim lying on top (*Yellowstone*, p. 84).

Novelist Owen Wister, who visited Yellowstone in 1887, wrote that the Hoodoo Basin rocks looked "like a church organ that has met with a railroad accident" (*Harper's Monthly*, March 1936, p. 479). *Hoodoo* is a word that means a person or thing that causes bad luck.

THE HOODOOS*   Map #1
As early as 1883, this area of massively tumbled travertine limestone blocks just below and east of Terrace Mountain

above Mammoth Hot Springs was known as the "Limestone Hoodoos." G. L. Henderson may have named the area because of its ghostly, strange shapes and the somewhat spooky appearance of the fallen rocks. The rocks in the Hoodoos are believed to have been deposited by hot springs thousands of years old and toppled from the east face of Terrace Mountain sometime before records were kept.

HORNADAY CREEK* Map #2

This stream, which flows west from Mount Hornaday to Slough Creek, was first named "Plateau Creek" in 1885 by members of the Hague survey parties. The name was derived from the creek's location on Buffalo Plateau. In 1981, a Park place-names committee renamed it Hornaday Creek in an effort to eliminate duplicated names. There is another Plateau Creek south of Yellowstone Lake on Two Ocean Plateau.

HOT LAKE* Map #3

A. C. Peale first described this thermal spring in the Firehole Lake Group (or Black Warrior Group) of the Lower Geyser Basin in 1871. But the lake did not receive a name until 1883 or 1884, when Walter H. Weed of the Hague survey named it the "Great Hot Lake." By 1887, Arnold Hague had decided to call it simply Hot Lake.

G. L. Henderson had a more colorful name for the lake—he named it "Walpurgia Lake," from a poem by Johann Goethe. In German mythology, April 30, the day preceding May Day, was Walpurgia, the occasion for witches to gather to celebrate a sabbat.

Hot Lake is some 1,000 feet long and over 300 feet wide. Its depth is unknown, but there are a number of powerful hot springs in the lake that can be seen at its surface when they are agitated. Canada geese occasionally nest on the western end of Hot Lake.

HOURGLASS FALLS Map #3

Hourglass Falls are located on the Phillips Fork of the Bechler River about 1,500 feet above Quiver Cascade. David Lentz of the U.S. Fish and Wildlife Service named this falls in 1978. "This waterfall," Lentz wrote, "drops at least 30 m[eters] and is unique because midway in its drop, the falling water is pinched off by rocks so that the flow narrows in the middle and spreads at the bottom, resembling a long hourglass. We called it Hourglass Falls" (letter to author, 1979).

HOWELL CREEK† Map #4

Howell Creek flows from Eagle Pass to Mountain Creek on the Park's eastern boundary. The namesake for this creek is "Uncle" Billy Howell, a longtime guide and dude rancher from Cody, Wyoming, who led horse parties into Yellowstone from the east side. The name, which came into use during the 1950s, applies to this creek because Howell often led his horse parties down it. Billy Howell was the original owner of the Holm Lodge near Cody. Mary Shawver, a cohort of his at Holm Lodge, remembered that "Mr. Howell's greatest pleasure was to show guests all the wonders and beauties that he loved" (*Sincerely, Mary S.*, p. 17).

HOYT PEAK* Map #4

In 1881, Park Superintendent P. W. Norris named this 10,506-foot-high peak of the Absaroka Range, northeast of Eleanor Lake, for John W. Hoyt, the first territorial governor of Wyoming. In that year, Governor Hoyt made a trip into Yellowstone to scout a route into the Park from the east so that Wyoming residents could visit the Park easily. Accompanying Hoyt were his son Kepler (see Kepler Cascades), Maj. J. W. Mason (for whom Mason Creek, to the east of the Park, was named), an escort of soldiers, and Norris. Hoyt may well have selected the peak that was to bear his name.

John Wesley Hoyt (1831-1912) was born in Ohio and educated as a doctor and a lawyer. He was primarily known as an educator and was the first president of the University of Wyoming (1887-1890). He was a member of Wyoming's constitutional convention, and he prepared the memorial for the state's admission into the Union in 1890. Hoyt is also known for having personally intervened in 1878 to aid Chief Washakie and the Shoshone Indian tribe in getting promised rations from the federal government.

HURRICANE VENT* Map #1

This hot spring—formerly a geyser—in the Porcelain Basin of Norris Geyser Basin evidently underwent spectacular changes early in its recorded history. The spring was first described in 1884 by geologist Walter Weed, who wrote that it was "a—basin with rough rhy[olite] floor—covered with gray muddy dep[osit]—spg—10′ diameter. rock in center—wat[er] blue . . . spouts const. on S.E. side 1′ –2′ –3′ –no overflow . . ." (USGS, Box 47, vol. 6., p. 7).

In 1885, G. L. Henderson called the geyser the "Enchanted Hurricane" because it resembled an immense wheel in continuous motion. By the summer of 1886, Hurricane had become a "perpetual geyser, dashing its turbid water down a quadrangular rocky basin over 30 feet" (Henderson, *Manual and Guide*, p. 2). But still more changes occurred. As Henderson reported in the June 18, 1887, *St. Paul Pioneer Press*, Hurricane Geyser's boiling flood shoots out over the wall where we formerly sat. August Kelly, who has been the only resident of this basin during the winter, informs me that he noticed a marked change in the quantity of water discharged and the energy displayed at this basin after the earthquakes of December 9, 1886.

Henderson's "Enchanted Hurricane" later became "Hurricane Geyser" and finally Hurricane Vent.

HYGEIA SPRING*   Map #3

This hot spring in the Lower Geyser Basin is located just south of the place where the Fountain Flats Drive crosses Nez Perce Creek. The spring got its name in 1884 from the owners of the nearby Marshall's Hotel, who named it for Hygeia, the Greek goddess of health. Marshall's Hotel used the spring's waters for bathing and culinary purposes. On June 4, 1886, geologist Arnold Hague wrote: "I believe [G. G.] Henderson and Claymore called it the Hygeia Spring which is a very good name" (Hague papers, Box 1, Book 2C, pp. 106-107). Throughout its known history, Hygeia has been a quiet warm spring.

HYMEN TERRACE   Map #1

This travertine hot springs terrace of the Mammoth Hot Springs is located immediately north of Liberty Cap. It was probably either Walter H. Weed or G. L. Henderson who named it in 1882 or 1883 for Hymen, the Greek god of marriage. Henderson, who came to Mammoth in 1882, lived near Hymen Terrace and was fond of giving classical names to Yellowstone features. He probably gave the name because Hymen had become a place where lovers bathed together.

During the 1880s, some claimed that Mammoth's hot spring waters could cure diseases such as rheumatism and vertigo. Hymen Terrace water was conveyed to the new National Hotel in 1884, and by 1885 several Mammoth-area hotels were using the water.

Since the 1870s, the behavior of Hymen Terrace has been characterized by extreme variability, and during its times of activity it has been one of the most exquisitely beautiful springs in the Park. This 1912 description by Park photographer Jack E. Haynes is typical:

> Hymen Terrace [is] one of the most beautifully colored spots in the Park.... This new addition to the number of distinct terraces at Mammoth... is easily the gem of the collection because of its exquisite coloring. The veil of steam softens and blends the vivid colorings, while innumerable water-glazed knobs reflect the sunlight like a thousand mirrors (*Haynes Official Guide*, p. 17).

ICE BOX CANYON*   Map #2

Ice remains until late summer on the walls of this small canyon on Soda Butte Creek, just east of Round Prairie on the East Entrance Road. The name was in local use at least as early as 1929 to 1932.

ICE LAKE†   Map #1

This small lake, located 4 miles southeast of Norris, was named in about 1900 because the ice supply for the Norris Hotel (1900-1917) was cut here.

IMPERIAL GEYSER*   Map #3

This geyser in the Twin Buttes area is located about 200 yards west of Spray Geyser in the Lower Geyser Basin. In 1927, hot spring researcher E. T. Allen reported the geyser's first recorded eruption, noting that it was about 25 feet high.

The name Imperial was given on July 31, 1929, as the result of an election held at Old Faithful among members of the visiting National Editorial Association, which included newspapermen from all over the country. Stephen Mather, the head of the National Park Service, had decided that the NEA members would be allowed to vote on a name for the new geyser from a list of 17 names submitted by William H. Holmes (see Mount Holmes). Originally, the scheme was more of a contest, with the winner getting a trip to the Park in order to stimulate interest in Yellowstone. A tie between "Columbia Geyser" and Imperial was resolved in favor of the latter.

In late 1928, Imperial Geyser continued to erupt from 80 to 150 feet high every 10 to 14.5 hours for periods of 4 to 6 hours. The geyser became dormant in late 1929 and did not rejuvenate (that we know of) until sometime in August of 1966. During its early years, the discharge of Imperial Geyser was said to be one of the greatest in the Park, at around 878,000 gallons per eruption.

INDIAN CREEK*   Map #1

In 1878, members of the third Hayden survey (possibly W. H. Holmes—see Mount Holmes), noticed that an Indian trail passed down the north side of this creek. It was part of the Great Bannock Trail, which was used by Shoshone and Bannock hunting parties during the nineteenth century as a route through the Yellowstone country on their way to and from eastern and northern hunting grounds.

INDIAN POND*   Maps #2 and 4

This is the correct historic name of what was once called "Squaw Lake," which is located just north of Yellowstone

Ice Box Canyon on Soda Butte Creek

B.L. Brown, Haynes Studio

Lake, about 3 miles east of Fishing Bridge. Park Superintendent P. W. Norris named the lake Indian Pond in 1880, because Indians used it for camping. He mentioned its "decaying brush, corrals, wickeups, and lodgepoles." Later, geologist Arnold Hague noted: "Indian Pond . . . appears to have been a favorite camping ground for manufacturing implements, being convenient to quarries, and nearby the hunting grounds of Pelican Valley and the fishing resorts of Yellowstone Lake" (*Monograph 32, Part 1*, p. 40). For unknown reasons, a Park superintendent changed the name to "Squaw Lake" during the 1920s. A Park place-names committee restored the name Indian Pond in 1981.

INDIGO SPRING* Map #3

This hot spring in the Excelsior Group of Midway Geyser Basin was named for its color. In 1878, members of the third Hayden survey called it Indigo Spring, describing it as dark blue, triangular, 20 by 25 feet, and 196°F.

Assistant Park Superintendent G. L. Henderson named the spring "Mystic Lake" in 1882, and he also referred to it as "Lake of Magic Bells" or "Magic Lake." This name referred to the bell-shaped silver bubbles that arose in double columns from the depths of the spring. As Henderson explained: "when . . . [the bubbles] reach the surface, [they] dissolve rather than explode, making scarcely a visible ripple" (*Livingston Post*, January 11, 1900).

INKWELL SPRING* Map #3

James D. Landsdowne, a naturalist during the 1920s, wrote of this hot spring in the Giant Group of Upper Geyser Basin: "The Inkwell is so named because it presents two colors, red and black. The red is due to algae, the black to a peculiar deposit of sulphides. The water is 200 degrees Fahrenheit" (NPS, *Ranger Naturalists Manual*, 1926, p. 11).

Inkwell Spring is located on the left bank of the Firehole River just above Oblong Geyser and the footbridge. The name of the spring seems to have been in local use by 1914. The spring was also occasionally referred to as the "Devil's Inkwell."

INSIDE MOUNTAIN Map #2

This 9,681-foot-high peak in the Washburn Range is located about 2 miles northwest of Dunraven Peak. This may be the mountain that geologist J. P. Iddings named "Crows Foot Mountain" in 1883. Arnold Hague appears to have given the name Inside Mountain to the peak in about 1902, referring to the location of the mountain inside the semi-circle of peaks in the Washburn Range.

INSPIRATION POINT* Map #2

This point on the north rim of the Grand Canyon of the Yellowstone River is probably the same one that W. H. Holmes (see Mount Holmes) named "Promontory Point" in 1878. He gave this name because the point protrudes into the canyon. G. L. Henderson probably named it Inspiration Point in about 1884, a reference to the great display of color in the canyon at this place.

In 1896, writer Charles Dudley Warner described his impressions of Inspiration Point:

> From this point is the finest display of color. The body of color is yellow, but of all shades, and intermingled with it is much brown and red, spots of deep red and vermilion and white, astonishingly brilliant. The slopes of the Cañon are of friable, decadent, crumbling rock, and the colors run much together, so that you get often an iridescent appearance. . . . The magnificence is in the great depth, and the supernal beauty in the brilliant color. The scene is mightily impressive and unwearying. The different shades in morning and evening light, in a gray sky and in the bright sunlight, are so varied that the picture is always new, and the more wonderful the more one gets to know it. I should say that it is the sort of spectacle that would grow upon one the longer and oftener he saw it (in Schullery, *Old Yellowstone Days*, p. 164).

IRIS FALLS* Map #3

This 45-foot-high waterfall on the Bechler River is located between Treasure Island and Colonnade Falls. In 1885, members of the Hague survey named it possibly for a Greek mythological character, Iris, or for the wildflower. It is most likely, however, that they named the falls because of its irised spray, which creates a rainbow.

IRIS POOL* Map #3

This hot spring in the Midway Geyser Basin, located some 200 feet southeast of Tromp Spring, is the largest of several springs in the area. Hague survey members named the spring sometime before 1904. The origin of the name is unknown, but it probably referred to the pool's colors. A 1904 map showed the name in plural form ("Iris Pools"), referring to 7 or so different springs. The singular form was officially approved in 1937.

IRON POT Map #3

Iron Pot is a hot spring and geyser in the Sentinel Group of the Lower Geyser Basin. Located in a grove of trees about 350 feet south of Steep Cone, Iron Pot was named in 1872 by Frank Bradley of the second Hayden survey because of its color ("reddish brown . . . and mainly siliceous"). In 1984, Iron Pot was a geyser, erupting to about 4 feet above the top of its general water level.

IRON SPRING*   Map #1

During the 1890s, this spring in the Gibbon Canyon just north of Gibbon Falls was a favorite stop for thirsty travelers on the stage road. It is not known who named the spring or when, but Hiram Chittenden referred to it in 1895 as "Soda and Iron Spring" and in 1897 T. C. Porter found it "strongly impregnated with iron and soda, tasting like ink" (*Impressions of America*, p. 37).

The name Iron Spring appeared on the 1912 Park topographic map at a location just north of the mouth of Secret Valley Creek. There is a spring today that roughly corresponds to the 1912 location, at a point .1 mile north of the mouth of Secret Valley Creek. This spring is probably the remains of the original Iron Spring. Located on the west side of the road, it shows bright orange ferric-oxide coloring in rocks of the area and in its runoff water in the ditch at the roadside. Photographer Jack Haynes's *Guide* (1939, 1966) locates the original Iron Spring on the east side of the road; it has probably been covered by roadwork. The 1961 Park topographic map erroneously moved the name to a location one-half mile north, where it referred incorrectly to a spring one-half mile north of the mouth of Secret Valley Creek.

IRON SPRING CREEK*   Map #3

This creek originates south of Old Faithful and Fern Cascades and flows north to the Little Firehole River near Biscuit Basin. Named in 1871 by members of the first Hayden survey, the creek got its name when A. C. Peale mistakenly attributed its red color to the presence of iron. Geologist Arnold Hague later wrote that the name was a misnomer as

> neither the water nor its banks [is] in any manner more characterized by iron than other tributaries of the Firehole. Its name is . . . owing to the exceptionally large amount of reddish-brown algae accompanying its thermal waters (Hague papers, "The Geyser Basins," Box 11, p. 81).

ISA LAKE*   Map #3

Hiram Chittenden of the U.S. Corps of Engineers claimed to have discovered this lake on the Continental Divide at Craig Pass in 1891. Chittenden, who built many early roads in Yellowstone, was searching for a practicable route to locate his new road between Old Faithful and West Thumb. It was not until 1893 that Northern Pacific Railroad officials named the lake for Isabel Jelke of Cincinnati. Little is known about Jelke or about her relationship to Chittenden, the NPRR, and Yellowstone Park. Chittenden's 1916 poetic tribute to the lake and his discovery includes the puzzling line: "Thou hast no name; pray, wilt thou deign to bear/The name of her who first has sung of thee" (*Verse*, p. 53). Perhaps Isabel Jelke was already associated with the lake when Chittenden "discovered" it.

Isa Lake is noteworthy as probably the only lake on earth that drains naturally to two oceans *backwards*, the east side draining to the Pacific and the west side to the Atlantic.

JACKSON GRADE   Map #2

This hill, located just north of the Northeast Entrance Road and northeast of the mouth of Soda Butte Creek (marked 6,583 feet on the 1961 USGS topographical map), is named for "Old Man" George J. Jackson. A squatter in the Park, Jackson received verbal permission from Park Superintendent Patrick Conger in 1882 to live on Rose Creek where the present-day Lamar Ranger Station and Yellowstone Institute are located. When Jackson refused an eviction order by Superintendent Robert Carpenter in October 1884, Park officials removed him from his cabin. Little else is known of Jackson, except that he continued to hang around the Park for several years after his eviction. The story of the naming of Jackson Grade has it that George Jackson was the first to skid wagons down this steep grade using a log jammed in the wheel.

JACKSTRAW BASIN†   Map #1

In 1958, USGS topographer Raymond E. Hill named this fallen timber area along an intermittent creek, about 5 miles southeast of West Yellowstone, Montana. Hill named the area "because of a massive jumble of down[ed] timber, making ascent extremely difficult" (letter to author, April 28, 1980).

JAY CREEK   Map #2

Jay Creek flows into the Yellowstone River from the hills west of the Chittenden Bridge between Otter Creek and the Upper Falls. During his reconnaissance of the Park in 1875, Capt. William Ludlow named the creek. In his 1876 *Report*, Ludlow wrote:

> [We] followed down the left bank of Alum Creek until the main trail down the Yellowstone was reached. This was pursued for 2 or 3 miles farther, and camp made in a drenching rain on a small creek, which we named "Jay Creek," and near the point where the two trails from Cascade Creek had united coming up (p. 29).

Ludlow probably named the creek for the jays (perhaps Gray's Jay) that inhabit Yellowstone.

JELLY SPRING* Map #3

It appears that geologist Walter Weed named this geyser in the Fountain Group of Lower Geyser Basin in 1887 or 1888. Weed described the spring as a deep, oblong, fissure bowl with a light gray lining. It was filled to its rim with clear-as-glass green water, which boiled quietly and discharged constantly. Weed believed that some algae helped in depositing sinter and that the progression was from "algous jelly" to hard sinter—hence, the name Jelly Spring.

JOFFE LAKE Map #1

This small lake in the Mammoth area is located just south of the old Mammoth water supply reservoir. The lake was named in about 1949 for Joseph Joffe (1896-1960), who came to Yellowstone Park in 1922 and assisted Jack Haynes in the preparation of the *Haynes Guide to Yellowstone National Park*. Because Joffe devoted his leisure time to fishing, he was nicknamed "Beautiful Water Joffe." He often caught fish illegally in the Mammoth water supply reservoir (now drained) and claimed that they were caught in "CCC Lake" (present-day Joffe Lake). The name "CCC Lake" came from the old Civilian Conservation Corps camp nearby.

For a time, Joffe Lake was also known as "Hoodoo Lake" because of the nearby stone Hoodoos and was called "Demonstration Pond" because fire equipment used to be demonstrated there.

JONES PASS* Map #3

This mountain pass in the Absaroka Range, located south of Mount Chittenden, is accessible only by trail. P. W. Norris named the pass in 1880 for Capt. William A. Jones (1841-1914), who had discovered it in 1873 during a military reconnaissance of Wyoming and Yellowstone Park. Jones, who had served in the Civil War, was an assistant professor of engineering at the U.S. Military Academy and an army engineer officer during the construction of the Union Pacific Railroad in 1869. In 1873, Jones wrote of his exploration:

> After the Indian guides, I was the first to reach the summit of the pass, and, before I knew it, had given vent to a screeching yell, which was taken up with a wild echo by the Indians; for there, seemingly at their feet, and several miles nearer than I had expected, was spread out a scene of exceeding beauty—Yellowstone Lake—embosomed in its surrounding plateau, and a mass of green forest extending as far as we could see (*Report*, p. 20).

Jones named the pass "Stinkingwater Pass" because he thought it was the head of the "Stinkingwater River" (now Shoshone River), but P. W. Norris later changed that name to Jones Pass.

JORDAN FALLS Map #1

This 30- to 50-foot waterfall is located about 1.5 miles above the mouth of Canyon Creek, a westward-flowing tributary of the Gibbon River near Gibbon Falls. John Varley of the U.S. Fish and Wildlife Service named the falls in 1975 for David Starr Jordan (1851-1931). Jordan was a fish expert, naturalist, teacher, peace advocate, and the first fish investigator in Yellowstone Park. He made a reconnaissance of Yellowstone Park in 1889 with Elwood Hofer to find out which Park lakes and streams were barren of fish and why. Jordan's visit resulted in a program to stock Yellowstone's lakes and streams with game fish. He wrote the highly influential *Manual of the Vertebrates of the Northern United States* (1876), earned an M.D. degree, was president of Indiana University from 1885 to 1891, and was the first president of Stanford University (1891-1913).

JOSEPH PEAK* Map #1

In 1885, members of the Hague survey named this 10,494-foot-high peak in the Gallatin Range southwest of Electric Peak for Chief Joseph of the Nez Perce Indians. The Nez Perces traveled through Yellowstone Park in 1877 on a heroic 1,300-mile trek from their Idaho reservation while being pursued by the military. Chief Joseph (1840?-1904), known to members of his own tribe as Hin-mut-too-yah-lat-kekht or "Thunder-rolling-in-the-mountains," was one of several Nez Perce chiefs who led the 800 men, women, and children away from their reservation. Cavalry troops finally halted the Nez Perces' flight just 50 miles south of the Canadian border and freedom. At the surrender near present-day Chinook, Montana, Joseph told his chiefs in council: "Hear me my chiefs, I am tired; my heart is sick and sad. From where the sun now stands I will fight no more forever."

JOSEPHS COAT SPRINGS* Map #2

This group of hot springs is in an isolated region along Broad Creek on the Mirror Plateau some 5 miles west of Hot Spring Basin Group. Capt. W. A. Jones explored this area in 1873 and named it "Orange Rock Springs," which survives as an alternate official name.

In 1884, geologists Arnold Hague and Walter Weed visited the area. When they saw the multicolored rocks, they named it Josephs Coat Springs in reference to Joseph's coat of many colors in the Bible. Hague found the place "unsurpassed in beauty of color by any other locality in the Park." He described the area for the *American Journal of Science* in 1887:

Lt. Dan Kingman of the U.S. Army Corps of Engineers (left) with Lt. R. C. Stivers

Tourists camping at the YPC Company Canyon Camp

This group of springs is situated along both sides of the stream bed between rhyolite ridges which rise abruptly for two or three hundred feet. Solfataric action has completely decomposed the rhyolite into smooth, rounded slopes of soft earthy material . . . orange, yellow, vermilion, and white are interblended in a most striking manner" (September 1887, p. 171).

JUG SPRING   Map #3

This hot spring in the Thud Group of Lower Geyser Basin was named in 1872 by A. C. Peale of the second Hayden survey because of its jug-like shape.

JUNCTION BUTTE*   Map #2

This 6,598-foot-high square-shaped butte is located at the junction of the Yellowstone and Lamar rivers. Although Capt. J. W. Barlow reported that the butte was known as "Square Butte" at the time of his visit in 1871, members of the third Hayden survey named it Junction Butte in 1878.

JUNCTION VALLEY   Map #2

Located west of Junction Butte, southeast of Garnet Hill, and east of Crescent Hill, this large, treeless valley was named in 1878 by members of the third Hayden survey (probably by W. H. Holmes or Henry Gannett). They gave it this name because it borders the junction of the Yellowstone and Lamar rivers and nearby Junction Butte.

JUPITER SPRING(S) and
JUPITER TERRACE   Map #1

Jupiter Springs form Jupiter Terrace just south of Mound Terrace at Mammoth Hot Springs. The name Jupiter, from the chief of the Roman gods, appears to have been given to these springs in 1871 by members of the first Hayden survey: "To these [natural bathing basins] some of our party gave the names of Jupiter's Baths and Diana's pools" (A. C. Peale in Hayden, *Fifth Annual Report*, p. 177). Artist Henry Wood Elliot, who sketched "Jupiter's Baths" for the September 30, 1871, issue of *Frank Leslie's Illustrated Newspaper*, may have named these springs. A. C. Peale of the Hayden survey wrote that "the whole mass looked like some grand cascade that had suddenly been arrested in its descent, and frozen" (in Hayden, *Fifth Annual Report*, p. 174).

KALEIDOSCOPE GEYSER   Map #3

The namesake geyser of the Kaleidoscope Group of the Lower Geyser Basin first appeared on maps in the 1904 Hague Atlas. The geyser must have been active in some form when it was named during the period of the later Hague survey studies, but the origin of the name is not certain. A 1927 reference to the geyser suggests one origin for the name: "The Kaleidoscope has a slight periodic action that produces a play of colors suggesting that nearly forgotten toy" (NPS, *Ranger Naturalists' Manual*, p. 131). But Park Geologist George Marler has suggested that the name was given instead from the brilliant iron and algal coloration about the spring.

KELP POOL   Map #3

This hot spring in the Black Sand Basin of Upper Geyser Basin is located on the east bank of Iron Spring Creek several hundred yards below Sunset Lake. The pool, which is shaped like a long trough, runs into the creek. Arnold Hague and Walter Weed named it in 1888 because of its algous growths that resemble kelp (a greenish-brown seaweed). In 1888, Weed reported that Kelp Pool was 100 feet long and 20 to 30 feet wide, with a temperature of 122.5°F.

KEPLER CASCADES*   Map #3

These 100- to 150-foot waterfalls are located on the Firehole River above Old Faithful. The falls got their name in 1881 when Park Superintendent P. W. Norris honored Kepler Hoyt, "the intrepid twelve-year-old son of Governor [John] Hoyt, of Wyoming, who unflinchingly shared in all the hardships, privations, and dangers of the explorations of his father" (*Calumet of the Coteau*, p. 262). Kepler Hoyt and his father explored Yellowstone in 1881 with Maj. J. W. Mason, Lt. J. F. Cummings, four civilians, five enlisted men, and some packers. The group was searching for a practicable route into Yellowstone from Wyoming Territory. Superintendent Norris and gamekeeper Harry Yount guided the party around the cascades that now bear Kepler's name.

In 1870, Lt. G. C. Doane of the Washburn party described the cascades: "These pretty little falls if located on an eastern stream would be celebrated in history and song; here amid objects so grand as to strain conception and stagger belief, they were passed without a halt" (in Bonney and Bonney, *Battle Drums*, p. 340).

KIDNEY SPRING   Map #3

In 1872, A. C. Peale of the second Hayden survey named this northernmost named hot spring of the Thud Group of Lower Geyser Basin for its renal shape.

KING GEYSER*   Map #3

King Geyser is located in the Lower Group of the West Thumb Geyser Basin, east and north of Black Pool near the shore of Yellowstone Lake. King Geyser may have been named for Crown Prince Gustaf of Sweden, who visited the West Thumb area in 1926. King Geyser erupted twice on August 5, 1938, at 10 a.m. and at 4 p.m., to heights of 6 to 8 feet for 10 minutes.

KINGMAN PASS*   Map #1

This pass on the main road between Terrace Mountain and Bunsen Peak was named for Dan C. Kingman (1852-1916) of the U.S. Corps of Engineers. Kingman built the first road through the pass in 1883-1885. The original road from Mammoth Hot Springs to Norris Geyser Basin, built in 1878, ran west from Liberty Cap, up Clematis Gulch, and through Snow Pass. The road up to Snow Pass (a trail today) was so steep that stage drivers regularly swore at it. New York Senator Roscoe Conkling was so scared by the road in 1883 that "he packed his trunk and went back home without going further into the Park" (*Cheyenne Weekly Leader*, September 27, 1883).

Lt. Kingman returned to the Park in 1883 to build a new road, and within a year someone—possibly Kingman's associates Oscar Swanson and Ed Lamartine—had named the new pass for him. The road through Kingman Pass was, in Kingman's words, "by far the most difficult and expensive piece of work undertaken in the Park" (in Baldwin, *Enchanted Enclosure*, p. 92).

Dan Kingman had been graduated second in the West Point class of 1875, had served with the Engineer Battalion at Willet's Point, New York, and had taught engineering at West Point. During his three years in Yellowstone, he completed some 30 miles of permanent roads and initiated the idea of today's Grand Loop Road system. Kingman planned his road system to "enable tourists to visit the principal points of interest in the Park without retracing their steps; and to take a long or short trip, according to the time and the means at their disposal." He based his plan "upon the supposition, and in the earnest hope that [the Park] will be preserved as nearly as may be as the hand of nature left it—a source of pleasure to all who visit it, and a source of wealth to no one" (in Baldwin, *Enchanted Enclosure*, pp. 85, 88, 93). Kingman later became chief of the U.S. Corps of Engineers.

KITCHEN SPRING*   Map #3

A. C. Peale of the third Hayden survey in 1878 probably named this hot spring of the Orion Group of Shoshone Geyser Basin near the Shoshone Lake Trail. Peale wrote:

> This spring was so named from the fact that during our stay in the Shoshone Geyser Basin it was utilized almost every day by our cook. The spring has two openings, in which the water is constantly boiling. The largest measured about 18 inches in diameter, just large enough to allow a kettle to be sunk in it (in Hayden, *Twelfth Annual Report*, p. 254).

KITE HILL   Map #1

Kite Hill is an eastern spur of Sepulcher Mountain, just northwest of Mammoth where the first Mammoth Cemetery is located. The hill was named in recent years because children of National Park Service families fly kites there. The hill has also been locally referred to as "Sepulcher Hill."

KNOTTED WOODS HILL   Map #4

This place name recalls an old stretch of road between the present-day crossing of Arnica Creek and Natural Bridge on the west shore of Yellowstone Lake. Replaced in 1927-1930 by the present-day route, the old road ran over Knotted Woods Hill just east of Arnica Creek on its way to Natural Bridge. A stretch of knotted lodgepole pine trees called the "Knotted Woods" or "Knotted Pines" dominate this hill, which got its name at least as early as 1926.

KNOWLES FALLS†   Map #1

This 15-foot-high waterfall on the Yellowstone River is located just downstream from Crevice Creek and 4 miles upstream from Gardiner. Lt. G. C. Doane called it "Cañon Fall" in 1876, and it seems to have received its current name in about 1930 by National Park Service personnel or other local persons. The waterfall is named for John S. Knowles, a miner who lived in a cabin at the mouth of Crevice Creek "for more than twenty years. When the north boundary of the Park was surveyed he was forced to move out."

Knowles came to the area as early as 1876, working a claim at Emigrant Gulch in the Paradise Valley north of Yellowstone. By 1882, he had begun mining on Crevice Creek and had built his cabin at the mouth of Crevice Creek near the falls by 1898. After the government discovered that Knowles was living in the Park, they told him to move out. Knowles had made a good strike of about $40,000 the year before, and, as the story goes, he boarded a train for Chicago, where he rented the Old Iroquois Theater for one night and opened it to the public. At the end of each act, he announced "this party is on me, folks. I would like to have you all come out to the nearest saloon and have a drink on old J. S. Knowles after the show" (Randall, *Footprints*, p. 62).

LACTOSE SPRING   Map #3

This hot spring in the Myriad Group of Upper Geyser Basin was named by naturalists in 1959 following the

Yellowstone earthquake. Lactose is a white sugar found in milk, and the naturalists named this spring because of its white milky appearance. A. C. Peale of the Hayden survey called it "spring #10" in 1878. By 1887, observers were referring to Lactose Spring as "White Geyser," a name that was later transferred to a spring farther southeast.

LADIES' LAKE   Map #1

This spring, located at Mammoth Hot Springs just south of Bath Lake and on the other side of a travertine ridge, was famous during the 1880s. Originally called "spring #33" in A. C. Peale's 1878 report of Yellowstone thermal features, Ladies' Lake appears to have been named in 1882-1884 by G. L. Henderson. At the time, Henderson was promoting bathing in nearby Bath Lake, which was open to swimming for men only. As early as 1885 Henderson suggested that "Ladies Lake . . . might be enclosed at small expense and used by the fair sex exclusively" (*Livingston Enterprise*, June 27, 1885).

Bathing in Yellowstone's hot springs today is illegal because of potential danger to swimmers (temperatures of natural springs can change very suddenly) and because of potential damage to the springs themselves.

LAKE OF THE WOODS*   Map #1

Lake of the Woods is located about one mile southwest of the hill known as the Landmark. Park Superintendent P. W. Norris named the lake in 1879 because of its setting in the timber. Believing that he had discovered the lake, Norris wrote that it was "thus appropriately named at the time of its discovery, when I was searching for water which was not poisonous for one of my men, severely injured by the fall of his horse in a bear-fight" (*Calumet of the Coteau*, p. 249). Unknown to Norris, members of the third Hayden survey had already discovered the lake in 1878 and had named it "Gibbon Lake." The lake was also called "Pine Lake." His original tourist road, built in 1878, passed Lake of the Woods and dropped down Solfatara Creek to Norris Geyser Basin.

LAKE VIEW   Map #3

This point on a hill west of the West Thumb of Yellowstone Lake on the Grand Loop Road is west of Duck Lake at the spot where the road suddenly curves west. Hiram Chittenden probably named this spot in 1891 while he was directing the tree cutting for the West Thumb to Old Faithful Road. From this spot there is a magnificent view of Yellowstone Lake.

LAKE WYODAHO*   Map #3

This small lake in the Cascade Corner country is located a mile west of Ouzel Falls on the edge of the Madison Plateau and 4 to 5 miles east of the Idaho-Wyoming state line. Chief Naturalist David Condon suggested the name in 1956, and a Park place-names committee took the name from its local use by parties visiting the area. Many of those visitors were from Jack Young's Wyodaho Ranch nearby. The lake's name was taken from the ranch because ranch tourists camped there for years.

LAMAR RIVER*   Map #2

One of the Park's major rivers, the Lamar originates in the Hoodoo Basin on the slopes of Lamar Mountain and flows northwesterly for 66 miles to the Yellowstone River. Father Pierre DeSmet's map in 1851 showed this stream as "Beaver Creek," but in 1869 the Washburn General Land Office map called it the "East Fork" of the Yellowstone River. In 1885, Arnold Hague renamed the stream for his boss, Lucius Quintus Cincinnatus Lamar, Secretary of the Interior from 1885 to 1888. Hague wrote: "He has done so much for the park, and has been so good a friend, that it seems only the proper thing to perpetuate his name in the Park" (Hague papers, Hague to G. L. Henderson, February 22, 1887, Box 1, Book 2C, pp. 403-405).

A Mississippi lawyer, legislator, and Confederate army veteran, L. Q. C. Lamar (1825-1893) was an associate justice of the U.S. Supreme Court at the time of his death. As Secretary of the Interior under Cleveland, Lamar incorrectly interpreted Congress' original purpose in establishing Yellowstone as a wilderness preserve. But his action gave credibility to the movement to protect Yellowstone from railroads and other development.

LAMAR VALLEY   Map #2

This is the general name for the valley drained by the Lamar River, extending from about the mouth of Cache Creek to the Lamar Canyon. Fur-trapper Osborne Russell was the first to describe the valley. He referred to it in 1835 as "Secluded Valley" and later wrote in his journal for August 20, 1836:

> There is something in the wild romantic scenery of this valley which I cannot nor will I, attempt to describe but the impressions made upon my mind while gazing from a high eminence on the surrounding landscape one evening as the sun was gently gliding behind the western mountain and casting its gigantic shadows accross [sic] the vale were such as time can never efface from my memory but as I am neither Poet Painter or Romance writer I must content myself to be what I am a humble journalist and leave this beautiful Vale in obscurity until visited by some more skillful admirer of the

The Folsom-Cook-Peterson Expedition

This journey by "two yankee quakers and a Dane" is considered by many to have been the first attempt at organized exploration of what is now Yellowstone National Park. Accepted as part of the Washburn expedition of 1869, Charles Cook, David Folsom, and William Peterson set out on their own when that expedition fizzled. From Diamond City, Montana, the three rode south on three horses (and packing two more) with supplies for six weeks.

Riding up the Yellowstone River, they entered what is now the Park by crossing over Mount Everts and Blacktail Deer Plateau. They forded the river at Tower Fall, advanced up the Lamar Valley, turned south up Flint Creek to cross the difficult Mirror Plateau, and struck the Grand Canyon of the Yellowstone at Point Sublime (q.v.). Continuing upriver, the men saw Mud Volcano and then Yellowstone Lake, where they left a carved rock in the mortise of a tree (which has never been found). Trekking westward to West Thumb and up a hill (see Lake View) toward Shoshone Lake, the Folsom party dropped down White Creek to Great Fountain Geyser, which they saw erupt to at least 80 feet high. Taking off their hats and yelling "with all our might," they celebrated that natural wonder before continuing down the Firehole and Madison rivers to Diamond City.

Folsom's account of that 36-day trip was published in the July 1870 issue of *Western Monthly* magazine. In addition to that rather obscure magazine article, the Folsom party contributed an improved map and planted the germ of the idea that this phenomenal area of the country should be preserved. They also gave direct encouragement to members of the Washburn party, which explored the Park in 1870. The definitive account of their trip is in Aubrey Haines's *Valley of the Upper Yellowstone* (1965).

Although the Folsom party gave no place names to the Park, their verbal and written accounts greatly influenced subsequent name-givers, such as members of the Washburn and Hayden parties, and two place names (Point Sublime and Buffalo Pool) may have come directly from their narrative of the trip.

Upper Falls of the Yellowstone, 1914

Elliott W. Hunter, Haynes Studio

beauties of nature who may chance to stroll this way at some future period . . . (*Journal of a Trapper*, p. 46).

Russell was too modest.

Geologist Arnold Hague, who named the Lamar River in 1885, probably transferred the name to the valley.

LAMBREQUIN SPRING   Map #3

This hot spring in the Quagmire (formerly Camp) Group of Lower Geyser Basin is located west and southwest of Snort Geyser. Geologist Walter H. Weed called the spring #30 of the "Camp" Group in 1887, describing it as a

> Basin 25' × 27' —Water surface 11' × 12' —Temp. 179.6°— No recent deposit of hard sinter—Water apparently boils at the east edge. Bottom of basin of soft sintery sand into which the foot sinks—Deposit under water [is] white—water clear green (USGS, Box 53, vol. 28, p. 61).

Weed also called the spring "Curtain Spring." He probably used the name lambrequin, which means a scarf or valance, because he saw the spring as having a curtain in it.

LANDSLIDE CREEK†   Map #1

This stream flows north into the Yellowstone River from Sepulcher Mountain west of Mammoth. A member of the third Hayden survey to Yellowstone named it in 1878, because the creek runs down the north slopes of Sepulcher Mountain, which slide regularly.

LANGFORD CAIRN†   Map #4

This 8,842-foot-high peak is the first knob above Terrace Point on the east side of the Southeast Arm of Yellowstone Lake. The peak seems to have been named because of Chief Naturalist David Condon's misconception that it was from this hill in 1870 that N. P. Langford observed and sketched Yellowstone Lake. A cairn is a pile of rocks often used by Indians and explorers to mark travel routes and tops of mountains.

Park photographer Jack Haynes made a trip around Yellowstone Lake and built a cairn of rocks on top of this hill on August 29, 1924. This may be the source of Condon's misinformation. Haynes also thought this was the hill climbed by Langford and Lt. G. C. Doane, but the one they climbed was actually present-day Colter Peak.

LAUNDRY SPRING   Map #3

This hot spring in the Myriad Group of Upper Geyser Basin is a shallow spring connected to and immediately west of Abuse Spring. A. C. Peale described it in 1878 as only a "basin one to two feet deep, with a hole" (Hayden, *Twelfth Annual Report*, p. 240). Connected to Abuse Spring, Laundry Spring was the more active of the two springs in 1878. During the 1880s, geologist Walter Weed did some renumbering of springs in the Myriad Group and reversed the positions of the springs. But in 1886, Weed noted the correct location of Laundry Spring, which was described as having a ledge that had been physically cut out a bit to make room for people to boil their clothing. Tourists used Laundry Spring during the early 1880s to wash their clothes. At that time, Laundry Spring boiled and foamed from 2 to 3 feet high, from heat or soap or both. In recent years, Laundry Spring has been improperly referred to as "West Spectacle Pool" or "West Pool."

LAVA CREEK*   Map #1

Called "Falls Creek" in 1877 by Col. O. M. Poe, this stream flows north to the Gardner River from the Washburn Range. Members of the third Hayden survey called it "East Fork of the Gardiner River" in 1878, but in 1885 members of the Hague parties renamed it Lava Creek because of the basaltic and rhyolitic lavas that dominate the area.

LAVENDER SPRING   Map #3

This hot spring in the Grand Group of the Upper Geyser Basin is located north and a little east of Calida Pool. Geologist Walter Weed named the spring in 1887. He described it as

> Lavender Spg—5' × 8½' —bowl—2½' × 3' —10' deep— Hard brown gray deposit at border. Apple-green sinter about springs nearby. Coloring proved to be organic—4 springs, the largest 4½' × 6' —(USGS, Box 53, vol. 28, p. 121).

There is also a Lavender Spring in the Camp Group of Shoshone Geyser Basin.

LEATHER POOL   Map #3

This hot spring in the Fountain Group of Lower Geyser Basin seems to have been called "Mystic Lake" in 1881 by F. Jay Haynes, who used the name in a caption for one of his photographs. By 1904, however, the USGS map labeled the spring "Leather" because of its thick brown coating of low temperature algae. Capt. J. W. Barlow noted in 1871 that this hot water algae was "formed in large sheets resembling raw hides in a vat," and Lt. G. C. Doane saw in these hot springs "what appear to be raw bullock hides, as they look in a tanner's vat" (in Bonney and Bonney, *Battle Drums*, p. 330).

The local name for the spring soon became "White Sulphur Spring" because of the spring's white border of sinter and its sulphury smell. Around 1927, however, Jack Haynes and Horace Albright, as part of a Park place-names committee, revived the name Leather.

Throughout its known history, Leather Pool appears to have changed temperature, water level, and general appearance several times. In 1915, it had clear boiling water from two vents and was still notable for its sinter rim. But sometime between 1915 and 1959, the temperature of the spring again lowered, allowing the leather algae to grow again. This change may have occurred by the 1920s and prompted the name change back to Leather Pool. The 1959 Yellowstone earthquake caused a drop in water level in Leather Pool and a rise in temperature, which again killed the leathery algae. Also, geyser-like eruptions occurred from the spring, leaving the spring with an opaque, turquoise hue. The earthquake also created the Red Spouter Geyser nearby, which Park Geologist George Marler believed to be the reason for the loss of heat and the drop in water level of Leather Pool.

Leather Pool is probably most famous for having served as a hot water supply for the "geyser baths" of the Fountain Hotel from 1891 to 1916, about a quarter-mile to the north on a tree-covered hill. A cut was made in the north side of Leather Pool, and a pipe was laid from the pool across the meadow to the hotel. The route of the pipe (laid in 1890 during construction of the hotel) can still be seen across the meadow.

LeHARDYS RAPIDS† Map #2

These cascades on the Yellowstone River are located about 3 miles north of the Fishing Bridge area. Members of the W. A. Jones expedition (see Jones Pass) named the rapids for Paul LeHardy (1845-1929), a civilian topographer with that expedition. On August 7, 1873, LeHardy and his partner (a man named Gabbet) left the main party at the outlet of Yellowstone Lake for a raft trip down the Yellowstone River to sketch the stream and make soundings. Expecting to meet the rest of their party at the Lower Falls, the two men loaded guns, bedding, food, and a gridiron onto their makeshift raft. About 3 miles later they ran into rapids, and the rear end of the raft was sucked to the bottom next to a conical rock. Saving what they could and caching the rest, they followed a game trail down the river, where they spent the night near present-day Mud Volcano.

Paul LeHardy was born in Belgium in 1845. After his imigration to the U.S., he helped survey the Tennessee Valley in 1871 and later worked on New York's Oswego Canal.

LEMONADE CREEK† Map #1

This intermittent stream, which originates at Ampitheater Springs and flows west to Obsidian Creek, was known as "Green Creek" as early as 1880 because of its color. The creek's light green color later suggested the name Lemonade Creek. During the 1880s, the tourist road forked at Lemonade Creek and went over Hibbard's Pass and past Ampitheater Springs, following "Green Creek" for a short distance. Stories of stagecoach drivers dipping water from the creek and carrying a "small bag of sugar along to treat their party to cold lemonade hardly distinguishable from the real article" (Randall, *Footprints*, p. 57) probably were responsible for the name. Jack Haynes and Horace Albright restored the name to the stream in 1927-1928 after it had been in local use since at least the turn of the century. The water from Lemonade Creek, although clear and green, is warm, acidic, and unfit to drink.

LEMONADE LAKE† Map #1

This small, intermittent, acidic, and shallow pond is located at the west base of Roaring Mountain. In 1929, Park Superintendent Roger W. Toll named the pond because of its yellow-green color or its proximity to Lemonade Creek or both.

LEWIS CANYON FALLS Maps #3

This place name refers to two separate waterfalls on the Lewis River in Lewis Canyon, about 2 miles south of Lewis Lake: an upper one 80 feet high and a lower one 50 feet high. In 1895, Hiram Chittenden referred to "Lewis Canyon Falls, upper," possibly present-day Lewis Falls, and "Lewis Canyon Falls, lower." Government scientist Barton W. Evermann noted in 1892:

> About halfway between the Upper Falls and the mouth of Crawfish Creek, they came upon a very beautiful fall of considerable size. The stream is divided by a small island into two parts, the larger portion of the water flowing around to the right of the island. This part was estimated to be at least 50 feet wide and to fall almost perpendicularly at least 30 feet, then descend about 20 feet more in a very steep raid, in which the stream widens out very much. That part of the stream passing around to the left of the small rocky island is about 8 feet wide, and it comes down in a series of very steep cascades and two principal falls, each apparently vertical ("A Reconnaissance," p. 21).

The upper Lewis Canyon Falls is a cascade of about 80 feet, of which 20 feet at the top is perpendicular.

LEWIS LAKE*   Map #3

At 108 feet deep, Lewis Lake is Yellowstone's third largest lake. Frank Bradley of the second Hayden survey to Yellowstone, who named the lake in 1872, wrote: "As it had no name, so far as we could ascertain, we decided to call it Lewis's Lake, in memory of that gallant explorer, Captain Merriwether [sic] Lewis" (Hayden, *Sixth Annual Report*, p. 249). In 1804-1806, Meriwether Lewis and William Clark led a government expedition to explore the newly acquired "Louisiana Purchase" lands. They were to make trade agreements with Indians, find a water route to the Pacific Ocean for commerce, and collect scientific information about the western environment. The expedition passed north of Yellowstone Park by about 50 miles, so Lewis never saw the lake. The first record of Lewis Lake appeared in fur-trapper Osborne Russell's journal of 1839.

LEWIS RIVER*   Map #3

This river drains Shoshone and Lewis lakes and is a tributary of the Snake River. In 1872, members of the second Hayden survey called the river "Lake Fork" because it was a fork of the Snake that began in those two lakes. An 1876 map showed the river marked "Lewis Fork" (of the Snake), named from Lewis Lake.

LIBERTY CAP*   Map #1

This 37-foot-high extinct hot spring cone of travertine is located at Mammoth Hot Springs. F. V. Hayden named the cone in 1871 for its resemblance to the peaked caps worn during the French Revolution. Hayden believed that the cone was an extinct geyser, but geologists now think that it was once merely a flowing hot spring that was eventually sealed off by travertine that deposited at its top. Dormant at the time of its discovery in 1871, Liberty Cap is estimated to be 2,500 years old.

Park Superintendent P. W. Norris, fearing that the dry cone would fall over, braced it with timbers in 1878. In 1888, G. L. Henderson, who lived near Liberty Cap, wrote:

> it looks like a silent sentinel guarding the gate of Wonderland; or like an ancient witness who could, if it would, reveal the sealed secrets of the past. It has more faces than Janus and more eyes than the fabled Argus (*Yellowstone Park Manual*, p. 1).

LIBERTY POOL*   Map #3

This hot spring in the Sawmill Group of the Upper Geyser Basin, located about 350 feet southeast of Sawmill Geyser, has an interesting history. Liberty Pool was not always so quiet as it is now. Yellowstone's first military superintendent, Captain Moses Harris, named Liberty Pool on July 4, 1887, the day that a party of tourists first observed it spouting 50 to 75 feet high. That year, Walter H. Weed, who also observed eruptions of Liberty Pool, wrote:

> At present the geyser basin is circular, 7 ft. in diameter, formed of hard gray deposit, and rudely funnel-like in shape.... In action, it sends up a jet or rather succession of jets, 50 to 75 feet high. The duration is brief, 15-20 seconds. As yet its period, if it have [sic] any definite interval, is unknown. The Geyser has been christened the Liberty, by Capt. Harris, acting Superintendent of the Yellowstone Park, the name being suggested by the date of the first observed eruption ("The Liberty," pp. 1-2).

LIGHTNING HILL   Map #1

This 8,975-foot-high hill is located immediately south of the junction of the East and North forks of Specimen Creek in the northwest corner of the Park. Lightning Hill seems to have been named during the 1920s because rangers climbed it after electrical storms to look for signs of forest fires.

LILY PAINT POTS   Map #4

This nearly extinct thermal mudpot area is located on the southeast side of the Southeast Arm of Yellowstone Lake near the mouth of Beaverdam Creek. Park photographer F. Jay Haynes named it in about 1891 for his wife, Lily V. Snyder Haynes. The name appeared on an 1892 map in a guidebook written by A. B. Guptill and later on maps in editions of *Haynes Guide*, 1902-1908.

LIMEKILN SPRINGS*   Map #3

This group of several small hot springs in the Grand Group of the Upper Geyser Basin is located about 175 feet west of Witches Caldron. In 1878, members of the third Hayden survey (probably A. C. Peale) named these springs. Peale wrote: "The Limekiln Springs are so called from the fancied resemblance of the mound on which they are located to a deserted limekiln" (Hayden, *Twelfth Annual Report*, p. 219). A limekiln is a furnace in which limestone, shells, and so forth are burned to make lime. The resemblance of some thermal areas to limekilns has been noted since the earliest days in the Park.

LINEN SPRING   Map #3

This hot spring in the Myriad Group of Upper Geyser Basin is located just east and a little south of Cousin Geyser. In 1878, Henry Gannett or J. E. Mushbach of the

Lone Star Geyser, 1884

F.J. Haynes

third Hayden survey named Linen Spring and included it on their hand-drawn notebook map. An investigation of the area in 1981, using the Gannett/Mushbach map and A. C. Peale's descriptions, indicated that Linen Spring is two round springs very close together, each about 6 feet in diameter and separated by a sinter bridge 4 feet wide. The complex is acid in nature and was partly dried up in 1981. It is not known why the name Linen was selected for this spring complex, but the survey members also named two other Myriad Group springs "Silk Spring" and "Cotton Spring."

LION GEYSER*   Map #3

Lion Geyser is a major geyser in the Lion Group in the Upper Geyser Basin. Park Superintendent P. W. Norris named it in 1877 evidently because of the sound the geyser made during eruption—a sudden gush of steam accompanied by a hollow "roar." In 1886, tourist George Wingate wrote that

> the clump of geysers known as the "Lion," the "Lioness and Cubs," are close together and derive their name[s] from the growling noise which they emit even when not in a state of eruption (*Through the Yellowstone Park*, p. 109).

G. L. Henderson also noted in 1885 that the names of the Lion, Lioness, and Cubs "are given on account of the grumbling and growling that accompanies their eruption" (*Yellowstone Park Manual*, p. 4).

LITTLE AMERICA FLATS   Map #2

This is the name of the flat meadow area along the Northeast Entrance Road between Junction Butte and the east road crossing of the Lamar River. The name was in local use as early as 1956, apparently because the flag was raised and lowered here at a National Park Service road camp.

LITTLE GIBBON FALLS   Map #1

Originally named "Upper Falls of the Gibbon" in about 1920, this 25-foot-high waterfall on the Gibbon River is located about a half-mile southeast of Ice Lake. Fish researcher John Seamans re-named it in 1939 because it resembled the larger Gibbon Falls some distance downstream.

LITTLE MEADOWS   Map #1

This little-known place name was given to the very small meadow southeast of Capitol Hill in the Mammoth area by Park Superintendent P. W. Norris in 1881.

LITTLE SPECIMEN CREEK   Map #2

This creek is a long branch of Crystal Creek and runs immediately east and parallel to that stream on the north side of Specimen Creek. Geologist Walter Weed named the creek in 1888, transferring the name from the western end of Specimen Ridge, which Arnold Hague had called "Little Specimen."

LITTLE TRUMPETER LAKE   Map #2

In 1977, the U.S. Fish and Wildlife Service gave this name to the small lake just northwest of Trumpeter Lake.

LITTLES FORK*   Map #3

W. C. Gregg and USGS topographer C. H. Birdseye named this branch of the Gregg Fork of the Bechler River in 1921-1922 for Ranger Raymond G. Little. Gregg explored the Bechler region in 1920-1921 and later wrote: "Of those rangers I have found only two, [James] McBride and Little, who have ever been through this section [of the Park] and know all its beauty" (*Saturday Evening Post*, November 20, 1920).

Ray Little worked in Yellowstone as a civilian army scout from late 1911 until the end of the military administration in the Park and then as a ranger until 1922. Little later reminisced about the naming of Little's Fork:

> there was some disagreement [in 1920] among the scouts and others who had explored the Bechler River country. McBride and others claimed there were only three forks of the river, but I had been riding the country between Old Faithful and Bechler river, and I knew there were four forks, and I came in for a lot of kidding. . . . When . . . Col. C. H. Birdseye . . . got into the Bechler river country and he found I was right about that fourth fork, [he] told me that since I had found it and had been on the receiving end of so much ridicule over it, he would name it Little Fork. And he did (*Park County News*, June 19, 1952).

Little died in 1961 at Corwin Springs, Montana.

LONE SPRING   Map #3

This hot spring in the Thud Group of Lower Geyser Basin is located about 500 yards east of Thud Geyser. Visitors at the Fountain Hotel, which was open from 1891 to 1916 and was razed in 1927, used the area around Lone Spring as a dumping ground. In 1948, workers found broken dishes, bottles, cans, and other trash from the hotel in the spring's crater. Also during the Fountain Hotel period, there was a bath house built near Lone Spring. Apparently, the water cooled in the pipes laid between the spring and the bath house. After the hotel was abandoned, the bath house was left to disintegrate and the pipes to rust.

LONE STAR GEYSER*   Map #3

This major geyser in the Third Geyser Basin of the Firehole River is located about 5 miles upstream from Old Faithful. In 1872, the Hayden survey party under Frank Bradley saw the geyser and mentioned "a fine profile of a mild-featured human face done in the bead-work" of the cone (Hayden, *Sixth Annual Report*, p. 242). Bradley reported that it spouted 20 to 70 feet high about every 2 hours, and he named it "Solitary" because of its isolated position. But who named it Lone Star Geyser?

S. P. Panton (a Northern Pacific Railroad surveyor), A. H. Sanborn, and several other men surveying the Park in 1882 claimed that they named Lone Star. Panton recalled that the party named the geyser while searching for a pass south of the Upper Geyser Basin. He mentioned that "in talking of old times, Sanborn expressed his belief that it was on his suggestion that we named Lone Star Geyser" (*Billings Gazette*, December 26, 1961).

This may be, but Park visitor Joseph M. V. Cochran remembered naming the geyser 8 years before Panton surveyed Yellowstone:

> To the best of my recollection it was in 1874 when I was out with Col. W. D. Pickett of Louisville, Kentucky on a hunting trip. We were camped near Old Faithful Geyser. I went out hunting for a bear and was on a high butte overlooking the basin when I saw the steam from a geyser above the trees and went down to it. There were game trails near but no blazed trails nor trails showing signs of having been traveled by horses, nor any signs of old campfires—in fact, nothing to show that anyone had ever been there before.
>
> The next day I returned with Col. Pickett and took with me a board off a cracker box and nailed it up on a tree and printed on it the name "Lone Star Geyser." On this trip we did not see anyone in either the upper or lower basins but on the way out met Mr. [H. B.] Calfee and Mr. Catlan near Sulphur Mountain. They were on their way into the basins to take pictures of the geysers. I told them about the Lone Star Geyser and gave them directions how to find it from Old Faithful Geyser. If they took views, as they intended, they would be the first ever taken of Lone Star Geyser ("The Naming of Lone Star Geyser," YNN, p. 47).

Col. W. D. Pickett, in his *Hunting at High Altitudes*, confirmed that he visited the Park with Joseph Cochran, but he gave the year as 1879. During the 1880s, photographs of the geyser by F. Jay Haynes popularized the name Lone Star Geyser. The name has nothing to do with Texas, the Lone Star state.

LONE TREE ROCK   Map #1

Lone Tree Rock is located in the Gibbon Canyon .3 mile north of Beryl Spring and near the west bank of the Gibbon River. During stagecoach days, from 1880 to 1916, stagecoach drivers pointed out this boulder to tourists. This large rhyolite boulder was a prominent feature during those early days, because the road forded the Gibbon River nearby and a lodgepole pine grew right out of the rock. Lone Tree Rock appears to have been named in 1881 by Park photographer F. Jay Haynes, who included it in his photo catalogue that year.

LOOKOUT CLIFFS   Map #1

Park Superintendent P. W. Norris gave this name to the high south walls of the Madison Canyon west of Mount Haynes in 1880. From the top of these cliffs, which are prominently visible from the Targhee Pass area west of Yellowstone Park, Norris could see to the west of the Park for miles.

LOOKOUT POINT*   Map #2

In 1880, Park Superintendent P. W. Norris either named this spot or took the name from local use. An observation point on the north rim of the Grand Canyon of the Yellowstone River, Lookout Point was used as a viewing point by many early tourists. Norris built a railing at the point, and it subsequently was known as "Point Lookout," "Mount Lookout," "Lookout Rock" and "Prospect Point." Since the 1870s, writers have romantically described the beauty of the view from Lookout Point. Robert Strahorn wrote in 1880: ". . . one seems suspended 'tween heaven and earth" (*Enchanted Land*, p. 30). And H. Banard Leckler's impression in 1881 was "even standing before it one can hardly realize it is not fairyland" (*American Field*, March 22, 1884, p. 286). Two other places in the Park bear the name Lookout Point: one at Mammoth and one on Shoshone Lake.

LOOKOUT TERRACE   Map #1

This hill is located on the old Norris stagecoach road between Canyon Creek and the far south end of the Firehole Canyon. In 1880, this hill was on the main tourist road, which ran from the east side of Gibbon Falls down a long hill, crossed Canyon Creek, ascended the plateau that separates the Gibbon and Firehole rivers, and reached the Firehole about 3 miles above the Cascades of the Firehole. Today, the road is a portion of the Howard Eaton Trail, but wagon wheel ruts from the early days can still be seen.

Park Superintendent P. W. Norris probably named the hill because of the view that visitors standing on the plateau had of the Lower Geyser Basin. First named in 1878 when Norris built the road, Lookout Terrace got its formal designation in 1880. Many early accounts of visits to the Park mention this spot.

By 1887, stagecoach driver guides, such as Elwood "Billy" Hofer, referred to the hill as "Teton Hill," because tourists could also see the Teton Mountains from that vantage point. As late as 1895, when the road was falling into disuse because of the newer Mesa Road to Firehole Falls, a guidebook still mentioned the well-known view of the Tetons.

To reach Lookout Terrace, follow the old road north from a point about 3.5 miles south of the Firehole Cascades and near an intermittent pond on the east side of the old road. The road at that point begins the ascent of Lookout Terrace hill for the next half mile or so.

LOST CREEK* Map #2

Lost Creek flows northeast into Elk Creek from Prospect Peak, due west of Tower Fall. The stream had several early names. In 1871, Capt. John W. Barlow named it "Meadow Brook," and the Hayden surveys in 1871-1872 called it "Meadow Creek." Col. O. M. Poe, who visited the Park in 1877 with Gen. William T. Sherman, found wild strawberries growing along the stream and named it "Strawberry Brook." Geologist William H. Holmes named it Lost Creek in 1878. As he explained "I have called [it] Lost Creek, because it apparently sinks from sight in the lower part of its course . . ." (Hayden, *Twelfth Annual Report*, p. 44).

LOST LAKE Map #3

This mysterious lake evidently existed at one time somewhere near the headwaters of Big Thumb Creek on or near the Continental Divide between Shoshone Lake and West Thumb Village. In 1871, F. V. Hayden reported: "We camped at night on the shore of a lake which seemed to have no outlet. It is simply a depression which receives the drainage of the surrounding hills. . . . the lake was about two miles long and one wide, and it is doubtful whether it had ever been observed by human beings before" (Hayden, *Fifth Annual Report*, p. 127). The several maps of the Hayden surveys variously showed this unnamed lake on both sides of the Continental Divide.

Superintendent P. W. Norris's maps in 1879 and 1880 showed the lake resting squarely on the Divide; he labeled it "Two Ocean Pond." In 1886, a USGS map showed it on the Atlantic side of the divide. Shown on maps since 1871 and named in 1885, Lost Lake could not be found by the 1930s.

In 1937, following many inquiries from fishermen and others as to why this good-sized lake could not be found, Ranger Trusten Peery asked the advice of old-timers in the area. He was told that Billy Ferrell had succeeded in finding the lake in 1915 while searching for a lost horse. Ferrell had reportedly tried his luck fishing at Lost Lake with splendid success. A packer named Jack Mears told Peery that he had often visited the lake to fish, saying it was about 3 miles southwest of West Thumb Village and had been misplaced on the map.

Intrigued by the mystery, Ranger Frank R. Oberhansley set out to find the lake on August 8, 1938. He took four and one half hours to find it and reported that it drained into Shoshone Lake. Nonetheless, the lake does not show up in aerial photographs. It is possible that Lost Lake, like other glacial lakes, has filled with vegetation.

Two other lakes in the Park have been named Lost Lake: one near Tower Fall and one in the Mammoth area.

LOVELY PASS† Map #2

Lovely Pass is a low pass between Mist Creek and the headwaters of Willow Creek east of Pelican Valley. In 1881, Park Superintendent P. W. Norris opened a trail that crossed this pass between Raven Creek and Mist Creek. His map that year showed "Pass Lovely" on it, and he referred to one of his campsites in the area as "Camp Lovely."

**LOWER FALLS OF THE
YELLOWSTONE RIVER*** Map #2

This 308-foot-high waterfall on the Yellowstone River is the Park's highest. The earliest claim of white explorers seeing the falls came from Baptiste Ducharne, an early trapper who at the age of 102 remembered seeing the Lower Falls in 1824 and 1826. Ducharne was also a member of an 1839 party that claimed to have seen the falls. Jim Bridger and a small party that included James Gemmell visited the falls in 1846, and in 1851 Bridger drew a map for Fr. Pierre-Jean DeSmet that showed "Falls 250 Feet."

During the 1860s, newspapers carried outrageous stories of a huge mythical waterfall. An 1867 story described the falls as on

> the face of a mountain thousands of feet, the spray rising several hundred. A pebble was timed by a watch in dropping from an overhanging crag of one perpendicular fall, and is said to have required eleven and a half seconds to strike the river below (in Haines, *Yellowstone National Park*, p. 38).

In 1868, another story claimed that "where the water of the lake breaks over the northern face of this cross ridge, there is a perpendicular fall of fifteen hundred feet over one cliff . . ." (in Haines, *Yellowstone National Park*, p. 39).

In 1869, the Cook-Folsom-Peterson party made the first detailed observations of the Lower Falls, measuring it at 360 feet. David Folsom wrote that "language is entirely

James C. McCartney's 1871 cabin, October 4, 1887

F. Jay Haynes in his Twin Six Packard on the Madison River road, 1916

inadequate to convey a just conception of the awful grandeur and sublimity of this masterpiece of nature's handiwork" (*Western Monthly*, July 1870, p. 64). The celebrated 1870 Washburn party waxed poetic in their descriptions of the falls. N. P. Langford wrote: "A grander scene than the lower cataract of the Yellowstone was never witnessed by mortal eyes" (*Scribner's Monthly*, May 1871, p. 13). And Cornelius Hedges penned that it was "the grandest waterfall in the world, and surely destined at no distant day to become a shrine for a world-wide pilgrimage" (*Helena Daily Herald*, October 15, 1870).

During the highest runoff period of the year (usually June), some 63,500 gallons of water per second are estimated to pass over Lower Falls. By November, the amount has usually dropped to about 5,000 gallons per second.

The green color of the water that extends part-way down the falls is caused by a notch in the riverbed at the top of the falls, which allows the river to retain some of its natural green color instead of immediately breaking into spray.

MADISON LAKE*   Map #3

This small lake at the head of the Firehole River and due west of Shoshone Lake is the source of the Madison River. Frank Bradley of the second Hayden survey named the lake in 1872. In the September 1873 *American Journal of Science and Arts*, Bradley reported: "we found the source of the stream [Firehole River] . . . in a pond covering about sixty acres, to which we were obliged to transfer the name Madison Lake" (p. 201). He made the transfer because "as the ultimate lake-source of the Madison River, [it] is the only proper possessor of the name Madison Lake" (Hayden, *Sixth Annual Report*, p. 243).

In 1895, Hiram M. Chittenden noted that Madison Lake was "with possibly the exception of Red Rock Lake, the source of the Jefferson, . . . further from the sea by direct water-course than any other lake on the globe" (*Yellowstone*, p. 237).

MADISON RIVER*   Map #1

The Madison is one of the three main tributary branches of the Missouri River. Beginning in the Park at Madison Junction, at the confluence of the Firehole and Gibbon rivers, the river was named by explorers Meriwether Lewis and William Clark on July 27, 1805. Lewis wrote:

> On examining the two streams [Madison and Jefferson rivers at Three Forks], it became difficult to decide which was the larger or real Missouri. They are each ninety yards wide, and so perfectly similar in character and appearance that they seemed to have been formed in the same mould. We

were therefore induced to discontinue the name of Missouri, and gave to the southwest branch the name of Jefferson in honor of the president of the United States, and the projector of the enterprise. We called the middle branch Madison, after James Madison secretary of state (in Coues, *History of the Expedition*, 2:446).

The river contains brown and rainbow trout as well as small numbers of whitefish, grayling, and brook trout, and is a nationally known blue-ribbon trout stream. In their project reports, members of the U.S. Fish and Wildlife Service rate the Madison River as the world's second best trout stream after the Yellowstone River.

MAE WEST CURVE   Map #2

This 180° curve on the Grand Loop Road is located less than a mile north of the Chittenden Road on Mount Washburn. The name seems to have been given sometime before 1940. Tour bus drivers probably named the sharp curve because of its resemblance to film star Mae West's famous bustline.

MAIDENS GRAVE SPRING   Map #3

In the old Marshall's Hotel area of the Lower Geyser Basin, this hot spring is on the right bank of the Firehole River, about 650 yards south of Hygeia Spring. Apparently, guidebook writer W. C. Riley named this spring in 1889 and included it in a book of Park photos. The spring's name came from its location about half a mile upstream from the grave of Mattie S. Culver, which is at the present-day Nez Perce picnic area near the confluence of the Firehole River and Nez Perce Creek.

Mattie Culver was the wife of E. C. Culver, the winter keeper of the Marshall Hotel during the 1880s. She died in childbirth (or shortly thereafter) in early March 1889, just before Riley wrote his guidebook. Because the ground was frozen, Mrs. Culver was put inside of two barrel halves until the spring thaw. A baby girl survived and was sent to live with her aunt in Spokane, Washington. E. C. Culver remained in the Park for years after his young wife's death. "While all know the story of his faded dreams," an acquaintance wrote in 1901, "not even the roughest cowpuncher or mountaineer will allude to it in his presence."

MAIN SPRING(S)   Map #1

Main Spring refers to one or more of the intermittent large hot springs located in the center of the eastern edge of the Main Terrace of Mammoth Hot Springs. Originally, the spring had the largest reservoir and discharged the greatest volume of water of any of the hot springs at Mammoth. The 1871 Hayden survey map showed the name "Main

Hot Sp" and listed the temperature of the spring as 155°F. Tourist H. Banard Leckler wrote an excellent description of the Main Springs in 1881:

> It was a boiling pool, fifty feet in diameter, of the clearest water that ever was seen. The water shaded the sides and bottom with most charming tints of blue and green. The basins made by the overflow from this spring were superb; such delicate formations covered the walls and bottoms as one would never believe possible unless he looked upon them; many were colored with the most magnificent, varied and exquisite shades conceivable (*American Field*, April 12, 1884, p. 360).

MAMMOTH CRYSTAL SPRING   Map #4

Mammoth Crystal Spring, located below Sylvan Pass, is the source of Middle Creek. In 1901, while surveying the East Entrance Road, Hiram Chittenden noticed this large, cold spring about a mile east of present-day Eleanor Lake: "Just at the foot of this descent [from Sylvan Pass] and within a short distance of the North Fork of Middle Creek is a very large cold-water spring from which a strong, clear stream flows" (in Baldwin, *Enchanted Enclosure*, p. 106).

In 1904, tourist Carrie McLaughlin passed the spring on what was then Chittenden's new road and saw a sign at the spring that inexplicably said "polywater." A 1905 tourist, Charles Heath, referred to the spring as the "Mammoth Crystal Spring, the largest in the Park" (*Trial of a Trail*, p. 42).

MAMMOTH HOT SPRINGS*   Map #1

These famous travertine hot springs are located near Park Headquarters not far from Gardiner, Montana. The earliest map reference to these springs is on Capt. Washington Hood's 1839 map, which showed "Boiling Spring White Sulphur Banks" at a location on "Gardner's Fork." Hood drew his map with information provided by fur-trapper Bill Sublette, and the name could have been Sublette's. Jim Bridger included a "Sulphur Mt." on "Gardener's Cr." in 1851 for Fr. DeSmet's map, but J. W. Gunnison, in *The Mormons, or, Latter-Day Saints* (1852), wrote that Bridger had described to him the "Great Springs, so hot that meat is readily cooked in them, and as they descend on the successive terraces, [they] afford at length delightful baths" (pp. 151-152).

An 1869 map showed the area only as "Hot Spgs" on "Hot Spring Ck," and in 1871 Hayden gave the name "White Mountain Hot Springs" to the locale. Other names were later applied to Mammoth, including "Great Soda Mountain," "Soda Mountain Springs," "Snowy Mountain," "White Mountain," "White Sulphur Mountain," "White Sulphur Springs," "Hot Springs Terraces," "Pink Terraces," "Springs Mountain," "Grand Terraces," "Terrace Mountain Hot Springs," and variations of "Gardiner's River Hot Springs."

Visitors were at Mammoth quite early. There is one report of a visit to Mammoth in 1830 by Louis Bleau and about 15 Crow Indian families. But probably the first whites to see Mammoth were a party of 40 men led by fur-trapper Baptiste Ducharne in 1839. Other early visitors may have included James Gemmell and Jim Bridger in 1846, "Uncle" Joe Brown in 1866, and James Dunlevy in 1867.

In 1870, the Washburn party failed to see the Mammoth Hot Springs, but the loss of Truman Everts from their party resulted indirectly in the naming of the springs. Harry R. Horr, one of the volunteers who helped rescue Everts, visited the springs and decided to locate a business there. He and James McCartney returned to the area in 1871 and built bath houses to serve as a crude spa. Twenty years later, on May 16, 1891, while trying to recover some money for his original "improvements" that the government had confiscated, Horr wrote, "I gave the springs the name they now bear" (doc. #1049, YNP Archives).

A. C. Peale, whose 1871 party under F. V. Hayden received credit for discovering the springs, wrote:

> We were totally unprepared to find them so beautiful and extensive. Before us lay a high white hill, composed of calcareous sediment deposited from numerous hot springs. The whole mass looked like some grand cascade that had been suddenly arrested in its descent, and frozen (Hayden, *Fifth Annual Report*, p. 174).

Hayden noted that a number of invalids were already living at the springs in tents, "and their praises were enthusiastic in favor of the sanitary effects of the springs. Some of them were used for drinking and others for bathing purposes" (*Scribner's Monthly*, February 1872, pp. 389-391).

Park Superintendent P. W. Norris selected Mammoth Hot Springs as the site for Park Headquarters in 1878. He was attracted by its "nearness and accessibility throughout the year, through one of the ... main entrances to the park ... as well as accessibility to the other prominent points of interest in the Park" (*Fifth Annual Report*, p. 23).

The Mammoth Hot Springs deposit about 2 tons of travertine (calcium carbonate) limestone per day. The material is soft, compared to the quartz-like material in the geyser basins farther south, and it is believed that the water temperatures here are too low for geysers to form. Individual springs can deposit as much as 22 inches per year of travertine. As a whole, the springs are estimated to discharge about 500 gallons of water per minute. Although the individual locations of springs change constantly, the amount of water discharged from the area is believed to remain fairly constant. Travertine buildup covers most of the area between Terrace Mountain and the Gardner River, and it is thought to be as much as 200 feet thick in some places.

Walter Weed's 1883 summation of the activity of the Mammoth Hot Springs still holds true:

> There is reason to believe that the springs of this group vary, somewhat from year to year, and in a lesser degree from month to month, so that a change in the flow of a spring (affecting the temperature), or in the temperature of the water cannot be accepted as proof of a permanent increase or decrease in activity (USGS, Box 56, vol. 3, p. 79).

MANTRAP CONE — Map #3

This hot spring in the Lower Group of West Thumb Geyser Basin is located some 500 feet north of King Geyser on a peninsula that extends into Yellowstone Lake. Walter Weed named it "Pier Spring" in 1886 because of a nearby boat dock. In 1946, naturalist John F. McMillan gave the name Mantrap Cone because several fishermen stepped into the spring and were burned.

MARBLE CLIFF SPRING* — Map #3

In 1872, members of the second Hayden survey gave the name Gray Spring to this spring in the Orion Group of Shoshone Geyser Basin. In 1937, the USBGN approved Gray Spring and Marble Cliff Spring as official names. Park personnel thought they were two separate springs, but they are in fact one and the same. The spring was named after what appear to be miniature marble cliffs in it.

MARBLE TERRACE — Map #1

Marble Terrace, located just south of Pulpit Terrace, refers to the east vertical side of the Main Terrace of Mammoth Hot Springs. In about 1887, USGS members applied the name "Marble Basins" to some of the hot spring pools on the eastern edge of the Main Terrace. Geologist Arnold Hague retained this name and included Marble Terrace on his map in 1904. The name refers to the alabaster-like quality and color of the travertine limestone.

MARIPOSA LAKE* — Map #4

This small lake is located in a meadow on Two Ocean Plateau about a mile south of Plateau Falls. It appears to have been named "Fish Lake" by members of the Hague parties of the USGS in about 1887. Sometime between 1896 and 1904, survey members changed the name to Mariposa Lake after the mariposa lily, which grows in the Park. *Mariposa* is the Spanish word for butterfly or moth.

MARSHALL'S PARK — Map #3

This large meadow is located on the north side of Madison Plateau on the Old Fountain Pack Trail, about 7 miles west of the mouth of Nez Perce Creek. Park Superintendent P. W. Norris probably named the meadow in 1880 for George W. Marshall (1846-1917), who built Marshall's Hotel (the second hotel in Yellowstone Park) near the mouth of Nez Perce Creek in 1880. The Old Fountain Pack Trail, one of the main Park roads from 1880 until after the turn of the century, was the route Marshall's guests took to reach the hotel. Marshall's daughter, Rosa Park Marshall, was the first white child born in Yellowstone Park.

MARY BAY* — Maps #2 and 4

Mary Bay on Yellowstone Lake is located north of Steamboat Point and south of the Pelican Valley. Artist Henry Wood Elliot of the 1871 Hayden survey named the bay for his girlfriend, Mary Force. Survey member A. C. Peale wrote in his diary: "The bay just before us is Mary's Bay, so named by Elliot after some lady to whom he has promised to introduce me next winter" (diary, p. 40). But the bay that Peale described was located east and south of Steamboat Point. In 1878, the survey transferred the name to present-day Mary Bay. Elliot returned from Yellowstone and married Alexandra Melovidov in 1872.

MARY LAKE* — Map #3

Rev. Edwin J. Stanley, who made a trip through the Park in 1873, named this small lake on Mary Mountain at the head of Nez Perce Creek. Five years later, Stanley wrote in *Rambles in Wonderland*:

> We passed along the bank of a lovely little lakelet, sleeping in seclusion in the shade of towering evergreens, by which it is sheltered from the roaring tempests. It is near the divide, and on its pebbly shore some members of our party unfurled the Stars and Stripes, and christened it Mary's Lake, in honor of Miss Clark, a young lady belonging to our party (p. 123).

Stanley remembered Miss Clark as "a young lady from Chicago, with vocal gifts that all admired." W. H. Todd, another member of the party, later recalled saving Miss Clark after she had been knocked from her horse by a low-hanging branch into a swampy place.

MASTIFF GEYSER* — Map #3

It was probably Walter Weed of the USGS who named this geyser in the Giant Group of the Upper Geyser Basin in about 1886. Weed did not give a reason for the name, but C. M. Bauer suggested in his 1937 book, *The Story of*

Hymen Terrace, the Mammoth Hotel, and a "Coated Specimen" tent at Mammoth Hot Springs, c. 1885

F.J. Haynes

Yellowstone Geysers, that the name was given "for its position as a watchdog close to the Giant Geyser" (p. 105). Its "growling" sound could also have been a factor in giving it the name. Mastiff eruptions were only 3 to 15 feet high until 1951, but that year it shot up to 100-foot-high eruptions in concert with nearby Giant Geyser.

McBRIDE LAKE† Map #2

The name of this small lake on the Buffalo Plateau near Slough Creek and northwest of Bison Peak was in local use as early as 1936. James McBride (1864-1942), who probably came to Yellowstone during the 1880s, worked and lived on the lake as a ranger at the upper Slough Creek station. An army private, who could be the same James McBride, was stationed at Upper Geyser Basin in 1886. Horace Albright has identified McBride as "a driver for a quartermaster wagon" and probably an army scout and one of the "first Park rangers" in the 1880s (*Oh Ranger!* pp. 18-19).

In 1900, McBride was an army scout in the Park, and in 1903 he guided President Theodore Roosevelt around Yellowstone. He had been a friend of Roosevelt's in Medora, North Dakota. In Gardiner, Roosevelt called him to the speakers' platform to personally thank him for the trip, saying, "Mac, oh Mac. Come up here, I want to see you." Another source, Dorr Yeager ("Some Old Timers of the Yellowstone," 1929), claimed that McBride had personally suggested building the North Entrance arch at Gardiner, which Roosevelt dedicated. McBride became an NPS ranger, and in 1920 he became Yellowstone's first chief ranger. He was stationed at Slough Creek from 1924 to at least 1927. F. Dumont Smith described him as

> a quiet man, big and silent like his habitat, with something of the free wildness of his friends. . . . Once in a while you will find him, in his forest clothes, in one of the great hotels, rolling and smoking endless cigarettes and observing the foolish ways of civilization (*Summit*, pp. 40-42).

McBride retired in 1929 and worked a gold mine at Crevice during his later years. He died on May 3, 1942, and was buried in the Gardiner cemetery in his Park Service uniform.

McCARTNEY CAVE* Map #1

This cave is a travertine sinkhole located in the field north of Capitol Hill and just southwest of the Horace Albright Visitor Center at Mammoth Hot Springs. Probably named by Park Superintendent P. W. Norris in about 1878, the cave honors James C. McCartney (1835-1907?), who built the first hotel in Yellowstone and served as the first mayor of Gardiner, Montana, in 1892.

If, as reported, McCartney discovered this cave in 1869, he was one of the earliest people to enter the Yellowstone area. Originally from Missouri, McCartney first came to Montana Territory in 1866 and later joined the mining stampede to Cooke City in 1870.

In 1871, McCartney and Harry Horr built the first hotel in Yellowstone, a log cabin located just northwest of Liberty Cap at Mammoth Hot Springs in what was then known as Clematis Gulch. McCartney tried to capitalize on the supposedly curative powers of the Mammoth Hot Springs waters, and even after the creation of the Park his crude "hotel" was the only accommodation until 1880.

Evicted from the Park by the government in about 1883, McCartney moved to Gardiner where he became a landowner and got a contract to supply grain to Camp Sheridan, the new army post at Mammoth. As mayor of Gardiner, he introduced President Roosevelt in 1903 at the laying of the cornerstone of the official Park entrance arch. He was so nervous at the ceremony that all he could say was "Ladies and Gentlemen, the President" (*Livingston Enterprise*, June 20, 1903).

McCartney's Cave was visited in the 1930s and reported on in *Yellowstone Nature Notes*. Explorer Scouts who studied the cave in some detail in 1954 discovered elk bones at a depth of 100 feet below the surface.

McMINN BENCH† Map #1

The McMinn Bench is the northern shoulder or extension of Mount Everts, the mountain ridge east of Mammoth Hot Springs. Army scouts applied this name to the rocky bench as early as 1897. As early as 1885, Silas McMinn took a claim for a coal mine on the bench with E. C. Clark to supply fuel to the National Hotel at Mammoth. In 1885, geologist Arnold Hague wrote about McMinn's coal operation on the face of Mount Everts:

> A tunnel has been run in on the coal, and several tons have been mined for domestic purposes at Mam[moth] Hot Sp[rings], but the coal is of a very poor quality, disintegrates readily, and leaves much ash. . . . The hotel pays $5 per ton for the coal. . . . The mine yields a little more than two tons per day (Hague papers, Box 12, "Notes on Mammoth Hot Springs," p. 18).

The name McMinn Bench was accepted by a 1956 Park place-names committee.

MEDUSA SPRING Map #1

Medusa Spring in the Back Basin of Norris Geyser Basin is located about 700 feet southwest of Green Dragon Spring and 250 feet west of South Gray Lake. In 1887, members of the Hague parties of the USGS (probably Walter Weed) named the spring, probably because the shape of the spring with its runoff channels reminded him of a giant medusa jellyfish. The spring may also have been named for the beautiful maiden in Greek mythology who was transformed into a winged monster with snakes for hair.

Medusa Spring is geologically unusual. Its deposits are hard sinter instead of the loosely sedimented silica that is characteristic of acidic springs. In 1984, Medusa erupted all summer to heights of 7 to 8 feet at 2-hour intervals.

MELDRUM MOUNTAIN†   Map #1

This turret-shaped, 9,552-foot-high peak in the Gallatin Range rises between Crescent Lake and the East Fork of Specimen Creek in the northwest corner of the Park. Known as early as 1933 as "Turret Peak," Meldrum Mountain got its new name in 1962, when Park photographer Jack Haynes suggested honoring John W. Meldrum (1843-1936), who was U.S. commissioner for Yellowstone National Park from 1894 to 1935.

Born in New York, Meldrum moved to Wyoming Territory in 1867, became clerk of the circuit court and was surveyor general; he was acting governor when Wyoming became a state in 1890. Having "read law," Meldrum was appointed U.S. Commissioner when that position was established in Yellowstone by the Lacey Act of 1894. He presided over trials of game poachers and stage robbers during his tenure.

MICROCOSM BASIN   Map #3

Microcosm Basin is located in the far southwestern portion of the Mud Volcanoes area (just west of Rush Lake) in the Lower Geyser Basin. Tour guide G. L Henderson named the area in 1884 because he saw a miniature world in the basin's pasty mud. Henderson had left Mammoth in November 1884 with Park Assistant Superintendent J. W. Weimer to explore "several hitherto almost unknown geyser basins in the vicinity of Marshall's Hotel" (*Livingston Enterprise*, November 29, 1884). After adding George Marshall to their party, the men discovered this basin and the area that the Hague survey would later call the Mud Volcanoes. In the December 6, 1884, *Livingston Enterprise*, Henderson described this area as:

> the most wonderfully beautiful spot we had seen and in so small a space, the circumference being only 120 yards. As the name implies it is a world in miniature.... The Microcosm Basin has been so seldom visited that it has escaped mutilation.

MIDWAY BLUFF*   Map #3

This 7,425-foot-high bluff is on the east side of Midway Geyser Basin and overlooks that basin. Over the years, it has been a favorite spot for photographers to get exceptional views of Grand Prismatic Spring and Excelsior Geyser. In 1878, members of the third Hayden survey named it "Bluff Point," but in 1979 a Park place-names committee recommended the name Midway Bluff to avoid duplication. The USBGN approved the change in 1981.

MIDWAY GEYSER BASIN*   Map #3

This group of hot springs had been named the "Half-way Group" in 1871 because it was between Lower and Upper geyser basins. In 1878, members of the third Hayden survey renamed it "Egeria Springs." The name Egeria has since been moved to a single spring in Midway Geyser Basin. Midway Geyser Basin has had a number of other names during its history, including "Excelsior Geyser Basin," "Middle (Geyser) Basin," "Hot Spring Lakes," "Devil's Half Acre," and, the most famous, "Hell's Half Acre."

Although Park Superintendent P. W. Norris used the name Midway Geyser Basin for the area in 1878, the name "Hell's Half Acre" was more popular. Rudyard Kipling, who visited Yellowstone in 1889, had this story told to him by his stagecoach driver:

> Once upon a time there was a carter who brought his team and a friend into the Yellowstone Park without due thought. Presently they came upon a few of the natural beauties of the place, and that carter turned his team into his friend's team howling: "Get back o' this, Jim. All Hell's alight under our noses." And they call the place Hell's Half Acre to this day (in Singleton, *Wonders of Nature*, p. 357).

This is a good example, even if it is unverified, of how local names gain currency.

MILLER CREEK*   Map #2

This creek flows west from Hoodoo Peak on the Absaroka divide to the Lamar River. Park Superintendent P. W. Norris named the stream in 1880 for prospector Adam "Horn" Miller (1825?-1913) after Miller had accompanied Norris, Henry Calfee (see Calfee Creek), George Rowland (see Rowland Pass), W. H. Parker (see Parker Peak), and a man named Handford on a trip to the area. "Five miles further on," Norris wrote in 1880, "we reached the creek which Miller recognized as the one he descended in retreating from the Indians in 1870, and which, on this account, we called Miller's Creek" (*Report of the Superintendent*, p. 7).

Called "Montana's Toughest Man," Adam "Horn" Miller came up the Missouri River in 1854 from St. Louis and settled in Emigrant, Montana, as early as 1864. He became friends with local prospectors Ed Hibbard (see Hibbard's Pass), A. Bart Henderson, James Gourley, Sam Shively, and "Uncle" Joe Brown. He first visited Yellowstone in 1864 with John C. Davis and participated in the naming of Cache Creek and Pelican Creek. In 1870, he discovered (with Pike Moore) his beloved Shoo Fly Mine on the south end of Miller Mountain near Cooke City, Montana, and he guided Norris on the new superintendent's arrival trip of 1877. Gay Randall was a child when Miller made frequent visits to his parents' OTO Ranch at Gardiner. He remembered him this way:

> Horn's steady, brown eyes with deep crow-foot wrinkles at the corners were clear and watchfully alert from long habit. He was a big man, over six feet, heavy-boned, deep-chested, with sinewy muscles like steel that bulged his knotted chest and arms with the free movement of his body. His hands were large and knotted, misshapen with crooked fingers and enlarged broken knuckles that came from bare knuckle fighting. His hair, usually long uncut, was streaked with an undeterminable shade of yellow that blended with his gray stained beard. The nose was large and crooked from being broken many times, the deep-lined, leathery skin, etched with a spiderweb of fine purplish veins, was as weather-beaten as old saddle leather. In the features of his broad heavy face, strong character was written in every seam . . . (*Footprints*, p. 96).

Miller died in 1913 in Cooke City, where he is buried.

MILLERS VALLEY   Map #2

Park Superintendent P. W. Norris named this long, narrow meadow on Miller Creek in 1881. It is probably the meadow 3 to 5 miles above the mouth of the stream.

MINERVA SPRING and
MINERVA TERRACE   Map #1

Located in the Mammoth Hot Springs, Minerva Spring creates Minerva Terrace. In 1878, A. C. Peale referred to Minerva Spring as "Cleopatra Spring" and wrote that it had been named by "some of the earlier visitors to the springs" (Hayden, *Twelfth Annual Report*, p. 75). Park Superintendent Patrick Conger may have changed the name to Minerva in 1882, but it is just as likely that G. L. Henderson named it. Henderson gave classical names to many Mammoth features, and he referred to this spring in 1884 as the "Fountain of Minerva." A third possibility is F. Jay Haynes, the official Park photographer, who published a captioned photo of Minerva in 1884.

Regardless of who gave the name, the change from "Cleopatra" to Minerva probably occurred because of the name confusion with "Cleopatra's Bowl" (see Cupid Spring), which had become quite large and well-known by that time. As early as 1886, Minerva was also known as the "Coating Terraces" because people used it for coating specimens with travertine to be sold as souvenirs.

Minerva was the Roman goddess of artists and sculptors.

MINUTE GEYSER*   MAP #1

Located some 250 feet northwest of Monarch Geyser Crater in the Back Basin of Norris Geyser Basin, Minute Geyser was named because it erupted about every 60 seconds during the 1880s. It was sometimes called "Minute Man" during the early days of the Park and was one of the Norris area's most watched geysers. Minute Geyser was also one of the most vandalized. A loading dock for stagecoach passengers was located here, and it appears that passengers threw items into the geyser as they waited for coaches.

Minute Geyser was amazingly regular and erupted quite often between 1878 and 1902, and it sometimes had larger than normal eruptions, varying from 5 to 40 feet. After 1902, Minute Geyser appears to have become gradually more unpredictable. In recent years, it has continually erupted a 4-foot-high spray only from its southeast (mound) vent. Its last recorded major eruption from its northwestern vent was in 1947, to heights of 50 feet.

A Park place-names committee in 1927 decided on the name "Minute Man" as opposed to Minute, but Chief Naturalist C. M. Bauer believed that the name did not refer to time but to min*ute*, as in small. In 1937, Bauer pushed that name through the official approval channels of the USBGN. While he saved the geyser's historic name, he was wrong about the pronunciation and meaning of the word.

MIRROR LAKE* and MIRROR PLATEAU*   Map #2

In 1871, members of the first Hayden survey discovered this small lake, which is located about a mile east of the headwaters of Wrong Creek on the Mirror Plateau. First known as "Divide Lake," because it was on the divide between the Lamar and Yellowstone rivers, Mirror Lake got its name in 1878 because it was "a natural mirror." The plateau took its name from the lake.

MODEL GEYSER*   Map #3

This geyser in the Geyser Hill Group of Upper Geyser Basin is located about 50 feet north and a little east of Dragon Geyser. Walter Weed of the USGS named the geyser in 1886 or 1887. In about 1911, geologist Arnold Hague described Model Geyser as

> Midway between the Giantess and Sponge [geysers], and in striking contrast to both . . . the smallest natural geyser on record. Its shallow circular bowl only 15 inches in diameter, is so obscure that when empty one might step into it without being aware of its presence, yet it is a typical geyser in all respects. . . . the column of water thrown out seldom exceeded 10 inches in height, and lasted only three minutes (Hague papers, Box 11, "The Geyser Basins," pp. 30-31).

Hague's references to it as "the smallest geyser on record" and "a perfect geyser" are the reasons for the name.

Oscar Swanson and his road crew and equipment in front of the Mammoth Hotel, c. 1885

The Burlington wheel party at the Mammoth Hotel, 1896

MOL HERON CREEK* Map #1

This stream flows north from Joseph Peak to the Yellowstone River just north of Gardiner, Montana. As early as 1884, locals called it Mol Heron for "Frisky" John H. Mulherin (1832-1904), who once lived at the mouth of the creek.

Mulherin and his wife came to Deer Lodge, Montana, in 1869 and moved to Emigrant Gulch, Montana (just north of Yellowstone Park) as early as 1876. He started out in mining, but by 1883 Mulherin and his family had moved to Cinnabar (about 3 miles west of present-day Gardiner), where he operated the C. B. Saloon. In 1886, petitions were sent to Washington for a post office at the mouth of "Mulhern creek" to be called "Mulhern." The stream was renamed "Cinnabar Creek" (from nearby Cinnabar Mountain) in about 1893. Through some confusion in spelling, the creek became known as Mol Heron Creek, a name that was officially approved in 1932.

MOLLY ISLANDS* Map #4

These two islands, located in the Southeast Arm of Yellowstone Lake, were named in 1878 by members of the second Hayden survey for Molly Gannett, the wife of Henry Gannett. Henry Gannett was the astronomer and topographer for that survey, and he may have given the name to the islands himself. Gannett was the founder of the U.S. Board of Geographic Names and its chairman for 20 years. The December 1914 *National Geographic* claimed that Gannett did more work on place names "than any other American."

The Molly Islands, which were individually named Sandy and Rocky, constitute the only breeding colony of white pelicans in Wyoming and the only one in a national park. To protect the young pelicans, regulations have forbidden boats to land on these islands since 1921. Regulations now forbid boaters from approaching the islands closer than one-quarter mile.

MONARCH GEYSER* Map #1

Often referred to as Monarch Geyser Crater because of its dormancy since 1913, Monarch Geyser is the official name of this feature in the Back Basin of Norris Geyser Basin. It is not known who named this geyser, but the earliest known use of the name is P. W. Norris's notation in 1881. An 1883 guidebook implied the reason for the name when it stated that Monarch "spouts in regal splendor."

Monarch's reported eruptions spanned only 36 years, from 1878 to 1913, during which time it was also dormant on a number of occasions. But in its day, Monarch was a major geyser that erupted to heights of 125 feet. Geologist Arnold Hague described an eruption in 1884 "when suddenly suppressed steam was ejected with great force, being thrown to a height estimated at 60 feet. The eruption from start to finish took 3 minutes and 30 seconds, followed after an interval of 1 hour and 50 minutes by another outburst similar in all respects to the former one" (Hague papers, Box 13, "Norris Geyser Basin," pp. 37-39).

There may be underground connections between Monarch and Steamboat geysers. Monarch is known to have been dormant in 1889, 1902, and 1911, years when Steamboat had major phase eruptions. Monarch was also apparently dormant in 1888 and 1894, years when Steamboat probably had major eruptions.

MONUMENT GEYSER* Map #1

This tall, thermos-bottle-shaped namesake geyser in the Monument Geyser Basin west of Gibbon Canyon was named by Park Superintendent P. W. Norris in 1878 or 1879. He named the entire area the Monument Geyser Basin for the gravestone-like thermal features he found there. Monument Geyser is no doubt the same feature that G. L. Henderson referred to in 1886 as "Pluto's Chimney." Henderson described it as 8 feet high with a 3-inch in diameter black crater. He called it "an active atomizer," indicating that there was some escape of water in the form of spray; but whether the feature is actually a geyser is subject to some disagreement.

MONUMENT GEYSER BASIN* Map #1

In 1878, P. W. Norris discovered and named this area on the east slopes of the high ridge located south of Gibbon Meadows. This is one of the strangest spots in the Park. High on the side of the mountain once known as "Mount Schurz," this area boasts a number of strangely formed gravestone-like sinter cones, "a deposit of hot springs, but strongly suggesting the work of human hands; some ancient memorial to the dead in this remote and secluded spot" (Allen and Day, *Hot Springs*, p. 491). These "monuments" are surrounded by a number of acid hot springs, typically muddy, gaseous, and associated with sulphur.

The Monument Geyser Basin was once a major tourist attraction with 12 monumental cones and features named "Sulphur Cone" and "Trip Hammer." Henry J. Winser described the cones in his 1883 guidebook:

> one . . . resembles a crouching lioness; another, a headless man; a third, like a slender chimney, pours out a cloud of smoke; a fourth whistles like a locomotive; a fifth belches out steam with a whizzing sound which is quite deafening as you stand by, and is audible for miles (*Yellowstone*, p. 30).

MONUMENT PEAK Map #1

This 9,689-foot-high peak of the Gallatin Range is located on the north end of an unnamed ridge and immediately south of Fawn Pass. The mountain appears to have been named in about 1887 by scientists working with the Hague parties of the USGS, perhaps as a reference point in mapping the region.

MOOSE POOL Map #2

This hot spring in the Mud Volcano area is located 700 feet southeast of Sour Lake. Ann and Jerry Mosser, who were conducting micro-organism studies in the area with Dr. Thomas Brock, named it in the 1970s for a moose they saw near the spring.

MORAN POINT Map #2

This viewpoint on the north rim of the Grand Canyon of the Yellowstone is located just east of Lookout Point. Members of the first Hayden survey, probably in 1871, named it for Thomas Moran (1837-1926), the artist who accompanied them on the trip.

Moran was the first artist to see and record the Yellowstone and Grand Teton areas, "the most remarkable scenery" in the American West. His watercolors from that trip along with the photographs taken by W. H. Jackson influenced a skeptical Congress to name Yellowstone the first national park. Jackson described Moran this way:

> despite his lack of horsemanship, he made a picturesque appearance when mounted. The jaunty tilt of his sombrero, long yellowish beard, and portfolio under his arm marked the artistic type, with some of local color imparted by a rifle hung from saddle horn (in Fryxell, *Thomas Moran*, p. 54).

Moran's friends on the expedition soon began calling him "T. Yellowstone Moran," and later he would sign his paintings in a colophon, incorporating a "Y" into his initials. Years later, his daughter wrote:

> Every artist of genius experiences during his life a great spiritual revelation and upheaval. This revelation came to Thomas Moran as he journeyed on horseback through an almost unbelievable wilderness. To him it was all grandeur, beauty, color, and light—nothing of man at all, but nature, virgin, unspoiled and lovely. In the Yellowstone country he found fairy-like color and form that his dreams could not rival (in Fryxell, *Thomas Moran*, p. 9).

The Grand Canyon of the Yellowstone enchanted Moran, and it was his large, 7- by 12-foot painting of the canyon that launched his career. As his friends watched the painting take shape, they judged it "was like keeping one's eyes open during the successive ages of world crea-

tion." "There is no doubt," Hayden later wrote to Moran from Montana, "that your reputation is made" (in Wilkins, "Moran," p. 24).

MORNING FALLS Map #3

This waterfall is on an unnamed branch of Mountain Ash Creek about 2 miles northwest of Union Falls and north of the campground on Mountain Ash Creek in the southwestern corner of the Park. Guidebook writer Thomas B. Carter suggested this name in 1976, because it faces east and catches the rays of the morning sun.

MORNING GEYSER Map #3

This geyser in the Fountain Group of Lower Geyser Basin is located immediately north of Fountain Geyser. The first record of Morning Geyser's eruption was in 1899:

> At 9:20 yesterday [June 26] morning and continuing until 10:25 without intermission there was an eruption from a crater about fifty feet north of the Fountain Geyser.... The size of the opening is about the same as that of the Fountain, and I do not exaggerate when I say the height it played was from 200 to 250 feet, and was the grandest I have ever witnessed in the park (Scrapbook 4210, YNP Research Library, p. 34).

As still sometimes happens today, eruptions of this geyser (which guidebook writers called "New Fountain") caused dormancy in Fountain Geyser. Although it has erupted rarely over the years (recently in 1983), an eruption of Morning Geyser is one of the most spectacular thermal sights in Yellowstone Park. Its eruptions are often followed by a chain-like sequence of activity in nearby Clepsydra, Fountain, Spasm, and Jet geysers, indicating its underground connections with those features and probably others in the area.

MORNING GLORY POOL* Map #3

The namesake spring of the Morning Glory Group in the Upper Geyser Basin is one of Yellowstone's most famous hot springs. Mrs. E. N. McGowan, the mother of Coda Finch, who ran the tent hotel at Old Faithful in 1883 and 1884, may have named Morning Glory Pool in 1883. The caption on a photo by F. Jay Haynes may have helped put the name into common use. Guidebooks during the 1880s seized on the name almost immediately.

Alice Rollins's description of the spring in 1887 is typical of the reactions early visitors had to its beauty:

> It is exquisitely named; for it is precisely like a morning glory flower. Its long and slender throat, like the tube of the blossom, reaching from unknown depths below, branches out in ever-widening snowy walls, forming at last a perfectly sym-

metrical and exquisite chalice, which is filled with water of the loveliest, clearest, robin's egg blue. The rim of the chalice is delicately and regularly scalloped, like the flower, and is edged with a tiny line of hard coral [sinter] from the deposit (*Harper's New Monthly Magazine*, May 1887, p. 886).

Morning Glory Pool was vandalized early in the Park's history. The spring originally had a scalloped border, described by geologist Arnold Hague as a sinter fringe 6 to 10 inches wide and 2 to 5 inches high, broken in only two places for runoff water. It seems incredible that souvenir hunters could have dismantled this entire thick rim, but it happened. Morning Glory Pool has been the victim of so much vandalism that Park staff during the 1950s called it the "garbage can." During the 1970s, the main road was routed away from the area, and the comparatively less visitation to the spring has resulted in some rejuvenation.

MOTTLED POOL*   Map #3

This hot spring in the Geyser Hill Group of the Upper Geyser Basin is located about 50 feet northeast of Infant Geyser. Park photographer Jack Haynes gave it the name "Oyster Spring" in 1912, but by 1926 it had acquired a new name—Mottled Pool. Naturalist Charles Phillips, who may have named it, located the spring "at the edge of the timber . . . an extinct vent with vegetation growing down to the water level" (in NPS, *Ranger Naturalists' Manual*, 1927, p. 143). *Mottled* means "blotchy," but the reason for the name is unknown.

MOUNT CHITTENDEN*   Maps #2 and 4

This 10,181-foot-high peak in the Absaroka Range is located at the headwaters of Sedge Creek, directly east of Mary Bay on Yellowstone Lake. Members of the third Hayden survey named this peak in 1878. Survey member Henry Gannett wrote: "of the prominent peaks in this . . . range may be mentioned Mount Chittenden, named for Mr. George B. Chittenden, whose name has long been identified with this [U.S. Geological] survey" (Hayden, *Twelfth Annual Report*, p. 483). Chittenden had nothing to do with any of the Yellowstone surveys, and this place name is an example of "taking care of one's friends." Little is known about Chittenden other than that between 1873 and 1877 he worked with Hayden, Gannett, Peale, and many of the other Yellowstone survey members in surveys of Colorado (1876) and portions of Wyoming, Idaho, and Montana (1877). As a topographer, Chittenden was in charge of various divisions of those surveys. He died in 1939 at East River, Connecticut.

Geologist Arnold Hague considered Mount Chittenden one of the best points of observation in the Park and thought that it would become a tourist objective "after a trail has been built to it. On its eastern slopes is a remarkably fine glacial canyon" (*Science*, February 1884, pp. 135-136).

MOUNT DOANE*   Map #4

In 1871, F. V. Hayden named this 10,656-foot-high peak in the Absaroka Range for Gustavus Cheyney Doane, "who wrote the first official report on this [Yellowstone] country" (Hague papers, Box 10, p. 135). The peak is located at the head of Rocky Creek east of Yellowstone Lake.

Doane (1840-1892) rose from private to 1st lieutenant during the Civil War, was mayor of a Mississippi town during Reconstruction, commanded the Second Cavalry during the Indian Wars, and explored North America from the Arctic to the Rockies. He is most famous for commanding the military escort that accompanied the 1870 Washburn expedition, the party that received credit for "discovering" Yellowstone Park. Of this party's many writings, historians consider Doane's journal to be the best narrative. It created great interest in the area, and as a result Doane became known as "the man who invented Wonderland."

MOUNT EVERTS*   Map #1

This high plateau east of Mammoth Hot Springs was first called the "Great Plateau" by Lt. G. C. Doane in 1870. In late 1870 or early 1871, Gen. Henry D. Washburn applied the Mount Everts name to this plateau on the map he drew of the Yellowstone area. Cornelius Hedges, another member of that party, had given the name "Mt. Everts" to the north end of Two Ocean Plateau (just south of the Southeast Arm of Yellowstone Lake). Washburn appears to have transferred the name to the northern Park area, possibly because he was one of those who thought that Truman Everts (1816-1901) had been found near this mountain.

Everts, a member of the 1870 Washburn expedition, was lost in the Yellowstone wilderness for 37 days. As fellow expedition member Lt. Doane wrote:

> he [Everts] subsisted on thistle roots boiled in the springs. . . . Twice he went five days without food, and three days without water, in that country which is a network of streams and springs. . . . [When he was found] a heavy snowstorm had extinguished his fire; his supply of thistle-roots was exhausted; he was partially deranged and perishing with cold. . . . It was a miraculous escape, considering the utter helplessness of the man, lost in a forest wilderness, and with the storms of winter at hand (in Bonney and Bonney, *Battle Drums*, p. 385).

Two old mountaineers, Jack Baronett and George Pritchett, found Everts on the west side of Crescent Hill just east of the canyon known as The Cut. Everts was ungrateful for his rescue and refused to pay the rewards that had been offered. He received Jack Baronett so coldly that

The Hayden Surveys, 1871, 1872, and 1878

In late 1870, geologist Ferdinand V. Hayden (see Hayden Valley) attended a lecture given by N. P. Langford, who was reporting on his experiences in Yellowstone as a member of the 1870 Washburn expedition. Hayden, who had been studying the geology of the American West for over 15 years, was intrigued. His curiosity led him to persuade Congress to allot $40,000 for his U.S. Geological and Geographical Survey to explore Yellowstone.

On June 1, 1871, 21 men with 7 wagons left Ogden, Utah, for Yellowstone. Managed by Hayden's brilliant assistant, James Stevenson (see Mount Stevenson), the group included mineralogist A. C. Peale (see Peale Island), artists Henry Elliot and Thomas Moran (see Moran Point), photographer William H. Jackson (see Mount Jackson), and zoologist Campbell Carrington (see Carrington Island). Accompanying them were Capt. John W. Barlow (see Barlow Peak) and his party of military explorer-engineers, along with about 20 packers, cooks, hunters, and guides.

In their 38 days of traveling through the Yellowstone region, the expedition confirmed the discoveries made by the Washburn party and made many of their own. They climbed Mount Washburn, gave place names to at least 60 features, and drew several new maps. They marveled at the beauty of the Grand Canyon of the Yellowstone, recorded the temperatures of hot springs, felt earthquake tremors at Yellowstone Lake, and launched the first known boat on the lake. And they produced hundreds of photos, sketches, and paintings, which would be used to persuade Congress that Yellowstone should be preserved. Through his reports, his articles for *Scribner's Magazine* and the *American Journal of Science and Arts*, and his own lobbying of powerful members of Congress, Hayden became an articulate advocate for the national park idea.

Congress appropriated $75,000 to continue the survey work that Hayden had begun. A vastly larger Hayden survey composed of over 60 men set out for the new park in 1872 to become arguably the best-known of the great surveys of the American West. Over the years, Henry Gannett, William H. Holmes (see Mount Holmes), Gustavus Bechler (see Bechler River), John Merle Coulter (see Coulter Creek), Rudolph Hering (see Hering Lake), and other prominent men joined in the effort to explore and map as much of Yellowstone as possible.

The Hayden surveys left their mark on Yellowstone in the form of hundreds of place names. And they left their imprint on the history of the American West in voluminous literature, in expanded knowledge, and in an awareness in the American people that the western landscape was to be cherished and preserved.

Hayden expedition in camp

Baronett said years later that "he wished he had let the son-of-a-gun roam" (*Helena Independent*, February 6, 1887). The plant that Everts ate to survive his ordeal grows abundantly in Yellowstone and is today known as the Everts Thistle.

MOUNT HANCOCK*   Map #4

This 10,214-foot-high peak on the Big Game Ridge south of Heart Lake was named in 1871 by Capt. John W. Barlow. Barlow wrote: "while upon the summit of the mountain, which I named Mount Hancock, I enjoyed an unparalleled view of a vast extent of country" (in Baldwin, *Enchanted Enclosure*, p. 39).

Barlow named the peak for Gen. Winfield Scott Hancock (1824-1886) who issued the orders for the military escort that accompanied the 1870 Washburn expedition. Hancock's military career began in the Mexican War. He was named brigadier general in 1861, and he fought at Antietam, Fredericksburg, Chancellorsville, Gettysburg, the Wilderness, and Spotsylvania (where he took 4,000 prisoners in 1864). Hancock also served as military governor of Louisiana. Nominated for president in 1880 following the Indian Wars, he lost to James A. Garfield.

MOUNT HAYNES*   Map #1

In 1921, Park Superintendent Horace Albright named this 8,235-foot-high mountain in the Madison Canyon for Park photographer F. Jay Haynes (1853-1921). The mountain appears to have been named "Mount Burley" as early as 1912, probably for D. E. Burley, general passenger agent of the Union Pacific Railroad at Salt Lake City. The Union Pacific began service to the Park's West Entrance in 1907.

Haynes came to Yellowstone for the first time in 1881. In 1883, he became Yellowstone's official photographer and accompanied the party of President Chester A. Arthur through the Park. Haynes's original studio was at Mammoth Hot Springs, but eventually he had Haynes photo shops at a number of locations throughout the Park. He received his first concessions permit in 1884.

Haynes spent some 40 years in the Park as a concessionaire, operating his photo shops, the Yellowstone Western Stage Lines, and the Cody-Sylvan Pass Motor Company, the first motor line in Yellowstone. For almost 30 years, from 1876 to 1905, Haynes was the photographer for the Northern Pacific Railroad.

In 1890, Haynes published the first *Practical Guide to Yellowstone National Park*, a series of guidebooks that was continuously published through 1966. Following Haynes's death in 1921, his son Jack took over the Park photo operations and ran them until he died in 1962.

MOUNT HOLMES*   Map #1

This 10,336-foot-high peak in the Gallatin Range directly west of Obsidian Cliff is probably the mountain shown on the 1860 Raynolds map as "Mount Gallatin." It was called "Mount Madison" prior to 1878, probably because of its location near the head of the Madison River.

On October 8, 1878, Henry Gannett and William H. Holmes of the Hayden survey ascended the peak, and Gannett wrote: "I have named it after Mr. W. H. Holmes, who has been connected with the survey as geologist and artist since 1872" (Hayden, *Twelfth Annual Report*, p. 485). William Henry Holmes (1846-1933) wrote the first detailed geological descriptions of Yellowstone in 1878, but he was more than a geologist. Historian William Goetzmann called him "perhaps the greatest artist-topographer and man of many talents that the West ever produced" (*Exploration and Empire*, p. 512). Anthropologist, ethnologist, and archaeologist, Holmes variously served as director of the National Collection of Fine Arts, head of the Bureau of American Ethnology, and curator of the National Gallery of Art.

MOUNT HORNADAY*   Map #2

Mount Hornaday is a 10,036-foot-high peak located west of Pebble Creek in the Absaroka Range. The mountain was named in 1938 for William Temple Hornaday (1854-1937), former director of the New York Zoological Gardens and one of the most famous naturalists of his day. Hornaday became interested in bison during the mid-1880s, and he came to Montana and Wyoming territories to collect some of them for the Smithsonian Institution. In compiling the first bison census, he found that in 1885 there were only about 285 wild bison in the U.S., most of them in Yellowstone Park and about 550 in Canada. He wrote "The Extermination of the American Bison" in 1887, the standard work on the subject, and became the first president of the American Bison Society in 1905.

A dedicated preservationist, Hornaday angrily denounced poaching in Yellowstone of not only buffalo but also elk. In his 1913 book, *Our Vanishing Wildlife*, he wrote:

> If the people of Gardiner [Montana] can not refrain from slaughtering the game of the Park . . . then it is time for the American people to summon the town of Gardiner before the bar of public opinion, to show cause why the town should not be wiped off the map (pp. 336-337).

MOUNT HUMPHREYS*   Map #4

This 10,965-foot-high peak in the Absaroka Range east of Yellowstone Lake was named for Gen. Andrew Atkinson Humphreys (1810-1883), an early supporter of F. V. Hayden's geological surveys. Members of Hayden's 1878 survey transferred the name from present-day Turret Mountain, which had been named for Humphreys in 1871.

MOUNT JACKSON*   Map #1

Located on the north side of Madison Canyon, this 8,257-foot-high peak was named for William Henry Jackson (1843-1942). Park Naturalist C. M. Bauer suggested the name in 1935, but Jackson was still living and the suggestion languished for a couple of years. In 1937, Jackson personally approved the mountain that would carry his name.

Born in New York, Jackson was a photographer, artist, explorer, historian, and pioneer. While taking photographs near Cheyenne, Wyoming, in 1869, he met F. V. Hayden. Hayden was impressed with Jackson's photos and suggested that the photographer join Hayden's geological expedition in 1871. While on the expedition, Jackson became fascinated with the Mammoth Terraces, taking many pictures of them and using the warm spring water for the final rinse of his plates. The next summer, Jackson again accompanied the survey into Yellowstone and the Tetons, and from 1873 to 1876 he joined Hayden's surveys in the southern Rockies. He returned with the survey to Yellowstone in 1878 before moving to Denver and establishing a studio. Jackson remained active into his 90s, painting 4 murals for the museum of the new Department of the Interior building at the age of 92. He made his 26th and final visit to Yellowstone in 1940 at age 97.

MOUNT LANGFORD*   Map #4

The naming of this 10,440-foot-high peak in the Absaroka Range has a confusing history. The original "Mount Langford" is known today as Colter Peak, which is also in the Absaroka Range. Henry Washburn named that mountain "Mt. Langford" in 1870 following the ascent of the peak by G. C. Doane and N. P. Langford, who made the first accurate sketch of Yellowstone Lake. In 1871, F. V. Hayden moved the name Mount Langford to its present-day location at the head of Beaverdam Creek.

Nathaniel Pitt Langford (1832-1909) was a member of the 1870 Washburn party of explorers, the author of a book on that expedition, one of a group who worked for the establishment of the Park, and the Park's first superintendent. Langford's series of articles in *Scribner's Monthly* in 1870 revealed Yellowstone to the world for the first time. Known as "National Park Langford" for his promotion of Yellowstone in his lectures and articles, Langford was U.S. Bank Examiner at the same time that he was superintendent of Yellowstone. As a result, he made only one brief report and about three visits to the Park.

MOUNT NORRIS*   Map #2

Mount Norris is a 9,936-foot-high peak in the Absaroka Range, located just south of The Thunderer and above Soda Butte Creek. Philetus Walter Norris (1821-1885) named the mountain in 1875 during his explorations with mountaineers George Huston, C. W. Wyman, and Jack Baronett. Norris wrote: ". . . we being doubtless the first white explorers of this peak towering [southeast] from Soda Butte. I deem it but just that as promised by the mountaineers, it shall retain my name. Though not the highest peak of the range, it is the plainest land mark in ascending the east fork of the Yellowstone [Lamar River]" ("Meanderings," letter 21).

Norris was a native New Yorker who developed an early interest in nature tour guiding. During service in the Civil War, he resolved to go to Yellowstone. "Conversations with several military officers during the war," Norris wrote, "developed the opinion that, notwithstanding the failure of the Reynold's [Capt. W. F. Raynolds] and other expeditions to the Yellowstone Lake, still it was possible to reach it through or near the great cañon from below, and that would be our route for future effort, if we survived the war, and ever again visited the mountains" ("Meanderings," p. 9).

Norris made a trip through Yellowstone in 1875 and became the Park's second superintendent in 1877, serving in that capacity until early 1882. He constructed the first real roads in the Park, built the first administration building, and explored extensively. Norris was a vigorous, honest administrator who accomplished much for the Park, including the recording of its human and natural history.

MOUNT SCHURZ*   Map #4

This 11,139-foot-high peak in the Absaroka Range, located just northwest of Mount Humphreys and east of Yellowstone Lake, is the second highest peak in Yellowstone National Park. Either this peak or a low saddle at the headwaters of nearby Cabin Creek was the summit named "Mount Doane" by Henry D. Washburn in 1870. In 1885, geologist Arnold Hague named the mountain for Secretary of the Interior Carl Schurz (1829-1906), because "throughout his administration [he] took a deep interest in the welfare of the [Yellowstone] reservation" (Hague papers, Box 10, p. 32).

Born in Germany, Schurz (pronounced *shirts*) received a doctorate degree from the University of Bonn. Because of his involvement in the 1848 revolution, he fled the country and later emigrated to the United States. Statesman, author, and diplomat, Schurz was appointed Secretary of the Interior in 1877 by President Rutherford Hayes. He was head of Interior from 1877 to early 1881, and in 1880 he became the first secretary to visit Yellowstone. As Secretary of the Interior, Schurz also was the first to propose a system of national forests, something that came about in 1891. He also led the fight to improve living conditions for Indians.

MOUNT SHERIDAN* Map #4

The main peak of the Red Mountains, Mount Sheridan towers 10,308 feet on the west side of Heart Lake. In 1870, members of the Washburn party named this peak "Brown Mountain," and Lt. G. C. Doane of the same party referred to it as "Yellow Mountain." A year later, F. V. Hayden named it "Red Mountain," a name that was soon transferred to nearby Factory Hill and ultimately to the whole range. It is curious that each man saw this peak as a different color.

J. W. Barlow, who in 1871 was the leader of Hayden's military escort, first used Doane's designation "Yellow Mountain." After ascending it, however, he named the peak for one of his superiors, Gen. Philip H. Sheridan (1831-1888). Civil War hero and commander of all forces in the West during the Indian wars, Sheridan staunchly defended the integrity of Yellowstone National Park. As historian Louis C. Cramton wrote in 1932: "without his interest and championing from 1875 and for ten years thereafter the whole national park story might have been much different" (*Early History of Yellowstone*, pp. 33-34).

Many early explorers climbed Mount Sheridan to view the magnificent panorama. Among them were Frank Bradley (who thought it might have been the "Mt. Madison" of early maps), W. A. Jones, Yellowstone Kelly, Henry Gannett, W. H. Holmes, Arnold Hague, George B. Grinnell, and Billy Hofer.

MOUNT STEVENSON* Map #4

This 10,352-foot-high peak in the Absaroka Range is located just south of Mount Doane and west of Mount Langford. F. V. Hayden named the mountain in 1871 for his principal assistant, explorer, and scientific surveyor James Stevenson (1840-1888). Reportedly, Hayden gave this place name against Stevenson's wishes. In 1853, during his exploration in the badlands of Dakota, Hayden first met the 13-year-old Stevenson, who had run away from home. Stevenson had grown up with military men before and during the Civil War, and he was Hayden's assistant from 1866 to 1879. During his career, Stevenson spent several winters among the Blackfeet, guided artist Thomas Moran (see Moran Point) to the Mount of the Holy Cross of Colorado, and claimed the first ascent of the Grand Teton with N. P. Langford. Stevenson spent his later years studying the Indians of the Southwest. He died in 1888 of mountain fever.

MOUNT WASHBURN* Map #2

This main peak of the Washburn Range is probably Yellowstone's best-known mountain. It rises 10,243 feet above the west edge of the Grand Canyon of the Yellowstone. Capt. W. F. Raynolds, who attempted to explore the Yellowstone area in 1859 with Jim Bridger as guide, drew a map of the region, showing a mountain in the location of present-day Mount Washburn. Raynolds called it "Elephants Back Mt," a name that may have come from Jim Bridger, considering that Raynolds did not actually see the area.

In 1871, F. V. Hayden transferred the name "Elephants Back" to another location far to the south and accepted the 1870 Washburn expedition's designation of the peak as Mount Washburn. The expedition members had unanimously named the peak for their leader after he made the first recorded climb of the mountain on August 28, 1870.

Gen. Henry Dana Washburn (1832-1871) spent his early years in Ohio and Indiana, where he was a teacher, lawyer, and auditor. After serving in the Civil War, he became Surveyor General for Montana Territory and led one of the most important early explorations of Yellowstone. He materially contributed to its designation as the first national park. Washburn had contracted tuberculosis during the Civil War, and while searching for Truman Everts in bad weather south of Yellowstone Lake he caught a cold. He died at the age of 39, just a few months after the party's return to civilization.

MOUNTAIN CREEK† Map #4

This creek flows west from Overlook Mountain to the upper Yellowstone River south of Turret Mountain. In 1885, members of the Hague parties of the USGS named Mountain Creek and included it on their 1886 map. Because of a boundary survey in 1904 by John Scott Harrison, officials called the stream "Monument Creek" for a time because Harrison placed a stone monument at the Park boundary near the creek. The name reverted back to Mountain Creek in 1965, however, when it became apparent from 1886 Park maps that Mountain Creek was its original name.

MOUNTAIN TERRACE Map #2

This little-known thermal area of dying hot springs is located on the north slopes of Little Saddle Mountain on an unnamed southern branch of Miller Creek. Park Superintendent P. W. Norris discovered this area in 1880 and named it Mountain Terrace in 1881, because he thought the springs here had once built small terraces. Walter Weed and Arnold Hague later characterized the area as having a strong smell of sulphur and small discharge of water, with sulphur deposits but no real springs.

Canyon Hotel employees, June 5, 1904

Tourists at Mud Volcano, 1911

MUD GEYSER   Map #2

Mud Geyser was one of Yellowstone's most famous geysers in the early days of the Park. It is located in the trees south of Mud Caldron and west of the Grand Loop Road, about 4 miles north of Fishing Bridge. Now a quiet bubbling hot spring, Mud Geyser seems to have been a geyser for about 30 years, with active periods from 1870 to 1878, from 1889 to about 1895, and from 1901 to 1905. There was at least one possible eruption in 1922, but there have been no known eruptions since then.

Members of the 1870 Washburn party described Mud Geyser as "the most singular phenomenon which we called the Muddy Geyser" (*Scribner's Monthly*, May 1871, p. 16). The crater was 35 to 45 feet by 75 feet, and eruptions of muddy water occurred about every 6 hours to heights of 20 to 50 feet. The eruptions, which lasted 30 minutes, shot a column of water that was 7 to 10 feet in diameter.

MUD POTS*   Map #2

This group of mud hot springs is located north of Dragons Mouth Spring and south of Turbulent Pool on the hillside just south of and above the Grand Loop Road. This place name seems to have been given in about 1935 by Park Naturalist C. M. Bauer or Park photographer Jack Haynes.

MUD VOLCANO*   Map #2

One of the Park's most famous mud hot springs, Mud Volcano is located just south of Dragons Mouth Spring off the Grand Loop Road. Members of the Washburn party named it in 1870 because it was shaped like a cone volcano. Most of their accounts described the booming sounds from the spring, which could be heard a mile away "like the discharge of artillery." Lt. G. C. Doane averred that "it was with difficulty we could believe the evidence of our senses, and only after the most careful measurement could we realize the immensity of this wonderful phenomenon" (in Bonney and Bonney, *Battle Drums*, p. 293). Members of the Washburn expedition also reported that Mud Volcano splashed in the topmost branches of trees 100 feet high and 200 feet away.

N. P. Langford returned to Mud Volcano in 1872 to find that a major explosion had greatly changed the crater and the cone. He found that only "a large excavation remained, and a seething, bubbling mass of mud, with several tree-tops swaying to and fro in the midst, told how terrible and how effectual must have been the explosion which produced such devastation." Today, Mud Volcano is flatter and considerably less cone-shaped, with eroded and flattened-out edges.

MUD VOLCANOES   Map #3

This group of mud springs is located west of Rush Lake and east of Pocket Basin. The name Mud Volcanoes appears to have been applied by members of the Hague parties of the USGS sometime before 1904, when it appeared on their map. This area was probably the one named "Lindern's Basin" in 1884 by George Marshall (owner of the nearby Marshall's Hotel) for Baron F. H. von Lindern of Holland who had visited the area earlier that year.

In 1878, this was probably the group of springs known as "Goose Lake Mud Springs," from nearby "Goose Lake," present-day Rush Lake. The area is also known as Pocket Basin Mud Pots from Pocket Basin, which lies to the west.

MUSHROOM POOL   Map #3

This hot spring in the Great Fountain Group of Lower Geyser Basin, is located at the edge of the trees some 1,200 feet east and a little south of White Dome Geyser. In about 1894, a new road passed very close to it and it may have been named at that time "on account of the vegetable formation growing in it" (Scrapbook #4209, YNP Archives, p. 135). Another source pegged the name as "characteristic of its appearance."

Guidebook writer Olin Wheeler used the name often and early, suggesting that he may have named it. Geologist Walter Weed described the spring in 1883 as "in woods . . . a shallow golden . . . lined basin 20′ × 35′ with cavern like hole at one end . . . water steams but is perf[ectly] quiet" (USGS, Box 47, vol. 3, p. 13).

MUSTARD SPRINGS*   Map #3

These two springs, named East Mustard and West Mustard, are located about 100 and 150 feet northwest of Black Pearl Geyser in the Biscuit Basin of Upper Geyser Basin. They are 10 to 15 feet in diameter and similar in appearance. It appears that in 1887 either geologist Walter Weed or Arnold Hague (or both) gave the name Mustard to the spring located the farthest north of all springs in Biscuit Basin—probably present-day North Geyser—because of the color of the spring's deposits. Three sources make it clear that Weed and Hague's "Mustard Spring" was north of the two springs that are now known as East Mustard and West Mustard. In 1927-1928, a Park place-names committee, confused about which spring was "Mustard," gave the plural name Mustard Springs to these features that are south of the original "Mustard Spring."

MYRIAD CREEK*   Map #3

Myriad Creek originates southeast of the Old Faithful area and flows northwest behind Old Faithful Inn, across a meadow, and into the Firehole River. The stream has had a variety of names over the years. The name Zipper Creek, a reference to the Old Faithful-area laundry, is also acceptable because of local use. During the early 1880s, the stream was called "Little Creek" and then "Crystal Creek" (for unknown reasons). It was also known as "Laundry Creek" during the 1920s or 1930s because it flowed past the area laundry.

Chief Park Naturalist David Condon named the creek Myriad in 1956 because "no name is shown on the maps for this feature and a variety of names are used locally depending on whom you talk to. The creek flows along the edge of the Myriad Hot Spring group and the name was selected to identify it with this group" (letter to J. M. Lawson, October 1, 1958, USGS files, Denver). During the 1970s, Old Faithful-area employees made many jokes about selling "Zipper Creek float trips" to tourists, a reference to the gullibility of some Park visitors.

MYSTIC FALLS*   Map #3

This 70-foot-high waterfall is on the Little Firehole River near Biscuit Basin. Members of the second Hayden survey named it "Little Firehole Falls" in 1872, but it was renamed Mystic Falls in 1885 by members of the Hague parties of the USGS for unknown reasons.

NAIAD SPRING*   Map #1

Sometime before 1904, members of the Hague parties named Naiad Spring, located on top of Mound Terrace at Mammoth Hot Springs. In Greek and Roman mythology, *naiads* were nymphs and water spirits who lived in and around and gave life to springs, fountains, rivers, and brooks. Naiads were thought to sometimes "weep copiously," thus giving birth to a spring or brook. Seeing Yellowstone as a kind of enchanted mythological land, the classically educated members of the Hague survey named many Yellowstone natural features for various mythological characters.

NARCISSUS GEYSER*   Map #3

This geyser in the Pink Cone Group of the Lower Geyser Basin is located about 550 feet north of Pink Cone Geyser. In 1887, geologist Walter Weed described Narcissus Geyser: "Eruptions consist of the bursting of spheres of steam, 2' in diameter, throwing water 3' on an average, with a maximum of 10 ft" (USGS, Box 53, vol 28, p. 80). Weed probably named the geyser in 1887, but it is not clear why. Park geologist George Marler thought that Narcissus Geyser had taken its name from the flower. The geyser cone resembles the narcissus flower, and it may be the feature that G. L. Henderson called the "Flower Pot" in 1885. The name could also refer to the Greek youth Narcissus, who spurned the nymph Echo. The gods punished him by making him fall in love with his own image, which was reflected in a fountain.

NARROW GATE   Map #3

This narrow canyon in the southwest corner of the Park on the Thirsty Fork of Snake River is located one-half mile due south from the point where Wyoming, Montana, and Idaho touch. Members of the Hayden surveys in 1871 or 1872 named the canyon.

NARROW GAUGE TERRACE and NARROW GAUGE SPRINGS   Map #1

This long, narrow terrace of the Mammoth Hot Springs is located north of Cheops Mound and above the Esplanade. The Narrow Gauge was probably named during 1883, when the name first appeared in a photo caption in a rare book, *Journey Through Yellowstone National Park and Northwest Wyoming, 1883*. The book was published as a memento of President Chester A. Arthur's trip to Yellowstone.

G. L. Henderson, a Mammoth-area resident who named many Park features, may have given the name earlier. Whoever applied the name, it slipped readily into local use with tour guide Henderson using it repeatedly. "The Narrow Gauge terrace," he wrote for the April 2, 1900, *Helena Daily Herald*, "resembles a graded road bed ready for tie and rail; hence its name." By 1904, the USGS had placed Narrow Gauge Springs on its map.

NATIONAL PARK MOUNTAIN*   Map #1

This mountain is the 7,560-foot-high edge of the Madison Plateau, located at the junction of the Firehole and Gibbon rivers. Calling it a "mountain" seems to have become part of local use in about 1905. The alternate name, "Mount Yellowstone," seems to have come into use shortly after that time.

National Park Mountain got its name because it overlooks the place where members of the Washburn expedition camped on September 19, 1870. It was here that they discussed what they should do about the wonders they had discovered. One party member, Cornelius Hedges (see Hedges Peak), has been partially credited with suggesting that there should be no private ownership of the area and that the land should be preserved as a national park. The other members of the group thought the idea a good one, and they returned to Montana Territory, where they began to give speeches and write magazine articles promoting the idea. During the summer of 1871, a government survey team—the Hayden survey—documented the reported wonders; and in March 1872, President U. S. Grant signed the act that made Yellowstone the world's first national park. Thus, the name commemorates the birth of not only Yellowstone but also of all national parks.

NATURAL BRIDGE†   Map #4

In 1871, F. V. Hayden discovered this natural bridge of rhyolite rock on a tributary of Bridge Creek just west of Bridge Bay. Hayden wrote: "At one point . . . we found a most singular natural bridge . . . which gives passage to a small stream. . . ." Hayden named this stream Bridge Creek. The name Natural Bridge eventually slipped into capitalized form from Hayden's use. The Natural Bridge has an arch span of about 30 feet and rises some 10 feet. The top of the bridge is about 40 feet above the stream.

THE NEEDLE*   Map #2

This 9,907-foot-high peak in the Absaroka Range is located southeast of The Thunderer in the northeast corner of the Park. The mountain's two summits and "needle's eye" arch are responsible for the plural name, "The Needles," that members of the Hague parties of the USGS gave it in 1885. Although maps as late as 1921 show the name as plural, the USBGN approved the singular form in 1930.

While searching in 1881 for natural bridges other than the one near Bridge Bay, P. W. Norris found this "storm worn tunnel" arch located "between the first and second peaks from the southwestern slopes of Mount Norris . . . showing a clear cut out-line of blue sky directly through the craggy crest, from the great terrace of Cache Creek" (*Fifth Annual Report*, p. 22). The opening was so hidden that Norris's assistant, George Rowland, wagered a new hat that it was but an adjacent snowdrift and not a bridge at all. Rowland lost the bet.

THE NEEDLE*   Map #2

This rock spire of volcanic breccia rises some 260 feet on the west bank of the Yellowstone River about a mile north of the mouth of Tower Creek. David Folsom, a member of the Cook-Folsom-Peterson expedition in 1869, discovered this tall slender column in 1869 and wrote:

> A short distance above us, rising from the bed of the river, stood a monument or pyramid of conglomerate, circular in form, which we estimated to be forty feet in diameter at the base and three hundred feet high, diminishing in size in a true taper to its top, which was not more than three feet across. It was so slender that it looked as if one man could topple it over (*Western Monthly*, July 1870, p. 62).

The following year, members of the Washburn party named this feature or another one nearby "Column Rock." A 1901 guidebook referred to the feature as "Cleopatra's Needle," a name taken from the rose-red column of Egyptian granite that had been shipped to England in 1878 as a gift from Egypt.

Hiram Chittenden noted in 1903 that Folsom had seen the column in 1869 "and [he had] then forgotten [it] until it was rediscovered a few years ago." Chittenden suggested to geologist Arnold Hague that it be named "Folsom's Column," but Hague wrote back that he did not like "Folsom's Column," because the Park had enough personal names attached to its features. Hague suggested classic references such as "Pompey's Pillar," "Sentinel Tower," "Watch Tower," "Alarm Tower," or something-or-other "pinnacle." Were it not for Hague's disapproval, the feature probably would have been called "Folsom's Column."

NEW CRATER GEYSER*   Map #1

See Steamboat Geyser

NEW HANDKERCHIEF POOL   Map #3

This hot spring in the Black Sand Basin of Upper Geyser Basin is located about 50 feet east of Handkerchief Pool. The name seems to have been in local use by Park personnel by about 1933, when the original Handkerchief Pool (q.v.) no longer "swallowed" handkerchiefs.

NEZ PERCE CREEK*   Map #3

Nez Perce Creek flows west from Mary Lake to the Firehole River. In 1871, F. V. Hayden named this stream "East Fork of the Madison River," but the next year Frank Bradley of the second Hayden survey christened the stream "Hayden's Fork." The 1878 survey showed the name of the stream as "East Fork of the Firehole," but the creek got its present name because of events in 1877. When the Nez Perce Indians entered Yellowstone National Park, they traveled up this stream (see Joseph Peak and Cowan Creek). In about 1885, geologist Arnold Hague suggested naming it Nez Perce Creek "to commemorate General [O. O.] Howard's pursuit of that tribe of Indians, who followed up the valley through which the stream runs" (Hague papers, Box 1, Book 2C, Hague to G. L. Henderson, February 22, 1887).

NEZ PERCE FORD*   Map #2

This ford on the Yellowstone River, about 2 miles below LeHardys Rapids, was named in about 1880 by Park

P. W. Norris and his party entering the Upper Firehole Basin, August 30, 1878

Looking at Obsidian Cliff from Beaver Lake

Superintendent P. W. Norris. Norris wanted to commemorate the Nez Perce Indians' crossing of the river at this point during their flight through Yellowstone Park in 1877. Also called "Chief Joseph's Crossing," the ford became known as "Buffalo Ford" in about 1946 after rangers Bob Murphy and Hugh Ebert discovered a number of bison frozen in the ice here. Apparently, the buffalo had tried to cross the frozen river and had fallen through. The Park place-names committee officially changed the name to Nez Perce Ford in 1981.

NIOBE CREEK   Map #3

Members of the Hague parties of the USGS named this branch of Iron Spring Creek in about 1891. The stream flows into Iron Spring Creek from the west, and its mouth is a short distance north of Black Sand Basin. It is not known why this name was selected for the stream, but survey members had a penchant for giving classical names to Park natural features. In Greek mythology, Niobe was the daughter of Tantalus who so angered the gods that they killed her children and changed her into a rock. The wet rocks along streambanks represent Niobe, always in tears.

NO NAME CREEK   Map #4

The mouth of this creek on Two Ocean Plateau is about 4 miles west of the Trail Creek Patrol Cabin on the Trail Creek Trail. No Name Creek flows north into the South Arm of Yellowstone Lake between Grouse and Chipmunk creeks. The creek was named in about 1887 by Arnold Hague of the USGS. Hague needed to describe the stream in his geological notes and apparently couldn't come up with a better name. He used the name a number of times in his notes.

NORRIS GEYSER BASIN*   Map #1

John Dwight Woodruff, accompanied by E. S. Topping, discovered this well-known thermal area in 1872. In 1877, Gen. William Sherman referred to the area as "Firehole Basins on Gibbon's Fork," and in 1878 members of the Hayden survey named the area "Gibbon Geyser Basin." Park Superintendent P. W. Norris (see Mount Norris), who explored the area in 1875, built a wagon road through the basin and described it by 1878. He appears to have named it for himself that year, referring to it as "Norris Geyser Plateau."

Norris had a penchant for giving his own name to many natural features in the Park, but this one stuck. In the Park for the last time in the autumn of 1884, Norris became seriously ill at the home of the Park superintendent. Believing he was on his deathbed, Norris entreated geologist Arnold Hague to put Norris Basin on government maps as the official name of that strange place that he loved so well. Norris died on January 14, 1885, and Hague kept his promise.

NORRIS PASS*   Map #3

This mountain pass, which is accessible only by trail, is located between two unnamed hills of the Continental Divide about a mile southwest of Craig Pass and Isa Lake. Although P. W. Norris has been credited with naming the pass in 1879, the year he discovered it, he claimed that Yellowstone Kelly named it "upon its discovery by myself, after fruitless search by himself and others for any pass in that vicinity" (*Calumet of the Coteau*, p. 262). Norris was looking for a route to connect the Upper Geyser Basin with the West Thumb area.

NORRIS VALLEY   Map #1

Norris Valley is the long meadow valley that begins about 2 miles south of Lake of the Woods and extends south along Solfatara Creek. Park Superintendent P. W. Norris named it for himself sometime between 1881 and 1883.

NUPHAR LAKE†   Map #1

Members of the Hague parties of the USGS (probably geologist Walter Weed) named this small lake of the Norris Geyser Basin in about 1888. *Nuphar* is a genus of yellow pond lily that is the common waterlily of high mountain lakes. The name is a Greek word derived from the Egyptian word for lily of the Nile River. The Yellowstone pond lily is *Nuphar polysepalum*. Apparently, this plant was growing on or near the pond at the time when it was named.

NYMPH LAKE*   Map #1

This small acidic lake is located about one-quarter mile north of Frying Pan Spring and west of the Grand Loop Road, 2.5 miles north of Norris. This is probably the lake that G. L. Henderson named "Quadrant Lake" in about 1888. Henderson did not list the reason for giving this name, but he included the lake in a tour of his "Seven Lake Avenue." In 1931, Hermon C. Bumpus, who placed an interpretative exhibit here in 1933, named Nymph Lake for *nymphaea*, a genus of waterlily.

NYMPH SPRING*   Map #2

The spring or group of small hot springs, located just east of the present-day horse corrals at Roosevelt Lodge, was famous during the early days of the Park. It has deteriorated considerably since the mid 1880s when geologist Walter H. Weed named it Nymph Spring. Weed's 1883 notes make it clear that people bathed in the spring, and Hiram Chittenden reported that the spring had been used for bathing since the early 1870s. A 1907 brochure of the Wylie Camping Company advertised "hot sulphur baths" at Camp Roosevelt (later Roosevelt Lodge), using water from Nymph Spring. The name probably came from Greek mythology. Nymphs were beautiful water spirits who inhabited streams, brooks, springs, and ponds.

OBLIQUE GEYSER   Map #1

This geyser in the Geyser Springs group of the Gibbon Geyser Basin is located in the center of the far southern end of the small valley that includes the Geyser Springs. Oblique Geyser is the correct name of the geyser that has been known as "Avalanche Geyser," "Talus," "Rockpile," "Marvelous," "Geyser Creek," and "Spray Geyser." In 1878, A. C. Peale, who may have named the geyser, wrote: "about 2 miles down the cañon is another small group in which there is a geyser which we call 'Oblique,' that spouts out obliquely over the road" (Hayden, *Twelfth Annual Report*, p. 133). Walter H. Weed's sketch map of the area in 1884 shows the geyser clearly. Weed described it as "[Spring] No 1 Oblique Geyser spurts about every 2-3 min—obliquely vent covered with masses of rock and debris from slope behind. Deposit beaded, brn gray when dry—dur[ation] 20 sec" (USGS, Box 47, vol. 6, pp. 18-19).

OBSIDIAN CLIFF*   Map #1

This is the famous "mountain of glass" that Park Superintendent P. W. Norris named in 1878. The cliff extends from Obsidian Lake south beyond Lake of the Woods and east for some 2.5 miles, making it one of the largest obsidian deposits in North America. The mountainside is composed of a hard, glass-like volcanic rock called obsidian. In building a road past the cliff in 1878, Norris built fires at its base to heat the rock. He then poured cold water on the rocks to break them up. Norris called this "the only road of native glass upon the continent" (*Report of the Superintendent*, pp. 980, 982, 989). Contrary to Norris's story, this is probably not the "glistening mountain of glass" that Jim Bridger mentioned in his tall tales. Bridger's mountain is probably in southeast Wyoming, but Norris no doubt applied Bridger's characterization to Obsidian Cliff.

Obsidian is believed to form when rhyolitic lava cools so quickly that no crystals have time to form in the rock, thus leaving a volcanic glass, usually in black but sometimes in red or brown. Obsidian Cliff was an important quarry site for Indians, who used the rock and may have traded it to tribes as far away as Ohio. "In the early days of white visitation," Arnold Hague wrote, "obsidian implements 4 and 5 inches in length, such as knives, scrapers, and arrowheads, could be picked up near-by abandoned obsidian quarries" (Hague papers, Box 10, p. 40). Collecting rock specimens is now expressly forbidden in national parks.

OJO CALIENTE SPRING*   Map #3

A hot spring in the River Group of the Lower Geyser Basin, Ojo Caliente Spring is on the group's northwest side. It is the farthest north of the springs that run into the Firehole River. In about 1889, Arnold Hague of the USGS named Ojo Caliente, which means "hot spring" in Spanish. It is not known why Hague gave it this name, but he could have taken it from New Mexico's Ojo Caliente Springs.

Ojo Caliente is probably the spring that G. L. Henderson referred to in 1884 as "Effervescent Spring": "When a stick is thrust into the spring anywhere it immediately effervesces like champagne when it sparkles and froths on being poured into a glass" (*Livingston Enterprise*, December 6, 1884). The hot water (198°F. and higher) was also no doubt responsible for the effervescing mentioned by Henderson. Ojo Caliente Spring is known to have boiled at least one large buffalo, which rushed pell mell into its superheated waters.

OLD BATH LAKE*   Map #3

This lake or "hot spring" is actually a large collecting basin in the Pink Cone Group of Lower Geyser Basin. It is known by three names: Old Bath Lake, Ranger Pool, and Tank Spring. Park Geologist George Marler believed that the tree sections embedded in its earthen walls make it likely that people (perhaps in prehistoric times) constructed the basin. People used the basin for bathing as early as 1885, when tour guide G. L. Henderson named it "Othello's Fountain." This name and others, such as "Ebony Basin," "Black Warrior," and "Walpurgia Lake," refer to the black-colored deposits in the vicinity. By 1904, however, the USGS had named the basin Tank Spring because of its resemblance to a water tank.

As early as 1908, the basin was also known as "Bath Pool" or "Bath Lake," and a bath house was built on its south shore. The USBGN officially approved the name Old Bath Lake in 1930. The word *old* was added to help prevent confusion with the Bath Lake in the Mammoth

Hot Springs area. In recent years, Old Bath Lake has become locally known as Ranger Pool, because Park rangers must prevent tourists from swimming in it. This lake is considered one of Yellowstone's most important archaeological sites.

OLD FAITHFUL GEYSER* — Map #3

The name of this geyser is practically synonymous with Yellowstone National Park. There is no record of who first saw this famous geyser, but it got its name in 1870 from members of the Washburn expedition. They named it Old Faithful "because of the regularity of its eruptions" (Langford, *Discovery of Yellowstone*, p. 169). It is uncertain which party member actually gave the geyser its name, but Gen. Henry Washburn, N. P. Langford, and Lt. G. C. Doane have all been given credit. One of the expedition members wrote: "we emerged from the woods opposite Old Faithful just as it was giving vent to its internal motion. From that time our spirits rose and all our personal woes and sufferings were forgotten."

Old Faithful's regularity (at an interval of from 33 to 120 minutes) is incredible, considering the highly erratic nature of geysers. Old Faithful has never been so regular as to erupt "every hour on the hour," an old myth that refuses to die. Even a *National Geographic* (April 1916) article reported that Old Faithful erupted "every hour on the hour." The majority of Old Faithful intervals have been 63 to 75 minutes.

Old Faithful's popularity has made it a victim of more vandalism than any geyser in Yellowstone. P. W. Norris reported in 1875:

> As stumps and poles as large as several men can carry and throw into the orifice of Old Faithful, at close of one eruption, are surely hurled out at commencement of the next, [so] the universal Yankee has already learned to utilize it for a self-operating, cheap and efficient washing machine. All blankets or other cloth garments thrown into it at the close of an eruption descend from sight; are thoroughly boiled in hot mineral water, scrubbed along the bead-like opal lining of the orifice and hurled high in the air, well cleaned within an hour, all without a patent on the machine or a cent for the use of it; truly a beneficient provision for the poor wifeless, homeless, often dirt begrimmed [sic] mountaineer ("Meanderings," letter 23).

In 1877, tourists described dumping thousands of pounds of trees, stones, stumps, and other rubbish into Old Faithful just to watch the geyser throw it out. One soldier from President Arthur's party in 1883 "took a long pole [and] pried off a piece from the mouth of 'Old Faithful' geyser, that weighed over 150 pounds" (Guie and McWhorter, *Adventures in Geyserland*, p. 64). A comparison of W. H. Jackson's 1871 close-up photograph of the Old Faithful Geyser crater with photos of today shows profound differences. The tendency of visitors to vandalize thermal features was one reason that the U.S. Army took over administration of the Park in 1886.

Old Faithful is not Yellowstone's tallest geyser, nor is it the hottest, and it does not discharge the most water. It is not even the most regular (see Bead Geyser and Riverside Geyser), but it does erupt 20 to 23 times per day every day, year after year. And its statistics are impressive:

    Age of tube: estimated to be 25,000 years
    Height: 106 to 184 feet, average 130 feet
    Shortest recorded interval: 33 minutes
    Longest recorded interval: 120 minutes
    Temperature before eruption: 204°F.
    Gallons discharged during an eruption: 3,700-8,400
    Depth of tube: 70 feet to constriction

OPAL TERRACE* — Map #1

Opal Spring forms this terrace of the Mammoth Hot Springs. The reason for its name is undocumented, but it probably originally referred to the opalescent blue color of the spring's water. In 1926, a large spring broke out at this location and near the tennis court belonging to Park concessionaire Harry Child. The spring increased significantly, and by 1933 Adelaide Child had named it Opal Terrace. The spring and terrace were active between 1926 and 1974, but they became dormant in 1978 and have been active intermittently since then. The tennis courts were removed in 1947.

OPALESCENT POOL — Map #3

This hot spring in the Black Sand Basin of Upper Geyser Basin is located north and west of Spouter Geyser. Probably named "Cerulean Spring" in the late 1920s or early 1930s for its deep azure color, the spring was also called "Algal Pool" by 1939 because of its colorful algae growths. In 1957, naturalist Herbert Lystrup commented that from the top of the nearby Madison Plateau ridge "the unnamed pool revealed an opalescent azure as lovely as the sky above" ("Disneyland in Real Life," p. 23). He is the apparent inadvertent namer of the spring. *Opalescent* means "iridescent like opal."

ORANGE ROCK SPRINGS* — Map #2

This place name, which was originally approved in 1937 to refer to hot springs thought to be at the head of Moss Creek, actually refers to present-day Josephs Coat Springs. The Orange Rock Springs name originated in 1873 with Capt. W. A. Jones: "On Orange [Broad] Creek ... occurs a notable mass of springs that have so cut down and discolored the rocks that I have named the locality Orange Rock Springs" (*Report*, p. 27).

Auto stage crossing the old Tower Fall road near Oxbow Creek

G.C. Axelrod, Haynes Studio

Old Faithful geyser crater in the Upper Geyser Basin, 1886

F.J. Haynes

ORANGE SPRING MOUND — Map #1

This is one of the most famous thermal springs at Mammoth Hot Springs. It was one of the first features named by Park tour operator G. L. Henderson, who wrote that "the form and color suggested to me its name early in 1882" (*Helena Daily Herald*, May 3, 1888). When he named it "Orange Geyser," Henderson and other observers still were unsure of the differences between a geyser and a hot spring. In 1871, A. C. Peale had named the spring "Oyster Shell Mound" because of its form. F. V. Hayden called it "Grotto in the Glen" and showed it on his map as "Upper Geyser."

A photo of Orange Spring Mound (c. 1883-1884) showed the entire mound to be only about two-thirds as high as it is today, with much spouting activity on its summit. An 1885 description mentioned "two pulsating jets of . . . water issuing from the top" (Henderson, *Manual and Guide*, p. 1). The spring continued to be very active through at least 1914, and records show it flowing during the 1920s until the famous small spouting jet of water on the top of the mound ceased in 1924.

A 1927 Park superintendent's committee on place names changed the spring's name from "Orange Spring" to Orange Spring Mound to prevent confusion with a spring at the Upper Geyser Basin. But the spring on top of the mound is still called Orange Spring, and its activity has been fairly constant since 1955. Springs on top of the mound in general have been active since at least 1871. The small cones to the east of Orange Spring Mound are known as Tangerine Spring, and a small sputtering jet at the foot of Orange Spring Mound was named "Whistling Willie" in 1924.

ORPIMENT SPRING — Map #1

This orange-colored, oval hot spring in the Back Basin of Norris Geyser Basin is located some 500 feet west of Palpitator Geyser on the east bank of Tantalus Creek. Sometime between 1889 and 1904, geologist Arnold Hague named Orpiment Spring, because his chemist found orpiment (a lemon-yellow colored trisulphide of arsenic) in the deposits of the area. Nearly 100 years after Hague's chemist made his observations, USGS scientists confirmed that the material in this and other Norris areas is not orpiment at all, but *metaorpiment*, a new term they have suggested for this material.

OSPREY FALLS* — Map #1

In 1885, members of the Hague parties of the USGS named this 150-foot-high falls on the Gardner River after the fishhawk. Past names for the falls include "Gardiner's Falls," "Middle Gardiner Falls," "Gardiner's River Falls," and other variations.

OUTLET CANYON and OUTLET CREEK* — Map #4

Outlet Creek flows southwest from Outlet Lake to Surprise Creek. Outlet Canyon is between Channel Mountain and Overlook Mountain, on the west slope of the Continental Divide just east of Heart Lake. In 1889, geologist Arnold Hague discovered this "outlet," where Yellowstone Lake once drained south to the Pacific Ocean. Hague wrote:

> For a number of years I have had good reasons to believe that the Yellowstone Lake formerly drained to the southward, although the [ancient] outlet has never been recognized. This year I was gratified in finding unmistakable evidence that the lake, which now adds its waters to the Atlantic, formerly drained toward the Pacific . . . (Hague papers, Box 2, Book 2F, p. 219).

Hague's evidence was probably the thick sediments in the area that may have changed the lake's drainage. In 1891, Hague named Outlet Creek, and by 1896 the name was applied to the canyon.

OUZEL FALLS* — Map #3

In 1885, members of the Hague parties of the USGS named this 230-foot-high waterfall on Ouzel Creek, just north of Bechler Meadows. Yellowstone's third highest waterfall, it was named for the water ouzel or American dipper (*Cinculus Americanus*), a small slate-colored bird that feeds underwater by diving and walking along the bottoms of streams.

OXBOW CREEK* — Map #1

This creek flows north to the Yellowstone River from above Phantom Lake. The name was in local use as early as 1887. The area near the mouth of this creek was named "Oxbow" because the Yellowstone River is in an oxbow at the point where the stream enters. This "ox-bow" was known early as one of only three places in present-day Yellowstone Park where the Yellowstone River could be forded (along with Nez Perce Ford and the famous crossing at Tower Fall). The Hayden survey named Oxbow Creek "Geode Creek" in 1878, but the name Oxbow later became so entrenched in local use that the names were officially switched sometime between 1915 and 1921.

PAINTED CLIFFS — Map #2

These cliffs are the hydrothermally altered west walls of the Grand Canyon of the Yellowstone River, about 4 miles below the Lower Falls. Park Superintendent P. W. Norris named the cliffs in 1881 because of the intense coloring of the walls. Norris found the colors to be "only skin deep." The material beneath is often nearly white, and the brilliant coloring is only brought out by surface oxidation of various minerals.

PAINTED POOL† — Map #1

There is some confusion about the name of this hot spring, which is located south of Ladies Lake and over an intervening ridge at Mammoth Hot Springs. Recent area maps of Mammoth incorrectly show Painted Pool as the thermal spring just south of Bath Lake and south of an intervening ridge; this is actually Ladies Lake. Painted Pool, which has been dry since at least 1927, is located farther south and a little west of Ladies Lake.

In 1884, Park tour guide G. L. Henderson named the pool and put up a sign that read: "Snow cave and bubbling painted pool containing poisonous gas." There was a shallow, cave-like structure (now gone) at the west end of the pool. The pool itself bubbled with carbon dioxide gas and was brightly colored with thermal algae. Geologist Walter Weed visited the site in 1884, noted the sign, and accepted the name Painted Pool.

The 1904 Hague Atlas of maps showed Painted Pool at its proper original location, but in the late 1920s Park personnel transferred the name to Ladies Lake and referred to the original spring (then dry) as "Old Painted Pool Spring."

PAINTPOT HILL* — Map #1

This 8,055-foot-high hill is located at the north end of Gibbon Canyon. In 1879, Park Superintendent P. W. Norris named the hill "Johnson Peak" for N. D. Johnson. Norris had requested that Johnson be appointed U.S. Commissioner for Wyoming Territory, hoping that he would help control crime in the Park. Members of the Hague parties of the USGS named the hill Paintpot Hill in 1885, because the Artists Paintpots thermal area is located at its north base.

PALETTE SPRING — Map #1

This hot spring of the Mammoth Hot Springs is located south of and just above the Devil's Thumb. Members of the Hague surveys of the USGS appear to have named Palette Spring sometime before 1904. The name probably referred to the heavy coloration in the area caused by thermal algae, bacteria, and deposits. The spring appears to have dried up around 1890, and it was not active again for some 40 years. In late 1928 or early 1929, Palette Spring rejuvenated in grand style. It remained active and beautiful until the mid-1930s, and it has been generally active since 1948.

PALPITATOR SPRING* — Map #1

In 1884, geologist Walter Weed described this spring in the Back Basin of Norris Geyser Basin as number "121" (Palpitator), "probably a small geyser, with two orifices" (USGS, Box 52, vol. 15, p. 85). When he saw the spring in 1887, Weed noted that a signboard at spring #121 read "Palpitator." Either a Park superintendent or Park tour guide G. L. Henderson probably named it because the steam from the spring produced uncanny rhythmic beats, "like the pulse of some subterranean monster" (NPS, *Ranger Naturalists' Manual*, 1927, p. 126).

PAPER PICKER SPRING — Map #1

During the early 1970s, National Park Service paper pickers named this hot spring of the Mammoth Hot Springs when it suddenly broke out from nothing. Located about 100 feet west of Poison Spring, the spring quickly built itself a travertine cone 2 to 3 feet high.

PARK CREEK — Map #1

Park Creek flows northwesterly from Gibbon Hill into the Gibbon River at Elk Park. Francis Gibson, an army officer who traveled through Yellowstone in 1882 with Gen. Phil Sheridan, recorded in his diary that Park Creek had been "named by Jon Tanly." Gibson probably meant John E. Tansy, a packer, cook, and guide who came to Yellowstone in the 1870s and remained in the area for many years. Tansy probably named the creek for the Elk Park meadow, a favorite camping place for early visitors to the Park.

PARK POINT* — Map #4

In 1871, members of the first Hayden survey (probably A. C. Peale) named this point on the east shore of Yellowstone Lake. Peale wrote in his diary: "we went over and found camp in a beautiful place at the edge of the trees, looking out on a beautiful little park with a stream of water running through it" (YNP Research Library, p. 36). Members of the Washburn expedition camped here in 1870, and geologist Arnold Hague noted in 1884 and 1888 that Park Point was one of the most beautiful places to camp in Yellowstone Park.

PARKER PEAK* — Map #2

Park Superintendent P. W. Norris named this 10,203-foot-high peak in the Absaroka Range in 1880. Norris gave the name for William H. Parker, one of the men who accompanied him on his explorations of the area. Parker lectured on Yellowstone Park for H. B. Calfee (see Calfee Creek) at presentations of the photographer's stereopticon views of the Park. Parker also drew the sketches of Hoodoo Basin that Norris included in his 1880 report.

PASS CREEK   Map #1

Pass Creek flows east into Grayling Creek about one mile south of Divide Lake, between mile posts 270 and 271 of the Montana-Wyoming state line. Boundary surveyor A. V. Richards (see Richards Creek) named Pass Creek in 1874 because of its location on the pass between the waters of Grayling Creek, which flow south to the Madison River, and those of the Gallatin River, which flow north to the Missouri River.

PASSAGE CREEK†   Map #4

In about 1960, Park officials named this creek because it provides a route from the southern part of Two Ocean Plateau and the Continental Divide to Yellowstone Lake. The creek flows north to Chipmunk Creek.

PAYCHECK PASS   Map #4

This pass is on the Heart Lake Trail between Heart Lake and the Grand Loop Road trailhead. It was named Paycheck Pass because National Park Service employees stationed at Heart Lake could hardly wait to hike or pack out to the main road and "civilization" to get their paychecks.

PEALE ISLAND*   Map #4

Members of the 1878 Hayden Survey named this island in the South Arm of Yellowstone Lake for one of their own, Albert Charles Peale (1849-1913). A doctor of medicine who later specialized in mineralogy, Peale was the great-grandson of Charles Willson Peale, the scientist, painter, man of letters, and friend of George Washington. A. C. Peale joined the Hayden surveys in 1871 and accompanied Hayden on all three of his surveys of Yellowstone. Peale was the author of the huge report on Yellowstone's hot springs and geysers in 1878, and he named many places in Yellowstone. He was the foremost authority of his day on the world's mineral springs.

Hayden's maps of 1871, 1874, and 1878, and Henry Gannett's report of 1878 indicate that there were two islands in the South Arm during early Park days. Geologist Walter Weed referred to the second island (now gone) as "St. Jacob's Isle" in 1887. In 1926, Park Superintendent Horace Albright took Sweden's Crown Prince Gustaf to this remote island at the tip of the South Arm of Yellowstone Lake. In 1891, geologist Arnold Hague reported that during his exploration of the island a single rabbit was the only wildlife present. Hague described the scene: "He turned up at different parts of the island wherever we happened to go, and seemed much astonished that anyone should have invaded his island home" (USGS, Box 55, vol. 1, p. 52).

PEANUT POOL   Map #3

This small hot spring in the Geyser Hill Group of Upper Geyser Basin is located about "twenty feet northwest of Butterfly Spring." In local use as early as 1909, the name Peanut Pool refers to its small size and peanut shape.

PEARL GEYSER*   Map #1

A. C. Peale of the Hayden survey named this geyser in the Back Basin of Norris Geyser Basin in 1878. Located just northwest of Double Bulger Spring, Pearl Geyser was named for semi-transparent geyserite "pearls" in the deposits that surround the spring. Pearl Geyser erupts erratically from 2 to 4 feet in height and occasionally to 7 feet.

PEBBLE CREEK*   Map #2

In 1872, members of the second Hayden survey named this stream "White Pebble Creek" because of the chalky white sedimentary pebbles and rocks at its headwaters. The stream flows from the Park's northeast corner to Soda Butte Creek. Members of the third Hayden survey shortened the name in 1878.

PELICAN CREEK*   Map #2

This major stream flows south and west to Yellowstone Lake from the Mirror Plateau. A splinter party of the James Stuart prospecting expedition named Pelican Creek in 1864. The group included Adam "Horn" Miller and John C. Davis, who wrote:

> We camped on this creek, and noticed several large birds which appeared to be wild geese. I shot one, which managed to fly out some distance in the lake before it fell. I swam out after it, and became very much exhausted before I reached it. It looked as if it might be good to eat so I skinned it, and then the boys concluded it would hardly do. I hung the pelican—for that was what it was—on a tree, and it was found, afterward by Miller, who came by with his party (*Livingston Enterprise*, April 21, 1884).

Miller probably named the creek, for Davis reported that "none of our party thought to give names to anything in the valley."

In one of the few recorded Indian skirmishes within present-day Park boundaries, Blackfeet Indians attacked Osborne Russell and a party of fur trappers near the mouth of Pelican Creek in 1839.

PELICAN CREEK MUD VOLCANO   Map #2

This mud hot spring is located near Pelican Creek about 3 miles north of the Mudkettles and Mushpots and some 75

The Hague Surveys

The Hague surveys (1883-1902) may not be as well-known in Yellowstone history as the Folsom, Washburn, and Hayden parties, but in terms of the time they lasted and the information they generated they were just as important. USGS geologist Arnold Hague (see Hague Mountain) first visited Yellowstone in 1883, beginning studies that were to absorb him for 34 years. Hague's influence on place names, maps, studies, and even the politics of Yellowstone became all-pervasive. Although he was especially interested in the Park's thermal features, for many years he maintained a general oversight of all geological investigations in the area. His giant treatise, *Geology of the Yellowstone National Park*, was published in 1899, and his 1904 atlas of colored maps is still a mainstay of Yellowstone literature.

Many of Yellowstone's place names came from Hague or his assistants: geologists Walter Weed, Joseph Iddings, T. A. Jaggar, George Wright, and Louis Pirsson, physicist William Hallock, and geographer Henry Gannett. At least 85 other people (including packers and cooks) assisted the survey at various times.

For 20 years, the Hague surveys worked in Yellowstone Park, producing maps, photos, geologic studies, and thousands of pages of unpublished notes and correspondence. Hague himself was not in the Park during some years, but his assistants always filled in, often serving as hosts to important Park visitors. Their published works number more than a hundred, but the bulk of Hague's work was never published.

Hague continued his work in Yellowstone for 14 years after the surveys officially ended—making it a true labor of love. He even visited the Park in his later years, in 1911 and 1915, and made extensive notes. With P. W. Norris, F. Jay and Jack Haynes, and G. L. Henderson, Arnold Hague was one of the Park's most eloquent tour guides. And his surveys in the Park, although unheralded and unsung, have no peer.

Arnold Hague, 1896

Portrait 122, U.S. Geological Survey

Members of the Hague survey at Yellowstone Lake, 1884

National Archives

yards east of the Pelican Creek trail. A. C. Peale of the third Hayden survey named the hot spring between 1880 and 1883. Peale wrote that it had been described to him in 1871 by some of his men as being "east of us as we traveled up Pelican Creek" but that he had not seen it that year.

Dr. S. Weir Mitchell, who passed the spring in 1879, described it as

> a cone of regular form about thirty feet across at top and five feet at the bottom.... The outbreak of imprisoned steam at intervals of a half minute or more threw the mud in small fig-like masses from five to forty feet in air with a dull, booming sound, sometimes loud enough to be heard for miles through the awful stillness of these lonely hills (*Lippincott's Magazine*, July 1880, pp. 30-31).

PELICAN ROOST* Map #4

Members of the Hayden survey named this small rocky island on Yellowstone Lake in 1871. This island is located about 1.5 miles southwest of Steamboat Point off the northeast shore of the lake.

PELICAN VALLEY† Map #2

The name for this large and open valley along Pelican Creek came into general use very early. Hayden referred to it in 1871 as the "valley of Pelican Creek," and Park Superintendent P. W. Norris used the name officially in 1880.

PENTAGONAL SPRING Map #3

This hot spring in the Black Sand Basin of the Upper Geyser Basin is located 150 to 200 feet northwest of Opalescent Pool. Geologist Walter Weed named Pentagonal Spring in 1884 because of its five-sided shape.

PEQUITO GEYSER Map #1

Pequito Geyser in Porcelain Basin of the Norris Geyser Basin is located 10 feet west of Pinwheel Geyser. Naturalist Tom Pittenger named the geyser in 1976, when it first broke out and erupted 10 feet high. *Pequito* is Spanish for "little one."

PETRIFIED TREE Map #2

Petrified Tree is located just east of Yancey Creek at the end of a small spur road off the Grand Loop Road 1.5 miles east of Tower Junction. This petrified tree was originally one of two in the area, but souvenir hunters completely destroyed the other one piece by piece. A fence was built in 1907 to protect the one that remains. John Yancey, who operated a hotel in nearby Pleasant Valley from 1882 to 1903, probably named the area "Yancey's Fossil Forest," a name that geologist F. H. Knowlton adopted. By 1905, however, the name Petrified Trees (for the two trees) was included on a map drawn by Hiram Chittenden.

PHANTOM FUMAROLE* Map #3

In 1956, a Park place-names committee named this "steam vent in a small thermal area at the head of Crawfish Creek," located southwest of Lewis Lake. The 1956 report noted:

> It is difficult to locate except on cool humid days when condensing vapor forms huge steam clouds and it is easily seen.... The name "Phantom" was selected because of the feature's changing characteristics and hidden site (USBGN folder file).

PHANTOM LAKE† Map #1

This small, intermittent lake is located along the Grand Loop Road near the headwaters of Oxbow Creek, about 11 miles east of Mammoth. In 1935, Park Superintendent Roger Toll gave the lake this name because it dries up each fall. There are no fish in Phantom Lake.

PHELPS CREEK† Map #1

Phelps Creek flows south from Sheep Mountain (above Gardiner, Montana) to the Yellowstone River. Only the mouth of the stream is within the boundaries of Yellowstone Park. Although the name Phelps Creek was used by locals as early as 1919, it may have been current in 1885. George H. Phelps, hunter, scout, and prospector, came to Montana Territory from New York in 1863 and settled at Grasshopper Creek near Bannack. He prospected the Yellowstone region with James Stuart in 1864, and he gave members of the Folsom party information on Yellowstone before they explored the area in 1869. He also worked for P. W. Norris in his 1881 explorations of remote parts of the Park. Norris called Phelps "our intelligent, observant mountaineer comrade" and named Phelps Pass southeast of Yellowstone Park for Phelps's crossing of it in 1864. Phelps prospected in the Jardine area during the 1880s and 1890s and supervised the building of Park roads under Ed Lamartine in 1888.

PHELPS PEAK Map #2

In 1883, geologist Joseph Paxton Iddings named this small peak, located about 4 miles east of Mount Washburn, for mountaineer George H. Phelps (see Phelps Creek). Iddings referred to the peak as "the small cone standing just above the river" (USGS, Box 54, p. 54). It is the small but prominent knob about 1.5 miles west of the Yellowstone River. Phelps Peak is best viewed from the summit of Amethyst Mountain.

PHILLIPS CALDRON* Map #1

In 1927, Park Superintendent Horace Albright and Park photographer Jack Haynes named this hot spring in the Back Basin of Norris Geyser Basin. Located just north of Green Dragon Spring, Phillips Caldron honors Charles Phillips (1890-1927), a Park naturalist who arrived in Yellowstone in 1925 and became very interested in hot springs and geysers. Phillips spent the winter of 1926-1927 at Old Faithful and died there suddenly from eating wild water hemlock (it grew in the thermal areas even in winter), which he thought was a wild parsnip. The *Saturday Evening Post* carried the story of removing his body by sleigh during the winter.

Phillips Caldron is one of only four names that violates a long-established rule against naming thermal features for people.

PHILLIPS FORK (of the Bechler River)* Map #3

This is the most northerly of the three forks that come together at Three River Junction to form the Bechler River. In 1921, explorer W. C. Gregg (see Gregg Fork) and Park photographer Jack Haynes named Phillips Fork for William Hallett Phillips, who was sent to Yellowstone in 1885 and 1886 as a special agent of the Department of the Interior to investigate conditions. His report, published as a government document, suggested ways to stop various forms of lawlessness in the Park and made recommendations about concessionaires, public health conditions, and unauthorized buildings and structures. Phillips opposed building a railroad in the Park, and in 1894 he appeared before a congressional committee to argue against further commercial spoiling of Yellowstone. N. P. Langford's description of Phillips appears in the 1923 edition of *The Discovery of Yellowstone Park:*

> If we were asked to mention the two men who did more than any other two men to save the National Park for the American people, we should name George Graham Vest and William Hallett Phillips, co-workers in this good cause. There were other men who helped them, but these two easily stand foremost (pp. 52-53).

PHILLIPS FORK FALL Map #3

This waterfall of the Phillips Fork of the Bechler River is the first one on that stream above Three River Junction. In 1921, explorer W. C. Gregg named this waterfall because of its location on Phillips Fork.

PILLAR OF HERCULES Map #1

The Pillar of Hercules, a large stone shaft that stands near the north end of Golden Gate bridge above Glen Creek, was named in about 1884. Tour operator G. L. Henderson named it as he watched the building of the Golden Gate bridge and the road through Kingman Pass (q.v.), between 1883 and 1885. Henderson may have selected this name because the pillar was so heavy. The Pillar of Hercules was moved during each renovation of the bridge—in 1902, 1934, and 1977—and it was moved 4 feet in 1889 to make room for the steamboat *Zillah*, which was being trucked to Yellowstone Lake. Henderson saw the pillar as a sentinel guarding the gate into the upper regions of Yellowstone.

PINTO SPRING Map #3

This hot spring in the Cascade Group of Upper Geyser Basin is located between Gem Pool and Sprite Pool. Although A. C. Peale did not include this spring in his "River Group," geologist Walter Weed designated it spring #33 in 1878 and gave it the name Pinto Spring in 1885. He gave it this name because of its small size compared to nearby Gem and Sprite pools. In 1887, Weed described it as "13 by 14 feet, clear, no overflow, no algae" (USGS, Box 53, vol. 28, p. 106).

PINYON TERRACE* Map #1

Members of the Hague parties of the USGS named this long extinct travertine terrace of the Mammoth Hot Springs sometime before 1904. This terrace abuts Clagett Butte and is the most westerly of the Mammoth terraces. The name could have been given as early as 1887. Early writers sometimes referred to juniper trees growing on these old terraces and in the general area as "pinion trees." This misidentification was probably responsible for the name.

PITCHSTONE PLATEAU* Map #3

One of Yellowstone's seven named plateaus that comprise the Yellowstone Plateau, Pitchstone Plateau is located southwest of Shoshone and Lewis lakes. Members of the third Hayden survey (probably topographer Henry Gannett) named the plateau in 1878 after pitchstone, a kind of obsidian and one of Yellowstone's more common volcanic rocks. The Pitchstone Plateau is much like a moonscape, with a little water and vast untimbered areas of very young volcanic rocks, visible flow lines, and swirls.

PLENTY COUPS PEAK* Map #4

This 10,937-foot-high peak of the Absaroka Range is located just north of Atkins Peak and southwest of Mount Langford. Members of the Cody Club of Cody, Wyoming, suggested the name in early 1932 to honor Crow Indian Chief Plenty Coups. The name was originally spelled "Plenty Coos Peak."

Chief Plenty Coups (1848-1932) was born near present-day Billings, Montana, and by 1889 was one of the most influential men of the Crow tribe. His grandfather gave him his name, saying, "I have dreamed that he shall live to count many *coups* and be old. My dream also told me that he shall be a chief—the greatest chief our people will ever have." The name given him was Aleekchea-ahoosh, which means "many achievements" or "plenty coups." As a child, Plenty Coups visited the Yellowstone Park area and remembered later that he had seen "hot water."

PLOVER POINT* Map #4

Plover Point on the west shore of the South Arm of Yellowstone Lake was named in 1885 by members of the Hague parties of the USGS. They named it for a plover, a type of quail. The killdeer and the snowy plover are plovers that live on Yellowstone Lake.

POCKET LAKE* Map #3

This small lake is located about 1.5 miles west of the most northern part of Shoshone Lake. Chief Naturalist David Condon named Pocket Lake in 1956 because "the lake occupies a definite pit or pocket in the edge of the plateau."

POINT SUBLIME* Map #2

In 1923 or 1924, Beulah Brown named this point on the south rim of the Grand Canyon of the Yellowstone River, just east of Artist Point. Park Superintendent Horace Albright agreed to the name, which probably was a reference to David Folsom's description of the canyon on September 21, 1869. Where the Cook-Folsom expedition had emerged from the woods on the east side of the canyon, Folsom wrote that the view was "pretty, beautiful, picturesque, magnificent, grand, sublime, awful, terrible" (in Haines, *Valley of the Upper Yellowstone*, p. 34).

POISON CAVE Map #1

This travertine sinkhole in the Mammoth Hot Springs is located on a ridge 165 feet southwest of the center of Bath Lake. The cave has an orifice of about 2 feet across. Park Assistant Superintendent J. W. Weimer, who may have named the cave, mentioned Poison Cave as early as 1883. In 1930, a Park guidebook described the cave as giving "off a gas that suffocates birds, mice and squirrels." Three decades earlier G. L. Henderson wrote:

> We had seen the famous Carbonic Acid Gas cave situated between Great and Ladies' Bath lakes, in which a flame was instantly extinguished at a depth of one foot. If a living animal dropped into this cave death would follow before reaching the bottom—about ten feet below (Ash Scrapbook, p. 23).

A number of sinkholes and vents in the Mammoth Hot Springs give off carbon dioxide gases that kill birds and other small animals. Around the turn of the century, chicken wire was stretched over some of these openings to prevent animals from being killed. In 1940, the Park posted a sign that read: "Danger. Cave filled with carbonic acid gas. It suffocates birds mice and squirrels."

POISON SPRING Map #1

Only recently called Poison Spring, this gaseous hot spring of the Mammoth Hot Springs has been called "Cave Spring," "Crimson Cave," "Poison Cave," and "Gaseous Hot Spring." The spring is located at the base of a cave-like ridge about 150 feet southeast of Soda Spring and over 500 feet southwest of Bath Lake. It has often been confused with Poison Cave.

Carbon dioxide gas bubbles freely at the surface of the algal-coated (green-scummed) water. In 1885, Park tour guide G. L. Henderson referred to this spring as "Crimson Cave" and warned that it "must be approached with caution, keeping on the wind side on account of its poisonous gases" (*Manual and Guide*, p. 1). In 1938, Park photographer Jack E. Haynes named it "Gaseous Hot Spring," and he included the feature in his *Haynes Guide*. In 1940, Park Naturalist W. E. Kearns described Poison Spring as a natural gaseous deathtrap that had killed 78 birds in a month and a half. Similarly, Park Naturalist Mildred Ericson found 6 kinds of birds dead at the spring in 8 days during 1946. Poison Spring finally got its name to differentiate it from Poison Cave to the northeast.

POLLUX PEAK* Map #2

Pollux Peak is a 11,067-foot-high mountain in the Absaroka Range just east of Castor Peak and south of the upper Lamar River. Members of the Hague parties of the USGS named it in 1893-1897 for a character in Greek mythology. Pollux and his half-brother Castor were gods of athletes and protectors of sailors and travelers. Geologist Arnold Hague (who probably named the peak) reported in 1899 that Pollux Peak was a twin of nearby Castor Peak, and this twin kinship was the reason for the name.

Preaching at Pulpit Terrace, Mammoth Hot Springs

Tourists at Punch Bowl Spring, 1917

PONUNTPA SPRINGS*   Map #2

This group of hot springs on the Mirror Plateau just west of Fern Lake was named in about 1885 by members of the Hague parties of the USGS. *Ponuntpa* is a Shoshone word that can be translated as "this water has power." *Pa* means water, and *poha* is the root of the word *power*. *Nunt* was probably pronounced *ghant* or *gaunt*. Another possible meaning is "one who has power." Nothing else is known about the circumstances of naming these springs, which are mostly small and inactive.

PORCELAIN BASIN*   Map #1

Porcelain Basin is one of the three major divisions of Norris Geyser Basin. Park Superintendent P. W. Norris named this area "Porcelain Vale" in 1881 because of the grey-white porcelain-appearing geyserite that covers most of the basin. In 1884, geologist Walter Weed of the Hague survey changed the name from "Porcelain Vale" to Porcelain Basin.

PORCELAIN TERRACE SPRINGS and PORCELAIN TERRACE   Map #1

Porcelain Springs are located in the Porcelain Basin of Norris Geyser Basin, on the west slopes of Porcelain Terrace and southeast of Opal Springs. These springs broke out in 1971 and were named by researchers because of their location on Porcelain Terrace. Rapid deposition of siliceous sinter occurs here at a rate of up to 10 centimeters in 12 months, making it more changeable "than any other locality in Norris Basin and Yellowstone Park." The changes are so great that current springs will be unrecognizable in a few years.

PORCUPINE CONE   Map #2

Porcupine Cone is a low, 8,979-foot-high hill located just southeast of Pelican Cone and north of Raven Creek. Geologist Arnold Hague named the hill sometime in the 1890s.

PORCUPINE HILLS†   Map #3

These low hills on the north side of the Lower Geyser Basin are actually thermally cemented glacial moraines. In 1887, geologist Arnold Hague named the hill nearest the present-day main road Porcupine and named the other hill "Nez Perce Butte" after nearby Nez Perce Creek. The name Porcupine Hill has been expanded over the years to include the whole range of small hills in the area, and the name "Nez Perce Butte" has long since disappeared.

PORKCHOP GEYSER   Map #1

This geyser in the Back Basin of Norris Geyser Basin is located 300 feet west of Double Bulger Spring. Don White of the USGS named Porkchop Geyser in 1961, when he was doing thermal research in the area. White originally named the feature "Dr. Morey's Porkchop" for a colleague of his and because the spring is shaped like a porkchop. The name was changed to Porkchop Geyser in 1978 in accordance with the rule against naming thermal features for people.

Porkchop Geyser is a strange but beautiful geyser that appears to erupt without boiling. In 1984, observer Rocco Paperiello recorded that Porkchop Geyser erupted 15 to 20 feet high, had a duration of 1 to 1.5 hours, with an interval of 3 to 3.5 hours. At times, the geyser spouts continuously for long periods.

POTTS HOT SPRING BASIN*   Map #4

In 1956, Chief Park Naturalist David Condon named this thermal area on the west shore of Yellowstone Lake (and north of West Thumb Geyser Basin) for Daniel T. Potts, a fur trapper who wrote the earliest known description of Yellowstone's thermal features. A member of the 1822 Ashley-Henry fur-trading expedition, Potts wrote a letter to his brother Robert that was published in the September 27, 1827, *Philadelphia Gazette and Daily Advertiser*. Potts's description may have referred to this area, which he visited in 1826:

> . . . that [river] of the Yellow-stone has a large fresh water Lake near its head on the verry top of the Mountain which is about one hundrid by fourty miles in diameter and as clear as crystal on the south borders of this lake is a number of hot and boiling springs some of water and others of most beautiful fine clay and resembles that of a mush pot and throws its particles to the immense height of from twenty to thirty feet in height. The clay is white and of a pink and water appears fathomless as it appears to be entirely hollow under neath. There is also a number of places where the pure suphor [sulphur] is sent forth in abundance. . . .

Although there were no active geysers here in 1961, at least 15 geysers are now known in the Potts Hot Spring Basin.

PRIMROSE SPRINGS   Map #3

Geologist Walter Weed of the USGS named Primrose Springs in 1897. The first hot spring south of Fissure Spring in the Firehole Lake Group of Lower Geyser Basin, Primrose Springs probably got its name from the spring's yellow color. It was originally designated spring #17 of the "Fissure Group" by A. C. Peale in 1878. There is another set of Primrose Springs at Norris Geyser Basin.

PROMETHEUS SPRING   Map #4

This hot spring in the Rustic Group of Heart Lake Geyser Basin was named in 1878 by members of the third Hayden survey, probably by A. C. Peale. The reason for the name Prometheus is undocumented, but it was no doubt named for the Greek mythological character who gave fire to man.

THE PROMONTORY*   Map #4

In 1871, members of the first Hayden survey named this peninsula of Yellowstone Lake "Promontory Point." Lt. G. C. Doane also called it a promontory the previous year. "We traveled across a high promontory running into the lake," Doane wrote (Bonney and Bonney, *Battle Drums*, p. 315). This may have been Hayden's inspiration for the name. Locals later named it "Alligator Head," because of what its shape looked like from the north.

PROPOSITION CREEK*   Map #3

This creek flows west to Mountain Ash Creek from the base of Pitchstone Plateau west of Falls River Basin in the southwestern corner of the Park. For unknown reasons, geologists of the USGS named this stream "Ampitheatre Creek" in about 1885. In about 1896, U.S. Army soldiers named it Proposition Creek. As the story goes, Acting Superintendent George S. Anderson (1891-1897) used to say on arriving at a campsite: "I'll make you a proposition. You furnish the water and I'll furnish the whiskey." At this creek one of his men reportedly said: "Captain, we'll just name this creek for your proposition" (Bauer, "Place Names"). Anderson appears to have enjoyed an evening nip while sitting around a campfire.

PROSPECT PASS   Map #2

Sometime before 1917, geologist Arnold Hague named this pass located between Folsom and Prospect peaks and northwest of Tower Creek.

PROSPECT PEAK*   Map #2

This 9,525-foot-high peak of the Washburn Range is located west of Tower Fall. Members of the Hague parties of the USGS, for unknown reasons, named it "Surprise Peak" between 1883 and 1885. Park Superintendent P. W. Norris had named the peak "Mt Stephens" in about 1880 after one of his assistants, C. N. Stephens (see Stephens Creek), but geologist Arnold Hague changed the name to Prospect Peak in 1885. It is not known why Hague selected this name, but he could have been honoring a name that Cornelius Hedges gave in 1870 to a high point on Overhanging Cliff near Tower Fall, which Hedges called "Prospect Point."

PROSPECT POINT   Map #3

Prospect Point refers to a historic intersection of roads (which are now gone) located about a mile northeast of the intersection of Nez Perce Creek with Firehole River and near the bridge across Nez Perce Creek.

During the 1880s, three roads came together at Prospect Point: one from the north ran down the Firehole toward its confluence with the Madison River; one from the east ran up Nez Perce Creek to Mary Lake and Yellowstone Lake; and one from the south ran toward Old Faithful through Lower Geyser Basin. Famous during early days in the Park, this place was known as the "forks of the road" or Prospect Point, as in "what prospects will await us at the forks of the road?" P. W. Norris used the name in 1880 and may have named the intersection.

PSEUDO GEYSER   Map #3

This little-known geyser, which is located on the west bank of the south fork of Alum Creek in Glen Africa Basin, was discovered in 1871 by Capt. John W. Barlow. Barlow described the geyser as "constantly throwing up boiling water to a height of several feet. The crater is of . . . rock, 6 feet in diameter, and bears a strong resemblance to a human ear" ("Reconnaissance," p. 19).

In 1878, F. V. Hayden and A. C. Peale named this strange, nearly perpetually spouting thermal feature Pseudo Geyser. They reported that "almost all constantly boiling springs have periods of increased activity, and those which spurt a few feet into the air have been classed as *pseudo-geysers*" (Hayden, *Twelfth Annual Report*, pp. 302, 417).

PUFF 'N STUFF GEYSER   Map #1

This geyser in the Back Basin of Norris Geyser Basin is located just northeast of Black Hermit Caldron. Geologist Rick Hutchinson named it in 1971-1972. Its original name, "H and S Puff and Stuff," meant "H" for heat and "S" for steam, with a humorous side-reference to the television show of the same name. Puff 'n Stuff Geyser gurgles and growls and sprays water a few feet into the air but does little else.

PULPIT TERRACE   Map #1

Pulpit is a long inactive terrace of the Mammoth Hot Springs. It is evident from Peale's 1878 map that water then flowed over this terrace from the Main Springs. Hayden survey members (probably Peale) gave the name "Pulpit" to a mass of travertine deposit on the far western side of the Main Terrace, not anywhere near present-day Pulpit Terrace. It is not known who gave the present name or when, but it was given sometime during the 1870s as visitors began to notice the natural "pulpits."

By 1879, traveler Henry Drummond reported that there were basins here or near here called "The Pulpits" and he reported that "one place has fifty" of them (in Smith, *Henry Drummond*, p. 172). They were "cream colored" in the shade and "spotless white" in the sunshine, and travertine stalactites could be seen here and there around them. In 1882, a visitor wrote: "the Natural Pulpit is no more or less than one of these old deserted [travertine hot spring] basins, with one side broken through to admit the speaker" (*Omaha Bee*, August 31, 1882). The late 1870s or early 1880s photo by H. B. Calfee showed a mock sermon being "preached" from Pulpit Terrace, with the speaker standing in the "pulpit," Bible open.

PUNCH BOWL SPRING*   Map #3

This hot spring in the Daisy Group of Upper Geyser Basin was named "Punch Bowl" in 1871 by members of the first Hayden survey. They chose the name because of the spring's shape and form. Capt. John W. Barlow noted that it had "a beautiful curbing of rock, built up in silicate scollops of a perfect pattern" (*Enchanted Enclosure*, p. 33). In 1875, Capt. William Ludlow wrote that Punch Bowl "played frequently during the day, some of its exhibitions being very fine" (in Baldwin, *Enchanted Enclosure*, p. 79). Guptill's 1890 guidebook referred to Punch Bowl Spring as possibly exhibiting geyser action, but there have been no other such references. Punch Bowl has been a quiet hot spring for many years.

In 1882, William Wylie named the spring "Fairies' Well." Later the spring was called the "Devil's Punch Bowl," a name that it carried for many years.

PURPLE MOUNTAIN*   Map #1

Purple Mountain is an 8,433-foot-high hill located just north of Madison Junction. In about 1904, geologist Arnold Hague named the mountain because of its color, probably caused by orthoclase feldspar.

QUADRANT MOUNTAIN*   Map #1

This 10,216-foot-high mountain in the Gallatin Range is located west of Gardner's Hole and Swan Lake Flat. Members of the third Hayden survey named it in 1878. Topographer Henry Gannett wrote that it "has a very peculiar shape. The summit, with the northern and western slopes, forms a curved surface, roughly resembling a segment of a sphere" (Hayden, *Twelfth Annual Report*, pp. 484-485).

QUEEN ELIZABETH'S RUFFLE   Map #1

This name was given to the rhyolite cap on Mount Everts, especially the part of it on the south side of the mountain. Tour operator G. L. Henderson named the cap in about 1885. Why he named it after Queen Elizabeth is not known, although it is believed that the imaginative Henderson fancied her skirts in the ruffly form of the rock.

QUEENS LAUNDRY*   Map #3

Members of the second Hayden survey discovered this beautiful blue hot spring in the Sentinel Group of Lower Geyser Basin (on the west side of Sentinel Meadows) in 1872. In 1878, A. C. Peale named the large spring Red Terrace Spring and described it as "conspicuous on account of the brilliant color displayed on its terraces. These terraces are like those of [Mammoth Hot Springs] on a very small scale" (Hayden, *Twelfth Annual Report*, p. 178). The terraces he mentioned were formed on the north and west sides of the spring; they are nearly gone today, victims of thermal change and vandalism.

In 1880, Park Superintendent P. W. Norris and his men, while engaged in building a road across the Madison Plateau (shown on today's maps as Old Fountain Trail), spied steam rising below and south of them. Norris named the spring Queens Laundry, noting:

> . . . during a Sabbath's rest and bathing recreation, some of the boys crossed from our camp to the attractive bordered pools below this great boiling fountain, and in one cool enough for bathing discovered its matchless cleansing properties, and from the long lines of bright-colored clothing soon seen drying upon the adjacent stumps and branches, while their owners were gambolling like dolphins in the pools, the envious cooks and other camp attaches dubbed it the Laundry, with a variety of prefixes, of which that which I deemed the most appropriate adheres, and hence the name Queen's Laundry (*Calumet of the Coteau*, p. 252).

Bathing and doing laundry in this area were common for several years. In 1881, Norris began building a two-room bath house with an earth-covered roof, but it was never completed. One room appears to have been intended for bathing, and the second room was less finished. The building still stands, the "first government building constructed specifically for the use of the public in any national park" (in Haines, *Yellowstone*, 1:248-249).

RABBIT GEYSER   Map #3

Rabbit Geyser is the correct historic name of the geyser that is also known as Till Geyser in the Rabbit Creek Group of Midway Geyser Basin. In 1884, geologist Walter Weed drew a diagram of the vents of this geyser and named it for its proximity to Rabbit Creek. In about 1915, geologist Arnold Hague discussed Rabbit Geyser:

Republic Mountain and Cooke City, 1884

Ragged Falls on the Ferris Fork of the Bechler River, 1921

The most prominent geyser [in the Rabbit Creek area] has been named Rabbit Geyser. It is remarkable for its two vents playing in unison, one vertical with a jet 10 feet in height, the other oblique throwing a stream in 1888 . . . to a height of 30 feet. Similar conditions apparently existed at the time the region was revisited by the writer in 1902, and again in 1911. . . . In some ways Rabbit Geyser resembles the Monarch [Geyser] in Norris Basin (Hague papers, "Excelsior Geyser Basin," Box 11, p. 18).

Although the name Rabbit Geyser appeared in several of Hague's published works and on Maj. Charles J. Allen's 1888 road map, Hague's failure to publish the bulk of his work resulted in obscurity of the name. In 1959-1960, changes in the area because of the earthquake brought Rabbit Geyser to the attention of Park Geologist George Marler, who called it "Mud Spring." During the early 1960s, "Mud Spring" erupted from 3 to 15 feet high for 10 to 15 minutes every 6 to 8 hours. In 1971, not knowing about the name Rabbit Geyser, Marler renamed it Till Geyser (to prevent confusion with Mud Spring at Norris), from the glacial till that composes the nearby embankment.

RAGGED FALLS*   Map #3

This 45-foot-high waterfall of the Ferris Fork of the Bechler River is near Three River Junction and east of the Bechler River Trail. Park photographer Jack E. Haynes named the falls in 1921 because of its ragged shape. His companion, W. C. Gregg, did not like the name and suggested "Rugged" instead, but Haynes prevailed and his name for the falls was adopted.

RAINY LAKE†   Map #2

Park Superintendent Roger Toll named this small lake near Tower Junction sometime between 1929 and 1935. Toll chose the name because small springs in the lake make it appear to be raining on its surface. Rainy Lake was where President Theodore Roosevelt's military entourage camped in 1903 during his visit to Yellowstone.

RANGER POOL   Map #3

See Old Bath Lake

RATTLESNAKE BUTTE†   Map #1

This 6,749-foot-high butte is located on the northern Park boundary about 4 miles east of the North Entrance. Gardiner townspeople named the butte Rattlesnake during the 1930s because of rattlesnakes that inhabit this area. It is one of the few places in the Park low enough in elevation to support rattlesnakes.

On his 1879, 1880, and 1881 maps, Park Superintendent P. W. Norris showed "Sheep Mountain" at a site close to present-day Rattlesnake Butte. But USGS surveyors apparently transferred this name to the peak north of Gardiner.

REALGAR SPRINGS*   Map #1

This group of hot springs in One Hundred Spring Plain of the Norris Geyser Basin forms the head of Realgar Creek. Realgar Springs got their name in 1889-1891 from geologist Arnold Hague, who named them for the presence of bright red realgar (arsenic sulphide).

RED CANYON   Map #4

This canyon of the Snake River is located on the west side of Big Game Ridge south of Heart Lake. During his winter boat exploration of the river in 1876, Lt. G. C. Doane named the canyon because of its color.

RED JACKET SPRING   Map #1

This hot spring in Glen Africa Basin of the Hayden Valley is located on the west bank of Alum Creek. In 1887, geologist Walter Weed named this hot spring, which lies immediately north of Pseudo Geyser and on the same bank of Alum Creek.

RED MOUNTAINS*   Map #4

This small range of mountains, located just west of Heart Lake, is completely contained within the boundaries of Yellowstone National Park. In 1871, F. V. Hayden named present-day Mount Sheridan "Red Mountain." In 1872, members of the second Hayden survey transferred that name to the entire range. The name was "derived from the prevailing color of the volcanic rocks which compose them" (Hayden, *Twelfth Annual Report*, p. 470). In 1878, Henry Gannett reported that there were 12 peaks in the range, with 10,308-foot-high Mount Sheridan being the highest.

RED ROCK*   Map #2

This tall pinnacle below the Lower Falls of the Yellowstone River is colored red by oxides of iron. This is probably the feature that P. W. Norris called "Red Pinnacles" in 1883. Another writer called it "Cinnabar Tower," although the rock is not composed of cinnabar, a reddish mercuric sulphide.

Park photographer F. Jay Haynes named the pinnacle Red Rock in about 1886 because he needed a caption for a photograph of Lower Falls that he had taken from the rock. Other artists have also taken advantage of the spectacular view from Red Rock, such as artist Albert Bierstadt who painted a well-known picture of the canyon and falls from this point during his 1881 trip to Yellowstone. In 1926, geologist R. M. Field of Princeton University discovered sediments of a much older Yellowstone riverbed at this point, which added to the knowledge about the age of the Grand Canyon of the Yellowstone.

RED SPOUTER GEYSER   Map #3

This geyser in the Fountain Group of the Lower Geyser Basin did not exist before the 1959 earthquake. By mid-September of that year, Park Geologist George Marler had named it Red Spouter Geyser because it was ejecting reddish-colored muddy water. During the winter it is still a red spouter, but often in summer and fall it dries up and is only a steaming hole.

RED TERRACE SPRING*   Map #3

This is the other name of Queen's Laundry (q.v.) in the Lower Geyser Basin.

REESE CREEK†   Map #1

Reese Creek flows north from Cache Lake east of Electric Peak to the Yellowstone River 4 miles north of Gardiner. Members of the third Hayden survey named the stream "Cache Creek" in 1878 because it flowed from Cache Lake. In about 1881, Park Superintendent P. W. Norris took the name Reese from local usage.

George W. "Tough" Reese (1838?-1913) was in the Yellowstone country as early as 1867 in the company of Lou Anderson and a party of prospectors. Reese had a ranch at the mouth of this stream as early as 1883 and had a peripheral role in naming Crevice and Slough creeks (q.v.). He took part in the skirmish with the Nez Perce Indians at James Henderson's ranch in 1877. By 1882, Reese was placer mining on the upper Yellowstone, and in 1884 he guided a party of tourists into the wilds of the Hoodoo Basin. With Walter Hoppe, he established the first school at Cinnabar. Reese later carried mail from Horr to Aldridge for 4 years and worked in the train dispatcher's office at Livingston in 1907.

REPUBLIC PASS†   Map #2

This pass of the Absaroka Range is located between Republic Peak and an unnamed summit at the head of Cache Creek on the eastern boundary of the Park. The pass got its name during the 1930s from nearby Republic Mountain (outside the Park between Silver Gate and Cooke City, Montana). Republic Creek flows northeast from the pass.

REPUBLIC PEAK   Map #2

This 10,440-foot-high peak of the Absaroka Range is located immediately south of Republic Pass. Republic Mountain is 4 miles to the north. Republic Peak seems to have been named in 1928-1929, but it is not known how long before this the name had been in local use (probably from Republic Creek, which flows from the peak). The name Republic comes from the most prominent mining company in the Cooke City area.

RESCUE CREEK*   Map #1

Rescue Creek flows east to Blacktail Deer Creek from the east side of Mount Everts. In 1870, N. P. Langford of the Washburn expedition named it "Antelope Creek," because the expedition's advance party had killed an antelope in the vicinity. Sam Hauser, a member of the same party, named the stream "Lost Trail Creek" because the group lost Lt. G. C. Doane's trail on the creek. In 1878, F. V. Hayden gave the creek its present name because he misunderstood where Truman C. Everts (see Mt. Everts) was found in 1870. Everts had been lost from the Washburn expedition and had wandered in the Yellowstone wilderness for 37 days. Two old mountaineers, Jack Baronett and George Pritchett, found Everts "on the summit of the first big mountain beyond Warm Spring Creek," that is, on the west summit of Crescent Hill beyond Tower Creek (*Helena Daily Herald*, October 21, 1870). Hayden understood this description to mean present-day Mount Everts and the Gardner River, since both Tower Creek and the Gardner River were known as "Warm Spring Creek." Hayden's error still stands in the name Rescue Creek.

RESERVATION PEAK*   Map #4

Reservation Peak is a 10,629-foot-high mountain in the Absaroka Range just northeast of Arthur Peak. In 1895, the Hague parties of the USGS named the peak because it marks the boundary of the great "reservation" of Yellowstone National Park, forever "reserved and withdrawn from settlement, occupancy, or sale" (Chittenden, *Yellowstone*, p. 306).

RESTLESS GEYSER*   Map #3

In 1937, a Park place-names committee mistakenly gave official approval of this name to refer to Atomizer Geyser in the Upper Geyser Basin (q.v.).

RESTLESS GEYSER   Map #3

This geyser in the Cascade Group of the Upper Geyser Basin is located on the right bank of the Firehole River 60 feet west of Atomizer Geyser. In 1878, A. C. Peale reported: "to the upper or southern one [geyser of his "River Group"] we gave the name Restless Geyser although its periods are not known" (in Hayden, *Twelfth Annual Report*, p. 188). Some researchers subsequently assumed that Peale was referring to present-day Artemisia Geyser, but evidence suggests that he meant present-day Atomizer Geyser. The 1904 Hague Atlas showed the name "Restless" applied to present-day Atomizer Geyser, as Peale had intended, but the entrenched use of G. L. Henderson's popular name Atomizer created confusion.

It is not known who first used the name Restless to apply to a third spring in the Atomizer-Artemisia area, but Chittenden used all three names in 1895, presumably for three different features. In 1909, guidebook writer Reau Campbell used all three names and noted that Restless Geyser was "little more than a boiling spring," in an apparent reference to the present-day feature Restless (*Complete Guide*, pp. 162-163).

RICHARDS CREEK†   Map #1

Richards Creek located on the northeast side of the Madison Valley, flows west to Gneiss and Duck creeks. USGS topographer Raymond Hill named this stream in 1958 for Alonzo V. Richards, deputy surveyor and astronomer. In 1874, Richards surveyed the southern and western boundaries of Wyoming Territory, including the Park's southwest corner. Richards contributed four place names to the Yellowstone map: Narrow Gate, Pass Creek, Sinking Water Canyon, and Cascade Creek.

RIDDLE LAKE*   Map #4

This small lake is located about 3 miles south of the West Thumb bay of Yellowstone Lake. Rudolph Hering (see Hering Lake) of the Hayden survey named Riddle Lake in 1872. Frank Bradley of the survey wrote:

> "Lake Riddle" is a fugitive name, which has been located at several places, but nowhere permanently. It is supposed to have been used originally to designate the mythical lake, among the mountains, whence, according to the hunters, water flowed to both oceans. I have agreed to Mr. Hering's proposal to attach the name to the lake, which is directly upon the [Continental] divide at a point where the waters of the two oceans start so nearly together, and thus to solve the insolvable "riddle" of the "two-ocean water" (in Hayden, *Sixth Annual Report*, p. 250).

This "insolvable riddle" of the "mythical lake among the mountains" where water flowed to both oceans probably originated from (or at least was fueled by) "Lake Biddle," which appeared on the Lewis and Clark map of 1806 (named after their editor, Nicholas Biddle). The lake then appeared on the Samuel Lewis version of the map in 1814 as "Lake Riddle." Riddle Lake is not "directly on the divide"; it drains to the Atlantic Ocean by way of its outlet, Solution Creek, which flows to Yellowstone Lake. Thus, the name was the result of a mapping error combined with fur-trapper stories of two-ocean water.

RIVER STYX   Map #1

River Styx is a mostly subterranean hot water creek that originates from the upper Mammoth Hot Springs and flows to unknown regions (see Stygian Caves). As of 1985, the creek is visible in the bottom of spring craters between Stygian Caves and White Elephant Back Terrace. River Styx was named in about 1885 by Park tour operator G. L. Henderson for the infernal river that surrounds the underworld in Greek mythology.

RIVERSIDE GEYSER*   Map #3

Riverside is a geyser in the Grotto Group of the Upper Geyser Basin, located 500 to 600 feet above and southeast of Fan Geyser. In 1871, F. V. Hayden named a geyser Riverside and made an error that caused confusion for 13 years. Hayden showed Riverside Geyser on his map in the location of present-day Riverside Geyser and captioned a woodcut "Riverside Geyser," but the illustration showed present-day Mortar Geyser. By 1883, the name Riverside was applied to present-day Riverside Geyser. It was at about that time that observers began noticing the geyser's "phenomenal regularity."

When regularity is defined as a percentage of variation from the total interval, Riverside has been the most regular geyser in Yellowstone Park. Since 1930, Riverside Geyser has maintained an amazingly regular interval of 6 to 9.5 hours. For a short time after the 1959 earthquake, the interval was 5 hours, but this soon increased. During most seasons, for a period of about 5 to 7 days, Riverside's interval will suddenly shorten by 30 to 60 minutes, but it will then shift back to its regular interval. The shift was noticed as early as 1911, and its cause is unknown.

ROARING MOUNTAIN*   Map #1

This mountainside of steaming fumaroles is located east of Twin Lakes and north of Norris on the Grand Loop Road. Arnold Hague and Walter Weed of the USGS named the mountain in 1885. Hague noted:

> It takes its name from the shrill, penetrating sound of the steam constantly escaping from one or more vents located

Roaring Mountain, 1934

J.E. Haynes

near the summit, and on a calm day, or with a favorable wind, the rushing of the steam through the narrow orifices can be distinctly heard from the wagon road ("Yellowstone Park," p. 350).

Geologist Weed added in 1885:

> At the summit of the cliff there is a cavern-like hole from which a loudly roaring steam jet issues. The emission of steam is nearly constant and has given the name to the place (USGS, Box 52, vol. 17, p. 87).

The mountain is known to have been loud from 1883 until about 1897, when it became quieter. In 1902, it resumed its former activity and a half a mile of trees were killed. In 1911, Roaring Mountain was roaring in much the same way as it had in 1883-1890, and it got louder the next year. But by the mid-1920s, both the sound and activity had diminished.

ROBINSON CREEK* Map #3

This creek flows south and west into Warm River (in Idaho) from an area south of Buffalo Lake in the southwest corner of the Park. As early as 1898, army scouts Felix Burgess and James Morrison referred to "Robinson's river or creek." The creek was probably named for Jim Robinson, a thief and rustler who with Ed Harrington (alias Ed Trafton, the Teton bandit) and Columbus Nickerson stole cattle in 1887 in Teton Valley, Idaho. The men were pursued and Robinson was shot. He died a few days later at Rexburg, Idaho.

ROCK CREEK† Map #3

Rock Creek flows southwest to Robinson Creek from Robinson Lake just west of the Bechler Ranger Station. Army scouts and old mountaineers named this stream as early as 1896 for Richard W. Rock, a hunter and poacher who lived near Henry's Lake, Idaho, in the early days of the Park. According to Nolie Mumey's *Rocky Mountain Dick* (1953), Rock was an Indian scout for Gen. George A. Custer, but he is mainly remembered for his sometimes illegal efforts to capture and protect wild animals from the Park. Rock's ranch near Island Park, Idaho (now known as the Diamond D), was a stopping place for early Yellowstone-bound tourists.

As early as 1887, Rock was suspected of poaching in Yellowstone, but nothing could be proven. During the 1890s, he was in the business of selling wild animals, and in 1891 he traveled to Alaska to make a collection for the World's Fair. A friend to animals, including bears, lynxes, goats, and a moose named Nellie, Rock was killed when a buffalo gored him on March 22, 1902. He was buried east of Dunham Creek on his ranch. Yellowstone's buffalo keeper, Buffalo Jones, remarked about Rock's death:

> a tame wild animal is the most dangerous of beasts. My old friend, Dick Rock, a great hunter and guide out of Idaho, laughed at my advice, and got killed by one of his three-year-old bulls. I told him they knew him just well enough to kill him, and they did (in Easton and Brown, *Lord of Beasts*, p. 146).

ROCKET GEYSER Map #3

This geyser in the Grotto Group of the Upper Geyser Basin is located immediately north of Grotto Geyser. Rocket Geyser was probably named in 1886 (but possibly in 1887) by Arnold Hague and Walter Weed of the USGS. The reason for the name is undocumented, but it may have been given for the rocket-like pattern of the geyser's eruptions. A less likely explanation is that geologist Hague gave the name for one of his horses, something he may also have done in naming Daisy Geyser.

ROSA LAKE Map #1

Rosa Lake, located at the head of Indian Creek west of the summit of Mount Holmes, was named in 1882 by Northern Pacific Railroad surveyors (probably Carl Hals and S. P. Panton) for Rose (or Rosa) Park Marshall, the first white child born in Yellowstone Park.

Rose Marshall was born on January 30, 1881, to George and Sarah Marshall (see Marshall's Park), who were custodians of the Marshall Hotel at the junction of the Firehole River and Nez Perce Creek. Visiting Wyoming Territorial Governor John Hoyt (see Hoyt Peak) named her because "roses were scarce in the Park and she was born in same" (*Livingston Enterprise*, January 1, 1884).

ROUND PRAIRIE† Map #2

This meadow is located between the Thunderer and Mount Hornaday south of the Northeast Entrance Road near Pebble Creek Campground. Park Superintendent P. W. Norris may have named the meadow in 1881 for its shape. By 1887, squatter T. R. "Red" Siwash had established a saloon here.

ROWLAND PASS Map #2

This pass in the Washburn Range is located east of Mount Washburn on the trail between Antelope Creek and Washburn Hot Springs. Park Superintendent P. W. Norris, Adam "Horn" Miller (see Miller Creek), and R. B. "George" Rowland discovered, explored, and named the pass in 1878. As Norris wrote in his *Calumet of the Coteau* in 1883, the pass was discussed and named "while Miller shot an elk and Rowland used a portion of the flesh in the preparation of our welcome evening's repast" (p. 214). Norris also called the pass "Grizzly Pass."

George Rowland first visited the Yellowstone country in July 1870, and he remained in the area for many years after that. With Norris, he explored Hoodoo Basin in 1878, where his party narrowly escaped a conflict with Indians. Norris sent Rowland and H. C. Wyman to the geyser basins in 1881 to record geyser observations and weather and to prevent vandalism.

RUDDY DUCK POND Map #2

This small glacial pond is located near the main road and just south of Junction Butte near Tower Junction. It is the larger and more easterly of two ponds in the area. NPS rangers and maintenance personnel probably named the pond by 1970 after the ruddy ducks that frequent the area. In 1881, Superintendent P. W. Norris referred to a small lake in this area, possibly this one, as "Duck Lake."

THE RUIN* Map #3

This ancient geyserite deposit is located behind Old Faithful Inn just south of the TWS employee pub. Members of the Hague parties of the USGS named the deposit as early as 1889, apparently because of its appearance. At one time it was a large spring.

RUSTIC FALLS* Map #1

This 47-foot-high waterfall of Glen Creek is on the east side of the Grand Loop Road at Golden Gate. Park Superintendent P. W. Norris named the falls in 1879. In his 1879 report, he wrote: "another of the season's discoveries is a rustic fall upon the West Gardiner, near the summit of nature's rocky fence to our pasteurage." J. W. Barlow had already seen and described the falls in 1871. Park photographer F. Jay Haynes sold pictures of the falls in 1887 under the name "West Gardiner Falls." Another later name for Rustic Falls was "Rural Falls."

Although water has been added to the falls' flow by a pipeline from Indian Creek, which empties in above the falls, the shape of the falls remains similar to that photographed in the early 1870s by W. H. Jackson.

SADDLE MOUNTAIN* Map #2

This 10,670-foot-high peak of the Absaroka Range is west of Parker Peak and north of the upper Lamar River. Park Superintendent P. W. Norris named the mountain in 1880 because of its marked resemblance to a riding saddle when viewed from Lamar Valley.

SAFETY VALVE GEYSER Map #2

This geyser in the Grand Canyon of the Yellowstone River is located on the trail to Seven Mile Hole on the slope above the first river campsite. P. W. Norris named the geyser in 1880 "from its powerful and distinct reverberations along the cliff," which were quite audible (*Report of the Superintendent*, p. 11). Safety Valve Geyser has built up beautiful geyserite deposits, and it erupted a few feet high in 1982. To Norris, the geyser seemed to be a kind of safety valve through which the earth's underground forces were safely released.

SAGE CREEK Map #4

Sage Creek flows northwest from Mount Chittenden into Pelican Creek about 4 miles northeast of Turbid Lake. It is the more southerly of two long streams. Arnold Hague named the stream in 1888 for the presence of the common sagebrush (*Artemisia tridentata*).

SAND GEYSER Map #3

This geyser in the River Group of the Lower Geyser Basin is located about 25 feet downstream from the runoff channel of Mound Geyser. The geyser is actually *in* the Firehole River, and it erupts when the river level is low. At other times, it behaves as a spring that stirs the obsidian sand particles in the river. Park photographer Jack E. Haynes gave the geyser its name in 1925 "because with each eruption it throws the sand a foot or two into the air." Haynes's guidebook, however, lists Sand Geyser's height as only a few inches, its duration variable, and its interval several per day.

SAND SPRING Map #1

This cold spring is located about 100 feet below the west side of the Grand Loop Road, 5.8 miles east of Mammoth Hot Springs or 12.4 miles west of Tower Junction. Photographer Jack Haynes named the spring in about 1949 because it emerges through black sand.

There are two other features that bear the name Sand Spring in the Park: one at Norris Geyser Basin and the other at Heart Lake Geyser Basin.

SANDY BUTTE Map #1

This 6,948-foot-high hill is located just west of the confluence of Campanula and Gneiss creeks about 7 miles north of West Yellowstone. Army scouts, possibly James Morrison or Elmer Lindsley, named the hill in about 1897. Lindsley wrote that the butte "near the junction of Campanula and Clematis [Gneiss] Creeks is called Sandy Butte. It is a landmark in the whole basin and might well be named on the [USGS] map" (Hague papers, Box 5). Arnold Hague probably left the name off his maps because Lindsley mistakenly identified Gneiss Creek as Clematis.

SANDY CREEK   Map #4

Sandy Creek is an intermittent stream that flows northeast from northwest of Riddle Lake through the Grant Village campground to West Thumb. The name "Sandy Creek" was originally given to present-day Big Thumb Creek in 1882 by Northern Pacific Railroad surveyors, who proposed that a spur railroad line run down this creek to Yellowstone Lake and that the main line follow the Lewis River to Lewis Lake. Guptill's 1890 map, which was modeled after the 1882 railroad survey map, showed the name Sandy Creek on the present-day stream, with present-day Big Thumb Creek unnamed and too far to the north. The confusion of names and streams remained until the 1930s and 1940s, when place-names researchers recognized the name Sandy Creek.

SAPPHIRE POOL*   Map #3

This is the namesake hot spring of the Sapphire Group of Biscuit Basin in the Upper Geyser Basin. Between 1883 and 1886, geologists Walter Weed and Arnold Hague named Sapphire Pool because of "the color of its water." Geologist Hague thought that it was the finest hot pool in the Park. F. Jay Haynes used the name Sapphire Pool in captioning a photograph of it in 1886.

Following the 1959 earthquake, Sapphire became a large geyser, erupting from 125 to 150 feet high. At first, its eruptions occurred every 2 hours and lasted up to 5 minutes, but gradually they subsided in height until by 1964 they were only about 20 feet high. The initial large eruptions tore out many of the beautiful "biscuits" in Biscuit Basin and washed them into the Firehole River. The eruptions harmed Sapphire's plumbing as well, and now there is no geyser activity. Sapphire Pool still boils and overflows constantly.

SAVAGE HILL   Map #3

As early as 1969, this summit located one mile west of West Thumb became known as Savage Hill because employees used it as a romantic rendezvous spot. Yellowstone Park employees are known as "savages," a term that originated during the stagecoach era when it applied to stagecoach drivers. Elizabeth Frazer explained the term in the May 1, 1920, *Saturday Evening Post*: "they [the drivers] used to hell-for-leather round those narrow mountain curves in order to hear the doods [sic] and tourist ladies screech. So we got to calling them savages because they were such a raw bunch" (p. 40).

SAWMILL GEYSER*   Map #3

This is the namesake geyser in the Sawmill Group of the Upper Geyser Basin. Topographer Antoine Schoenborn of the 1871 Hayden survey named the geyser, probably because of its whirring whistling sound or from its rotary motion or both.

A. C. Peale wrote in 1878 that Sawmill erupted with a whirling motion, and an 1890 reference suggested that Sawmill received its name "from the peculiar [whirring] noise accompanying activity." Geologist Arnold Hague wrote: "at times the water in the bowl takes on a characteristic rotary motion, while from the vent issues a shrill whistle suggestive of a factory or mill" (Hague papers, Box 11, "The Geyser Basins," p. 40). Several early accounts mentioned that the geyser sounded "like a large sawmill in operation," and one reported that "its stream rises and falls constantly, somewhat resembling the gait of an old-fashioned upright saw, hence its name" (Dudley, *National Park*, p. 87).

During the 1870s and 1880s, Sawmill Geyser was also known as "Rustler" ("a word much used in the mountains, indicative of energy and activity") and "The Fountain." Sawmill is a fascinating and typical fountain-type geyser that has erupted in separate noisy bursts from 3 to 40 feet high in recent years.

SCORODITE SPRING   Map #2

This hot spring in the Josephs Coat Springs is located on the left bank of Broad Creek directly across the stream from the Whistler Geyser complex on the Mirror Plateau. The spring, which discharges into Broad Creek, is about 4 miles east of the Grand Canyon of the Yellowstone. In 1884, geologists Arnold Hague and Walter Weed of the USGS named Scorodite Spring because its runoff channel is lined with a green material that was thought to be scorodite (a hydrous arseniate of iron).

THE SEASHELL*   Map #3

This hot spring is in the Lime Kiln Springs of the Grand Group of Upper Geyser Basin. Mrs. Arthur Burney, wife of the Park engineer, named the spring in 1925 because the deposit of the spring resembles a seashell. Because Park Superintendent Horace Albright and Arthur Burney were close friends, Albright allowed the name to stand. The USBGN officially approved the name in 1937.

Guides to Yellowstone Park

The first two guidebooks to Yellowstone Park—James Richardson's *Wonders of the Yellowstone Region* and Harry Norton's *Wonderland Illustrated; Or, Horseback Rides Through the Yellowstone National Park*—were published in 1873, just one year after the area became a national park. *Wonders* was largely a reprinting of the reports of the Washburn and Hayden parties, so Norton's book, which contained original information, can be considered the first Park guidebook.

The next Yellowstone guidebook to appear was Robert Strahorn's beautiful little book, *The Enchanted Land or an October Ramble Among the Geysers, Hot Springs, Lakes, Falls and Cañons of Yellowstone National Park*, which Strahorn published himself in 1881.

William Wylie's (see Wylie Hill) *The Yellowstone National Park, or the Great American Wonderland* was published in 1882, and a year later Henry Winser's *The Yellowstone National Park a Manual for Tourists* was available. Winser's guide was very popular during the 1880s and was republished several times in editions by John Hyde and W. C. Riley. A rarer but more detailed guidebook was Herman Haupt's *The Yellowstone National Park* (1883), which was cleverly published in a foldaround binding that protected it from inclement weather. And Superintendent P. W. Norris published *Calumet of the Coteau* in 1883, a collection of his poetry and a guidebook. Beginning in 1884 with *The Wonderland of the World*, the NPRR published guidebooks illustrated with F. Jay Haynes's photographs. The books, which became known as the Wonderland series, carried information about Yellowstone and about all of the places visitors could see along the railroad's northwestern route. These paperbound books were published from 1884 to 1906.

In 1890, F. Jay Haynes entered the guidebook market on his own. His books became the most famous of Park guidebooks and were later the official guides to the Park. Their titles ranged from *Practical Guide to Yellowstone National Park* (1890) to *All About Yellowstone Park* (1892). Haynes published a guide nearly every year from 1890 to 1966, with text written by Albert Guptill (1890-1909), by himself (1910-1915), and by his son Jack (1916-1962). After Jack Haynes died in 1962, two more editions of the *Guide* were published before the Haynes photo shops were sold to the Hamilton company.

Other Yellowstone guidebooks included Reau Campbell's guides, which appeared in 1909, 1913, 1914, and 1923 (*Campbell's New Revised Complete Guide*), and W. F. Hatfield's guides published in 1899, 1901, and 1902 under three different titles. And two very nice guidebooks were published in 1910: A. M. Cleland's *Through Wonderland* and Edward Colborn's *Where Gush the Geysers*. G. L. Henderson's newspaper guidebooks, *Yellowstone Park Manual and Guide*, were published in 1885 and 1888 and are probably the rarest of the Yellowstone guides.

F. Jay Haynes, 1887

Jack Ellis Haynes, 1922

SEA WEED SPRING   Map #3

Sea Weed Spring, which is part of the Sapphire Group in Biscuit Basin of the Upper Geyser Basin, is located about 30 feet east of West Geyser. In about 1887, geologist Walter H. Weed of the USGS named the spring and described it as having stringy, seaweed-like, and reddish-orange vegetable growths. Sea Weed Spring is probably the spring named "Spicule Spring" in 1959 by Park Geologist George Marler.

SEISMOGRAPH POOL   Map #3

During 1946-1961, this hot spring and nearby Bluebell Pool in the West Thumb Geyser Basin were called "Blue Pools." In 1961, area naturalists named this spring Seismograph Pool. The reason for the name is unrecorded, but it could refer to changes brought about in the spring by the 1959 earthquake. A seismograph is a device for measuring the intensity of earthquakes.

SEMI-CENTENNIAL GEYSER*   Map #1

Yellowstone Park's most northerly geyser, Semi-Centennial Geyser is located just north of Roaring Mountain on Obsidian Creek south of Clearwater Springs. Obsidian Creek flows through the geyser. Park Superintendent Horace Albright and Park photographer Jack Haynes named the geyser in 1922 because it erupted that year, the 50th anniversary of Yellowstone Park.

Apparently, this geyser first erupted in 1918. A report from that year stated:

> A large mud spring, 15 miles south of Mammoth Hot Springs, close to the main road, was seen to play thin mud to a height of about 50 feet for about five minutes on September 14th. A road gang working in that vicinity reported having seen the same spring play on June 19, 22, 26, and July 4 (*Monthly Report of the Superintendent*, September 1918).

On August 14, 1922, the geyser again erupted with a furious explosion. Scalding water carrying rocks and mud washed out the road and killed trees in an area several hundred feet across. The first eruption was estimated to be 300 feet in height. Later discharges were smaller and occurred at lengthening intervals (100 to 200 feet high, several times per day), until by the end of the season the geyser was dormant. It never erupted again after 1922, probably because the cool waters of Obsidian Creek flow through the geyser's crater.

SENTINEL CREEK*   Map #3

Named the "Sentinel Branch" (of the Firehole) by Frank Bradley of the second Hayden survey in 1872, Sentinel Creek flows north and east to the Firehole River from the Madison Plateau. Bradley named the creek for the high hot spring mounds of Steep Cone, Flat Cone, and Mound Spring, which "appear so much as if they were guarding the upper valley" (Hayden, *Sixth Annual Report*, p. 237).

SEPULCHER MOUNTAIN*   Map #1

Capt. J. W. Barlow named this 9,652-foot-high mountain northwest of Mammoth Hot Springs in 1871. In a May 26, 1885, letter, F. V. Hayden wrote to geologist Arnold Hague that he thought Barlow gave the name "on account of its low black appearance" (Hague papers, Box 5). But in 1878, W. H. Holmes of the third Hayden survey had wondered "why this mountain received such a melancholy appellation I have not been able to discover" (in Hayden, *Twelfth Annual Report*, p. 15).

In 1903, Hiram Chittenden speculated that a tomblike rock formation on the north slopes, suggesting the head and footstones of a grave, may have given the mountain its name. Where Chittenden got this information is not known, but his suggestion is logical and would have been readily apparent to Barlow as he came up the Yellowstone River in 1871.

SERENDIPITY SPRINGS   Map #3

This group of hot springs is located in Serendipity Meadow, south of Firehole Lake Loop Drive and west of White Creek. Microorganism researchers Richard G. Wiegert and Mary Louise Brock named the springs in 1968. They wrote that they named Serendipity "as a result of seeing the springs . . . by chance due to their steam trails appearing on a cold June morning" (Weigert to author, September 4, 1979).

SEVEN MILE HOLE†   Map #2

Seven Mile Hole is an area in the Grand Canyon of the Yellowstone River located about 7 miles downstream from the Lower Falls. Park Superintendent P. W. Norris opened a trail to the area in 1880. He wrote:

> Here, only between Tower Creek and the Great Falls of the Yellowstone, does a bridle-path reach the foaming, white-surfaced, ultramarine blue water of the "Mystic River," . . . in short, the seclusion, the scenery, and the surroundings of this hidden glen of the Wonder Land render it one of the most uniquely attractive so that the few tourists who fail to visit it will never cease to regret their neglect (*Fifth Annual Report*, pp. 20-21).

The Seven Mile Hole name was in local use as early as 1921. It probably came from fishermen who first referred to the area as "Seven Mile Fishery."

SHEEPEATER CLIFFS* Map #1

This name refers to the southern canyon walls of Sheepeater Canyon. The Sheepeater Cliffs extend from several miles above to several miles below Osprey Falls and eastward up Lava Creek to Undine Falls.

Park Superintendent P. W. Norris traveled through this area in 1879. His maps, texts, and road logs make it clear that the area he named Sheepeater Cliffs in 1879 was the southern wall of the canyon of the Gardner River above Osprey Falls. Later topographers apparently applied the name to the area downstream (below Osprey Falls), possibly because of local use of the name "Sheepeater Mountain." This name applied to the most easterly end of the cliffs, which is easily visible from Mammoth Hot Springs.

Confusion from Norris's map probably gave the singular name Sheepeater Cliff to the long columnar basalt cliff near the junction of Obsidian Creek and the Gardner River, even though the cliff is a good distance above the original Sheepeater Cliffs.

Norris gave the name to the canyon wall in honor of the Sheepeater Indian tribe, also known as the Tukudikas—the only Indian tribe known to have lived within the boundaries of Yellowstone Park. They were called Sheepeater because their staple food was the bighorn sheep. The Sheepeaters left Yellowstone in 1871 when Shoshone Chief Washakie invited them to settle on Wyoming's Wind River Indian Reservation.

SHOSHONE LAKE* Map #3

Shoshone Lake, the Park's second largest lake, is located at the head of the Lewis River southwest of West Thumb. It is possible that fur-trapper Jim Bridger visited this lake in 1833, and fellow trapper Osborne Russell certainly reached the lake in 1839. According to James Gemmell, he and Bridger visited the lake in 1846 (in Wheeler, "The Late James Gemmell," pp. 131-136). Gemmell referred to it then as "Snake Lake," a name apparently used by the hunters.

Fr. Pierre-Jean DeSmet's 1851 map showed a "DeSmet's L." in the approximate position of present-day Shoshone Lake. In 1863, prospector Walter DeLacy visited the lake and named it "DeLacy's Lake." The lake was also called "Madison Lake" because it was erroneously thought to be the head of the Madison River. Cornelius Hedges of the 1870 Washburn expedition named the lake after the party's leader, Gen. H. D. Washburn. By 1872, Shoshone Lake had already borne 4 or 5 names before Frank Bradley of the second Hayden survey added a sixth. Bradley wrote: "Upon crossing the divide to the larger lake, we found it to belong to the Snake River drainage, and therefore called it Shoshone Lake, adopting the Indian name of the Snake [River]" (*American Journal of Science and Arts*, September 1873, p. 201). Bradley's name thus returned in spirit to Gemmell and the fur trappers' name "Snake Lake."

Park Superintendent P. W. Norris thought that the name Shoshone Lake was "a fitting record of the name of the Indians who frequented it" (*Fifth Annual Report*, p. 44). The Shoshones lived mainly to the west and south of present-day Yellowstone Park, but there is evidence that they occasionally entered the area and may have visited the lake each summer. Their arrowheads and other artifacts have been found in various places around the Park.

The meaning of *Shoshone* has long been debated. Some authorities believe that the word represented an uncomplimentary Siouxian expression given to the tribe by their Crow neighbors. David Shaul, a University of Arizona linguist, believes that the word literally translates as "those who camp together in wickiups" or "grass house people."

Shoshone Lake is 205 feet at its maximum depth, has an area of 8,050 acres, and contains lake trout, brown trout, and Utah chubs. Originally, Shoshone Lake was barren of fish owing to waterfalls on the Lewis River; but two types of trout were planted beginning in 1890, and the Utah chub was apparently introduced by bait fishermen. This large lake is the source of the Lewis River, which flows to the Pacific Ocean via the Snake River system. The U.S. Fish and Wildlife Service believes that Shoshone Lake may be the largest lake in the lower 48 states that cannot be reached by a road. No motorboats are allowed on the lake.

SHOSHONE POINT Map #3

This point on the Grand Loop Road is located halfway between West Thumb and Old Faithful. It was named in 1891 because Shoshone Lake could be seen from here. In that year, Hiram M. Chittenden began constructing the first road between Old Faithful and West Thumb, and he probably named the point himself.

Shoshone Point was the scene of a stagecoach holdup in 1914. One bandit, armed and masked, stopped the first coaches of a long line of vehicles and robbed the 82 passengers in 15 coaches of $915.35 and about $130 in jewelry. Edward Trafton was convicted of the robbery and sentenced to 5 years in Leavenworth.

SHRIMP LAKE† Map #2

This small lake is located northwest of Trout Lake just off the Northeast Entrance Road about one mile southwest of Pebble Creek Campground. The name Shrimp Lake appears to have been given by fishermen and was in use as early as 1925. In his 1938 book, *The Waters of Yellowstone with*

Rod and Fly, Howard Back wrote: "up above Fish [Trout] Lake lies another little lake which abounds in freshwater shrimp" (p. 35). This was probably the reason for the name.

SICKLE CREEK*   Map #4

Sickle Creek flows southwest from Two Ocean Plateau to the Snake River just north of Barlow Peak. Members of the second Hayden survey in 1872 showed this stream as "Mounts Creek," probably for Frank Mounts, an obscure member of the party. In 1885, members of the Hague parties of the USGS named Sickle Creek because its path on the map was crescent-shaped, like a sickle.

SIGNAL POINT,* SIGNAL HILLS*   Map #4

This point on Yellowstone Lake is located on the east shore south of Park Point and due east of Frank Island. Two members of the 1871 Hayden survey, Henry Elliot and Campbell Carrington, made a survey of Yellowstone Lake by traveling out onto the lake in a small boat. A. C. Peale, another survey member, wrote that year: ". . . emerging from which [place] onto an open place on the edge of the Lake we camped so as to be in a conspicuous place for Elliot to see us if he happens to be on the bay." A little later, Peale added that Elliot and Carrington "saw the fire we built on the hill" (diary, pp. 34, 36). This incident seems to have been partially responsible for the names Signal Point and Signal Hills. Survey members also used the hills for signaling purposes during mapping. Signal Point did not appear on maps until 1878.

SILENT POOL   Map #3

In 1887, geologist Walter Weed named this hot spring in the Midway Geyser Basin. Silent Pool is located on the west side of the Firehole River, 600 feet north of the Fountain Freight Road iron bridge and across the Firehole River from Catfish Geyser. Weed gave the spring a name because of its proximity to the stagecoach road, which passed very close to it.

SILEX SPRING   Map #3

This hot spring is part of the Fountain Group in Lower Geyser Basin. The name appeared on maps in 1904, but it is not known who named the spring or when. The name may refer to silica, *silex* being the Latin word for that material. Silex Spring became a geyser in 1947, and it also erupted following the 1959 earthquake to heights of 10 feet. Silex did not exhibit geyser activity again until 1973. In 1977, the geyser erupted from 10 to 15 feet high at intervals of about 1.5 hours; it then abruptly became quiet in November 1979.

SILVER CORD CASCADE*   Map #2

This series of cascades is on Surface Creek, where that stream flows into the Grand Canyon of the Yellowstone River downriver from Artist Point on the east side of the canyon. The stories of 1,000-foot-high waterfalls hidden in the mountains may have had their origins with this cascade. Cornelius Hedges of the Washburn party wrote in 1870:

> The wild, floating stories about falls 1,000 feet in height are no doubt exaggerations as applied to the main stream [of the Yellowstone River]. That there are small streams from the high plateau above the brink of the canyon that fall the distance of 1,000 feet or more, perpendicular, is true and such were seen by some of our party (*Helena Daily Herald:*, October 15, 1870).

Samuel Hauser and Benjamin Stickney of the 1870 Washburn expedition discovered the cascade. Hauser wrote: "he [Stickney] also discovered a waterfall he named 'Silverthread fall'." On the very next page of his diary, Hauser added: "Discovered and named falls opposite side of [Yellowstone] river. Silver thread fall. They pitch and plunge down side of cannon [*sic*] over 1500 feet" (diary, pp. 9-10). Hauser's estimate was too high; the canyon at this point is 1,200 feet deep.

In 1883, former Superintendent P. W. Norris referred to this waterfall as "Sliding Cascade," and in 1885, members of the Hague parties of the USGS saw fit to change the name "Silverthread" to the present-day Silver Cord Cascade. The trail from Artist Point to Silver Cord Cascade was built in 1921.

SILVER GATE*   Map #1

This is a portion of the 1899 stagecoach road through the jumbled rocks known as the Hoodoos, which is preserved as a short drive off the Grand Loop Road south of Mammoth Hot Springs. Silver Gate, located about 2 miles north of the Golden Gate bridge, is a cleft between large travertine boulders.

The first stagecoach road from Mammoth to Swan Lake Flats passed west of Narrow Gauge Terrace and ascended Snow Pass. A second road (begun in 1883) passed east of the present-day Hoodoos rock formations and joined the current route just below the Golden Gate bridge (built for this purpose in 1885). In 1899-1900, Hiram Chittenden and the U.S. Engineers built the third road, which generally follows the route of today's road. This road passed just east of Marble Terrace, ascended Formation Hill in a northerly direction, turned back south

Carriage and riders passing through Silver Gate, 1899 — F.J. Haynes

Looking at Steamboat Point from Lake Butte, 1935 — J.E. Haynes

at the top of Main Terrace, and ran through the limestone blocks known as the Hoodoos.

In 1899, Helena tourist James L. Galen took the new road through a narrow picturesque cleft among the Hoodoos and reportedly exclaimed, "Why, this is the Silver Gate" (*Livingston Enterprise*, November 11, 1899). The name stuck. "Silver" was a reference to the silvery gray color of the rocks of the Hoodoos, and "Gate" referred to the already existing Golden Gate Canyon and bridge to the south.

SILVER GLOBE (SPRING)*   Map #3

This hot spring in the Sapphire Group of Biscuit Basin in the Upper Geyser Basin is located immediately south of Avoca Spring and is attached to Avoca. Park tour operator G. L. Henderson named Silver Globe in 1887 because of its ascending, silvery bubbles of gas. The name has nothing to do with "globular masses of sinter," as some sources have reported.

Over the years, there has been confusion about which spring is Silver Globe. Current maps incorrectly place the spring an entire complex south of the Avoca Spring complex. Confusion has also placed the name on the spring complex southwest of Avoca. But Walter Weed's 1884 map clearly shows his spring #14 (Silver Globe) attached to spring #7 (present-day Avoca Spring).

Activity at the Avoca Spring complex in 1986 caused its large catch basin on the south to fill nearly to the brim, and an increase in heat restored this basin to the look it apparently had during the 1880s when Henderson saw it. No other spring in the area satisfies Henderson's descriptions as well as this "new" spring, and Weed's map seems to confirm the location.

SILVER SCARF FALLS*   Map #3

This 250-foot-high waterfall of an unnamed branch of Boundary Creek is located less than a mile east of Dunanda Falls northeast of Bechler Meadows. William C. Gregg discovered this sloping cascade in 1920. Henry Van Dyke, former minister to Holland, named it from its appearance in 1921. Gregg later wrote: "Dr. Henry Van Dyke gave me 'Silver Scarf Cascade' as his way of adopting one of our nameless beauties" (*Outlook*, November 23, 1921, p. 476).

SINKING WATER CANYON   Map #3

In 1874, boundary surveyor Alonzo V. Richards (see Richards Creek) gave this name to the uppermost canyon of Little Robinson Creek. The canyon is located about 2 miles west of Dunanda Falls on the Idaho-Wyoming state line at mile post 226. Richards wrote that the canyon ran southwest "with [a] small stream in it that runs and sinks, at intervals. For convenience I have called it Sinking water Cañon" ("Field Notes . . . 1874").

SKELETON POOL   Map #3

This hot spring in the River Group of the Lower Geyser Basin is located between Crown Crater and Leaf Pool. Skeleton Pool's official name is Buffalo Spring. The spring has very thin sinter ledges that extend out over its hot water and break off quite easily, so that animals sometimes fell through into the pool to their deaths.

The names Skeleton Pool and Buffalo Spring were both given because the bones in the bottom of the spring were thought to be buffalo bones. The pool was named Buffalo Spring sometime between 1904 and 1912. The name Skeleton Pool came into local use during the 1920s. Yellowstone Park Transportation Company bus driver Gerard Pesman distinctly remembers old-timer Doc Way using the name in 1926. The name Buffalo Spring was officially approved in 1930.

SLEEPING GIANT   Map #2

This name refers to one peak or a group of several peaks in the Absarokas that resembles a giant's face looking skyward from Bridge Bay across Yellowstone Lake. According to one source, the Sleeping Giant is composed of parts of Castor and Pollux peaks. Another source claims that it is Saddle Mountain. In 1871, F. V. Hayden wrote:

> These [mountains] are all of volcanic origin, and the fantastic shapes which many of them have assumed under the hand of time, called forth a variety of names from my party. There were two of them that represented the human profile so well that we called them the "Giant's Face" and "Old Man of the Mountains" (*Fifth Annual Report*, p. 80).

SLOUGH CREEK*   Map #2

Slough Creek flows south and west to the Lamar River from a lake on Pinnacle Mountain in the Gallatin National Forest north of Yellowstone. Early in the summer of 1867, prospectors Lou Anderson, Ansel Hubble, George W. Reese, Caldwell, and another man went up the Yellowstone River. Hubble was sent ahead of the main party, and on his return he was asked what kind of stream was up ahead. "Twas but a slough," he is said to have replied. Slough Creek is probably the stream that Jim Bridger showed on his hand-drawn map of 1851 as "Beaver Creek." Fur-trapper Osborne Russell hunted for beaver on this stream in 1837.

More than one authority has referred to Slough Creek as "the finest natural cutthroat trout stream in America if not the world." Over 4 million trout were stocked into this stream between 1921 and 1954, and rainbow and grayling were planted here in 1936. The stream now contains almost all cutthroat with some longnose dace and longnose suckers. Catch-and-release regulations were instituted in 1973 due to heavy angler pressure.

SLUICEWAY FALLS* Map #3

This 35-foot-high waterfall is on the Ferris Fork of the Bechler River west of Pitchstone Plateau. Explorer William C. Gregg named the falls in 1921 because it looked like a prospector's sluice.

SMOKE JUMPER HOT SPRINGS* Map #3

In 1956, Assistant Chief Ranger William S. Chapman named Smoke Jumper Hot Springs, located about one mile west of Summit Lake and about 6 miles southwest of Old Faithful. Chapman named it because "smoke jumpers who jump on forest fires use the thermal area as a guiding land mark in making their jumps and in coming out from fires" (USBGN folder file).

SNAKE RIVER* Map #4

The Snake River is a major tributary of the Columbia River and has its headwaters just inside Yellowstone on the Two Ocean Plateau. Various stretches of this important river have had at least 15 different names. The name, which comes from the Snake (Shoshone) Indians, was applied to the river as early as 1812, making it one of the oldest place name in the Park. Shoshone Indians referred to some parts of the stream as "Yampa-pah," meaning "stream where the Yampa grows" (Yampa is a food plant) and later as "Po-og-way" meaning "road river" (an allusion to the Oregon Trail, which followed sections of the river) or, less likely, "sagebrush river."

In 1872, the second Hayden survey to Yellowstone gave the name "Barlow's Fork" (of the Snake) to the part of the river above the mouth of Harebell Creek, honoring J. W. Barlow who had explored that area in 1871. The group thought that Harebell Creek was the Snake River's main channel, an interpretation of the stream that was changed by the Hague surveys during the 1880s. Frank Bradley of the 1872 survey gave the name "Lewis Fork" (of the Snake) to the present-day Lewis River. The Snake name comes from sign language—a serpentine movement of the hand with the index finger extended—that referred to the weaving of baskets or grass lodges of the Snake or Shoshone Indians.

The source of the Snake River was debated for a long time. The problem was to find the longest branch in the Two Ocean Plateau, which is thoroughly crisscrossed with streams. Current maps show the head of the Snake to be about 3 miles north of Phelps Pass, at a point on the Continental Divide *inside* Yellowstone Park. In 1926, John G. White showed a photo in his hand-typed book *Souvenir of Wyoming* of the "true source of the Snake," writing that "it is near the Continental Divide upon two ocean plateau. A number of springs gush forth upon the hillside. Uniting, they form a small stream, which, at an altitude of two miles above sea level, begins its arduous journey . . . to the Pacific" (p. 309). The Snake River is the nation's fourth largest river; 42 miles of it are in Yellowstone Park.

SNOW PASS* Map #1

Snow Pass is located between Terrace Mountain and Clagett Butte, west of Mammoth Hot Springs. P. W. Norris discovered the pass in 1875 and named it "Terrace Pass" in 1879 after nearby Terrace Mountain. Norris also built the first road to Swan Lake Flat (and points south) through this pass in 1878. This road rose steeply from the Mammoth area, and many early accounts mentioned "the terrible hill on the only passable route from Mammoth . . . to the upper districts of the park." In 1883, this hill scared New York Senator Roscoe Conkling so badly that he reportedly "packed his trunk and went back home without going further into the park." Park tour operator G. L. Henderson noted that "Snow Gate" (Snow Pass) was

> usually blockaded with snow until late in the summer. It has been the terror of the packers, freighters, and guides. A shower of rain made it impossible to climb and equally dangerous to descend (*Manual and Guide*, p. 1).

In 1883, engineer Dan Kingman (see Kingman Pass) began work on a new road along Glen Creek to the Golden Gate, which avoided the hard pull up Snow Pass. By 1900, Hiram Chittenden referred to the pass as Snow Pass, but it was also known as "Wagon Road Pass" and "Hell Gate."

SNOWSHOE PASS* Map #1

This pass in the Gallatin Range, which is accessible only by traveling cross-country (there is no trail), is located at the headwaters of Stellaria Creek just southwest of Gray Peak. It is not known who named this pass or when the name was given, but it first appeared on the 1930 topographic map of the Park.

"Snowshoe" refers to the long heavy wooden skis (Norwegian snowshoes) that army personnel and others used in Yellowstone to travel in winter. The skis were 8 to 10 feet long, about 4 inches wide, and an inch thick in the middle.

SNOWY RANGE   Maps #2 and 4

See Absaroka Range

SOAP HILL   Map #1

This name refers to the hill over which the main road runs from Gardiner to Mammoth between the Mammoth Campground and the 45th parallel of latitude. The name was given locally in the 1890s because rain or snow often made this quarter-mile of unpaved road nearly impassable, as "slick as soap."

SODA BUTTE*   Map #2

This extinct hot spring cone of travertine in the Lamar River Valley near the junction of Soda Butte Creek and the Lamar River was named in 1870 by a party of prospectors that included A. Bart Henderson, Adam "Horn" Miller (see Miller Creek), and James Gourley. Henderson wrote in his diary in 1871: "We gave the cone the name of Soda Butte and the creek the name of Soda Butte Creek" (p. 54). In 1871, F. V. Hayden wrote that "this old ruin is a fine example of the tendency of the cone to close up its summit in its dying stages" (*Fifth Annual Report*, p. 138).

P. W. Norris noted in 1883 that near Soda Butte "is the legendary spring of the surrounding Indian nations for the cure of the saddle-galls of horse, or arrow or other wounds of warriors, and besides properties similar to those of the Arkansas Hot Springs, will soon fatten man or animal using it" (*Calumet of the Coteau*, p. 269). Norris's claim may be questionable, but there is no doubt that the spring was well-known. Apparently, its water has a terrible taste. As S. Weir Mitchell, who visited Yellowstone in 1879, wrote for *Lippincott's Magazine*:

> I do not distinctly recall all the nasty tastes which have afflicted my palate, but I am quite sure this was one of the vilest. It was a combination of acid, sulphur, and saline, like a diabolic julep of lucifer matches, bad eggs, vinegar, and magnesia. I presume its horrible taste has secured it a reputation for being good when it is down (July 1880, p. 33).

SODA BUTTE CANYON*   Map #2

This name refers to the canyon and much of the valley of Soda Butte Creek, which is located from near Soda Butte, north to the Montana-Wyoming state line and which includes Ice Box Canyon. The name was in use as early as 1877 by Gen. O. O. Howard, when his military force passed through the area in their pursuit of the Nez Perce Indians. Although Howard knew the name Soda Butte Canyon from nearby Soda Butte Creek, he tried to give the name "Jocelyn Canyon" to the area for one of his officers, Stephen Perry Jocelyn.

SODA SPRING*   Map #1

This thermal spring at Mammoth Hot Springs is located less than 200 feet west and a little north of Poison Spring. It is appropriate that a spring in Yellowstone still bears this name, because early fur trappers probably used the name "Soda Spring(s)" to refer to now unknown springs in the region during the 1830s. Soda Spring at Mammoth became quite well-known during the early days in the Park for its good drinking water, which tasted like soda.

Geologist Walter Weed appears to have given the name (or taken it from local use) in 1885. He described a spring that year as "Soda Spring... water milky, 53°, bulges and bubbles up constantly, slightly over 6 feet diameter" (USGS, Box 47, vol. 10, p. 85). Weed reported that the spring had been cleaned out and boards placed around it, apparently for the convenience of visitors who used the spring's drinking water. The main road ran close to this spring from the early days into the 1920s. The spring continued to be used for drinking at least into the 1940s.

Today, Soda Spring is a dry, grass-filled depression with a little water bubbling in a small hole in its bottom. The spring has been full as recently as 1976.

SOLFATARA PLATEAU*   Map #1

Solfatara Plateau, one of 7 named plateaus that make up the Yellowstone Plateau, has a mean elevation of 8,000 feet and is located west of Canyon Village. Labeled "Yellowstone Ridge" on an 1882 map, the plateau seems to have been given its current name in 1883 by geologist Walter Weed. The earliest known usage is his "Plateau Solfatara."

A solfatara is a thermal vent that emits hydrogen sulphide, steam, and other gases that are sometimes so strong that they can literally catch on fire. Solfataric areas are characterized by little water, much sulphur, and crumbling rocks due to acid decomposition. In Italian, *solfatara* means "sulphur mine."

SOLITARY GEYSER*   Map #3

This geyser in the Upper Geyser Basin is located north of and above the Geyser Hill Group. In 1872, Gustavus Bechler of the second Hayden survey included "Solitary Spring" on his map and probably named it. In 1915, Solitary Geyser was selected as the hot water source for a swimming pool to be built at Old Faithful:

> Its outlet channel was deepened and the water-level lowered, whereupon the spring began to play. The next year the channel was dredged out still farther, when the Solitary assumed its present [eruptive] behavior and has functioned in the same manner ever since (Allen and Day, *Hot Springs*, p. 261).

Monida-Yellowstone stage drivers at the Upper Geyser Basin, 1906

The water from Solitary Geyser was conducted over wooden cooling frames (dismantled in 1928) that eventually became heavily encrusted with sinter. The geyser erupted and overflowed about every 5 minutes, sending water down over the frames to the pool. The license for this concession was revoked in 1948, and the swimming pool was dismantled in 1950. Solitary Geyser was studied in 1958 and found to erupt 15 feet high at intervals of about 5.5 minutes.

SOLUTION CREEK*   Map #4

This stream flows north from Riddle Lake to the south shore of Yellowstone Lake east of Grant Village. Members of the Hague parties of the USGS named the creek in 1885 because it is the outlet of Riddle Lake. Earlier survey members had been confused about whether Riddle Lake drained to the Atlantic Ocean or to the Pacific Ocean. Discovery of the outlet solved the riddle.

SOUTH END HILLS   Map #1

This name is applied to the low, 8,934-foot-high hills of the Gallatin Range just south of Mount Holmes. Geologist Arnold Hague named these hills in about 1896 because of their location at the south end of the range.

SPA GEYSER   Map #3

Spa Geyser is part of the Grotto Group in the Upper Geyser Basin. Geologist Walter Weed of the USGS named the geyser in 1887 and described it as "The Spa": "Permanent water level 13′ × 18′ —basin 36′ diameter. Overflows and bulges intermittently" (USGS, Box 53, vol. 28, p. 109). Although the reason for the name is undocumented, Weed may have named it for the medicinal springs at Spa, Belgium.

In 1927, Spa Geyser was known as "Spa Pool" because the feature had apparently not been known to erupt on a large scale. But in 1927, the spring erupted to heights of 30 feet in July and was also active in November. During the 1930s, Spa Geyser erupted to 50 feet, and in recent years its eruptions have reached heights of 10 to 80 feet, with variable durations and infrequent intervals. Geyser researcher Rocco Paperiello recorded seeing 40-foot eruptions in 1982 and 1983.

SPECIMEN RIDGE*   Map #2

This long ridge, which separates the Lamar Valley and Mirror Plateau, can be seen from the Grand Loop Road at Tower Fall and south of the Northeast Entrance Road in the Lamar Valley. Capt. W. A. Jones described his visit to the ridge in 1873: "I went out today with the miners at the [Baronett] bridge to a place called by them 'Specimen Mountain,' a noted locality for amethysts, forms of chalcedony, opal, and silicified wood" (*Report*, p. 33). The name was in use prior to 1870 and was probably given by prospectors.

SPIREA CREEK†   Map #3

This stream flows south from Pitchstone Plateau to Crawfish Creek near the South Entrance of the Park. In 1882, members of a Northern Pacific Railroad survey team, including S. P. Panton, named this stream "Loud Creek" for Judge Charles H. Loud of Miles City, Montana. A member of the party, Judge Loud was an engineer who helped survey the NPRR's Park branch railroad. In 1885, members of the Hague parties of the USGS named the stream Spirea for a shrub called spirea or "meadowsweet" (*Spiraea sp.*), which grows in many parts of the American West.

SPLENDID GEYSER*   Map #3

Splendid Geyser is part of the Daisy Group in Upper Geyser Basin. Historian Aubrey Haines believes that this geyser was the one seen by fur-trapper Warren Ferris in 1834. If so, it would join springs at Shoshone Geyser Basin and Potts Hot Spring Basin, Grand Prismatic Spring, and Steamboat Springs as thermal features viewed very early by fur trappers.

The earliest known description of an eruption of Splendid Geyser is the Earl of Dunraven's report in 1874, when he saw it from a distance and estimated its height to be about 150 feet. In 1876, M. A. Switzer's party apparently saw the feature. Switzer wrote: "saw the new Geyser splendid. It throws probably 150 feet.... Splendid spouts for us in free style" ("Trip to the Geysers," pp. 4, 6). Some have thought that Park Superintendent P. W. Norris named the geyser in 1881, but Switzer's notes suggest an earlier naming or, more likely, how the name probably came about. The name was probably in local use before Norris recorded it in 1881.

Splendid Geyser was apparently dormant between 1878 and 1880, active between 1881 and 1891, dormant in 1892, active between 1893 and 1898, and then dormant from mid-1898 to 1931. On July 28, 1931, Splendid made its comeback, erupting 130 feet high and causing great excitement in the Park. There were no more eruptions until 1951. Splendid was active until 1959 and then again became dormant. Its most recent active cycles have been 1974-1977, 1978-1980, and 1983-1985.

SPONGE GEYSER*   Map #3

Sponge Geyser is in the Geyser Hill Group of the Upper Geyser Basin. In 1871, F. V. Hayden named this spring the

"Dental Cup" from its shape. Geologist Arnold Hague believed that the name Sponge was given "in 1883 by some visitor" because "it is perforated by numerous holes and cavities, giving it a porous look, which together with its light-buff color, suggests a huge sponge" (Hague papers, Box 13, vol. 16). Sponge Geyser was very famous during early days in the Park because of the beauty of its rim, which attracted much attention. The geyser was also well-known because it erupted often.

In 1884, guidebooks referred to Sponge Geyser as the "Terian" spring, a name that had also been applied to nearby Lioness Geyser. The reason for that name is not known. Beginning in about 1885, Park tour operator G. L. Henderson called it "Tyrian Boiling Spring." Sponge Geyser's action has remained essentially the same during recent years, erupting from 6 to 12 inches high for a few seconds, every minute or so. The geyser was inactive much of the time between 1973 and 1983, but it rejuvenated in 1983.

SPRING CREEK*   Map #3

Spring Creek, which flows from Norris Pass to the Firehole River, was named by members of the Hague parties of the USGS in 1885. Arnold Hague wrote in 1891: "Spring Creek is well named as there is a large amount of water coming out from beneath the rhyolite [along its course]" (USGS, Box 55, vol. 2, p. 45). Hague's reference was to cold springs.

SQUIRREL SPRINGS and
SQUIRREL SPRINGS RIDGE*   Map #1

These springs in Mammoth Hot Springs are located on top of the ridge that has been built up by the springs. Tour operator G. L. Henderson named the area "Jacob's Ladder Terrace" in 1885 and made the place one of the focal points for his tours of the Mammoth Hot Springs. Henderson also named the "three" caves under the ridge (see Stygian Caves) and described the area in some detail. As early as 1883, the small spouting springs on top of Squirrel Springs Ridge became known as "Pulsating Geyser." Henderson probably gave the geyser that name, because geologist Walter Weed found it on a signboard there in 1883.

The name Squirrel Springs was in local use by 1884 and was included on the 1904 map of the Park. In 1927, a Park place-names committee dropped "Jacob's Ladder" in favor of the name Squirrel Springs Ridge. The squirrel-like "twittering" sound made by the small springs was the reason for the name.

STEADY GEYSER*   Map #3

Steady Geyser is in the Firehole Lake (Black Warrior) Group of the Lower Geyser Basin. This geyser is a perpetual spouter, perhaps the world's largest, and erupts constantly. In 1871, F. V. Hayden included a drawing of "Steady Geyser, Lower Fire-Hole" in his report, giving the name but no other information.

Steady Geyser has two vents that alternate between eruptive and dormant periods. First one vent will show steady action and then the other, followed by a longer period when both vents will play in concert. The force and height of the eruption slowly (sometimes over many months) increase and decrease, from 15 feet high sometimes down to only one foot high.

Geologist Arnold Hague wrote about Steady Geyser in 1911: "A short distance back from the geyser is a second vent one foot in diameter, black-lined, and bulging from 1 to 2 feet intermittently" (Hague papers, "Firehole Geyser Basin," Box 11, p. 36). Apparently, the color of Hague's second vent (or perhaps the dark color of deposits or water nearby) was responsible for the geyser's second name, "Black Warrior Geyser." Park tour operator G. L. Henderson gave it a third name, "Margurite Geyser" from the writings of German author Johann Goethe. He described it as having a "white front wall [and] an ebony back ground [that] makes it the most unique and wonderful of all the active geysers" (*Manual and Guide*, p. 4). Henderson's name "Margurite" did not survive, and his name "Black Warrior" was to be gradually transferred to some nearby springs (see Black Warrior Springs).

STEAMBOAT GEYSER*   Map #1

This geyser in the Back Basin of Norris Geyser Basin is also officially named New Crater Geyser. Since the dormancy of New Zealand's Waimangu Geyser in 1917, Steamboat Geyser (when in its major phase) has become the tallest geyser in the world (300 to 400 feet). Its unpredictability (from 4 days to 50 years) makes it difficult to observe, however, and its short water phase (from 3 to 20 minutes) adds to the difficulty. Many more people have seen its powerful steam phase, which lasts for up to 12 hours following the water phase. In its minor phase, Steamboat emits splashes of up to 30 feet high every few minutes.

The 1878 Hayden party named it Steamboat Geyser because "the eruptions reminded one [member] of the sound of an old style paddle wheel steamboat." Guidebook writer Lester C. Hunt noted in 1941 that "the water is dashed out of the vent, as water is churned by a steamboat wheel" (*Wyoming*, p. 415).

Steamboat Geyser (New Crater Geyser) has been called "Fissure Geyser," "Double Crater Geyser," "Noble Geyser," and "Tippecanoe Geyser." Arnold Hague of the USGS named it "Fissure Geyser" in 1887 because of the geyser's vents or the fissure on which it is located or both. In about 1888, Park tour operator G. L. Henderson called it "Double Crater Geyser," and in 1890 Park Superintendent F. A. Boutelle named it "Noble Geyser" for Secretary of the Interior John Noble. Noble declined the honor and ordered that the geyser be called "Tippecanoe Geyser" for President Benjamin Harrison.

P. W. Norris claimed that the geyser "burst forth" on August 11, 1878, and that it had two types of eruptions: one 30 feet high every half hour and one 100 feet high every 6 to 7 days. A. C. Peale also thought in 1878 that the geyser was newly formed and named it "Steamboat Vent."

Steamboat Geyser had numerous powerful eruptions in 1881 to at least 100 feet. It is likely that these "heavy" eruptions continued during 1882 and 1883, combining with Steamboat's "normal" smaller eruptions from 5 to 30 feet high. The geyser also had large (major phase) eruptions in 1888, 1889 (probable), 1890, 1891, 1892 (probable), 1894, 1902, and 1911. These eruptions are estimated to have attained heights of from 100 to 350 feet. After 1911, Steamboat did not erupt again in major phase for 50 years. Recent major eruptions numbered 23 in 1982, 12 in 1983, and 5 in 1984. Jack L. Crellin described a major eruption of Steamboat in 1964:

> The only way that I can describe the initial burst of water from the north vent is to liken it to a rifle shot. There was no gradual advent as in the case of Old Faithful Geyser. It was rather a sudden, explosive action in which the maximum height was shortly to be achieved. Because of my location it became necessary to immediately remove myself to a more advantageous point from which to photograph the full eruption.... As I turned around, breathless from my retreat, I was astounded by the incredible height and power of this long maturing thermal giant. The main column of water from the north vent most certainly attained a height of 400 feet and possibly 500 feet. The column of water maintains a nozzle type discharge and does not separate appreciably. This undoubtedly accounts in part for its high altitude performance (letter, July 21, 1964, YNP Research Library).

STEAMBOAT POINT* Map #4

This point on the northeastern shore of Yellowstone Lake is located just south of Mary Bay and Holmes Point. Members of the 1871 Hayden survey named this "Steam Point" or "Steamy Point" because of nearby steam jets. F. V. Hayden also referred to it that year as Steamboat Point, which is the name that has survived. In 1878, A. C. Peale wrote that the point was named from the existence "of a powerful steam vent from which a vast column of steam escapes with a continuous roar that exactly resembles the escape from a huge steamboat" (in Hayden, *Twelfth Annual Report*, p. 115).

STEAMBOAT SPRINGS* Map #4

These hot springs are located on Steamboat Point along the northeastern shore of Yellowstone Lake south of Mary Bay. There are two individually named features: Steamboat Spring and Locomotive Vent. It is appropriate that the name Steamboat is given to some springs in the Park, for it is a name that was used in much earlier times to refer to Yellowstone area hot springs in general. Walter DeLacy wrote of his trip through the Lower Geyser Basin in 1863: "these [springs] were probably geysers, and the boys called them 'steamboat springs' " ("South Snake River," p. 132). Charles Wilkes's 1845 map showed the notation "Steamboat Sp." In 1878, the Hayden survey placed the name on its map.

STEAMVALVE SPRING* Map #1

This hot spring in the Norris Geyser Basin is located about 150 feet southeast of the Norris museum and east of Bathtub Spring. Steamvalve Spring has disappeared at times and has had several locations. In 1878, A. C. Peale mapped a feature in this area that he called "Locomotive Spring" in his report and labeled "No. 6 Sulphur Mud Spr." on his map. Peale described it as "a boiling sulphur mud-hole about 12 feet in diameter with a raised margin about 3 feet high, composed of mud coated with sulphur.... The spring is across the road from No. 1 [Bathtub Spring] on somewhat higher ground" (in Hayden, *Twelfth Annual Report*, p. 126). Geologist Walter Weed used the name Steamvalve in 1887, when he described it as roaring with no water but with copious steam. G. L. Henderson described the spring in 1888 as "The Steam Valve ... being alternately a steam, steam-aqueous and gas-aqueous geyser" (*Manual and Guide*, p. 2). Henderson could as easily have given the name to the spring as Walter Weed. Weed got some of his place names from Henderson (and vice versa). Steamvalve was at least partially active in 1914—two tourists saw it as it "sizzled and threatened"—but there were no reports of activity until May 22, 1946, at 9:33 a.m., when Steamvalve Spring made its modern reappearance, breaking through the blacktopped parking area at the Norris Museum and causing a cave-in. Within 48 hours a 12- by 15-foot crater formed that alternately boiled 3 feet high and then drained. By 1947, the spring was inactive, but its hole remained into the 1950s, when the crater was filled in. Steamvalve Spring broke out anew in February 1981.

STELLARIA CREEK* Map #1

This creek flows northwest to the East Fork of Fan Creek from Snowshoe Pass north of Fawn Pass and west of Gray Peak. Arnold Hague named the creek in 1885 for the small, white flower Starwort (*Stellaria sp.*).

STEPHENS CREEK† Map #1

Stephens Creek flows north to the Yellowstone River from Sepulcher Mountain, which is between Electric Peak and

Corkscrew bridge in Sylvan Pass

Comet Geyser, Upper Geyser Basin

Three River Junction on the Bechler River, 1921

Mammoth Hot Springs. Before 1878, this stream was locally named "Henderson Creek" after the James Henderson ranch, which had been established on the creek in 1871. James Henderson was the brother of prospector A. Bart Henderson; and in 1877, his ranch was the site of a minor skirmish between locals and a band of fleeing Nez Perce Indians.

In early 1879, Clarence M. Stephens came to the Park to serve as P. W. Norris's assistant. He was the first employee to spend a winter in the Park (1879-1880) and was its first postmaster (1880). Under Norris, Stephens was in charge of Park road building in 1879. An 1880 traveler referred to him as Norris's "jolly young assistant."

During his three years as assistant superintendent, Stephens purchased the Henderson ranch. He sold the ranch in 1883, and it was subsequently owned by George Huston, C. T. Hobart, and the H. J. Hoppe family. Stephens Creek was known as "Hoppe Creek" until the mid-1920s, when the government forcibly purchased the ranch to be added to the Park.

STEVENSON ISLAND*   Map #4

This island on Yellowstone Lake, 2 miles south of Lake, was named in 1871 by members of the Hayden survey. The name honors James Stevenson (see Mount Stevenson), whom F. V. Hayden considered "undoubtedly the first white man that ever placed foot upon it" (Hayden, *Fifth Annual Report*, p. 96). Stevenson and Henry Elliot reached the island, but Elliot appears to have been the one to name the island. A. C. Peale recorded in his diary on Saturday, July 29, 1871:

> This morning Jim and Elliot started off in the boat for the island. They used a blanket for [a] sail. . . . Sometime after dinner the boat came back. They went all around the island and say that it is a thick jungle and that the tracks of game are abundant. The boat worked splendidly. Elliot named the island "Stevenson's Island" (p. 21, YNP Research Library).

Although these two men are the first recorded persons to have reached the island, fur trappers, prospectors, or Indians may have reached it earlier. In 1874, tourist Mabel Cross Osmund and some government men visited the island when she was six years old. Osmund remembered that they collected raspberries and gooseberries and that the men named the island "Mabel's Island" because she was the first child to visit it.

STONE MOUNTAIN   Map #1

In about 1902, geologist Arnold Hague named this 9,548-foot-high peak of the Washburn Range, which is located immediately west of Hedges Peak and east of Observation Peak.

STORM PASS   Map #1

Storm Pass in the Washburn Range is located immediately north of Cook Peak. This place name was given by geologist Arnold Hague after 1904 and recalls the old name of Cook Peak, which was known as "Storm Peak" in Hague's day.

STORM POINT*   Map #4

In 1871, members of the Hayden survey gave the name "Bluff Point" to this point on Yellowstone Lake south of Indian Pond. Cornelius Hedges and N. P. Langford of the 1870 Washburn party had named the place the "Curiosity Shop" or "Curiosity Point" from the oddly shaped stone objects found along the beach here. A party of prospectors under A. Bart Henderson had found these same kinds of stones three years earlier and had wrongly attributed them to Aztec Indians (see Concretion Cove). Members of the 1878 Hayden survey named Storm Point, a focal location of northeastward-moving storms.

STYGIAN CAVES*   Map #1

Located under Squirrel Springs Ridge in the Mammoth Hot Springs, Stygian Caves were apparently larger and more spectacular during the 1880s than they are now. There were three caves in the summer of 1882, when tour operator G. L. Henderson made "frequent visits to this and the two adjoining caves." By 1883, Henderson had given the name "Stalactic Cave" to the most southwesterly cave and Stygian Cave to the northeast cave. He named the caves for the River Styx in Greek mythology, which surrounded the underworld with its 9 loops and was a place "from whence no traveler returns." The name Stygian was appropriate because of a hot water stream that was partly underground (see River Styx) and the presence of dead insects and birds killed by poisonous gases from the caves. The gases, which are carbon dioxide, sulphur dioxide, and hydrogen sulphide, did sometimes cause problems for humans, but they were especially lethal to smaller creatures. There was great concern over these dead animals during later years. Some 16 species of birds were found dead in Stygian Cave in 1902, and hundreds if not thousands of dead birds were found that year in other caves of the upper terraces area. For this reason, it became known as the "Cave of Death."

Henderson named the third cave "Hermit's Cave." It seems to have been less important than the other two, and its location is not certain.

SULLIVAN CREEK   Map #3

Sullivan Creek flows west and northwest from Grants Pass to the Firehole River. S. P. Panton, Carl Hals, Charles

Loud, and other Northern Pacific Railroad surveyors named Sullivan Creek for one of two Sullivans (and perhaps both of them) employed by the railroad.

John H. Sullivan was superintendent of transportation for the NPRR and a member of the construction department of the Yellowstone Division of the railroad, which built the National Park Branch to Cinnabar in 1883. The other John Sullivan, the survey team's cook, is probably the creek's namesake. Sullivan's creativity kept the men from starving when provisions ran low during the survey. Panton wrote that Sullivan gave the surveyors a "square meal" by taking a swan that the party had shot at Lewis Lake.

> Next morning we saw Sullivan holding the swan on the ground with one foot while he hacked it to pieces with an ax. He had tried to pluck it, but the feathers were fastened too tight, so he skinned it. He put the pieces to boil, and for some days we had rather thin soup from it. In a week of boiling the skin of that bird was so softened that we could strip it off the bones and eat it (*Billings Gazette*, April 22, 1945).

SULPHUR BEDS Map #2

This name is applied to the area just east of Tower Fall, where the Great Bannock Trail crossed the Yellowstone River and where John Colter probably crossed in 1807-1808. The name was used locally from the existence and odor of sulphur from the active hot springs.

SULPHUR CALDRON* Map #2

This hot spring of the Mud Volcano area is located on the east bank of the Yellowstone River just east of Turbulent Pool. This spring was probably seen by both the Folsom and Washburn parties in 1869 and 1870. It may have been the spring that traveler A. J. Thrasher called "Alum Spring" in 1871. Park Superintendent Edmund B. Rogers named the spring Sulphur Caldron in 1937 because it contains large amounts of free sulphur. Some have called this the most acidic spring in the Park with a *pH* of 1.3.

SULPHUR LAKE Map #1

This large thermal pond is located in the Mary Mountain area and in the true (southern) Highland Hot Springs. The old stagecoach road ran near the pond during the early days, and many observers saw it.

In 1873, T. B. Comstock described the lake as a large "sulphurous pond not more than one-quarter the size of Turbid Lake" (in Jones, *Report*, pp. 220-221). The place name seems to have been used as early as 1878, when geologist W. H. Holmes described it as "a sulphur lake of irregular slope—some 200 yards in length" (*Random Records*, 3:119). In 1889, Arnold Hague called the hot springs the largest and most active sulphur area in the Park. It lies exactly on the divide. . . . The whole basin presents a dreary view as there is almost no vegetation over an immense area of country. There is quite a large lake in the center of rather a dull, dirty, opalescent appearance. Southwest of the lake there are one or two remarkable hills covered with sulphur (USGS, Box 55, vol. 2, p. 94).

Today, there are two ponds here that were probably a single pond at one time.

SULPHUR MOUNTAIN* Map #2

This 7,937-foot-high hill is located just south of the Crater Hills in the Hayden Valley in an area of intense sulphur thermal activity. The name of the hill came from stories told by fur trappers and has been associated with an 1839 group who "told about the sulphur mountain" and other Yellowstone wonders (Hamilton, *My Sixty Years*, p. 95). Fr. Pierre-Jean DeSmet's 1851 map, drawn with information provided by trapper Jim Bridger, applied the name "Sulphur Mountain" to present-day Mammoth Hot Springs. Capt. J. W. Barlow showed the name in its proper place on his 1871 map. But N. P. Langford of the 1870 Washburn party had given the name "Crater Hill" to the main hill of the area in 1870, which created confusion for years. In many accounts, Sulphur Mountain was interchangeable with the name for the main hill of the Crater Hills. After the USBGN approved the name Sulphur Mountain in 1930, Park maps omitted the name Crater Hills until it was approved in 1937. Maps since then have carried both names.

SULPHUR ROCK Map #2

This boulder, located just above Tower Fall on the left bank of Tower Creek, is one of the "towers" of Tower Fall. Apparently, artist Thomas Moran, who painted a picture of the rock in 1874-1875, named it. Its yellowish color suggested the name, but there is no sulphur prevalent in this area.

SULPHUR SPRING* Map #2

This is the official name of a thermal feature of the Sulphur Springs at Crater Hills in the Hayden Valley. The spring has sometimes also been called Crater Hills Geyser. Because this area was well-known in the early days of the Park, many visitors saw Sulphur Spring and it became quite famous for its "restless vigorous energy."

Members of the Washburn party inadvertently named the spring in 1870, when Lt. G. C. Doane described it as "intensely sulphurous." N. P. Langford called it "a sulphur spring twelve by twenty feet." And Gen. H. D. Washburn described it in 1871 as:

... a large sulphuric spring, 20 feet by 12, filled with boiling water, and this water is thrown up from 3 to 5 feet. The basin of this spring is pure solid brimstone, as clear and bright as any brimstone of commerce. Quite a strong stream flows from the spring, and sulphur is found incrusting nearly everything ("Yellowstone Expedition," p. 215).

F. V. Hayden described the spring in 1871 and 1872, using the name Sulphur Spring and "Yellow Sulphur Spring." But photographer H. B. Calfee (see Calfee Creek) had visited the area before the Washburn party and had called it "Alum Geyser" (perhaps a reference to nearby Alum Creek). Other names applied at various times were "Hot Sulphur Spring," "Boiling Sulphur Spring," "Brimstone Bowl," "Devil's Bathtub," "Chrome Spring," "White Sulphur Spring" (from the "whitish cast" of the water), and "Plunging Pool" (probably because the spring plunges or sinks after an eruption).

In behavior, Sulphur Spring may be said to stand between the typical geyser and the perpetual spouter. Its temperature seldom, if ever, reaches boiling. Recent observers have placed Sulphur Spring in the category of "gas driven geyser." In 1984, geyser observer Rocco Paperiello saw it erupting from 20 to 25 feet high and discharging copiously toward the west.

SULPHUR SPRING CREEK   Map #2

This creek flows northeast from Crater Hills to the Yellowstone River between Alum Creek and Trout Creek. Lt. G. C. Doane of the 1870 Washburn party named it "Sulphur Run" from his observations of sulphur springs in the Crater Hills area—the source of the creek. By 1939, guidebooks were calling the stream Sulphur Spring Creek in accordance with the 1870 name, but they added the word "spring" to differentiate it from Sulphur Creek.

SUNDAY GEYSER   Map #1

This geyser in the Porcelain Basin of Norris Geyser Basin is located some 100 feet northwest of Hurricane Vent. Born on July 12, 1964, it was called "Milky Geyser" at first because of the milky color of its water. Park Naturalist William J. Lewis named it Sunday Geyser: "Since this was a Sunday, and since its water may clear (making the name Milky inappropriate), and since it promises to be a geyser of considerable interest, the name Sunday Geyser is suggested" ("Thermal Features," p. 67). Sunday's original eruptions were 30 feet high for a few seconds. In 1981, it rejuvenated and erupted to over 50 feet high.

SUNSET LAKE*   Map #3

Sunset Lake is a large hot spring in the Black Sand Basin of the Upper Geyser Basin. Lt. G. C. Doane described the spring in 1870 as "a lake of Bluestone water, a hundred feet in diameter" (in Bonney and Bonney, *Battle Drums*, p. 345), and members of the 1872 Hayden survey named it "Great Hot Basin." Geologist Walter Weed appears to have named this spring "Sunshine Lake" in 1887 for its intense flame-like colors. Arnold Hague wrote that the "display of red and yellow tints upon the surface" of Sunset Lake was only surpassed by those of Grand Prismatic Spring.

SUNSET POINT   Map #2

This overlook point is located just above the Lower Falls on the south side of the Yellowstone River. H. C. Bumpus (see Bumpus Butte) named the point in about 1937, because looking downstream from this spot at sunset, observers can see the Grand Canyon of the Yellowstone beautifully illuminated.

SURPRISE CREEK*   Map #4

Surprise Creek flows southwest from the Continental Divide to the Heart River between the South Arm of Yellowstone Lake and Heart Lake. Members of the Hague parties of the USGS named the creek in 1885 because its course, as mapped that year, was surprisingly different from the discoveries of earlier explorations. Geologist Walter Weed wrote in 1891:

> Surprise Creek is applicably named. The meadow with its outlet is deceptive, being seemingly the course of Heart River, for this stream now flows through a modern [geologically speaking] cutting bordered by deep woods, the canyon being somewhat obscure, while the Surprise Creek meadows are large, prominent, and appear to be the proper outlet for the [Heart] lake (Hague papers, Box 13, p. 16).

SURPRISE POOL*   Map #3

Surprise Pool is a hot spring in the Great Fountain Group of Lower Geyser Basin. The pool's name came into local usage sometime between 1891 and 1894. The "surprise" came from the boiling reaction when the water's surface was disturbed. In 1895, an observer wrote: "If a handful of gravel is thrown into it, it will bubble and sparkle, exactly like bromo seltzer." This happened because the water temperature was right at the boiling point threshold. By 1896, guidebooks called it "Surprise or Sand Spring," and in 1897, geologist Walter Weed reported that a signboard posted at the spring gave its name as Surprise. Guidebooks encouraged visitors to throw sand in the pool, and as late as the 1930s this was still common practice. Visitors today are reminded that throwing items into springs can destroy these beautiful features.

Explorer William C. Gregg at Tendoy Falls, 1921

J.E. Haynes

SWAN LAKE*   Map #1

This small, shallow (3 feet deep) lake along the Grand Loop Road 5 miles south of Mammoth Hot Springs was named by Park Superintendent P. W. Norris in 1879. An 1883 guidebook reported that "we were informed [that it] was once covered with ducks and swans; hence the name" (Haupt, *Yellowstone*, p. 50). Trumpeter swans are often seen on the small ponds of this area, and 26 whistling swans were reported on Swan Lake in 1958.

The lake has had other names as well—"Annie's Lake" and "Freda's Lake"—apparently given for girlfriends or wives of visitors. In 1885, Dan Kingman's (see Kingman Pass) boat, the *U.S. Pinafore*, was launched on Swan Lake for a test-run before putting it on Yellowstone Lake. The shallowness of Swan Lake must have made the voyage difficult.

TANGLED CREEK*   Map #1

Tangled Creek flows west from above Firehole Lake to the Firehole River. The Hague parties of the USGS named the creek "Tangle Creek" in about 1889 because it is a network of separate channels that cross and recross each other.

TANTALUS CREEK*   Map #1

This stream is a tributary to the Gibbon River and drains much of the Back Basin (formerly "Tantalus Basin") of the Norris Geyser Basin. In about 1888, geologists Walter Weed and Arnold Hague of the USGS named the creek for Tantalus, the son of Zeus in Greek mythology, who stole the immortal nectar of the gods and gave it to his mortal friends. As punishment for this and other crimes, Zeus placed over Tantalus's head a huge stone that was always on the verge of falling and crushing him. This myth provides the origin of the word "tantalize."

It is not known why the two geologists chose this name for the creek. Perhaps the stream water, being undrinkable because of thermals, could only tantalize; or perhaps the name was given from the rising and falling water level due to geyser eruptions along the creek.

TANTALUS GEYSER   Map #1

This geyser in the Back Basin of the Norris Geyser Basin was formerly known as "Decker Geyser" (see Decker Island). Because the name "Decker Geyser" broke a long-established rule against naming thermal features for people, in 1984 Rick Hutchinson, Don White of the USGS, and Lee H. Whittlesey agreed to apply the name Tantalus (from Tantalus Creek and "Tantalus Basin") to the geyser.

TARDY GEYSER*   Map #3

Tardy Geyser is located in the Sawmill Group of the Upper Geyser Basin. In 1878, members of the third Hayden survey named this geyser for unknown reasons. T. B. Comstock had given the name to present-day Turban Geyser in 1873, but A. C. Peale moved it to this geyser in 1878. Peale described it this way:

> No. 22. Tardy Geyser.—This geyser has a circular basin about 18 feet in diameter, much like the Saw-Mill which is only a few feet north of it. In the center is a funnel-shaped orifice 2 by 2 feet, sloping to a hole 6 inches in diameter (in Hayden, *Twelfth Annual Report*, pp. 219).

Peale reported that he saw the geyser spout during an eruption of nearby Sawmill Geyser, but it did not erupt as high as Sawmill. For unknown reasons, geologist Walter Weed transferred the name "Tardy" in 1886 to a feature northwest of Spasmodic Geyser. The name was later moved back to the present-day feature, and Weed's second "Tardy Geyser" is now Old Tardy Geyser.

TEMPE CASCADE*   Map #3

This 30-foot-high cascade on Littles Fork of the Gregg Fork of Bechler River was named in 1922 by explorer W. C. Gregg. Tempe is a Shoshone Indian word meaning "cavern," referring to a cave near the cascade. Gregg's original name was "Cavern," but a USBGN staffer noted in 1922: "As two names were suggested that were so nearly alike, Cave and Cavern, the Board deemed it better to substitute the Indian name 'Tempe' instead of Cavern for the cascade on Little's Fork" (C. S. Sloane to J. E. Haynes, March 8, 1922).

TENDOY FALLS*   Map #3

This 33-foot-high waterfall is on the Ferris Fork of the Bechler River, just over a mile upstream from Ragged Falls. In 1922, explorer W. C. Gregg and Park photographer Jack E. Haynes named these falls for Tendoy (1834?-1907), a chief of the Lemhi Shoshones who lived near Yellowstone Park in eastern Idaho. Born on the Boise River in about 1834, he became chief of the Lemhis in 1863 and held that position for 44 years. Tendoy refused to leave his beloved Lemhi Valley in 1907, when his entire tribe moved to a reservation at Fort Hall, Idaho. Tendoy died in the valley on May 9, 1907, reportedly from drowning in a stream. His name has been translated as "the climber" or "he climbs rocks." He was probably one of the last Bannock-Shoshone leaders to cross Yellowstone Park on the Great Bannock Trail.

TERMINAL MONUMENT CREEK†   Map #1

This creek flows west from the Montana-Wyoming state line into the Gallatin River, south of Specimen Creek and about 45 miles south of Gallatin Gateway on U.S. Highway 191. USGS topographer Raymond E. Hill named Terminal Monument Creek in 1958, because the wooden corner post that marked the most northwesterly corner of Wyoming is near the creek. The National Park Service suggested "Corner Creek," but Hill's name prevailed.

TERRA COTTA SPRING   Map #3

This hot spring in the Castle Group of the Upper Geyser Basin was identified as "Brick Spring" on 1959 maps. The spring is not a geyser, and it is not the spring that is located 200 feet west of the south end of the Castle Geyser footbridge.

Terra Cotta Spring, named in 1886 by geologist Walter Weed "from its unchanging red color, due to disseminated clay" (Hague, Box 11, "The Geyser Basins," p. 52), is the spring that A. C. Peale called spring #12 in 1878. Naturalists Watson and Higgins called it "Brick Spring" in 1959, probably because it was a "quiet boiling spring of brick red muddy water" (USGS, Box 52, vol. 17, p. 75). Because of misplaced letters on one of Arnold Hague's 1904 maps, Terra Cotta Spring was placed across the river from Teakettle Geyser instead of downstream from Teakettle and on the opposite bank of the river. Recent maps have incorrectly placed the spring near the Castle Geyser footbridge, but that spring is actually the one that A. C. Peale called 'Dishpan Spring' in 1878.

TERRACE MOUNTAIN*   Map #1

This flat plateau located above the Hoodoos seems to have been named "Soda Mountain" as early as 1873, probably from confusion with nearby Mammoth Hot Springs, which also carried that name. Hiram Chittenden wrote that members of the third Hayden survey in 1878 named Terrace Mountain. If that is true, survey members also used the name "White Mountain" to refer to both Terrace Mountain and Mammoth Hot Springs. Like the Mammoth terraces, Terrace Mountain is believed to have been formed by ancient hot spring activity that deposited these travertine limestone terraces.

TERRACE POINT*   Map #4

In 1878, members of the third Hayden survey named this point on the Southeast Arm of Yellowstone Lake. They had found geological evidence here proving that Yellowstone Lake was once at least 160 feet higher. Old lake terraces extend up the hillsides east of Yellowstone Lake, marking several old beaches and indicating that the lake did not drain continuously but in stages.

TETON POINT   Map #4

Teton Point is on the East Entrance Road, 11.8 miles west of the East Entrance station. It appears that Park photographer Jack Haynes named this point or took it from local use in about 1922. Motorists can see Yellowstone Lake and the Teton Mountains from this vantage point.

THOMPSON'S PEAK   Map #1

This low peak 2 miles southeast of Osprey Falls is marked "7717" on topographic maps. It was named in about 1879 by Park Superintendent P. W. Norris for Frank Thompson of the Northern Pacific Railroad (see Cook Peak). The name was transferred to present-day Cook Peak in 1880, but since the small "7717" hill has never borne any other name, it should retain the name of Thompson's Peak.

THOROFARE CREEK*   Map #4

This large, important tributary of the Yellowstone River south of Yellowstone Lake took its name from the entire valley of the Yellowstone River above the lake. During fur-trade days (1822-1840), the route down the Yellowstone River from Two Ocean Pass became well-known as an easy (and the only southern) route onto the Yellowstone Plateau. So well-used was the route that trappers called it Thoroughfare. Members of the Hague parties of the USGS saluted the old name and the members of the trapping fraternity who gave it by applying the name to the stream in 1885.

THREE BROTHERS MOUNTAINS†   Map #1

Three Brothers Mountains are three edges or "prongs" of the Madison Plateau that overlook the Madison River just west of Madison Junction. In 1871, visitor R. W. Raymond called these mountains "Family Buttes." In 1959, Park Superintendent Lemuel Garrison recommended that the name Three Brothers Mountains be included on the 1959 USGS map, writing that "this name . . . has been applied for a long time." No evidence has been found to support Garrison's statement or to tell us who might have named the buttes.

THREE KNOB PEAK   Map #2

This peak in the Absaroka Range on the eastern boundary of the Park is located next to Notch Mountain and just across from Castor and Pollux peaks. T. A. Jaggar, Jr., a geologist with the Hague parties of the USGS, named the peak in 1897. He wrote:

> On the NW are Castor and Pollux, on SW is Notch Mt., a remarkable table capped with basalt, next to it 3-Knob Peak and next to it E[ast] the "candle extinguisher" [Candlestick Mountain]—so-called from its form (USGS, Box 50, vol. 1, p. 33).

THREE RIVER JUNCTION*   Map #3

This is where Gregg Fork, Phillips Fork, and Ferris Fork come together to form the Bechler River in the southwest corner of the Park. Explorer W. C. Gregg, who named the junction in 1920, wrote in the November 20, 1920, *Saturday Evening Post*:

> Three rushing streams came together at one point with such a roar that we could scarcely tell each other that this must be the head of the Bechler River . . . we pitched our tents at the very point of the union of the streams, and named the place Three River Junction—named not because we thought it pretty or romantic but because neither we nor others would call it anything else (p. 78).

THREE RIVERS PEAK*   Map #1

This 9,956-foot-high peak in the Gallatin Range is located at the head of the Gallatin River just south of Gallatin Lake. In a March 31, 1898, letter to naturalist John Muir, geologist Arnold Hague wrote that he personally had named Three Rivers Peak in 1884 and that it was one of his favorite names in the Park. Hague named it because branches of the Madison, Gallatin, and Gardner rivers take their rise from its slopes.

THREE SISTERS SPRINGS*   Map #3

This large spring of several connected pools is located in the Myriad Group of the Upper Geyser Basin. This 123-foot-long chain lake spring consists of "ten craters, seven hot springs, and three geysers." It was named "Three Crater Spring" in 1878 by members of the third Hayden survey. A. C. Peale of the survey thought that it was "three basins connected by narrow passages" (in Hayden, *Twelfth Annual Report*, p. 242). In 1875, Gen. W. E. Strong mentioned a feature he called "The Three Sisters," although it is unclear which spring he meant. In 1887, however, both Weed and Arnold Hague used the name Three Sisters for the first time, and one or both of them appears to have given the name.

In 1884, "while the air was full of politics," G. L. Henderson called Three Sisters Springs "Mugwump." Mugwumps were Republicans who refused to support party candidate James G. Blaine in 1884 and voted instead for Grover Cleveland.

Three Sisters Springs contains two named geysers: Three Crater Geyser and Little Brother Geyser. Nearby is Cousin Geyser. Three Crater Geyser is in the east vent. When active, the north vent of Three Sisters erupts 3 to 4 feet high for 20 to 60 seconds every 4 to 12 minutes. The south vent has been known to erupt 6 feet high at rare intervals. These springs have sometimes been referred to as North Sister, Middle Sister, and South Sister.

THE THUNDERER*   Map #2

This long, 10,554-foot-high mountain ridge borders the east side of Round Prairie and is just north of Mount Norris. On early maps the ridge was included as part of "Mount Norris." In 1885, members of the Hague parties of the USGS separately designated it The Thunderer and placed the name Mount Norris on the lower but connected southwest ridge. The name The Thunderer was given because the mountain was "seemingly a great focus for thunderstorms" (Chittenden, *Yellowstone*, p. 310).

TILL GEYSER   Map #3

See Rabbit Geyser

TOPPING POINT   Map #4

This point on Yellowstone Lake is located on the west bank about a mile south of the river outlet and north of Lake Hotel. Park Superintendent P. W. Norris named the point in about 1880 for Eugene S. Topping, who with Frank Williams ran one of the earliest boats on Yellowstone Lake.

Born on Long Island in 1844, Topping appears to have received good schooling before going to sea when he was 12 years old. Eleven years later, in 1868, he set out for the West, where he worked as a railroad tie-contractor, prospector, hard-rock miner, and stock trader. Topping reached the Clark Fork mines of Montana Territory in 1871 and eventually made Bozeman, Montana, his home.

The July 31, 1874, Bozeman *Avant Courier* reported that Topping was sailing a boat on Yellowstone Lake as early as 1874. In 1875, he built an "earth-roofed cabin" at Topping Point and constructed a boat there named *Topping*. It was "a small sail-boat of green, whip-sawed timber . . . which, after perilous service during a small portion of the seasons of 1875 and 1876, was dismantled, abandoned, and finally lost" (Norris, *Report of the Superintendent*, 1880, pp. 36-37).

Topping helped discover Norris Geyser Basin in 1872, and he led part of the Hayden survey party that same year

Tower Fall

Haynes Studio

to Mammoth Hot Springs. In 1883, he wrote *The Chronicles of the Yellowstone*, which is still a major source of early Montana history.

TORTOISE SHELL SPRING* Map #3

This is a hot spring in the Castle Group of the Upper Geyser Basin. Under a different name, Tortoise Shell Spring was a popular spring that campers cooked in during early days in the Park. Guidebooks referred to it as the "Devil's Well," and a Mrs. Foster who visited the area in 1882 reported:

> Here many of the campers boil their potatoes, eggs or in fact anything that one wishes to boil in water by putting them into bags, or small sacks and attaching a rope, throw them in and they are cooked perfectly in an incredibly short time ("From Foster Ranch to Wonderland," p. 47).

Because of its use as a cook station, Tortoise Shell Spring was also called "Camper's Spring" as late as 1914.

The name Tortoise Shell was in use by 1922, but it is not known when the name was given or who gave it. A Park place-names committee accepted the name Tortoise Shell Spring in 1927. According to naturalist Charles Phillips, one is "able to trace not only the shell of the tortoise but his head, tail and legs (several of the latter missing) as well" (NPS, *Ranger Naturalists' Manual*, p. 142).

TOWER FALL* Map #2

This 132-foot-high waterfall on Tower Creek was named in 1870 by members of the Washburn party. Prospector A. Bart Henderson had seen the waterfall in 1867 and had called it "the most beautiful falls I ever saw" (diary, September 3, 1867). N. P. Langford recorded that the name "was suggested by some of the most conspicuous features of the scenery" (*Scribner's Monthly*, May 1871, p. 9). Gen. Washburn claimed that the name was given "by a vote of the majority of the party" (in Cramton, *Early History*, p. 93). Samuel Hauser credited himself with the name: "Campt near the most beautiful falls—I ever saw—I named them 'Tower falls'—from the towers and pinacles [sic] that surround them" (diary, p. 6).

Langford has told the most interesting story of the party giving the name to Tower Fall:

> While in camp on Sunday, August 28th, on the bank of this creek, it was suggested that we select a name for the creek and fall. Walter Trumbull suggested "Minaret Creek" and "Minaret Fall." Mr. Hauser suggested "Tower Creek" and "Tower Fall." After some discussion a vote was taken, and by a small majority the name "Minaret" was decided upon. During the following evening Mr. Hauser stated with great seriousness that we had violated the agreement made relative to naming objects for our friends. He said that the well known Southern family—the Rhetts—lived in St. Louis, and that they had a most charming and accomplished daughter named "Minnie." He said that this daughter was a sweetheart of Trumbull, who had proposed the name—her name—"Minnie Rhett"—and that we had unwittingly given to the fall and creek the name of this sweetheart of Mr. Trumbull. Mr. Trumbull indignantly denied the truth of Hauser's statement, and Hauser as determinedly insisted that it was the truth, and the vote was therefore reconsidered, and by a substantial majority it was decided to substitute the name "Tower" for "Minaret" (*Discovery of Yellowstone*, pp. 79-80).

There has been discussion over the years as to when the large boulder perched at the brink of Tower Fall would drop over the edge. It finally fell from its perch in June 1986.

TOWER PASS Map #2

This pass of the Washburn Range is located between Stone Mountain and Inside Mountain at the head of Carnelian Creek west of Mount Washburn. Members of the Hague parties of the USGS named the pass in about 1904 after nearby Tower Creek, which heads on the west side of the pass.

TRAPPERS CREEK* Map #4

This creek flows south and west to the upper Yellowstone River from the Absaroka Range just south of Colter Peak. Called the "East Fork of the Upper Yellowstone River" on J. W. Barlow's 1871 map, Trappers Creek was named in 1885 by geologist Arnold Hague to honor the fur trappers who hunted the area during the early 19th century.

TREASURE ISLAND* Map #3

Treasure Island is located in the Bechler River just above Iris Falls. In 1921, explorer W. C. Gregg named the island for unknown reasons. In 1920, he had described the area for the November 20, *Saturday Evening Post*: "Twice the river divided and came together again before our eyes, inclosing [sic] a charming island, the whole set at a slant . . . sufficient to make everything a roaring cascade" (p. 78).

THE TRIDENT* Map #4

This 10,969-foot-high mountain of the Absaroka Range is on the western side of the Trident Plateau, which extends east along the Park's far southeastern corner. Geologist Arnold Hague named this mountain in 1885 because the plateau had three westerly "fingers" like a trident or pitchfork.

TRILOBITE POINT*   Map #1

Trilobite Point is the 10,003-foot-high lower eastern summit of Mount Holmes, located west of Obsidian Cliff in the Gallatin Range. Geologist W. H. Holmes named the point in 1878 because of the trilobite fossils found in rocks here. Trilobites are ancient marine creatures with bodies composed of three lobes or segments.

TRISCHMAN KNOB*   Map #3

Trischman Knob is an 8,600-foot-high hill of the Continental Divide that is located southwest of Madison Lake and west of Shoshone Geyser Basin. In 1962, Assistant Chief Ranger William S. Chapman named the hill for Harry Trischman (1886-1950), a well-known personality associated with the early development of Yellowstone Park. Reportedly, Trischman often rode to the top of this knob to scan the countryside when he was making patrols in this part of the Park.

Born at Fort Custer, Montana Territory, in 1886, Trischman came with his parents to Fort Yellowstone in 1899. His father, George Trischman (1848-1929), was the post carpenter. Harry Trischman, described as a "man of tremendous physical endurance and a fine sense of humor" (Haines, *Yellowstone*, 2:294), entered government service in 1907 and was employed as an army scout from 1909 to 1915. He became a ranger in 1916 and later served as assistant chief ranger and chief buffalo keeper. He spent most of his life in Yellowstone Park and had a hand in building many of the early backcountry patrol cabins, including one on Boundary Creek in 1923.

When he retired in late 1945, Trischman left a simple, eloquent note in the Crevice backcountry patrol cabin: "they won't let me sleep in their cabins any more." This was the comment of a man who loved Yellowstone and his job and helped to make both great. He died in 1950.

TROUT BAY   Map #4

This small bay on Yellowstone Lake is located between the Yellowstone River outlet and Bridge Bay. It seems to have been named in 1881 by photographer F. Jay Haynes in the caption of one of his photos.

TRUMPETER LAKE   Map #2

This small lake is located about a mile and a half east of Junction Butte between the Northeast Entrance Road and the Lamar River. A smaller lake to the west is known as Little Trumpeter Lake. The names were given from the trumpeter swans that sometimes nest on the lakes. George M. Wright, Ben Thompson, and Joseph Dixon of the Wildlife Research Division of the National Park Service named Trumpeter Lake in about 1930. When the men studied trumpeter swans in the Park that year, there was great concern for the swans' survival. Wright stated in 1935 that there were "probably fewer than a hundred" left in the United States. One researcher believed that it was the existence of Yellowstone Park that ultimately saved the swans. One pair of swans nested on this lake from 1925 to 1930.

TUFF CLIFF   Map #1

This high rock bluff (a spur of Purple Mountain) is located just north of the Grand Loop Road about 1.6 miles north of Madison Junction. H. C. Bumpus (see Bumpus Butte) named this cliff in 1930 because it is made of compacted volcanic ash known as *tuff* and is overlaid by other lavas. This rock is believed to represent young volcanic material that was erupted about 600,000 years ago. A large section of Tuff Cliff was sheared off by the 1959 earthquake.

TURKEY PEN CREEK   Map #1

This stream, which runs north from Turkey Pen Peak to the Yellowstone River southeast of Gardiner, Montana, got its name as early as the 1880s from the nearby "Turkey Pen Road" (see Turkey Pen Peak). Mammoth resident G. L. Henderson used the name in the 1880s, and guide Elwood Hofer used the name in 1892.

TURKEY PEN PASS   Map #1

The Rescue Creek Trail east of Gardiner, Montana, goes through this pass between Turkey Pen Peak and the north end of Mount Everts. The name was in local use as early as 1918 from the trail that passed through it, known as the "Turkey Pen Trail" or "Turkey Pen Road." This trail, which took its name from George Huston's 1867 Turkey Pen cabin, was used first by Indians and later by miners on their way to the Cooke City mines. In 1918, Jay Wilcox and Jim Parker received a permit to cultivate land in Turkey Pen Pass for the purpose of raising potatoes for sale to stores and tourists. They operated the small business for only two years.

TURKEY PEN PEAK†   Map #1

This 7,001-foot-high hill near the Park's north boundary is just south of Rattlesnake Butte and east of Gardiner, Montana. M. E. Richey of the U.S. Geological Survey and Chief Park Naturalist David Condon named the hill in 1955. The Turkey Pen cabin, the first white residency in the Park area, was built in 1867 by prospector George Huston and was later occupied by Huston, John Evans, and a man named Groves. Located on Turkey Pen Creek, the cabin was where hapless Truman Everts was taken in 1870 following his "Thirty Seven Days of Peril" lost in the Yellowstone wilderness.

According to old stories, at the time that Huston was building the cabin, he was visited by some friends who commented that the building with its rough, unchinked walls "looks like a turkey pen!"

TURQUOISE POOL* Map #3

This hot spring is in the Excelsior Group of Midway Geyser Basin. A. C. Peale of the Hayden survey named the spring in 1878 "from the tint of the water, which is the blue of the turquoise." He described it as "100 by 100 feet . . . square lake-like blue-tinted spring" (in Hayden, *Twelfth Annual Report*, pp. 181, 179). A later writer thought that Turquoise Pool was the most appropriately named of all the pools in the Park that were named for precious stones.

Since earliest days in the Park, visitors have been captivated by the beauty of Turquoise Pool. It is unusual that a spring of such low temperature (50° to 60°F.) could maintain such a rich color. The color is the result of pulverized particles of mineral matter suspended in the water. Geologist Arnold Hague was amazed that the beautiful blue color remained essentially unchanged from 1883 to 1911. The spring still has that color today.

Park tour operator G. L. Henderson had his own name for Turquoise Pool as early as 1883. He called it "Curtain Lake": "This lake [spring] is divided by a beautiful curtain of deep blue, looped in the center, similar to that of a theater" (Ash Scrapbook, p. Adii).

TWILIGHT GEYSER Map #3

This geyser in the Marshall's Hotel area of the Lower Geyser Basin is located on the west bank of the Firehole River in the meadow west of Maidens Grave Spring. It is in a tiny mud flat surrounded by grass and near the center of the small meadow where the original Marshall's Hotel was located. The author proposed this name in 1977 because the geyser was often seen erupting during the "Twilight Bus Tours," offered each evening from Old Faithful Inn by the Park concessionaire. In 1976-1977, Twilight Geyser erupted from 1 to 5 feet high at short intervals and exhibited the well-known flickering gas effect. It became dormant in about 1981, but was seen in eruption in 1985 by researchers.

TWIN CREEK Map #2

This creek flows north to the Lamar River from Specimen Ridge just upstream and on the opposite side of the river from Cache Creek. This place name was given in 1888 by geologist Arnold Hague because the creek was a twin of either of its flanking streams, Flint and Opal creeks.

TWIN FALLS Map #2

This 200-foot-high waterfall on Glade Creek drops from the edge of the Grand Canyon of the Yellowstone River. In 1880, Park Superintendent P. W. Norris named this little-known double falls, writing in his *Report of the Superintendent*:

> Some of these streams [which run into Grand Canyon] descend by beautiful cascades or in dark narrow cañons, and others, as the Twin Falls, by cañons to the remnants of old [rock] slides, and thence, by a clear, beautiful leap of some two hundred feet, reach the river . . . (p. 11).

TWIN LAKES* Map #1

These two small lakes are located 1 to 2 miles south of Semi-Centennial Geyser and west of Roaring Mountain on the Grand Loop Road. The lakes are separately named North Twin Lake and South Twin Lake. Park Superintendent P. W. Norris, who first used the name in 1879, may have named them during the 1870s. But in 1872, traveler C. C. Clawson wrote for the January 13 *New Northwest*: "Again we saw, at a distance below us, two silvery sheets of water, with many lillies floating upon them. We named them the *Twin Lakes*. They were only separated by a strip of land a rod or two in width." This description could have been the source for Norris's use of the name in 1879. Park tour operator G. L. Henderson had his own names for these two lakes in the 1880s. For reasons not now known, he called them "Mystery Lake" (South) and "Myrtle Lake" (North).

North Twin Lake has a maximum depth of 11 feet and is inhospitable to fish, even though tourists are often seen fishing here. The colors of these two lakes are often different, and Hiram Chittenden claimed in 1895 that the two lakes "never simultaneously exhibit the same colors" (*Yellowstone*, p. 219).

The lakes are located right on a divide, and over the years there have been great disagreements about which direction these lakes drain. Forbes reported in 1890 that Twin Lakes drained north into Obsidian Creek, but *Haynes Guides* and other guidebooks claimed that they run south to the Gibbon River. U.S. Fish and Wildlife studies in 1966 and 1974 can't agree either, with the former stating that neither lake has an outlet and the latter giving the impression that the lakes drain north. Is it possible that the drainages of these two lakes sometimes shift?

TWISTER FALLS* Map #3

This 55-foot-high waterfall is on the Gregg Fork of the Bechler River south of Douglas Knob. Current maps show

Twister Falls on the Bechler River, 1921

Haynes Studio

this falls located too far upstream. Twister Falls, as mapped in 1921 and named by explorer W. C. Gregg, is three-quarters of a mile downstream and closer to the mouth of Littles Fork. The falls makes a characteristic twist as the water drops.

TWO OCEAN PLATEAU* Map #4

This large plateau south of Yellowstone Lake took its name from Two Ocean Pass (outside of the Park to the southeast) and appeared on maps of the Hague surveys in 1886. Cornelius Hedges and Truman Everts of the Washburn party climbed the north end of this plateau and named it "Mount Everts," a name that was subsequently transferred to another mountain.

The name of Two Ocean Pass goes back to the fur-trapping era and may have originated with Jim Bridger. Bridger definitely told Capt. W. F. Raynolds of the existence of Two Ocean Pass in 1859, although Raynolds's group did not visit it. In 1888, Walter DeLacy wrote Arnold Hague that Bridger had told him about "this [Two Ocean] Pass, . . . received a good general description of them in 1855 at Portland, Oregon, from old Joe Meek who had once been a trapper for years with Bridger" (Hague Papers, Box 5). Capt. W. A. Jones verified the existence of Two Ocean Pass in 1873, and subsequently a number of scientists studied it. Two Ocean Pass is a marshy meadow where the waters of North Two Ocean Creek and South Two Ocean Creek divide and flow in two directions: one to the Atlantic Ocean via the Yellowstone River and one to the Pacific Ocean via the Snake River. There are a few other places in the world where this kind of division occurs, but the phenomenon is rare (if it exists at all) in the Rockies.

UNCLE TOM'S POINT Map #2

Uncle Tom's Point is a viewpoint of the Upper Falls from the east side of the canyon. This name seems to have come into local use from nearby Uncle Tom's Trail, which was built into the Grand Canyon of the Yellowstone and to the base of Lower Falls (south side) by "Uncle" Tom Richardson in 1898. From 1898 to 1903, Richardson took tourists across the Yellowstone River at a point above present-day Chittenden Bridge, accompanied them to the base of the Lower Falls (sometimes via ropes), served them a picnic supper, and then took them back across the river. After the first bridge was built across the river at this point in 1903, the government revoked Richardson's permit and tourists crossed the river on their own.

UNDINE FALLS* Map #1

This double waterfall on Lava Creek was known variously as "Gardiner River Falls," "Gardiner's Falls" or variations of "East Gardner Falls," and "Cascade Falls of the East Gardiner." During the 1870s, Lava Creek was referred to as "East (Fork of the) Gardiner River." The upper falls are 60 feet high and the lower falls are 50 feet high.

The name Undine (pronounced UN deen) was given to the falls in 1885 by geologist Arnold Hague for mythological water nymphs. In folklore, undines were wise, usually female, water spirits that could acquire a soul by marrying a mortal man and bearing children. They lived in and around waterfalls.

UNION FALLS* Map #3

This 250-foot-high waterfall on Mountain Ash Creek is the second highest waterfall in Yellowstone Park. Located south of Pitchstone Plateau at the end of the Mountain Ash Creek trail in the southwest corner of the Park, Union Falls was named in 1884-1886 by members of the Hague parties of the USGS. Geologist J. P. Iddings described the falls and the reason for the name: "the water descends over rocks to 50 ft. below the crest where the branch stream joins the falls. Hence 'Union Falls' " (USGS, Box 53, vol. 21, p. 42). W. C. Gregg found the date "1884" carved on a tree here, perhaps put there by one of the USGS members.

UPPER FALLS (of the Yellowstone River)* Map #2

This 109-foot-high waterfall on the Yellowstone River was probably the site of many unrecorded visits by fur trappers to Yellowstone. Jim Bridger and James Gemmell were familiar with this falls and saw it as early as 1846. Prospector John C. Davis saw Upper Falls in 1864:

> The full grandeur of the scene did not burst on me at once. Men who have engaged in a hand-to-hand struggle for a frontier existence lose sentiment after a few years; but when I realized the stupendous leap of water, I could not help being impressed (*Livingston Enterprise*, April 21, 1884).

Another prospector, A. Bart Henderson, saw the Upper Falls on September 2, 1867, and recorded in his diary:

> I walked out on a rock and made two steps at the same time, one forward, the other backward, for I had unawares as it were, looked down into the depths or bowels of the earth into which the Yellow[stone] plunged as if to cool the infernal region that lay under all this wonderful country of lava and boiling springs (p. 45).

Members of the 1869 Folsom party were the first to refer to the falls as "upper falls," and they observed that "rushing through a *chute* sixty feet wide, [the water] falls in an unbroken sheet over a precipice one hundred and fifteen feet in height" (*Western Monthly*, July 1870, p. 64). This figure of 115 feet was accepted for many years, although Ludlow measured the falls at 110 feet in 1875.

For several years, there was a viewpoint of the falls (now not accessible) located *below* the present-day brink viewpoint. The brink viewpoint, or perhaps the lower one, was first visited in 1870 by N. P. Langford and Cornelius Hedges. Langford later wrote:

> Mr. Hedges and I made our way down to this table rock, where we sat for a long time. As from this spot we looked up at the descending waters, we insensibly felt that the slightest protrusion in them would hurl us backwards into the gulf below. A thousand arrows of foam, apparently aimed at us, leaped from the verge, and passed rapidly down the sheet. But as the view grew upon us, and we comprehended the power, majesty and beauty of the scene, we became insensible to the danger and gave ourselves up to the full enjoyment of it (*Discovery of Yellowstone*, p. 34).

VALENTINE GEYSER*   Map #1

In 1907, this geyser in the Porcelain Basin of Norris Geyser Basin was born from "Alcove Spring" or from one of the nearby steam vent breakouts. C. W. Bronson, the winterkeeper at nearby Norris Hotel, named the geyser. He later remembered:

> One morning, it was Valentine Day, I heard a lot of noise across the basin and went to tell my wife that something was blowing up on the other hillside. We both watched it and on coming closer found that it was coming from what had been a very small hot spring—one which up till then seemed to be just barely alive. While we watched it blow large amounts of rock, mud, water, and steam were blown out, and the huge pit around the geyser hole was blown out. As I remember when it quieted down the hole in the hillside was about the same size and shape as it is now. The same day I got a small piece of board and wrote "Valentine" on it and stuck it up near the hole by this new geyser (in Watson, "Valentine Geyser," July 8, 1935, YNP Archives).

VETERAN GEYSER   Map #1

Veteran Geyser is in the Back Basin of Norris Geyser Basin. Geologist Walter Weed named this spring Veteran Geyser sometime between 1883 and 1885 for unknown reasons. Weed may have been referring to the ancient age of the thermal area evidenced by the very old sinter deposits here. The spring may have seemed like a veteran to Weed.

VIOLET CREEK*   Map #1

This creek, which flows east to Alum Creek in the Hayden Valley, was named by members of the second Hayden survey in 1872. A. C. Peale recorded the naming: "we named the small stream Violet Creek, from the profusion of violets growing upon its banks" (in Hayden, *Sixth Annual Report*, p. 134).

VIOLET SPRINGS*   Map #1

This group of hot springs is at the head of Violet Creek on the northwestern edge of the Hayden Valley. William Blackmore, an English guest of the Hayden survey, claimed to have been at the springs in 1872 with "Dr. Hayden, B. H., John, [W. H.] Holmes, Tom Ticknor [packer], and [Adolph] Burke's party." Blackmore later wrote:

> We noticed some most beautiful little violets growing in the greatest profusion covering in fact the ground like a carpet. Very fragrant, very small and of a very light violet color[.] I christened the new Springs Violet Springs in honor of the violets (diary, p. 23).

In 1878, topographer Henry Gannett wrote of his visit to Violet Springs:

> Another extensive group of springs occurs on a small branch of this creek [Alum], at the base of the ridge. These springs are, from the color of their deposits, known as the Violet Springs, and the branch which they supply with water is known as Violet Creek (Hayden, *Twelfth Annual Report*, p. 476).

Gannett may have actually stumbled onto Factory Springs or another group instead of Violet Springs. It is unusual when two reputable sources disagree on the origin of a name.

VIRGINIA CASCADE*   Map #1

Virginia Cascade is a 60-foot-high sloping cascade of the Gibbon River along the Grand Loop Road, about 2 miles east of Norris. As early as 1880, Park Superintendent P. W. Norris appears to have named this cascade "Norris Falls." But 6 years later, Ed Lamartine, the foreman in charge of government road work in the Park, renamed it Virginia Cascade. Lamartine built the first wagon road between Norris and Canyon that year, and he named the cascade for Virginia Gibson, the wife of Charles Gibson, who became head of the Yellowstone Park Association in 1886. The name probably would not have survived, but Lamartine and others approached Arnold Hague of the U.S. Geological Survey and requested that it be placed on the map. Hague told them that he did not like personal names on beautiful scenic places. Because Yellowstone was the first national park, however, Hague had "for a long time believed that it would be a good thing to name several features of the Park after the different states of the Union" (Hague papers, Box 3, Book 3C, pp. 201-204). With this in mind, Hague accepted the name.

In 1886, Lamartine's road followed the Gibbon River to the foot of Virginia Cascade and then climbed steeply up "Cascade Hill" out of the canyon next to the cascade. Early supply wagons bound for Canyon had to double-team their wagons to make it up this grade. At the foot of

Virginia Cascade was a sharp 180° "Bend in the Road," which became known as the "Devil's Elbow." In his 1900 road report, engineer Hiram Chittenden called the hill and bend "a positive menace to the lives of travelers. Several accidents have occurred here, and one life has been lost. Stage drivers [coming from the east] are often compelled to make passengers alight and walk down the hill."

VIXEN GEYSER* Map #1

This geyser in the Back Basin of Norris Geyser Basin was named in 1881 by Park Superintendent P. W. Norris. Norris saw in the geyser the qualities of a vixen—a spiteful, unpredictable woman (an appellation that today would surely be considered sexist). Norris reported that the geyser erupted "from forty to 50 feet high, each two or three hours" (*Fifth Annual Report*, p. 58). In recent years, Vixen has erupted from 8 to 10 feet high for a few seconds every minute or so.

WAHB SPRINGS* Map #2

This group of hot springs is located in Death Gulch on the south side of Cache Creek near its confluence with the Lamar River. Death Gulch got its name in 1888, and numerous scientific investigations have been carried out over the years to determine how many animals have died here from gas fumes. Wahb Springs got its name between 1900 and 1904 as Park tourists fell in love with Ernest Thompson Seton's book, *Biography of a Grizzly*, which told the fictional story of a grizzly bear named Wahb. Wahb's name, according to Seton, is Shoshone for "white bear." In Seton's book, Wahb met his end by breathing the poison gases at Wahb Springs in Death Gulch.

WAHHI FALLS* Map #3

This 28-foot-high waterfall on the Ferris Fork of Bechler River was named "Two Step Falls" by explorer W. C. Gregg in 1921. The USBGN approved the name Wahhi Falls in 1922, from a Shoshone Indian word (*wahat hwa*) meaning "two step" or "double."

WASHBURN RANGE* Map #1

This is one of only two ranges of mountains that is entirely within the boundaries of Yellowstone Park. There are about 25 summits in the range, and 9 are individually named. Fur trappers called it "Elephants Back Mountain" or "Elephants Back Mountains," a name that appeared on Capt. W. F. Raynolds's map of 1859-1860. Raynolds's guide, Jim Bridger, probably supplied the name.

The Washburn party of 1870 named the main summit of this range Mount Washburn, and the subsequent Hayden surveys decided on the name Washburn Range for the whole complex of peaks. Park Superintendent P. W. Norris referred to a part of the range in 1880 as "Stephens Range" for one of his assistants (see Stephens Creek), and geologist Arnold Hague referred to a portion of the range as "Sherman Volcano," a reference to Gen. W. T. Sherman and the volcanic origin of these mountains.

The named summits of the Washburn Range are: Mount Washburn, Dunraven Peak, Hedges Peak, Inside Mountain, Stone Mountain, Observation Peak, Cook Peak, Folsom Peak, and Prospect Peak.

WELLS CREEK Map #4

This creek flows southeast and east into the west side of Bridge Bay of Yellowstone Lake from Elephant Back Mountain. Wells Creek is the more northerly of two permanent streams in this area. Members of a Northern Pacific Railroad survey team in 1882 named the creek after Eben T. Wells, an assistant engineer on the Yellowstone Division of the NPRR. Wells appears to have accompanied the party under M. G. Grant (see Grants Pass), which surveyed a railroad route through Yellowstone Park.

WEST THUMB (of Yellowstone Lake)* Map #4

Members of the 1870 Washburn party noted that Yellowstone Lake was shaped like "a human hand with the fingers extended and spread apart as much as possible," with the large west bay representing the thumb. By 1878, however, the Hayden survey used the name "West Arm" for the bay; "West Bay" was also used. Norris's maps of 1880 and 1881 used "West Bay or Thumb." During the 1930s, Park personnel attempted to change the name back to "West Arm," but West Thumb remained the accepted name.

WHISKEY FLATS Map #3

This small marshy meadow is located just south of the Grand Loop Road about a mile northeast of Midway Geyser Basin and immediately east of a picnic area. This place name, heavily entrenched in local use, is something of a mystery. Stories among Park personnel have it that soldiers or stagecoach drivers before 1916 used the meadow to hide or throw away their whiskey bottles. During the 1970s, the Old Faithful district ranger placed a sign here that read Whiskey Flats. But there is no documentary evidence to support the use of the name or to explain its origins.

Soldiers at the Upper Basin soldier station

Four-horse coaching party on the road above the Upper Falls

WHISKEY SPRING   Map #1

This cold spring on the Mammoth-Gardiner Road is located in a marshy swale 3.5 miles south of the Roosevelt Arch. When the army controlled the Park from 1886 to 1916, soldiers plodding from saloons in Gardiner, Montana, back to Fort Yellowstone at Mammoth Hot Springs named the spring. Evidently, stagedrivers also used Whiskey Spring, sometimes caching their whisky bottles here: "Regulations forbade them carrying it with them, so under the guise of getting water from this spring, they could halt the stages, slip out of sight in the brush around the spring, and ease a parched throat here" (Yellowstone Card File).

WHISTLE GEYSER   Map #3

In 1872, Gustavus Bechler named this geyser in the Black Sand Basin of Upper Geyser Basin "Conical Spring" because of its prominent cone. Park tour operator G. L. Henderson called it "Hazle Fairy Mound Builder" in 1899 for unknown reasons. The name Whistle Geyser came into local use sometime between 1904 and 1912. Jack Haynes's *Official Guide* for 1912 noted that it "performs only at great intervals; but when the rush of steam commences, as it does several times each season, a whistle-like roar is produced which is audible half a mile, and lasts several minutes" (p. 66).

There are only 20 recorded eruptions of Whistle Geyser before 1983: two in 1924, one in 1927, two in 1931, one in 1934, and two in 1947. There were single eruptions in 1948, 1954-1956, and 1968. The best year was 1957, when 7 eruptions were recorded. The August 1931 eruption was 40 feet high, lasted 30 minutes, and "sounded like about four locomotives at a distance, with a shrill, ringing tone to it" (*Livingston Enterprise*, August 9, 1931).

An eruption of Whistle Geyser usually lasts from 2 to 3 hours, but only during the first moments of play is any water discharged. A violent steam phase begins almost immediately. Water reaches heights of 30 to 40 feet, but steam shoots up over 100 feet high.

WHISTLER GEYSER*   Map #2

Whistler Geyser is a thermal feature of Josephs Coat Springs located on Mirror Plateau near the head of Broad Creek. Whistler Geyser is a steam vent; it is not a geyser and probably never has been one. In 1873, Capt. W. A. Jones discovered the vent, describing it as "an exceedingly large jet of steam, escaping under such pressure from a narrow fissure that the noise is deafening" (in Baldwin, *Enchanted Enclosure*, p. 54). In 1884, geologists Arnold Hague and Walter Weed visited the area for the first time, and Hague named the feature "The Whistler" from the noise it made. Weed mapped the area and wrote in his field notebook:

> On the east bank of the [Broad] creek, opposite [Scorodite Spring], and 75 ft. farther downstream, is the most noticeable vent of the basin. It is a vent 1½ in diameter from which a jet of steam under high pressure issues with a whistling noise. The steam as it issues from the vent is perfectly transparent but condensing above. The vent is some five ft. above and ten feet from the creek. It is orange-lined, and around the vent there is a soft gelatinous orange, and greenish-brown deposit, apparently viandite (USGS, Box 52, vol. 16, pp. 108, 110).

Today, it is difficult to determine which feature in a bank of steam vents might be Whistler Geyser.

WHITE ELEPHANT BACK SPRINGS
and TERRACE   Map #1

White Elephant Back is a travertine terrace and hot springs in the Mammoth Hot Springs. The name "Devil's Backbone," which was in use in 1871, was probably an early name for this very noticeable terrace. Not until 1883 is there another reference to the terrace. In that year, Charles R. Keese, a tourist from Cooperstown, New York, who was in a tour party guided by G. L. Henderson, named the feature and suggested that it resembled "the vertebral column of a gigantic quadruped" (*Helena Weekly Herald*, May 10, 1888). Henderson suggested that White Elephant Back Terrace, with its "two trunks" and 600-foot length, formed a natural bridge and footpath along the east side of the area that he called "Sulphur Pit Valley" or "Teller's Valley." For Henderson, White Elephant Back Terrace was a giant aqueduct:

> One of the phenomenal things in connection with the White Elephant is the large quantity of hot water that is conducted through its two trunks for three-quarters of a mile. Occasionally there is an opening on the top where the hot water is seen threading its way slowly through this natural hydrant until it finally sinks into an abyss known as the Mammoth cave [present-day Devil's Kitchen] (*Livingston Enterprise*, November 21, 1883).

WHITE LAKE*   Map #2

This small lake at the head of Broad Creek on the Mirror Plateau was named in 1885 by members of the Hague parties of the USGS. They named it White Lake because of the white-colored areas of thermal activity in the vicinity. Geologist Arnold Hague mentioned the area's numerous "white lake beds" several times in his field notes.

WHITEROCK SPRINGS*   Map #1

This small hot spring area northeast of Roaring Mountain was named in or about 1885 by members of the Hague party. It appeared on their 1886 map as "White Rock Springs" and was named for the presence of fragments of white quartzite at the springs.

WINEGAR LAKE*   Map #3

This small lake in the southwest corner of the Park is almost on the Park's southern boundary, just off the Boundary Trail about 3 miles east of Cave Falls campground. The name, which was in local use by 1961 (and perhaps as early as the 1930s), comes from the lake's proximity to Winegar Creek.

The Winegar family, who may have come to the area as early as 1879, lived southwest of Yellowstone Park in Idaho by the 1890s. By 1896, they had secured hard reputations for themselves as poachers. Yellowstone scout Elmer Lindsley mentioned training a fellow scout in 1897 on how and "where to scout for" the Winegars. Capt. G. L. Scott mentioned a cabin built by the Winegars (probably for poaching purposes) "on [the] bank of a little lake" near the Bechler River, probably present-day Winegar Lake. Explorer W. C. Gregg recorded evidence of the Winegars' presence in 1920:

> Near Iris [Falls] we found on a tree, carved perhaps thirty years ago, the name of W. L. Winegar. We had heard rumors of a man by that name, and this increased our interest in the find immensely. Later I heard that Winegar, now an old man, is still alive somewhere in the West (*Saturday Evening Post*, November 20, 1920).

W. L. Winegar seems to have been living in Jackson Hole as late as 1921. John Winegar, another family member, was arrested in Yellowstone in 1907 for possessing firearms in the Park and fined $100.

WITCH CREEK*   Map #4

This creek flows southeast from Factory Hill to Heart Lake. The stream was named in 1878 by members of the third Hayden survey, probably for the prevalence of hot springs along its entire course.

WONDERLAND

This sobriquet that stands for all of Yellowstone National Park was given even before Yellowstone became a national park. Prospector A. Bart Henderson used the name in his diary on July 24, 1871. In October 1871, the *New York Times* article, "The New Wonderland," was the first published use of the term, and in 1878 E. J. Stanley used it in the title of his *Rambles in Wonderland*. Olin Wheeler's later *Wonderland* series of books on Yellowstone helped establish the name, as did the Northern Pacific Railroad's use of the term in its promotional literature.

WRAITH FALLS*   Map #1

This 100-foot-high sloping cascade of Lupine Creek is near Lava Creek on the Grand Loop Road. Members of the Hague parties of the USGS named the falls in 1885. A wraith is a ghost or specter, but there is no documentation of the reason for the name.

WRANGLER LAKE†   Map #2

This small lake is located about 2 miles east of the Yellowstone River between Cottongrass and Sour creeks and about 4 miles southeast from Canyon. The name Wrangler Lake was in local use by 1934, when it was stocked with cutthroat trout. The name is probably a tribute to cowboys or wranglers employed by the Park concessionaire at Canyon Village.

WRONG CREEK†   Map #2

Wrong Creek flows west into Shallow Creek on the Mirror Plateau due east of Mount Washburn. For years, maps placed the creek in the wrong location—hence, the name. The 1878 map of the third Hayden survey came closer to mapping Wrong Creek correctly than many subsequent maps did. The Hague survey map of 1886, for example, showed Shallow Creek (then unnamed) flowing north into Deep Creek instead of into Broad Creek, and present-day Wrong Creek was represented as simply a long southeastern part of Deep Creek. These errors continued through the 1930 editions. It was not until 1959 that the error was corrected (on the USGS 15-minute maps).

WYLIE HILL   Map #3

This name is applied to the ridge between Red Mud Crater and Cyclops Spring (west of Grotto Geyser) in the Upper Geyser Basin. A Wylie Tent Camp set up on this hill just north of the Daisy Geyser complex is responsible for the name, which was in local use by 1927.

William Wallace Wylie (1851-1930), a Bozeman, Montana, school superintendent who first visited the Park in 1880, was perhaps the first commercial tour leader in Yellowstone. Wylie published a guidebook to Yellowstone that established him as an authority on the Park, and guided people through the Park for some 10 years before realizing that he had drifted into the tourist business.

Wylie filed for formal licenses to locate semi-permanent camps throughout the Park and had his coaches carry tourists from one camp to another. By substituting candy-striped tents for hotels, he avoided a large investment in buildings and reduced operating costs. In this way, Wylie was able to offer tourists a very affordable way to see Yellowstone. Despite constant harassment from the hotel company, Wylie's business thrived, but he could never get a long-term license and had to get by with a yearly renewal. He sold his operations to A. W. Miles of Livingston in 1905. Wylie later established Wylie Way camps in Zion and Grand Canyon national parks.

Wylie was the concessionaire who began the practice of hiring college students and teachers, a tradition that continues today in Yellowstone and other national parks. Nightly camp entertainments by these employees were forerunners of later interpretative programs put on by the National Park Service and Park concessionaires.

YANCEY CREEK†   Map #1

Yancey Creek flows northwest to Elk Creek from Lost Lake near the Petrified Tree off the Grand Loop Road. The creek was named for "Uncle" John Yancey (1826?-1903), whom author Owen Wister described as a "goat-bearded, shrewd-eyed, lank Uncle Sam type." Yancey ran the Pleasant Valley Hotel (1884-1906), also known as "Yancey's," which was on the site of the present-day stagecoach cookout location near the mouth of Yancey Creek. The five-room hotel was said to accommodate 20 guests for $2 per day, including meals. One local story had it that the glasses at Yancey's never held water, only whisky. Another claimed that Yancey never gave change. One dollar would buy four drinks or one drink, normally 25 cents, but the customer would never get any change.

It is not known when this stream received the name Yancey Creek, but it did not appear on the USGS maps until 1959. John Yancey is buried in the Gardiner cemetery.

YANCEY'S HOLE   Map #2

This popular fishing area is located along the west bank of Yellowstone River just below the mouth of the Lamar River. Whether the name came from the meadows of Pleasant Valley, which border the Yellowstone River, or from fishing holes in the river (or both) is uncertain, but the name "Yancey Meadows" was in use as early as 1885. In the early days, a "hole" referred to a valley or meadow. On early maps, "Yancey's" referred to John Yancey's Pleasant Valley Hotel, which was located nearby (see Yancey Creek).

YELLOWBELL BROOK   Map #3

This hot creek flows east from the base of the Madison Plateau into Iron Spring Creek, between Niobe Creek and the runoff from Hillside Springs. In or before 1904, members of the Hague parties of the USGS named the stream for unknown reasons. The name simply appeared on the 1904 map, and there are no references to it in any of the literature of the Hague surveys. The name may refer either to the wildflower yellowbell (*Fritillaria sp.*) or to bright yellow monkeyflowers (*Mimulus sp.*). The yellowbell is not common in this area, but monkeyflowers grow year-round along this hot stream.

YELLOWSTONE LAKE*   Map #4

The Park's largest lake, Yellowstone Lake is also one of the world's largest natural freshwater lakes. This "matchless mountain lake" was probably seen by John Colter on his famous winter trip of discovery in 1807-1808. Before that, Indians surely camped on its shores every summer. Although it is unlikely that Indians lived here, many arrowheads, spearheads, and other artifacts have been found near the lake.

William Clark's map of 1806-1811 showed what was probably Yellowstone Lake as "Eustis Lake," a name given for the Secretary of War under President Jefferson. An 1814 mapmaker changed Clark's "Lake Biddle" (probably Jackson Lake) to "Lake Riddle," which may at times have referred to Yellowstone Lake. The name "Bridger Lake" (now applied to a small lake southeast of the Park) may also have applied at times to Yellowstone Lake. In 1826, a party of fur trappers that included Daniel Potts, Bill Sublette, and Jedidiah Smith called Yellowstone "Sublette Lake," and some historians credit Sublette with discovering the lake. Daniel Potts, one of the chroniclers of that 1826 trip, wrote to his family on July 8, 1827, that near the headwaters of the Yellowstone River is "a large fresh water lake . . . on the very top of the mountain which is about one hundred by fourty miles in diameter and as clear as crystal" (letter, Yellowstone Park Research Library). Trapper Warren Ferris knew the name "Yellow Stone Lake" by 1831, and he showed it on his map of 1836. By the 1860s, Yellowstone Lake was well-known among former fur trappers, army personnel, and other frequent western explorers.

The *Anna* of the 1871 Hayden survey was the first recorded boat on the waters of Yellowstone Lake, although some fur trappers or Indians may have floated rafts on the lake much earlier. Other early boats used to explore the lake were the *Topping* in 1874 (see Topping Point), a raft containing government surveyors in 1874, the *Explorer* in 1880 (see Explorer's Creek), a USGS boat destroyed by lightning in 1885, the *Zillah* in 1889, and the *E.C. Waters* (test runs only) in 1905. A boat piloted by Billy Hofer and William D. Pickett made at least one trip in 1880.

Yellowstone Lake covers 136 square miles and is 20 miles long by 14 miles wide. It has 110 miles of shoreline.

"Uncle" John Yancey

Camping in the Upper Geyser Basin, 1882

Tourists at Wylie Camp Roosevelt, 1915

The lake is at least 320 feet deep (in the West Thumb area) and has an average depth of 140 feet. Situated at an altitude of 7,733 feet, the lake remains cold the year round, with an average temperature of 41°F.

Yellowstone Lake is the largest natural freshwater lake in the United State that is above 7,000 feet and is one of the largest such lakes in the world. Because of its size and depth and the area's prevailing winds, the lake can sometimes be whipped into a tempestuous inland ocean. During late summer, Yellowstone Lake becomes thermally stratified with each of several water layers having a different temperature. The topmost layer rarely exceeds 66°, and the lower layers are much colder. Because of the extremely cold water, swimming is not encouraged. Survival time is estimated to be only 20 to 30 minutes in water of this low temperature.

The lake has the largest inland population of wild cutthroat trout in North America. Just how these Pacific Ocean cutthroat got trapped in a lake that drains to the Atlantic Ocean puzzled experts for years. There is now a theory that Yellowstone Lake once drained to the Pacific Ocean (via Outlet Canyon to Snake River) and that fish could pass across the Continental Divide at Two Ocean Pass. There are no rainbow trout or other types of gamefish in Yellowstone Lake.

Yellowstone Lake freezes over completely in winter, with ice thicknesses varying from a few inches to over 2 feet. The lake's basin has an estimated capacity of 12,095,264 acre-feet of water. Because its annual outflow is about 1,100,000 acre-feet, the lake's water is completely replaced only about every 8 to 10 years. Since 1952, the annual water level fluctuation has been less than 6 feet.

YELLOWSTONE RIVER*   Maps #1, 2, and 4

This is the oldest place name in Yellowstone Park. Historian Hiram Chittenden believed that the French forms of the word *Yellowstone*—*Roche Jaune* and *Pierre Jaune*—were literal translations of the Minnetaree Indian term, *Mi tsi a-da-zi* but he was unsure why the Minnetarees used the name. More recent historians believe that the Minnetarees would not have known about the upper Yellowstone River. The Crow Indians referred to the Yellowstone River as "Elk River" or "Echeda-Cahchi-ichi." In the August 1981 *National Geographic*, Crow chief Daniel Old Elk asserted that the name Yellowstone came about simply as the result of a mistake: "In our language we always called it the Elk River. The words sound alike, and the French didn't understand Crow very well" (p. 272). A 1796 map was the first to show the stream as "Rock or Crow R." and a 1797 map showed it as "R. des Roche Jaune" (river of yellow rock). Three different 1796 journal references used the name *Yellowstone*.

Contrary to long-held beliefs, the name Yellowstone did not come from the yellow altered-rhyolite walls of the "Fourth Canyon," or Grand Canyon of the Yellowstone. Those who originally used the name lived hundreds of miles downstream and did not know of the short stretch of colored canyon at the Lower Falls. F. V. Hayden, writing on May 2, 1885, to geologist Arnold Hague, claimed:

> Yellowstone Lake and River are names given by the Indians and adopted by the old trappers and hunters—Bridger, [Robert] Meldrum, and the Crow Indians told me the name was given from the great amount of coloring matter as oxide of iron . . . along its banks and on the stones. This is noticeable in the dry season of Autumn when the water is low (Hague papers, Box 5).

Geologist Arnold Hague, who searched for the origin of the name Yellowstone, wrote:

> It seems to me very far fetched to suppose that the name of the Yellowstone River came from the Indian name of the [Grand] canyon. The river for 100 miles or more is bordered by high cliffs of yellow sandstone, and it is much more probable that the name came from these rocks than that it came from highly colored rocks for 2 miles way up near the sources of the river (Hague papers, Box 10, p. 3).

The source of the Yellowstone River is on the slopes of Yount's Peak, far to the southeast of Yellowstone Park. Arnold Hague traveled to the spot in 1887 and reported that the source of the river was "in a long snow-bank lying in a large ampitheatre on the north side of the [Yount's] peak" (Hague papers, Box 2, Book 2D, pp. 252-253).

The Yellowstone River remains the longest undammed river in the U.S. and the most important cutthroat trout stream in America.

ZOMAR SPRING   Map #3

Zomar Spring is a hot spring in the Black Warrior (Firehole Lake) Group of the Lower Geyser Basin. The name of this spring first appeared on the 1904 map of the Hague survey. There is no other known mention of the name in the writings of the survey members, and it is not known who gave the name or why.

ZYGOMATIC ARCH   Map #3

This arch of sinter is in and over Silver Globe Spring of Biscuit Basin in the Upper Geyser Basin. Park tour operator G. L. Henderson named Zygomatic Arch in 1887 because it reminded him of the bones that form the prominence of each cheek on a human face (see Silver Globe Spring).

Bibliography

The two best bibliographical sources for pre-1940 Yellowstone material are *Yellowstone National Park: A Bibliography* (Hazel Voth, Department of the Interior, 1940) and *Scientific Investigations in Yellowstone Park* (Carl Russell, 1933). Other helpful sources are H. M. Chittenden's *The Yellowstone National Park* (1895 ed.); F. V. Hayden's *Twelfth Annual Report of the U.S. Geological and Geographical Survey of the Territories*, pt 2 (1883); Aubrey L. Haines, *The Yellowstone Story* (1977) and *Yellowstone National Park: Its Exploration and Establishment* (1974); Merrill Beal's *The Story of Man in Yellowstone* (rev. 1960); H. Duane Hampton's *How the U.S. Cavalry Saved Our National Parks* (1971); and Paul Schullery's *Old Yellowstone Days* (1979).

Some of the best material on Yellowstone is at Park Headquarters at Mammoth Hot Springs. The Yellowstone Park Research Library contains over 10,000 volumes and many rare manuscripts and diaries. The YPR Library also contains many of the important sources on the fur trade in Yellowstone.

The Yellowstone National Park Archives have a remarkably complete administrative record of the Park. The pre-1916 records have been microfilmed and are available at Harper's Ferry, West Virginia, at Montana State University, Bozeman, and at the Montana Historical Society, Helena. The post-1916 records are available only at the Park archives at Mammoth.

Montana State University Special Collections has the excellent collections of photographer Jack E. Haynes, which include not only his but also many of his father's books, papers, and photos. The Montana Historical Society in Helena has the entire F. Jay Haynes and Jack E. Haynes photo collections.

The National Archives in Washington, D.C., holds many USGS and NPS maps and papers that are available in no other repository. The Library of Congress contains many items that I could find nowhere else, but their Yellowstone collection is still far from complete. The U.S. Forest Service in Washington, D.C., has a complete collection of Forest Service maps of areas surrounding Yellowstone, and the U.S. Geological Survey in Reston, Virginia, has all USGS maps drawn of Yellowstone. The U.S. Board on Geographic Names in Reston has filed information on place names relating to Yellowstone and surrounding areas, but their information is far from complete.

The Minnesota Historical Society in St. Paul holds the records of the Northern Pacific Railroad, which was so important in Yellowstone's early history. The Burlington Northern Railroad also has historical information at its headquarters in St. Paul. Finally, the University of Oklahoma's outstanding Phillips Collection of Western History and the collections of the university's excellent School of Geology were amazingly helpful in my searches.

MAPS

No-place names study can be completed without a meticulous scrutiny of the area maps. The earliest maps of the Yellowstone area have been cited and reproduced in Carl Wheat's monumental work *Mapping the Transmississippi West* (5 vols., 1957-1963) and in Aubrey L. Haines's *Yellowstone National Park* (1974). Between 1868 and 1912, a different map of Yellowstone was made for virtually every year.

Maps of the Whole of Yellowstone Park

U.S. Department of the Interior, Geological Survey, 15-minute Quadrangles, 30 of which make up Yellowstone Park. Individual sheets have individual names and are dated 1943-1959.

U.S. Department of the Interior, Geological Survey, 1961 topographic map, "Yellowstone National Park, Wyoming-Montana-Idaho."

"Topographic Map of the Yellowstone National Park, Wyoming-Montana-Idaho," partial rev. 1930, National Park Service.

"Topographic Map of the Yellowstone National Park, Wyoming-Montana-Idaho," 1922; partial rev. 1921, by C. H. Birdseye.

"Topographic Map of the Yellowstone National Park, Wyoming-Montana-Idaho," January 1912; partial rev. 1910, by E. P. Davis.

"Yellowstone National Park Compiled from the official records of the General Land Office . . . under the direction of Frank Bond . . . 1907," General Land Office.

Arnold Hague, *Atlas to Accompany Monograph XXXII on the Geology of the Yellowstone National Park*, Washington, D.C., GPO, 1904.

Absaroka Folio, Crandall and Ishawooa Quadrangles, Wyoming, folio no. 52, Washington, D.C., GPO, 1899.

Livingston, Montana, Quadrangle, folio no. 1, Washington, D.C., GPO, 1893.

Bibliography

Three Forks Folio, no. 24, Washington, D.C., GPO, 1896.

C. H. Birdseye, "Map of Cascade Corner Yellowstone National Park (from U.S. Geological Survey)," 1922.

"Yellowstone National Park and North Western Wyoming," Scale 1/125000, contour interval 100 feet, Henry Gannett, Chief Geographer. Surveyed in 1883-84-85. USGS file copy, Reston, Virginia. (This key map was published in limited form apparently in 1886.)

Thermal Area Maps

The U.S. Geological Survey offers closeup maps for thermal areas of Upper, Lower, and Midway geyser basins. These are variously numbered with a Roman numeral, a letter, and often a number (for example, III.A.1, Kaleidoscope Group, Lower Basin). The Norris, Shoshone, West Thumb, and Mud Volcano areas are available as well.

Thomas Brock's *Thermophyllic Microorganisms . . .* (1978) contains recent closeup thermal maps, as do Barry Watson's 1961 master's thesis and George Marler's USGS Professional Paper 435. Persons who have drawn thermal area maps in recent years are Harry Majors (Mammoth), Al Mebane and Dick Frisbee (West Thumb), William Phillips (Mammoth, 1962), Rick Hutchinson (Sylvan Springs, 1973-1974), Steve Hodapp (Norris, 1973), and Verde Watson (Norris, 1954). Important 1959 maps of the Upper Geyser Basin spring groups are by William Germeraad and Barry Watson.

Historic thermal maps are included in F. V. Hayden's 1870s reports; in the 1904 Hague atlas; in *Haynes Guides* 1890-1966; and in U.S. Department of the Interior, National Park Service, General Information pamphlets, 1914-1930.

Two little-known thermal maps from 1872 by Gustavus Bechler are "Map of the Upper Geyser Basin on the Upper Madison River, Montana Terr." in Carl Wheat's *Mapping the Transmississippi West* (1957-1963, vol. 5, pt 2, p. 347); and "Map of the Upper and Lower Geyser Basins" in the Earl of Dunraven's *The Great Divide* (1876 ed.).

Walter Weed's five important 1884 thermal maps (which are Peale's 1878 maps with Weed's handwritten additions) are in NA, RG 57, Cartography Division, filed under Arnold Hague. Weed's many hand-drawn closeup thermal maps are in his various unpublished notebooks.

Miscellaneous Area Maps

"Yellowstone National Park, Guide Map, Mammoth Hot Springs and Vicinity, January, 1929," drawn by LCR, traced by Chester Alan Lindsley.

East Boundary, Yellowstone National Park. Set of 5-6 maps, surveyed 1931 by W. R. Bandy, YNP Research Library.

"Trail Map, Mammoth Hot Springs and Vicinity," n.d., pre-1935.

"Detailed Map of Crest of Fissure Terrace," Fissure Group, Heart Lake Geyser Basin, D. E. White, Sept. 10-23, 1973, USGS.

"Hydrographic Map Bridge Bay Lagoon," #5455, Aug. 11, 1939, National Park Service.

"Mammoth Hot Springs, Yellowstone National Park, Wyoming 1962," William Phillips.

"Monument Geyser Basin, Yellowstone National Park, Wyoming," Richard Frisbee, 1961.

"The North Portion of Potts' Geyser Basin, Yellowstone National Park, September 1, 1959," Martin Miller.

"Geologic Map of the Sylvan Springs Thermal Area, Yellowstone National Park Wyoming, 1973 and 1977," Roderick A. Hutchinson.

"Norris Geyser Basin—1967 Lifted by E. E. Leigh from U.S. Geological Survey Map of 1966."

"Porcelain Basin Norris Geyser Basin," hand-drawn, April 1, 1966, Jerome S. DeSanto.

"Norris Geyser Basin, Yellowstone National Park, March, 1954," W. Verde Watson.

Other Full Park Maps

1871—Map of F. V. Hayden, included in N. P. Langford's 1872 Report of the Superintendent.

1874—Map of "The American National Park" in Carl Wheat, vol. 5, pt 2, opp. p. 350.

1876—Map of F. V. Hayden in Carl Wheat, vol. 5, pt 2, opp. p. 351. Originally published in Hayden, *The Yellowstone National Park, and Mountain Regions of Portions of Idaho, Nevada, Colorado, and Utah*, 1876.

1877—Map of P. W. Norris included in published government documents with his 1877 annual report.

1878-1881—Maps of P. W. Norris included with his superintendent's annual reports of 1878-1881.

1882—Map of Northern Pacific Railroad by Carl Hals and A. Rydstrom.

1884—Map of "Wyoming," George F. Cram, Chicago.

1885—YNP map included in *Forest and Stream* 24 (February 5, 1885):22-23.

1887—Elwood Billy Hofer's Park map in his article "Winter in Wonderland."

1888—Map in *Science* 11 (June 1, 1888):255-256, after USGS.

1888—"Map of the Yellowstone . . . to accompany Major Charles J. Allen's project dated November 14, 1888."

1889—Map included in David Starr Jordan's "A Reconnaissance of the Streams and Lakes of the Yellowstone. . . ."

1890—Map included in A. B. Guptill's, *Practical Guide*.

1894—Map included in A. B. Guptill, *Haynes Guide*, 1894.

1895—Map included in H. M. Chittenden, *The Yellowstone National Park*, 1895.

1896—Gallatin Sheet (USGS), edition of April 1896; Canyon Sheet (USGS), 1896; Shoshone Sheet (USGS), 1896; Lake Sheet (USGS), 1896.

1898—Map of forest routes, YNP, included in G. D. Meiklejohn's "Roads in Yellowstone National Park."

1897-1907—Maps included each year in the annual reports of Park superintendents.

1905—Map included in H. M. Chittenden's road report for Yellowstone National Park (SN-4948, 1905).

1967—"Landscape Alterations Map 1870 to 1967," Aubrey L. Haines, National Park Service, #6316, September, 1967.

1899—Crandall Sheet (USGS), March 1899.

Maps of Areas Around Yellowstone Park

There are 18 maps (1910-1936) that were published by the U.S. Department of Agriculture, Forest Service, and are at Forest Service Engineering Offices, Rosslyn, Virginia. They are important for the view they give of Yellowstone's boundaries.

BOOKS, PERIODICALS, AND PAPERS

Albright, Horace. *Oh Ranger! A Book About the National Parks*. Palo Alto: Stanford University Press, 1928.

Allen, E. T. and A. L. Day. *Hot Springs of the Yellowstone National Park*. Publication No. 466. Washington, D.C.: Carnegie Institution, 1935.

Alter, J. Cecil. *Jim Bridger*. Norman: University of Oklahoma Press, 1962.

Atwood, John H. *Yellowstone Park in 1898*. Kansas City, Missouri: Smith-Grieves, 1918.

Augspurger, Marie M. *Yellowstone National Park—Historical and Descriptive*. Middletown, Ohio; Naegele-Auer, 1948.

Bach, Orville E., Jr. *Hiking the Yellowstone Back Country*. San Francisco: Sierra Club Books, 1973.

Back, Howard. *The Waters of Yellowstone with Rod and Fly*. New York: Dodd Mead and Company, 1938.

Baldwin, Alice Blackwood. *Memoirs of the Late Frank D. Baldwin, Major General, U.S.A.* Los Angeles: Wetzel Publishing, 1929.

Baldwin, Kenneth H., ed. *Enchanted Enclosure: The Army Engineers and Yellowstone National Park, A Documentary History*. Washington, D.C.: Government Printing Office, 1976.

Ballou, Maturin M. *The New Eldorado*. Boston and New York: Houghton Mifflin, 1892.

Barber, John F. *Ribbons of Water: The Waterfalls and Cascades of Yellowstone National Park*. Yellowstone National Park: Yellowstone Library and Museum Association, 1984.

Barlow, J. W. and David P. Heap. *Report of a Reconnaissance of the Basin of the Upper Yellowstone in 1871*. 42nd Cong., 2nd sess., S. Ex. Doc. 66, SN-1479, vol. 2. Washington, D.C.: Government Printing Office, 1872.

Bartlett, Richard A. "Those Infernal Machines in Yellowstone Park." *Montana the Magazine of Western History* 20 (Summer 1970): 16-29.

_____. *Nature's Yellowstone*. Albuquerque: University of New Mexico Press, 1974.

_____. *Yellowstone: A Wilderness Besieged*. Tucson: University of Arizona Press, 1985.

Bauer, Clyde M. *The Story of Yellowstone Geysers*. St. Paul and Yellowstone National Park: Haynes, Inc., 1937.

_____. *Yellowstone—Its Underworld*. Albuquerque: University of New Mexico Press, 1948, 1953, 1962.

Bauer, C. Max. "Place Names of Yellowstone National Park," c. 1935, file no. 924.4/B344, YNP Research Library.

Beal, Merrill D. *The Story of Man in Yellowstone*. Rev. Yellowstone National Park: Yellowstone Library and Museum Association, 1960.

_____. *I Will Fight No More Forever*. Seattle: University of Washington Press, 1963.

Bergon, Frank, ed. *The Wilderness Reader*. New York and Scarborough: Mentor, New American Library, 1980.

Blackmore, William. Diary, 1872, #6, #7, photocopies in YNP Research Library.

(Bonneville, Benjamin). "Captain Bonneville's Letter." *Contributions to the Historical Society of Montana*, 10 vols. (Boston: J. S. Canner, 1966), 1:105.

Bonney, Orrin H. and Lorraine Bonney. *Battle Drums and Geysers*. Chicago: Swallow Press, 1970.

_____. *Field Book of the Absaroka Range, Yellowstone Park*. Denver: Sage Books, 1960, 1963.

Brock, Thomas D. *Thermophyllic Microorganisms and Life at High Temperatures*. New York and Heidelberg: Springer-Verlag, 1978.

_____ and M. Louise Brock. *Life in the Geyser Basins*. Yellowstone National Park: Yellowstone Library and Museum Association, 1971.

Brown, Mark H. *Flight of the Nez Perce*. New York: G. P. Putnam's Sons, 1967.

_____. *The Plainsmen of the Yellowstone*. 1961; reprint, Lincoln: University of Nebraska Press, 1967.

Bryan, T. Scott. *The Geysers of Yellowstone*. Boulder: Colorado Associated University Press, 1979, 1982, 1986.

Bumpus, Hermon Carey, Jr.: *Hermon Carey Bumpus, Yankee Naturalist*. Minneapolis: University of Minnesota Press, 1947.

Burroughs, John. *Camping and Tramping with Roosevelt*. Boston and New York: Houghton, Mifflin, 1907.

Burton, G. W. *Burton's Book on California and Its Sunlit Skies of Glory*. Los Angeles: Times-Mirror, 1909.

Campbell, Reau. *Campbell's New Revised Complete Guide and Descriptive Book of the Yellowstone National Park*. Chicago: H. E. Klamer, 1909. Three other editions of this guide were published under slightly different titles in 1913, 1914, and 1923.

Carter, Thomas B. *Yellowstone Backcountry Basics and Trail Guide*. Edited by Lee H. Whittlesey, Bozeman: Color World of Montana, 1978. The third edition of this book carries the unauthorized notation: "Compiled by John F. Barber." The fourth edition is titled *Day Hiking Yellowstone*, 1985.

Chapple, Joe Mitchell. *A 'Top O' The World: Wonders of the Yellowstone Dreamland*. Boston: Chapple Publishing, 1922.

Chase, Alston. *Playing God in Yellowstone: The Destruction of America's First National Park*. Boston, New York: Atlantic Monthly, 1986.

Cheney, Roberta and Clyde Erskine. *Music, Saddles, and Flapjacks, Dudes at the OTO Ranch*. Missoula, Montana: Mountain Press, 1978.

Chief Joseph. *Chief Joseph's Own Story As Told by Chief Joseph in 1879*. Billings, Montana: Council for Indian Education, 1983.

Chittenden, H. M. and A. T. Richardson. *Life, Letters and Travels of Father DeSmet*. 4 vols. New York: Francis P. Harper, 1905.

Chittenden, Hiram M. *The American Fur Trade of the Far West*. 3 vols. New York: Francis P. Harper, 1902.

_____. *Verse*. Seattle: The Holly Press, 1916.

_____. *The Yellowstone National Park, Historical and Descriptive*. Cincinnati: Robert Clarke, 1895. The many editions of this book were continuously changed and updated, and later editions omitted much material from earlier editions. This book relied on the editions for 1897, 1900, 1903, 1905, 1915, 1917, 1927, and 1964.

Cochrane, C. E. *Geyserland: Lines Descriptive of the Yellowstone National Park*. Chicago: Shea, Smith, 1888.

Coues, Elliott. *History of the Expedition Under the Command of Lewis and Clark*. 3 vols. New York: Francis P. Harper, 1893.

Cramton, Louis C. *Early History of Yellowstone National Park and Its Relation to National Park Policies*. Washington, D.C.: U.S. Department of the Interior, National Park Service, 1932.

DeLacy, Walter W. "A Trip Up the South Snake River in 1863." *Contributions to the Historical Society of Montana* 10 vols. (Boston: J. S. Canner, 1966), 1:113-143.

DeVoto, Bernard. *Across the Wide Missouri*. Boston: Houghton-Mifflin, 1947.

Dike, D. John. *Log of a Western Journey*. Privately printed, c. 1910. Copy in author's possession.

Dodds, Gordon B. *Hiram Martin Chittenden: His Public Career*. Lexington: University of Kentucky Press, 1973.

Driggs, B. W. *History of the Teton Valley, Idaho*. Caldwell, Idaho: Caxton, 1926.

Dudley, W. H. *The National Park from the Hurricane Deck of a Cayuse or the Liederkranz Expedition to Geyserland*. Butte City, Montana: Free Press Publishing Company/Frank Loeber, 1886.

Dunraven, Windham T. W.-Q., 4th Earl of. *The Great Divide: Travels in the Upper Yellowstone in the Summer of 1874*. New York: Scribner, Welford, and Armstrong, 1876. A 1925 edition was published under the title *Hunting in the Yellowstone*, but it did not contain the foldout maps of the first edition. A 1967 edition was published by the University of Nebraska Press.

_____. *Past Times and Pastimes*. 2 vols. London: Hodder and Stoughton, 1922.

Easton, Robert and Mackenzie Brown. *Lord of Beasts: the Saga of Buffalo Jones*. Tucson: University of Arizona Press, 1961.

Edwards, Ira C. "A Trip Through Yellowstone National Park." *Milwaukee Public Museum Yearbook* 6 (1926): 78-107.

Elliot, Henry W. *Profile, Sections, and Other Illustrations, Designed to Accompany the Final Report of the Chief Geologist of the Survey*. New York: Julius Bien, 1872.

Elliott, L. Louise. *Six Weeks on Horseback Through Yellowstone Park*. Rapid City: The Rapid City Journal, 1913.

Evermann, Barton W. "A Reconnaissance of the Streams and Lakes of Western Montana and Northwestern Wyoming." 52d Cong., 2d sess., H. Ex. Doc., SN-3129, Vol. 20. Washington, D.C.: Government Printing Office, 1893. Also published in *U.S. Fish Commission Bulletin* 11 (1893): 3-60.

Faris, John T. and Horace M. Albright. *Roaming the Rockies: Through National Parks and National Forests of the Rocky Mountain Wonderland*. New York: Farrar and Rinehart, 1930.

Forsyth, James W. and F. D. Grant. *Report of an Expedition up the Yellowstone River, Made in 1875, by James W. Forsyth and F. D. Grant . . . Under Orders of Lieutenant-General P. H. Sheridan . . . .* Washington, D.C.: Government Printing Office, 1875.

Foster, Mrs. "From Foster Ranch to Wonderland and Return, August 17, 1882." Handwritten letter and typescript, YNP Research Library.

Fryxell, Fritiof. *Thomas Moran: Explorer in Search of Beauty*. New York: East Hampton Free Library, 1958.

_____. "Albert Charles Peale, Pioneer Geologist of the Hayden Survey." *Annals of Wyoming* 34 (October 1962): 175-192.

Fuess, Claude Moore. *Carl Schurz, Reformer*. Port Washington, New York: Kennikat Press, 1963.

Gerrish, Theodore. *Life in the World's Wonderland*. Biddleford, Maine: n.p., 1887.

Gibbon, John. *Gibbon on the Sioux Campaign of 1876*. Bellevue, Nebraska: Old Army Press, 1970.

Glidden, Ralph. *Exploring the Yellowstone High Country: A History of the Cooke City Area*. Livingston, Montana: Livingston Enterprise, 1976.

Goetzmann, William. *Exploration and Empire*. New York: Alfred A. Knopf, 1966.

Gray, John S. "Trials of a Trailblazer: P. W. Norris and Yellowstone." *Montana the Magazine of Western History* 22 (Summer 1972): 54-63.

_____. "Itinerant Frontier Photographers." *Montana the Magazine of Western History* 28 (Spring 1978): 2-15.

Guie, Heister Dean and Lucullus Virgil McWhorter. *Adventures in Geyserland*. Caldwell, Idaho: Caxton Printers, 1935.

Gunnison, J. W. *The Mormons, or, Latter-Day Saints*. Philadelphia: Lippincott, Grambo, 1852.

Guptill, Albert B. *A Ramble in Wonderland*. Chicago: Rand McNally, 1892. St. Paul: Chas. S. Fee and Northern Pacific Railroad.

Hafen, Leroy and Ann Hafen, eds. *The Diaries of William Henry Jackson*. Glendale, California: Arthur H. Clark, 1959.

Hafen, Leroy. *The Mountain Men and the Fur Trade of the Far West*. 10 vols. Glendale: Arthur H. Clark, 1965-1972.

Hague, Arnold. Personal papers, U.S. Geological Survey RG 57, National Archives, Washington, D.C. The collection includes:

Box 3—3 large books of letters numbered 3A, 3B, 3C.

Box 5—Letters written by Hague 1904-1910, 1911-1916; correspondence with USGS and others, 1880-1906; personal letters to Hague.

Box 10—mss. for *Monographs 32 Part I*.

Box 11—Manuscripts and illustrations for *Monographs 32 Part one*; "Thermal Springs and Geysers"; Abstracts from field notebooks of Hague and Walter Weed; Weather observations; "Geography and Nomenclature"; "The Geyser Basins"; "Firehole Geyser Basin."

Box 13—Norris Geyser Basin; miscellaneous notes on geysers and hot springs; photographs.

_____. "The Yellowstone Park." *International Geological Congress, Compte Rendu, 5th Session*, Washington, D.C.: Government Printing Office, 1893, 336-359.

_____. "The Yellowstone National Park." *Scribner's* 35 (May 1904): 513-527.

Haines, Aubrey L., ed. *Valley of the Upper Yellowstone*. Norman: University of Oklahoma Press, 1965.

_____. *Yellowstone National Park: Its Exploration and Establishment*. Washington, D.C.: Department of the Interior, 1974.

_____. *The Yellowstone Story*. 2 vols. Boulder: Colorado Associated University Press, 1977.

Hamilton, Mrs. James. "Through Yellowstone National Park in 1883 with Mrs. James Hamilton." Ms., n.d., YNP Research Library.

Hamilton, W. T. *My Sixty Years on the Plains*. New York: Forest and Stream, 1905.

Hampton, H. Duane. *How the U.S. Cavalry Saved Our National Parks*. Bloomington: Indiana University Press, 1971.

Harriman-Brown, Alice. *Chaperoning Adrienne: A Tale of the Yellowstone National Park*. Seattle: Metropolitan, c. 1909.

Harrison, Carter. *A Summer's Outing and the Old Man's Story*. Chicago: Dibble Publishing, 1891.

Haupt, Herman, Jr. *The Yellowstone National Park*. St. Paul: J. M. Stoddart, 1883.

Hayden, F. V. *Preliminary Report of the U.S. Geological Survey of Montana and Portions of Adjacent Territories; being a Fifth Annual Report of Progress*. Washington, D.C.: Government Printing Office, 1872.

_____. *Sixth Annual Report of the United States Geological Survey of the Territories . . . for the Year 1872*. Washington, D.C.: Government Printing Office, 1873.

_____. *Twelfth Annual Report of the United States Geological and Geographical Survey of the Territories: A Report of Progress . . . for the Year 1878. In Two Parts. Part II. Yellowstone National Park. Geology—Thermal Springs—Topography*. Washington, D.C.: Government Printing Office, 1883.

Haynes, Jack Ellis. Personal files, Montana State University, Bozeman.

_____. *Haynes Guide . . .* , 1890-1966. Editions of the *Guide* were revised nearly annually and were written by A. B. Guptill (1880-1909), F. Jay Haynes (1910-1915), and Jack Ellis Haynes (1916-1962). Joseph Joffe sometimes assisted Haynes in the preparation of these guidebooks, which were designated the official guide to Yellowstone Park in the 1920s. Titles varied from *Practical Guide to Yellowstone National Park* to *All About Yellowstone Park* to *Haynes Guide Handbook of Yellowstone Park*. The Yellowstone Park Research Library has most editions, and Montana State University in Bozeman has a complete collection.

_____. "The First Winter Trip Through Yellowstone National Park." *Annals of Wyoming* 14 (April 1942): 89-97.

Heath, Charles A. *Trial of a Trail*. Chicago: The Franklin Press, 1905.

Henderson, A. Bart. Diaries, 1866-1872. Typescript, YNP Research Library.

Henderson, G. L. Ash Scrapbook. Newspaper clippings collected and written by G. L. Henderson, 1882-1905, YNP Research Library.

_____. *Yellowstone Park Manual and Guide*. Mammoth Hot Springs, Wyoming: Privately printed, 1885; 2d ed. 1888.

_____. *Yellowstone Park: Past, Present, and Future*. Washington, D.C.: Gibson Brothers, 1891.

Holmes, William Henry. "Biography of William H. Holmes." Random Records, vol. 2 and 3, National Collection of Fine Arts, New Museum Building, Washington, D.C. Random Records consist of 15 volumes of photographs, notes, letters, essays, and newspaper clippings. The first six volumes pertain to his work with the Hayden surveys, and vols. 2 and 3 refer to Yellowstone.

_____. "Extracts from the Diary of W. H. Holmes," 1872, 1878. Typescript, YNP Research Library.

Hornaday, William T. *Our Vanishing Wildlife*. New York: Scribner's, 1913.

Howard, Oliver Otis. *Nez Perce Joseph*. Boston: Lee and Shepard; New York: Charles T. Dillingham, 1881.

Hunt, Dr. Lester C. *Wyoming: A Guide to Its History, Highways, and People*. New York: Oxford University Press, 1941.

Irving, Washington. *Astoria or Anecdotes of an Enterprise Beyond the Rocky Mountains*. 2 vols. Philadelphia: Carey, Lea, and Blanchard, 1836.

Jackson, William H. *The Pioneer Photographer*. New York: World Book Company, 1929.

Jackson, William Turrentine. "Governmental Explorations of the Upper Yellowstone, 1871." *Pacific Historical Review* 11 (June 1942): 187-199.

_____. "The Washburn-Doane Expedition of 1870." *Montana the Magazine of Western History* 7 (July 1957): 36-51.

Jones, William A. *Report Upon the Reconnaissance of Northwestern Wyoming Including Yellowstone National Park Made in the Summer of 1873*. Washington, D.C.: Government Printing Office, 1875.

Josephy, Alvin M., Jr. *Chief Joseph's People and Their War*. Yellowstone National Park: Yellowstone Library and Museum Association, 1964.

_____. *The Nez Perce Indians and the Opening of the North West*. New Haven, Connecticut: Yale University Press, 1965.

Kirk, Ruth. *Exploring Yellowstone*. Seattle: University of Washington Press, 1972.

Lang, William L. "At the Greatest Personal Peril to the Photographer." *Montana the Magazine of Western History* 33 (Winter 1983): 14-25.

Langford, Nathaniel Pitt. *The Discovery of Yellowstone Park 1870*. 2d ed. St. Paul: J. E. Haynes, 1923.

Lewis, William J. Reports on thermal features, YNP Research Library.

Linderman, Frank B. *Plenty-Coups Chief of the Crows*. 1930; reprint, Lincoln: University of Nebraska Press, 1962.

Linton, Edwin. "Mount Sheridan and the Continental Divide." *Academy of Science and Arts of Pittsburgh, Transactions* (1892), 1-27.

Ludlow, William. *Report of a Reconnaissance from Carroll, Montana Territory, on the Upper Missouri to the Yellowstone National Park and Return, Made in the Summer of 1875 by William Ludlow*. Washington, D.C.: Government Printing Office, 1876.

Marler, George. *The Story of Old Faithful*. Yellowstone National Park: Yellowstone Library and Museum Association, 1969.

_____. *Studies of Geysers and Hot Springs Along the Firehole River: Yellowstone National Park, Wyoming*. Yellowstone National Park: Yellowstone Library and Museum Association, 1964, 1971, 1978.

Mattoon, A. M. "The Yellowstone National Park. Summer of 1889." YNP Research Library.

Merk, Frederick, *History of the Westward Movement*. New York: Alfred A. Knopf, 1978.

Mitchell, S. Weir. "Through the Yellowstone Park to Fort Custer." *Lippincott's Magazine* 25 (June-July 1880): 29-41, 688-704.

Monthly Reports of the Superintendent of Yellowstone National Park. April 1918 through December 1929, Yellowstone Park Research Library.

Montana Historical Society. *F. Jay Haynes, Photographer*. Helena: Montana Historical Society Press, 1981.

Muir, John. *Picturesque California, The Rocky Mountains and the Pacific Slope*. Vol. 9 of 12 vols. New York: J. Dewing, 1888.

_____. "The Yellowstone National Park." *Atlantic Monthly* 81 (April 1898): 509-522.

Mumey, Nolie. *Rocky Mountain Dick: Stories of His Adventures in Capturing Wild Animals*. Denver: Range Press, 1953.

Nash, Roderick. *Wilderness and the American Mind*. New Haven: Yale University Press, 1973.

National Park Service. *General Information Regarding Yellowstone National Park, Season of (year)*. Washington, D.C.: Government, 1912-1927. The guidebook to the Park was sometimes entitled *Rules and Regulations*. . . .

Bibliography

_____. *1926 Ranger Naturalists' Manual.* Yellowstone National Park: Department of the Interior, National Park Service, 1926.

_____. *Ranger Naturalists' Manual of Yellowstone National Park.* Yellowstone National Park: Department of the Interior, National Park Service, 1927.

_____. *Ranger Naturalists' Manual of Yellowstone National Park.* Yellowstone National Park: Department of the Interior, National Park Service, 1928.

Norris, Philetus W. *Annual Report of the Superintendent of the Yellowstone National Park to the Secretary of the Interior for the Year 1880.* Washington, D.C.: Government Printing Office, 1881. See also his reports for 1877, 1878, and 1879.

_____. *Fifth Annual Report of the Superintendent of the Yellowstone National Park by P. W. Norris, Superintendent. Conducted Under the Authority of the Secretary of the Interior.* Washington, D.C.: Government Printing Office, 1881.

_____. *The Calumet of the Coteau and Other Poetical Legends of the Border. . . .* Philadelphia: J. B. Lippincott, 1883, 1884.

_____. "Meanderings of a Mountaineer, or, The Journals and Musings (or Storys) of a Rambler over Prairie (or Mountain) and Plain." Ms. prepared from newspaper clippings (1870-1875) and handwritten additions, annotated about 1885. Original in Huntington Library, San Marino, California. The original newspaper articles were published as "The Great West" in the *Detroit Post.*

Northern Pacific Railroad. *Saint Paul and the Northern Pacific Railway—Grand Opening, September, 1883.* St. Paul: Brown and Treacy, 1883.

_____. *The Wonderland Route to the Pacific Coast.* St. Paul: Chas. S. Fee, NPRR, 1885.

_____. *Land of Geysers.* St. Paul: NPRR, 1909. There is also a 1907 edition of this book.

Norton, Harry J. *Wonderland Illustrated; Or Horseback Rides Through Yellowstone National Park.* Virginia City, Montana: Harry J. Norton, 1873.

Peabody, Henry G. *The Yellowstone National Park.* Pasadena, California: n.p., 1928.

Peale, Dr. A. C. Diary, 1871. Transcript from book #1971, USGS Field Records, Denver, Colorado, in YNP Research Library.

Pickett, Col. William D. *Hunting at High Altitudes, the Book of the Boone and Crocket Club.* Edited by George B. Grinnell, New York: Harper and Brothers, 1913.

Pomeroy, Earl. *In Search of the Golden West: The Tourist in Western America.* New York: Alfred A. Knopf, 1957.

Porter, T. C. *Impressions of America.* London: C. A. Pearson, 1899.

Powell, J. W. *Fifth Annual Report of the U.S. Geological Survey to the Secretary of the Interior, 1883-84, by J. W. Powell, Director.* Washington, D.C.: Government Printing Office, 1885.

_____. *Eighth Annual Report of the U.S. Geological Survey to the Secretary of the Interior, 1887-88, by J. W. Powell.* Washington, D.C.: Government Printing Office, 1889.

Quaw, M. M. and L. L. Quaw. *A Love Affair in Wonderland.* Des Moines: Kenyon Company, c. 1906.

Randall, L. W. "Gay." *Footprints Along the Yellowstone.* San Antonio: Naylor Company, 1961.

Raymond, Rossiter W. "Mineral Resources of the States and Territories West of the Rocky Mountains." Washington, D.C.: Government Printing Office, 1869.

Raynolds, William F. *The Report of Brevet Brigadier General W. F. Raynolds on the Exploration of the Yellowstone and the Country Drained by that River.* 40th Cong., 1st sess., S. Ex. Doc. No. 77. Washington, D.C.: Government Printing Office, 1868.

Reports of the Naturalist Division of YNP. All editions, 1930-1963.

Richards, Alonzo V. "Field Notes of the Survey and Establishment of the Western Boundary of Wyoming Territory by A. V. Richards, U.S. Astronomer and Surveyor, 1874." Ms. with maps, Bureau of Land Management, Cheyenne, Wyoming.

Riley, W. C. *Yellowstone National Park. The World's Wonderland.* St. Paul: W. C. Riley, 1889.

Rothschild, Isidor. "Bicycling Through Yellowstone National Park in 1894." Ms., YNP Research Library.

Runte, Alfred. *National Parks: The American Experience.* Lincoln: University of Nebraska Press, 1979.

Russell, Osborne. *Journal of a Trapper.* Edited by Aubrey L. Haines. Lincoln: University of Nebraska Press, 1965.

Saltus, J. Sanford. *A Week in the Yellowstone.* New York: The Knickerbocker Press, 1895.

Schullery, Paul. *Old Yellowstone Days.* Boulder: Colorado University Press, 1979.

_____. *The Bears of Yellowstone.* Yellowstone National Park: Yellowstone Library and Museum Association, 1980.

_____. *Mountain Time.* New York: Schocken Books, 1984.

Schurz, Carl. *Reminiscences of Carl Schurz.* New York: McClure, 1907-1908.

Shawver, Mary. *Sincerely, Mary S.* Casper, Wyoming: Prairie Publishing, n.d. Copy at Montana State University, Bozeman.

Singleton, Esther, ed. *Wonders of Nature As Seen and Described by Famous Writers.* New York: P. F. Collier, 1911.

Smith, F. Dumont. *Book of a Hundred Bears.* Chicago: Rand McNally, 1909. The 4th edition of this book was entitled *Summit of the World.*

Smith, George Adam. *The Life of Henry Drummond.* New York: McClure, Phillips, 1901.

Smith, Henry Nash. *The American West As Symbol and Myth.* Cambridge, Massachusetts: Harvard University Press, 1950.

Stanley, Edwin J. *Rambles in Wonderland: Or, Up the Yellowstone. . . .* New York: D. Appleton, 1878.

Strahorn, Robert E. *The Enchanted Land or An October Ramble Among the Geysers, Hot Springs, Lakes, Falls, and Cañons of Yellowstone National Park.* Omaha: New West Publishing, 1881.

Strong, General W. E. *A Trip to the Yellowstone National Park in July, August and September, 1875.* Edited by Richard A. Bartlett. Norman: University of Oklahoma Press, 1968.

Sunder, John E. *Bill Sublette Mountain Man.* Norman: University of Oklahoma Press, 1959.

Swain, Donald C. *Wilderness Defender—Horace M. Albright and Conservation.* Chicago: University of Chicago Press, 1970.

Switzer, M. A. "1876 Trip to the Geysers." Ms., YNP Research Library.

Synge, Georgina M. *A Ride Through Wonderland.* London: Sampson Low, Marston, 1892.

Thomas, George. "My Recollections of the Yellowstone Park." Ms., 1883, YNP Research Library.

Thwaites, Reuben Gold, ed. *Early Western Travels*. 32 vols. Cleveland: Arthur H. Clark, 1904-1907.

_____, ed. *Original Journals of Lewis and Clark Expedition*. 7 vols. New York: Dodd, Mead, 1904-1905.

Topping, E. S. *Chronicles of the Yellowstone*. . . . St. Paul: Pioneer Press, 1888.

U.S. Board on Geographic Names. *Sixth Report of the United States Geographic Board, 1890 to 1932*. Washington, D.C.: Government Printing Office, 1933.

_____. Place Names Folder File (subject file) of newer names, Reston, Virginia.

_____. "Yellowstone National Park," Subject file, Reston, Virginia.

U.S. Department of the Interior, Fish and Wildlife Service, YNP. *Annual Project Report, Fishery Management Program*. All editions, 1962-1983.

U.S. Department of the Interior, Geological Survey. Field Notebooks, USGS RG 57, Field Notebooks section, National Archives, Washington, D.C. The following were important in this project:

Box 43—Walter Weed, 1889, #3502, specimens sent to lab.

Box 45—Condit-Finch-Pardee, 1916, #3565.

Box 47—Walter Weed, 17 vols., 1883-1888, thermal activity and geology: vol. 1, 1883, #3832; vol. 2, 1883, #3833; vol. 3, 1883, #3834; vol. 4, 1884, #3835; vol. 5, 1886, #3836; vol. 6, 1884, #3837; vol. 7, 1884, #3838; vol. 8, 1884, #3839, specimen lists; vol. 9, 1885, #3840; vol. 10, 1885, #3841; vol. 11, 1885, #3842; vol. 12, 1885, #3843; vol. 13, 1886, #3844; vol. 14, 1886, #3845; vol. 15, 1886, #3846; vol. 16, 1886-7-8, #3847; vol. 16-A, 1887, #3848.

Box 48—Walter Weed notebooks 1887-1899, thermal activity: vol. 17, 1887, #3849; vol. 18, 1887, #3850; vol. 19, 1887, #3851 (geology); vol. 20, 1888, #3852; vol. 21, 1888, #3864-B; vol. 22, 1888, #3853; vol. 23, 1889, #3854 (geology); vol. 24, 1889, #3855; vol. 25, 1889, #3856; 1890, #3857, on coal, some thermal; 1890, #3858, on coal, some thermal; 1892, #3860; 1897, #3861; 1899, #3862; n.d., #3863, chemical analyses; n.d., #3864, specimens lists; n.d., #3864-A, index for 1883.

Box 49—Henry Gannett/J. E. Mushbach notebook, 1878, #3872.

Box 50—George M. Wright notebooks: no. 1, 1884, #3883; no. 2, 1884, #3884; no. 2, 1885, #3889; no. 3, 1885, #3890; no. 4, 1885, #3891; no. 5, 1884, #3887; T. A. Jaggar, Jr., notebook, vol. 1, 1897, #3892-C.

Box 51—Joseph P. Iddings notebooks: vol. IX, 1883, #3893-F; vol. X, 1884, #3893-G; George M. Wright notebooks: vol. IV, 1883, #3893-A; vol. IV, 1883-1884, #3893-C.

Box 52—vol. XIII, 1884, #3893-J. J. P. Iddings notebook: vol. XX, 1885, #3893-Q; Walter Weed notebooks: vol. XIV, 1884, #3893-K; vol. XV, 1884, #3893-L; vol. XVI, 1884, #3893-M; vol. XVII, 1885, #3893-N.

Box 53—J. P. Iddings notebook: vol. 21, 1886, #3893-R; Walter Weed notebooks: vol. XXII, 1886, #3893-S; vol. XXIII, 1886-1887, #3893-T; vol. XXVIII, 1887, #3893-Y; vol. XXIX, 1887-1888, #3893-Z.

Box 54—J. P. Iddings notebooks: 1883, #3893-Z-5; 1886, #3893-Z-6; 1889-1890, vol. XXXI, #3893-Z-2; Walter Weed notebooks: 1888-1889, vol. XXX, #3893-Z-1; 1888, vol. XXXIII, #3893-Z-4.

Box 55—Arnold Hague notebooks, 1884-1889, 1891, 1893, 1897, 1902, 1911, and 1915. The 26 volumes in this box are numbered 3894-A through 3894-Z, and most years of Hague's notebooks contain a volume one and a volume two. All of the notebooks are Hague's except one, which was written by Ernest Howe (#3894-V, 1911). T. A. Jaggar, Jr., notebook, vol. 2, 1897, #3892-D; F. P. King notebook, 1897, #3892-G.

Box 56—Walter Weed notebooks: 1883, vol. I, #3899-A; 1883, vol. II, #3899-B; 1883, vol. III, #3899-C; J. P. Iddings notebook, 1884, no. 2, #3942; W. E. Sanders notebook, 1884, #3937; S. L. Penfield notebook, 1886, no. 1, #3938; A. C. Gill notebook, 1887, #3940.

Box 57—J. P. Iddings notebooks: 1884, #3943; 1885, #3944; 1888, #3949; 1889, #3951.

Box 58—William C. Alden notebook, 1922, #6014.

Box 48—Paul J. Dashiell notebook, 1888, #3865; Louis V. Pirsson notebook, 1889, #3866; J. H. Ropes notebook, 1889, #3867; Arnold Hague notebooks: 1889, #3868; (1891), #3869; n.d., #3870; (1889?), #3870-A.

(Note: Weed's notebooks that bear a Roman numeral volume number are his *formal* notebooks, a recopying and refining of his field notebooks. All of his other notebooks are field notebooks. Dates of the formal notebooks are not absolute, as Weed made insertions of place names at later times and sometimes in different ink. There are also references in some of the formal notebooks that date them as later than the year given. The dates of field notebooks are correct.)

Varley, John and Paul Schullery. *Freshwater Wilderness*. Yellowstone National Park: Yellowstone Library and Museum Association, 1983.

Vinton, Stallo. *John Colter, Discoverer of Yellowstone Park*. New York: Edward Eberstadt, 1926.

Washburn, Gen. H. D. "The Yellowstone Expedition." *Mining Statistics West of the Rocky Mountains*. 42nd Cong., 1st sess., H. Ex. Doc. No. 10, SN-1470, pp. 213-216, March 21, 1871. This also appeared in: *Helena Daily Herald*, September 27, September 28, 1870; *New York Times*, October 14, 1870; and St. Paul *Pioneer Press*, October 9, October 14, 1870.

Weed, Walter H. "The Formation of Yellowstone Hot Spring Deposits." *International Geological Congress, Compte Rendu 5th Session*. Pp. 36-363. Washington, D.C.: Government Printing Office, 1893.

Weikert, Andrew J. "Journal of the Tour Through the Yellowstone National Park in August and September, 1877." *Contributions to the Historical Society of Montana* (Boston: J. S. Canner, 1966), 2:331-336.

Wheat, Carl. *Mapping the Transmississippi West*. 5 vols. San Francisco: Institute of Historical Cartography, 1957, 1958, 1959, 1960, 1963.

Wheeler, Olin D. The Wonderland series. St. Paul, Minnesota: Northern Pacific Railroad, 1884-1906. The series included *The Wonderland of the World* (1884) and *The Wonderland Route to the Pacific Coast* (1885); John Hyde and Lt. F. Schwatka, *Wonderland or Alaska and the Inland Passage* (1886) and *Thro' Wonderland with Lieut. Schwatka* (1886); John Hyde, *Wonderland or the Pacific Northwest and Alaska* (1888); Elia W. Peattie, *A Journey Through Wonderland or the Pacific Northwest and Alaska* (1890); and Albert B. Guptill, *A Ramble in Wonderland* (1892). From 1893 to 1906, Olin D. Wheeler, as the NPRR's advertising manager and historian from 1892 to 1923, wrote the series.

Wheeler, Olin D. *Six Thousand Miles Through Wonderland*. St. Paul: NPRR, copyright 1893.

_____. *Indianland and Wonderland*. St. Paul: NPRR, 1894.

_____. *Sketches of Wonderland*. St. Paul: NPRR, 1895.

_____. *Wonderland '96*. St. Paul: NPRR, 1896.

_____. *Wonderland '97*. St. Paul: NPRR, 1897.

_____. *Wonderland '98*. St. Paul: NPRR, 1898.

_____. *Wonderland '99*. St. Paul: NPRR, 1899.

_____. *Wonderland 1900*. St. Paul: NPRR, 1900.

_____. *Wonderland 1901*. St. Paul: NPRR, 1901.

_____. *Wonderland 1902*. St. Paul: NPRR, 1902.

_____. *Wonderland 1903*. St. Paul: NPRR, 1903.

_____. *Wonderland 1904*. St. Paul: NPRR, 1904.

_____. *Wonderland 1905*. St. Paul: NPRR, 1905.

_____. *Wonderland 1906*. St. Paul: NPRR, 1906.

_____. *Yellowstone National Park: Descriptive of the Beauties and Wonders of the World's Wonderland*. St Paul: W. C. Riley, 1901.

White, John G. "Souvenir of Wyoming (Being a Diary of a Fishing Trip in Jackson Hole and Yellowstone Park with Remarks on Early History and Historical Geography)." 3 vols., Cleveland, Ohio, typewritten, 1926, YNP Research Library, Missouri Historical Society, and Wyoming Historical Society.

Whittlesey, Lee H. *Drivers' and Tour Guides' Commentary Handbook for Yellowstone National Park*. Mammoth: Yellowstone Park Company, 1975, 1979.

_____. "Marshall's Hotel in the National Park." *Montana the Magazine of Western History* 30 (Autumn 1980): 42-51.

_____. "In Yellowstone Park, 1886-1889: George Tutherly's Reminiscences." *Montana the Magazine of Western History* 33 (Winter 1983): 2-13.

_____. *Drivers' and Tour Guides' Commentary Handbook for Yellowstone National Park*. Mammoth: T. W. Services, 1985.

_____. *Yellowstone National Park Mile by Mile Guide*. Yellowstone National Park: Yellowstone Park Company, 1975, 1979, T. W. Services, 1985.

Wilkins, Thurman. *Thomas Moran: Artist of the Mountains*. Norman: University of Oklahoma Press, 1966.

Wingate, George W. *Through the Yellowstone Park on Horseback*. New York: O. Judd Company, 1886.

Winser, Henry J. *The Yellowstone National Park. A Manual for Tourists. . . .* New York: G. P. Putnam's Sons, 1883.

Wister, Owen. "Old Yellowstone Days." *Harper's Monthly Magazine* 172 (March 1936): 471-480.

Wolf, Marie and Rocco Paperiello. "Report on Lesser Known Thermal Units of Yellowstone National Park, 1981-84." 1985.

Wylie, W. W. *Yellowstone National Park, Or The Great American Wonderland*. Kansas City: Ramsey, Millett, and Hudson, 1882.

Yeager, Dorr. "Some Old Timers of the Yellowstone." Ms., 1929, YNP Research Library.

Yellowstone Interpreter. All editions, July 10, 1963 to November-December, 1964.

Yellowstone Nature Notes. All editions, 1924 to 1958.

YNP SUPERINTENDENTS

Annual Reports of the Superintendent or Acting Superintendent of Yellowstone National Park, 1872, 1877-1883, 1885-1930, and selected reports after 1930 are available at the YNP Research Library. The Park superintendents were:

Nathaniel Pitt Langford
May 10, 1872, to April 18, 1877

Philetus Walter Norris
April 18, 1877, to March 31, 1882

Patrick Henry Conger
April 1, 1882, to September 9, 1884

Robert Emmett Carpenter
September 10, 1884, to June 30, 1885

David Walker Wear
July 1, 1885, to August 20, 1886

Capt. Moses Harris
August 20, 1886, to May 31, 1889

Capt. Frazier A. Boutelle
June 1, 1889, to February 15, 1891

Capt. George S. Anderson
February 15, 1891, to June 23, 1897

Col. Samuel B. M. Young
June 23, 1897, to November 15, 1897

Capt. James B. Erwin
November 15, 1897, to March 15, 1899

Capt. Wilber E. Wilder
March 15, 1899, to June 23, 1899

Capt. Oscar J. Brown
June 23, 1899, to July 24, 1900

Capt. George W. Goode
July 24, 1900, to May 8, 1901

Capt. John Pitcher
May 8, 1901, to June 1, 1907

Gen. Samuel B. M. Young
June 1, 1907, to November 28, 1908

Maj. Harry C. Benson
November 28, 1908, to September 30, 1910

Col. Lloyd M. Brett
September 30, 1910, to October 15, 1916

Chester Allinson Lindsley
October 16, 1916, to June 28, 1919

Horace Marden Albright
June 28, 1919, to January 11, 1929

Joseph Joffe
January 12, 1929, to February 1, 1929

Roger Wolcott Toll
February 1, 1929, to February 25, 1936

John W. Emmert
February 26, 1936, to May 25, 1936

Edmund B. Rogers
May 25, 1936, to October 31, 1956

Lemuel A. Garrison
November 1, 1956, to February 16, 1964

John S. McLaughlin
March 6, 1964, to October 6, 1967

Jack K. Anderson
October 8, 1967, to June 1975

John A. Townsley
August 4, 1975, to September 19, 1982

James B. Thompson
September 19, 1982, to December 8, 1982

Robert Barbee
January 9, 1983, to present

About the Author

Lee H. Whittlesey has lived and worked in Yellowstone National Park for seventeen summers and six winters. Over those years, he has worked at all of the locations possible in the Park and has filled a variety of positions, including bus tour guide, tour bus driver, and Park ranger. For five years, he was communications specialist and company historian for TW Services in the Park. In the spring of 1988, Whittlesey received a law degree from the University of Oklahoma in Norman. He is currently living in West Yellowstone, Montana, where he is working for the National Park Service as a Park ranger.

Farewell ye boiling fountains all!
Farewell Old Faithful, geyser queen;
Most wondrous Park on this round ball;
To understand, you must be seen.

—G. L. Henderson, "Song of the Geysers," 1884